'This authoritative book, which benefits from archival access, extensive interviews and authors' experiences of working there, tells how the NAO developed over 40 years. It shows how valuable it is for parliamentary democracy, how fragile public audit can be, and how much depends on who is Comptroller and Auditor General'.

—**David Heald**, *University of Glasgow, Scotland, UK*

'This is an overdue examination of an important but not always understood institution. The insider/outsider combination among the authors ensures sometimes technical developments in audit are deftly set in the context of 40 years of governmental change, ensuring the book's analysis rings true'.

—**Jeremy Lonsdale**, *NAO director until 2021*

'*Holding Government to Account* is a timely and incredibly important look at the development and history of the National Audit Office. In an era where governmental accountability is more important than ever, the book provides a finely tuned and well-written roadmap for other governments and governmental agencies to follow'.

—**Khalid Hamid**, *International Director, Chartered Institute of Public Finance and Accountancy*

HOLDING GOVERNMENT TO ACCOUNT

The National Audit Office has played an important role in the checks and balances of the UK parliamentary and political system over the last 40 years. This new book, more than just a history of the UK's supreme audit institution, examines the very definition of accountability through both an historic and an academic lens, critically exploring questions about the role of audit in a democracy and how well it is working.

Holding Government to Account draws on several unique sources of evidence, including interviews with senior officials from the National Audit Office and the civil service, as well as senior parliamentarians with experience of the NAO's relationships with government and legislature. These interviews are supplemented by an analysis of previously unpublished manuscript material in the National Archives, examination of NAO reports and parliamentary and other reports focused on accountability. The book begins with a history of the National Audit Office in the context of the UK's wider history. It then offers an overview of the constitutional, political and human legacies of the Exchequer and Audit Department, followed by a close examination of the National Audit Office's leadership and decision-making from inception in 1984 through to the present. The authors conclude with an exploration of the way in which the meaning of public sector audit has evolved over time, in accordance with its wider political, ideological and material context. In doing so, they demonstrate that any question about the National Audit Office's future and organisation is really a question about what democracy and good government mean in a modern bureaucratic state.

Holding Government to Account will be of keen interest to students enrolled in courses on accounting, public administration, law and politics as well as to politicians, civil servants and Supreme Audit Institutions internationally.

Henry C Midgley is an Associate Professor in the Accounting Department at Durham University, UK. He did his PhD at Cambridge University focused on the political thinking of the New Model Army during the Civil Wars. He worked at the NAO between 2008 and 2021 and, whilst on secondment to the House of Commons between 2015 and 2018, authored landmark reports examining the role of accounting in constitutional democracy and the democratic functions of public sector audit. He has written academically about the NAO and financial scrutiny in the UK.

Laurence Ferry is an award-winning Full Professor in Accounting for Democracy at Durham University, UK, where he holds a Chair and served as Head of the Accounting Department He is also the Senior Distinguished Visiting Fellow at Rutgers University, USA. He earned his PhD at Warwick Business School, UK, is a fully qualified Chartered Accountant with both the Chartered Institute of Public Finance and Accountancy (CIPFA) and Institute of Chartered Accountants in England and Wales (ICAEW), and holds a first-class accounting degree. As a world-renowned expert in international public financial management, he has published well over 100 outputs including prize-winning journal papers, books and reports on public sector accounting, audit and accountability. In addition, Laurence has been a Parliamentary Fellow and Adviser to Select Committees at the UK Parliament. Furthermore, he is on the International Advisory Panel of CIPFA and has recently led work with the International Organisation of Supreme Audit Institutions (INTOSAI), culminating in the Rio Declaration on changing audit and accountability arrangements for almost 200 Supreme Audit Institutions internationally.

Aileen D Murphie is an Honorary Professor at Durham University, UK. She worked at the NAO from 1983 to 2021, with two years on secondment to the Cabinet Office, serving from 2003 to 2013 as Director of Justice Value for Money, covering the Home Office and the Ministry of Justice, and from 2013 to 2021 as Director for Local Government Value for Money. She led on implementing new statutory powers granted to the NAO after the abolition of the Audit Commission. During her NAO career, she published 90 major reports and supported over 70 Public Accounts Committee sessions. Since retirement from the NAO, Aileen has been a Specialist Adviser to the Levelling Up, Housing and Communities Select Committee at the UK Parliament and Chair of the Practice Oversight Panel of CIPFA, issuing advice to the finance profession locally on matters of concern.

ROUTLEDGE PUBLIC BUDGETING AND FINANCE

EDITOR
BRUCE D. MCDONALD III
Professor of Public Budgeting and Finance and Director of the School of Public Service
Old Dominion University, Norfolk VA

Public budgeting is a core function of public administration. Regardless of the level of government, size of government, type of management, or the socio-economic and political characteristics of the government, the execution of policies and programs requires the expenditure of resources, and important funding decisions must be made. Yet public officials are faced with policy and program implementation in an environment of limited resources. The Routledge Public Budgeting and Finance series explores issues related to effective, ethical, and equitable budgeting and financial management in the context of public administration. Topics of interest to the series include, but are not limited to:

- Budgeting for times of uncertainty
- Sales taxes
- Budget and revenue forecasting
- Management of local government debt
- Public pensions
- Financial analysis of public budgets
- Social equity budgeting
- Financing of subgovernment structures
- Financials of economic development
- Law enforcement budgeting
- Managing and organizing budget offices
- Transportation and infrastructure finance

Authors interested in discussing book project ideas on these and other public budgeting topics are encouraged to contact series general editor Bruce D. McDonald, III, Old Dominion University, at bmcdonal@odu.edu.

RECENTLY PUBLISHED BOOKS

Holding Government to Account
Democracy and the National Audit Office
Henry C Midgley, Laurence Ferry, and Aileen D Murphie

HOLDING GOVERNMENT TO ACCOUNT

Democracy and the National Audit Office

Henry C Midgley, Laurence Ferry, and Aileen D Murphie

Routledge
Taylor & Francis Group
NEW YORK AND LONDON

Designed cover image: © Getty Images – Nick Brundle Photography

First published 2025
by Routledge
605 Third Avenue, New York, NY 10158

and by Routledge
4 Park Square, Milton Park, Abingdon, Oxon, OX14 4RN

Routledge is an imprint of the Taylor & Francis Group, an informa business

ISBN: 978-1-032-85843-2 (hbk)
ISBN: 978-1-032-85837-1 (pbk)
ISBN: 978-1-003-52008-5 (ebk)

DOI: 10.4324/9781003520085

Typeset in Sabon
by Deanta Global Publishing Services, Chennai, India

CONTENTS

FOREWORD

The National Audit Office is a critical player in the checks and balances of our parliamentary and political system. An auditor general has existed in various forms for hundreds of years. In this book the authors examine the modern National Audit Office in the 40 years since its creation.

But the book is far more than just a history of the modern incarnation of the UK's supreme audit institution (established in 1984 by the National Audit Act of 1983). Besides the mechanics of how the National Audit Office operates, is funded and interacts with Whitehall and Parliament, it examines what accountability looks like through an historic and academic lens. The authors use the 40-year period in question to frame important questions about the role of audit in a democracy and assess how well it is working.

As a member of the PAC since 2011 (and chair since 2015) I've worked with the NAO closely for over a decade. The clear, politically neutral, factual reports and studies of major projects have informed the work of the PAC. The NAO and C&AG will also hear representations from the committee (and other parliamentarians) and often conduct a study or value-for-money report based on these requests.

At times of national upheaval and heated debate (such as Brexit and COVID-19), the authority, independence and rigour of the NAO have been critical. The NAO's access rights to Whitehall (it can examine all government spending) also enabled it to act much faster than any other body in examining and challenging in almost real time (the PAC was able to look into COVID-19 spending from June of 2020).

The authors tease out some of the areas of potential tension for the NAO, which has to 'understand the political forces swirling around them' and 'serves as Parliament's chief instrument of accountability and that it is the executive's preferred consultant'. Whether or not readers agree with the conclusions (e.g. that the NAO acted too cautiously over Brexit), it helpfully explores the challenges for a non-partisan body operating in a highly political sphere.

On the mechanics of the modern NAO, the book lays out the fascinating story of how the Treasury restricted funding to the NAO's predecessor body until the reforms under the 1983 Act put Parliament in charge of funding the NAO. As someone who has only ever served in Parliament under this regime, I am grateful for those who argued for audit to be wrenched from Treasury control and to be properly resourced.

One of the authors, Aileen Murphie, was a long-serving director at the NAO with a ring side seat for much of the period in question. She had unrivalled access to the key players and those in Parliament and academia who know, use and understand the National Audit Office. This is just one of the factors that makes this book a must read – an insight partly from the inside, partly from the outside of this crucial part of the system of accountability in our democracy.

Dame Meg Hillier, MP
Chair, Public Accounts Committee

PREFACE

There has always been a close connection between power and money, so it should surprise no one that as Parliament evolved it was soon interested in the relationship between the two. It is over 600 years since the House of Commons – in 1401 during the reign of Henry IV – claimed the right to grant taxation only after complaints had been addressed and that within another half a dozen years the Commons had successfully asserted its right to originate all new taxes. To this day, as a reminder of this primacy, in the King's Speech, which opens Parliament, the monarch pauses when the subject turns to money. Having initially begun the Speech by addressing both Houses: 'My Lords and Members of the House of Commons', the King starts again, pointedly ignoring the entire Peerage with the words: 'Members of the House of Commons, estimates for the public services will be laid before you'. From Locke and Burke to de Tocqueville and Gladstone, the centrality of the connection between taxation and accountability has been a constant theme.

It is therefore right that Aileen Murphie, Henry Midgley and Laurence Ferry, authors of this important study of the history of the National Audit Office over the last 40 years, begin with a close examination of these constitutional concerns, while emphasising that the very nature of the state and of the expectations placed upon it have been transformed since the late 19th century and further still as the 20th century gave way to today. The book provides an essential insight into this transformation, which lies at the heart of the successful government of a modern and accountable democracy.

The system of public audit and accountability in the United Kingdom has seen enormous changes since the 1860s when Chancellor of the

Exchequer, William Gladstone set up the Public Accounts Committee and the office of Comptroller and Auditor General (C&AG) in its modern form. Perhaps the most significant change was the replacement of the Treasury's internal Exchequer and Audit Department by the National Audit Office, which opened its doors in January 1984. Over the last 40 years, the NAO has established a reputation as one of the leading supreme audit institutions in the world. Better resourced and more independent than its predecessor, it is now the auditor for all central government departments and agencies, as well as a wide range of other public bodies. In addition to auditing the financial accounts, the NAO also produces a wide range of value-for-money studies, reporting to Parliament independently on how wisely the government is spending public money.

The NAO has also overseen significant changes to government accounting, partly due to the introduction of accruals accounting and also because of the need to keep up with changing international accounting standards. The NAO has managed to maintain its reputation for objectivity and good judgement while navigating through sometimes choppy political waters, thanks to the outstanding calibre and abilities of the five individuals who have held the office of Comptroller and Auditor General since 1984. Having had the distinct pleasure and privilege of personally knowing and working with four of these five C&AGs, I can attest to the public's good fortune in having had such a fine and dedicated group of public servants over four decades.

But as Murphie, Midgley and Ferry point out, important issues remain. We must ensure that there are enough parliamentarians who take a serious interest in issues of finance and management in government. Repeated mistakes by governments of all political complexions remain a staple of public discourse: in policy design and execution, in procurement, in the delivery of computer systems which enable change and in building a corporate memory that allows governments to learn from previous errors.

An auditor can point out where things should be improved, but it is for governments themselves to take action. There are enough examples of success that intelligent people across Whitehall should be able to learn and to deliver sustained improvements. If this is to happen, then the quality of public expenditure must become one of the central concerns of the age.

Richard Bacon, MP
Chairman,
The Public Accounts Commission

ACKNOWLEDGEMENTS

The authors would like to thank the following parliamentary, civil service and NAO colleagues together with academics and commentators on Parliament, accountability and government who gave their opinions and thoughts so generously:

Philip Aylett: former Clerk to the Public Accounts Committee
Richard Bacon, MP: former PAC Member and Chair of the PAC
Clive Betts, MP: Chair, Levelling Up, Housing and Communities Select Committee
Lord Bichard: former Chair, NAO Board
Marcial Boo: former NAO Director
Lord Butler: former Cabinet Secretary
David Clarke: former Director, NAO
Sir Geoffrey Clifton Brown, MP: PAC Member
Gabrielle Cohen: former Assistant Auditor General, NAO
Steve Corbishley: NAO Director (speaking in a personal capacity)
Gareth Davies: Comptroller & Auditor General, 2019–
David Davis, MP: former Chair of PAC
David Dewar: former Assistant Auditor General, NAO
Patrick Dunleavy: Professor, LSE
Mark Etherton: former Clerk to the Public Accounts Committee
Irene Gordon: former Specialist Adviser, NAO
David Heald: Professor, Glasgow University
Dame Meg Hillier, MP: Chair of PAC
Dame Margaret Hodge, MP: former Chair of PAC
Helen Irwin: former Clerk to the Public Accounts Committee

Khalid Hamid: International Director, CIPFA
Edward Humpherson: former Executive Leader, NAO
Sir Bernard Jenkin, MP: PAC Member, former Chair, Public Administration and Constitutional Affairs Select Committee and Chair of the Liaison Committee
Adrian Jenner: former Clerk to the Public Accounts Committee
Lord Kerslake: former Cabinet Secretary
Sir Edward Leigh, MP: former Chair of PAC and former Chair of the PAC
Sir Andrew Likierman: former Chair, NAO Board
Jeremy Lonsdale: former Director General Value for Money, NAO
Lord Macpherson: former Permanent Secretary, HM Treasury
Lord Morse: Comptroller & Auditor General, 2009–19
H. David Myland: former Deputy C&AG, NAO
Mike Newbury: NAO Director
Lord O'Donnell: former Cabinet Secretary
Sarah Olney, MP: PAC Member
Sir David Omand: former Permanent Secretary, Home Office and Cabinet Office
Sir Richard Packer: former Permanent Secretary, Ministry of Agriculture, Fisheries and Food
Sarah Petit: former Clerk to the Public Accounts Committee
Tim Phillips: NAO Director and former PAC Chair Liaison
Dame Fiona Reynolds: Chair, NAO Board
Steve Richards: Journalist and Contemporary Historian
Sir Peter Riddell: Institute for Government
James Robertson: former NAO Director and Chief Economist
Jill Rutter: Institute for Government
Neil Sayers: former Director, NAO
Alex Scharaschkin: former Director, NAO
Martin Sinclair: former Executive Leader, NAO
Nick Smith MP: PAC Member
Christian van Stolk: RAND
Tony Travers: former Adviser PAC, Professor, LSE and Head of LSE London
Lord Turnbull: former Cabinet Secretary
Michael Whitehouse: former Chief Operating Officer, NAO
Rob Whiteman: former Chief Eexecutive, UK Border Agency and Chief Executive, CIPFA
Lord Wilson: former Cabinet Secretary
Nick Wright: former Clerk to the Public Accounts Committee

The authors would like to convey their immense gratitude to Jonathan Bourn (Jon), son of the late Sir John Bourn, KCB, C&AG 1988–2008, and his family for enabling their access to Sir John's private papers, notes and diaries, which have added immeasurably to the authors' insight and understanding of his time as C&AG. Thanks are also due to them for their unfailing hospitality and warmth.

The authors would also like to thank the National Audit Office, the C&AG, Gareth Davies and Rob Holmes for permission to use and help in acquiring the images of the C&AGs in the book.

Our expert reviewers, Michael Whitehouse, Jeremy Lonsdale and David Heald, are owed immense thanks for their words of wise counsel and generous comments. Any remaining errors are the authors' responsibility.

The authors would also like to thank many staff of the NAO, Parliament, thinktanks and civil servants across government for discussing the ideas behind this book informally. Over the years, the authors have discussed the concepts which lie behind this book with their colleagues in Whitehall, Westminster and academia, and many of the insights which are in this book would not have been possible without those discussions, including: Claire Hardy, Matthew Fright, Toby Evans, Charles Nancarrow, Dan and Ruth Ward, Richard Ratcliffe, Phil Larkin, Adam Evans, Larry Honeysett, Joshua Reddaway, Senthuran Rudran, Matthew Sinclair, Mark Simpson, Oliver Lodge, Joe Perkins, George Crockford, Denis Brennan, Andrew Maxfield, Jeremy Lonsdale, Alex Scharaschkin, Mark Allen, Abigail Marshall Bailey, Ria Gill Williams, Jenny Brown, Martin O'Reilly, Thomas Ahrens, Rhys Andrews, Chris Carter, Hugh Coombs, Peter Eckersley, Warwick Funnell, Giuseppe Grossi, Jim Haslam, Donald Halliday, Khalid Hamid, David Heald, Ron Hodges, Kevin Hunter, Mark Sandford, Bruce D. McDonald III, Pete Murphy, David Oldroyd, Lee Parker, Richard Slack and Ileana Steccolini. There are many more names which could have been included here and deserve thanks too.

The authors would also like to thank their families and close friends for sharing their lives with a company of both contemporary and historical auditors for the last couple of years. Laurence would like to specifically thank his mother, Hazel; father, Laurence (sadly physically departed, but still here in spirit); and brother, Kevin, for always supporting him to challenge authority and hold power to account for the public good, and his wife, Anchalee, and daughters, Dior and Eloise, who afford the same measure of fortitude. Henry would like to thank his mother, Daintry Midgley, and his brother, John Midgley, for all their support over the years. His father, Gordon Midgley, died before Henry joined the NAO, and one of the great losses of this book is that he isn't alive to discuss it! Thanks are also due to Louise Hall, who has been amazingly supportive and kind during the writing of the book. Aileen would like to thank her husband, Andrew Maxfield, and her children, Nathaniel and Iris, and their partners, Meredith and Claire. They have all contributed massively to the author's ideas, energy and morale and were a great source of IT and technical help. Like anything else, this book rests on the kindness of many, many people who have been supportive, thoughtful and helpful friends over the years. They are too numerous to mention, but you know who you are.

Lastly, an enormous thank you to the staff of the National Archives at Kew.

1

INTRODUCTION TO THE NATIONAL AUDIT OFFICE

1.1 Introduction

The purpose of this book is to consider public sector auditing in the United Kingdom (UK) through a critical examination of the evolution of the National Audit Office (NAO). In other words, this is a 40-year history of the UK's Supreme Audit Institution. It is much more than that though: the history of the NAO as a Supreme Audit Institution helps tell the important story of accountability of the state during a time in which the UK adopted many policies associated with neo-liberalism. Whilst this is of course a UK story, nevertheless it is of international significance as the democratic tradition of accountability and the Westminster model of audit have had great influence globally. Therefore, we believe this historical record will have an important impact as to how countries around the world reflect on their own arrangements for audit and accountability.

In this chapter, we set out the UK's public accountability and audit arrangements within the liberal or republican tradition, which has become internationally influential, then we determine why studying the NAO's history, from 1984 to 2024, is important. We then set out how the study will be done theoretically via the conceptualisation of regulatory space. In addition, we lay down what we will analyse and how, and lastly, we highlight how the book is structured.

1.2 Public accountability and audit arrangements in the UK

Accountability is a central relationship within modern democratic states (Bovens, 2010). Early democracies may have had different structures to

DOI: 10.4324/9781003520085-1

modern ones, but they share with them a strong emphasis on accountability (Mitchell, 2019). Modern democracies are distinguished by their faith in accountability. Democratic and non-democratic states responded similarly to COVID-19 using lockdowns and other restrictive measures, but democracies alone married those measures to clear accountability for the governments who took those decisions (Ferry et al., 2024). Accountability therefore is central to democracy, but it is often unclear what that accountability should be for, and there are many views of accountability in democracies that can be drawn upon (Mulgan, 2000; Sinclair, 1995). The meaning of accountability in democratic or republican states has changed over time. For example, accountability in ancient Athens is not the same as accountability in modern Greece; these fluctuations are connected with the chosen form of democracy in different places and the political economy in which those constitutional forms are enacted. As Mueller (2011) has demonstrated, the history of accountability in European politics fundamentally changed in the 20th century with the invention of the mass civil service and the welfare state.

One of the dominant ways of thinking about accountability within a republican or democratic tradition of thinking about political power has been to examine government spending and taxation. During periods in which the number of democracies grew globally (such as in the immediate aftermath of the First World War or after the fall of the Berlin Wall), these traditions became more dominant across the world. Edmund Burke told the Commons in 1780 that the distinguishing fact about Britain as a parliamentary regime was that 'under other governments a question of expense is only a question of economy and it is nothing more: with us in every question of expense, there is always a mixture of constitutional considerations' (Burke, 1854, p. 201). William Gladstone said that the 'finance of a country is ultimately associated with the liberties of the country' (Dewar and Funnell, 2016, p. 1). Burke and Gladstone were making points about British history and British constitutional traditions, but they drew on and contributed to an argument that taxation and expenditure required consent and accountability for a state to be constitutional. Alexis de Tocqueville argued that 'the right of levying taxes' is so vast a power for a government that it 'may be said to involve all other rights' (Tocqueville, 1856). Locke, writing over a hundred years before Tocqueville, Burke and Gladstone, agreed. For Locke, taxation without consent invalidated the government which claimed it: 'if any one shall claim a power to lay and levy taxes on the people and by his own authority, and without such fundamental consent, he thereby invades the fundamental law of property and subverts the end of Government' (Locke, 1988, p. 362). The fear of limitless and arbitrary taxation flows through pre-modern and modern controversies including those surrounding the origins of the English

Civil War and the American and French revolutions (Russell, 1973, p. 27; Bailyn, 2017, p. 340). Taxation and spending are intrinsically linked: Hobbes, using his argument that the state was an artificial person, compared taxation to the blood which circulates to the heart and expenditure to the blood which the heart sends out once more to make the limbs of the body (i.e. the functions of the state) vital (Hobbes, 1996, p. 175). For Burke, Gladstone, Locke and Tocqueville, all operating within a liberal tradition, the idea that taxation rested on consent and that expenditure must therefore be accountable were central features of their constitutional thinking.

The UK and its predecessor kingdoms have a long history of thinking about this question.[1] In both medieval Scotland and England, Parliament claimed the right to consent to taxation (Goodare, 1989; Maddicott, 2010). In England, the principle that once Parliament had granted money, it had the right to demand an inspection of whether that money had been spent as allocated goes back to the Parliament of 1406 (Givens-Wilson, 2016, p. 294).

Though the demand for audit has been consistent across the centuries, its meaning has not. At times, the demand for audit was part of the demand for a new settlement amongst the nations of the British Isles based on principles of incorruptible religious faith and an understanding that God would guide his honest saints to achieve peace (Council of the Army, 1652).

At times, the demand for audit was a demand to turn austerity into a constitutional principle and reduce the powers of departments to overspend their budgets (Funnell, 2004). Such demands were tied often to political values, such as liberty (Funnell, 2007, 2008; Ferry and Midgley, 2022). These 20th-century debates became increasingly comparative: defects in the UK's audit arrangements were identified because they were weaker than those in other countries (Normanton, 1966). No definition of audit has ever been attempted without opposition or debate within the political system: questions about 'what' auditors of the public sector should do, 'why' they should, 'when', 'how' authoritative they should be, 'where' this should occur and 'who' they should call to account have been debated for centuries.

These debates are still live (Ferry et al., 2022) and are not about audit per se, but encompass wider questions such as what the correct role of the state should be; how democratic (or non-democratic) states should be held accountable; what the relationship between taxation and consent should be; how important corruption is to undermining governments; what powers the legislature should have over the executive and what information citizens and Parliaments should receive from the executive (Ferry and Midgley, 2024).

This study examines a period when audit was both changing and changed, through a 40-year history of the NAO. The NAO, created by the 1983 National Audit Act, opened its doors for the first time in January 1984, so consequently our study examines the period from 1984 to 2024. We examine why the NAO was created and how its activities have been shaped and reshaped by the political context in which it evolved and by the actions of individuals within and without the office (Hopwood, 1983, 1984). We do this to identify precisely the constitutional questions which the NAO and Parliament grappled with in this period. Was the argument, made by Burke and Gladstone, that all questions of finance were questions about the constitution still true in the late 20th and early 21st centuries? If so, what was the constitution that was being enforced and what meaning did democracy have in this period? What part was the auditor supposed to play in defining democracy? Where did the NAO sit in the relationship between legislature and executive? How did Mueller's (2011) politics of bureaucracy interfere with the older constitutional tradition of thinking about expenditure and rights?

These are all questions which have historical as well as philosophical and political answers: we do not suggest that the NAO or the UK political system has answered these questions correctly or finally; rather what we identify is the set of provisional answers offered by civil servants, politicians and auditors to both questions about democracy and the dilemmas of survival and success in historical moments of time. This is not an unusual approach: Hoppitt (2021) did this on a much broader scale for the territorial fiscal constitution of the UK since 1707 and Dewar and Funnell (2016) did similarly for parliamentary audit in England and the UK over 800 years. By focussing more tightly on a contemporary period, our study illuminates a moment of massive change in that longer history of UK democracy. Given the global importance of the Westminster model of audit and the Thatcherite neo-liberal reforms to the public sector, we believe that this history casts a light on the modern development of public sector audit and accountability outside the UK too.

1.3 Why 1984–2024?

Charting the history of an institution such as the NAO across time is challenging. Histories can start at any point, and as we will demonstrate later, there were considerable continuities between the NAO after 1984 and its predecessor organisation, the E&AD.

However, there are good reasons why we have chosen to analyse the meaning of audit and hence accountability and democracy, between 1984 and 2024, not only because the NAO was founded on 1 January 1984 by an Act of Parliament passed in 1983, although that is fortuitous. The

NAO's foundation happened at a moment of huge change in UK politics: a turning point in 20th-century British history (Richards, 2023; Bevan, 2023). The advent of Margaret Thatcher as prime minister in 1979, four years before the NAO was created, ushered in a period of radical change to the social and political structures of the UK. Thatcher and her successors remoulded the ways in which public services were provided to British citizens, the way British democracy worked and the position of the UK as a state within the wider world.

In terms of public services, the role of the state changed fundamentally after Thatcher's election in 1979. In May 1979, the UK government still owned important stakes in the commanding heights of the economy, specifically energy, transport and steel; it ran social services, education and much (social) housing through local government and health through the National Health Service (NHS) (Millward, 2014). After 1979, governments sold industries and assets and contracted out services and, irrespective of party, maintained those industries in private hands, albeit regulated (Parker, 2009; Sloman, 2021; Wickham Jones, 2021). This was a deliberate change influenced by neo-liberal thinkers who saw government inefficiency and extravagance as a cause of British and wider Western decline (Jackson, 2012; Buggeln et al., 2017). These thinkers found a sympathetic audience amongst both politicians and officials (Turnbull, 2022; Kelsey, 2023). This changed the nature of the craft of government for the British state. Pre-1979, the UK state had to be an expert in managing services or superintending nationalised companies (Heald and Steel, 1981). In later decades, after the 1980s, even where the state directly managed a service, it often did so at arm's length through a separate body or agency (Cooper et al., 2023). Slowly, the UK state evolved new relationships with services. Either it became a manager presiding over contracts where the actual service was being managed by a third party, or it became a regulator defining how a service might be regulated to ensure public goods were maintained within a market. Where the state had performed these roles before, it had done so in a much smaller way (Midgley, 2016; Sturgess, 2018; Murphy, 2023). Where services could not be allocated to markets or private sector managers, civil servants functioned in a context of far greater suspicion and a demand for rules that would enforce efficiency (Roberts, 2011). Calls for greater efficiency continued and intensified over the period (Innes, 2023).

Secondly, British democracy itself was reshaped. The relationship between central and local government and the four nations of the UK was fundamentally altered. Although there were some precedents in the past (Evans, 2015, 2020), the New Labour programme of devolution constituted 'the most radical constitutional change this country has seen since the Great Reform Act of 1832' (Bogdanor, 2001). New institutions had to be established and older ones forced to adjust (Evans, 2019; Foster and Knox, 2022, 2023). In contrast, England faced greater centralisation under Thatcher (Leach et al., 2017). Scandals such as the Poulson affair in the early 1970s, and its long aftermath, increased pressure for centralisation of guidance to local authorities to avoid corruption, improve codes of conduct and foster (good) corporate governance over the next 40 years (Ferry, Oldroyd et al., 2023). A new system of local government audit was created in 1983, which although arguably successful under the Audit Commission, was ultimately criticised for being too expensive and having too large a remit (Ferry, 2019, p. 8) and eventually abolished in 2015. Combined with austerity and large cuts to local government funding, it left England with underfunded local government, a weakened audit regime and an imperfect system of local democratic accountability (Ferry et al., 2015; Ferry and Sandford, 2022; Ferry et al., 2022).

These changes to tiers of government were matched by changes to the relationship between the individual and the state. Disquiet over the powers of the state against the citizen had been growing before 1984, with scandals like the Crichel Down affair[2] (O'Hara, 2011). In 1991, John Major introduced the Citizen's Charter to give citizens assurance about what they would receive from public services (Taylor, 1991). The Human Rights Act (1998) and the Constitutional Reform Act (2005) threatened to change the relationship between the judiciary, the executive and Parliament (Norton, 2007). Referendums were increasingly used to resolve complex issues, with potential conflict between representative and direct democracy (White, 2022). Despite the state becoming more democratic, the overall regime still struggled to engage the public, with falling electoral turnout and falling party memberships (Mair, 2013). The COVID-19 pandemic of 2020–2022 created further anxiety about the powers of the state versus those of the individual and led the right of politics to embrace the language of rights. Consequently, by 2024 the UK had a lopsided devolution settlement, an incomplete local government settlement and a stronger antagonism developing between the individual and the state, mediated by the courts. These new developments put British citizens into a very different position from 1984.

The third of our changes concerns the UK's global position. Superficially, in many ways, the UK's global position did not change in this period: it remained a key ally of the United States of America (USA) and a member of the North Atlantic Treaty Organization (NATO) and an ally of other European states particularly in response to the Russian invasion of Ukraine in 2022. However, in significant respects, the UK's position in 2024 was fundamentally different from that in 1984.

Firstly, the UK's relationship with Europe changed. The UK had entered the European Community in 1973 and had been involved in the major projects of integration in terms of both the single market and the alignment of currencies through the 1980s. In 1992, the UK left the Exchange Rate Mechanism (ERM) and obtained an opt-out from membership of the single currency, which it exercised in 1999. However, despite these decisions, its destiny seemed firmly rooted in what by then was the European Union (EU), and which by the 2000s had expanded further with the UK's support (though as Thompson (2016) suggests there were tensions implicit in the UK's EU membership). Nevertheless, in 2016, the UK voted to leave the EU: a decision then followed by the UK deciding to leave both the customs union and the single market.

This change was dramatic, reflecting deep changes in UK politics, but it was not the only change in this period (Thompson, 2017; Edgerton, 2018). Thatcher's UK had spent a significant amount on defence: 5.4% of GDP in 1984. In 1989, the Cold War ended, which meant that the UK got a peace dividend. By the 2020s, the UK spent less on defence as a proportion of GDP and more on healthcare and benefits (Clark and Dilnot, 2001; Clark, 2023). The UK state therefore had shifted its posture from being a warfare state to a welfare state increasingly (Edgerton, 2018). This change and its relative decrease in economic power (Edgerton, 2018) made it a far less significant military player in Europe and the wider world: unable in 2021 to stay in Afghanistan independently of the USA, for example (although rhetoric about the UK's position in geopolitics does not always match the financial reality). This change was reinforced by the fact that whilst UK GDP has increased since 1980, its percentage of global GDP has roughly halved given the extraordinary growth of China and continued strong growth of the USA (International Monetary Fund, 2023).

These three changes created a very different sense in 2024 of British democracy from that in 1984. The British state had become less local and more national, more fragmented, less focussed on the broader public sector, based more around health, social care and pensions and less on defence, than it had been in 1984. All these factors changed the requirements of public sector accountability and democracy and fundamentally formed the patterns of the NAO's audit over the decades.

Understanding that process of change requires us to understand the regulatory space in which audit sits so we can see how that changed over time.

1.4 Regulatory space

Regulatory space is a concept within accounting literature. It is an attempt to deal intellectually with the dynamism and fluidity of audit practices, how the boundaries of audit have changed over time and the invention of new areas for auditors to examine (Andon et al., 2015). Andon et al.

(2015) proposed four dimensions of regulatory space to enable scholars to understand the development of the profession: independence, reporting, professional accreditation and the nature of the audit role. Subsequently, scholars have refined these categories for use in the public sector. The first attempt by Ferry and Ahrens (2021) defined for UK local government (England, Northern Ireland, Scotland and Wales) a set of categories which matched those identified by Andon et al. (2015) but were scoped for the public sector: organisation and fragmentation, independence and competition, audit scope, and reporting. This structure was then used to compare internationally local government audit across 14 countries by research teams in the respective countries (Ferry and Ruggiero, 2022; Ferry, Midgley et al., 2023) and then further built upon to analyse 20 different countries and their local audit arrangements (Ferry, Midgley et al., 2023).

Building on earlier research work, Ferry, Hamid et al. (2023) analysed 196 Supreme Audit Institutions (SAIs), which are members of the International Organization of Supreme Audit Institutions (INTOSAI), a non-governmental organisation with special consultative status with the United Nations' (UN) Economic and Social Council (ECOSOC) and an umbrella organisation for the external government audit community: for SAIs, they suggested organisational context (including independence), capacities and audit scope were the key determinants of the regulatory space. This work for INTOSAI was presented in November 2022 at the XXIV International Congress of Supreme Audit Institutions (INCOSAI), culminating in the Rio Declaration (INTOSAI, 2022). The Rio Declaration helps to accomplish UN Sustainable Development Goal 16 (UN SDG 16) 'Peace, Justice and Strong Institutions' that specifically highlights the importance of strong accountability of the state, which is underpinned by audit and accounting.

It is important to define what exactly those concepts mean before we use them in our analysis. Firstly, the organisational context for an SAI has long been seen as a key factor in its development. SAIs claim that they are independent (Cordery and Hay, 2020). In the UK, this independence has often been contested. The SAI was originally set up with strong links to the government, in particular HM Treasury (the Treasury) (Funnell, 1994). In the 1980s, this was, as we shall discuss later, changed, with the audit institution becoming more closely associated with Parliament (Ferry and Midgley, 2022). In the UK and overseas, the conflict between the auditor with their interest in opening up government and government with its interest in concealing information has been a crucial way of understanding what accountability means and how far it goes (Radcliffe, 2008, 2011; Funnell, 2011). There are alternative structures: an audit office which serves the legislature can be a servant of a democratic regime, whereas one whose activities are firmly controlled by the executive becomes a tool of government control (Pallot, 2003; Mir et al., 2018). The institutions around the SAI are also developing, so this space is constantly changing (Davis, 2022). So, the organisational context of an audit office illuminates the ways in which accountability and democracy have been conceived of in a particular political system.

Secondly, if analysing the organisational context of an audit office illuminates the degree to which it is genuinely independent and a servant of the legislature, as opposed to an enforcement regime for the executive, then it is important to have a discussion of the capacities of the audit office to undertake its role. Capacities can be conceived of in two ways. Firstly, there is the clear issue that whatever the organisational context or scope of the audit, the capacity to perform the audit will determine the ways in which the audit office can do its task. The accounting literature has been alert to this. Recent changes in technology, for example, have prompted scholars to examine what the consequences for SAIs might be (Otia and Bracci, 2022; Ferry and Midgley, 2023). More basically, the number of staff that an SAI employs, and their skills and abilities, all have a relationship with what the SAI can do. Dewar and Funnell (2016) argue this in the UK context: as the skills of the auditors increased, so did the capacity of the audit. However, this shades into another meaning of capacity. An ideological view of capacity has consequences for the scope of the audit and the meaning of independence. Radcliffe (1999), for example, shows how auditors in Alberta constructed an image of efficiency that enabled them to conduct their audits, but this construction of what a good efficiency audit meant carried ideological meaning. This can commonly be seen in the types of training that an SAI endorses for its staff. Capacity therefore is not a neutral concept, but the choice of capacities for an SAI represents an ideological choice about what forms of accountability it should prioritise and which not.

Thirdly, both the concepts of organisational context and capacities are related to the idea of scope of its audit, which in turn relates to accountability. Audit scope has been widely studied in the accounting literature. The scope of audits could include matters such as a traditional financial audit; a value for money audit, which examines economy, efficiency and effectiveness; or other forms of audit such as sustainability assurance (Hopwood, 1983, 1984; O'Dwyer et al., 2011). Arguments have been advanced for increasing the scope of audit to assess equity (Johnsen, 2005; Ferry, 2019) and ethics (Bringselius, 2018). All these arguments, for equity, ethics and even efficiency as part of audit, carry ideological freight and have implications for what democracy means (Radcliffe, 1998). Ferry, Hamid et al. (2023) suggest as well that the scope can take in the type of organisation that the SAI audits: for example, can the audit office examine the central bank or local government or other government agencies? The reasons that an SAI's scope may differ will depend on what democracy (or government) in each country means: for example, Ferry, Midgley et al. (2023) suggested that in local government the question of who does the audit depends on the constitutional foundations of local government in a particular country. Countries which see local government as autonomous will use regional or local audit offices to conduct audits; countries which view local government more from central government could use their SAI to audit local authorities (e.g. New Zealand), whereas the mark of a devolved system could be the creation of a devolved system of accountability (Foster and Knox, 2022, 2023). The extension of audit into new realms is also the extension of a different type of rationality, associated with business and accounting, into those realms (Power, 1999; Free et al., 2020). The scope of audit tells us about what accountability is and how far it stretches within the public sector and ultimately what democracy and accountability mean.

1.5 What we will analyse and how we will do so

The history of the NAO since 1984 is complex. One of the complexities arises from our use of several different sources of evidence. In the following section, we summarise the evidence we have used and highlight how it differs across the periods examined. There are two basic types of evidence: documentary evidence and the evidence of recollection. We describe these below.

As regards documentary evidence, we have examined three types: firstly, the NAO's own reports and other reports, for example, by select committees from 1984 to 2024. There are two categories of reports used in the book. In the first category, we have drawn on reports which concern public audit itself, written by select committees or commissioned by government. They were infrequent. Significant examples include a wave of reports that came out before the National Audit Act was passed in 1983 (cited in Chapter 2), the Sharman Report published in the early years of New Labour (dealt with in Chapter 5) and reports on government accounts published both in the 1980s (discussed in Chapter 3) and in the 2010s (discussed in Chapter 6). Where they exist, these are valuable for informing us about the state of thinking within or outside of government about the NAO. However, their lack of frequency and the fact they are normative accounts of what public sector audit should be means that they are less useful as a guide to what public sector audit actually was. In the second category are the NAO's own reports from 1984 to 2024: these have the opposite problem. They show us audit in practice and what auditors were actually doing, but they do not provide us with accounts of a change in auditing practices or a change in the principles underlying those practices. The audit reports, for their own legitimacy, if they mention previous work at all, normally suggest that they are a repetition or continuation of what the NAO has done in the past. These include both reports on accounts and reports on value for money. Both concepts are fluid, and we will return to them later.

Secondly, there are a range of other documents which contain public comment on the NAO. These include newspaper articles; debates in Parliament (transcribed by Hansard) from the House of Lords, House of Commons and select committees; and other material such as books published contemporaneously. These often illuminate what was going on within the NAO and explain externally why things were changing.

Thirdly, we have examined archival records, deposited by the NAO and government departments at the National Archives in Kew. These records were made by officials at the time and include minutes of meetings, correspondence between the NAO and departments, briefing for ministers or senior officials before meetings or parliamentary debates, letters within the NAO or within departments, draft documents for circulation internally and other records. Similarly to reports, these records were created for their own purposes and not as interventions in debates about the role or purpose of the NAO. The UK's data release system puts an embargo on when documents can be made public, which means that we can access these records only for the period running up to 2000: they are much more extensive as well in the earlier part than later. Consequently, our chapters on the E&AD, Sir Gordon Downey's term of office and Sir John Bourn's early period depend much more on our access to these documents than our analysis of the period after Sir John Bourn's departure in 2008. As part of these archival records, we have obtained access to a unique archive. In 2022, Sir John Bourn died, unfortunately before we could interview him. His heir, though, allowed us access to the documents that Bourn had kept from his time as Comptroller and Auditor General (C&AG) and before. These documents provide a unique insight into Bourn's tenure in the role and include papers, notes on books and articles, lectures and talks and his diaries.

In addition to the documents we have inspected, we have also carried out 54 interviews. These interviews included politicians; senior officials at the NAO, in government and in Parliament; and academics and commentators on civil society. A list of interviews is provided in the Acknowledgements section. This interview evidence covers the entire period but for obvious reasons is more constrained after 2019 given that issues discussed are still current within the NAO. The interviews we have conducted were taped and transcribed.

The authors have reviewed all these documents and interviews individually and discussed them together back and forth to elicit main themes and trends. Both Aileen Murphie and Henry Midgley worked at the NAO: Murphie from 1983 to 2021 and Midgley from 2008 to 2021. They therefore have a deep insight into the workings of the office. This has been combined with the knowledge and experience of Laurence Ferry, who has worked and researched in both central and local government for almost 30 years and so was able to provide a more independent perspective on events and documents pertaining to the NAO.

In this way, of eliciting main themes and trends, the authors have followed the methodology for qualitative research identified by Ahrens and Chapman (2006). Words have had to be parsed carefully, as a statement made in one context does not mean the same as a statement made at another point in the NAO's history. For example, we pick up in Chapter 2 on the prehistory of the NAO the fact that the C&AG was often described as an officer of the House, including by C&AGs, but the meaning of this changed after 1983 when that title had been granted to the C&AG under statute. What had once been a claim to independence became after 1983 either a reminder of the C&AG's ultimate subservience to Parliament or the assertion of an independence against the executive that had already been granted. This reading in context matters for the study of an institution like the NAO, which stresses how much it relies on precedent and an unchanging constitutional order to legitimate its work. A large part of this volume consists therefore of sifting through the language that C&AGs and other officials used to identify what changed and why, rather than reading words for their simple locutionary meaning.

1.6 How the book is structured

The NAO was created in 1984. The NAO's senior official is the C&AG. This person – always so far (and lamentably) a man – has a huge influence on the way that work is carried out within the office. Christian van Stolk[3] put it to us that 'you can always recognise the hand of the C&AG in all the work that the NAO does' (Christian van Stolk, interview). C&AGs have tended to serve for long periods of time: in the period since 1984, there have been five: Sir Gordon Downey (1981–1988), Sir John Bourn (1988–2008), Tim Burr (2008–2009), Sir Amyas Morse (2009–2019) and Gareth Davies (2019–ongoing).[4] Consequently, we have structured the book around these individuals and their time as C&AG, including Tim Burr within Bourn's chapters as his tenure as C&AG was brief due to the fact he was appointed after Sir John Bourn's resignation with the clear intention that a new C&AG would be appointed to replace Bourn. Consequently, the rest of the book is structured as follows.

In Chapter 2, we provide an analysis of the development of public sector audit in the UK between 1866 and 1984. During this period, given its length, we explain themes in the development of public sector audit from the 1860s to the 1980s. These themes are related to developments which informed the kind of organisation that the NAO became in 1984 and afterwards.

After our analysis of the period before the NAO's foundation, we move to examining the individual periods during which each C&AG was in office from 1984 to 2024. We analyse these terms of office in the same manner: firstly, by establishing the context within which the C&AG in question operated, then by using the categories of regulatory space to analyse the evolution of the NAO. Consequently, in each chapter we analyse the organisational context, capacities and audit scope of the NAO and how those evolved in each era.

In Chapter 3, we examine the period of Downey's time as C&AG from 1984 to 1988. This chapter sets out how Downey and his senior colleagues interpreted the new mandate of the NAO and how they operated against the context of the Thatcherite revolution. Choices made in this period especially around the NAO's relationship to Thatcherite reform initiatives would provide precedents for later NAO work.

In Chapter 4, we examine the first nine years (1988–1997) of Bourn's period as C&AG. Bourn attempted to push the NAO forward after Downey's period in office and to widen the NAO's value-for-money work. This period also saw the adoption of accrual accounting by the Treasury with related changes to the NAO's structure and organisation. We divide Bourn's reign in two around the election of a Labour government in 1997.

Chapter 5 covers the rest of Bourn's period in office from 1997 to 2008. In this chapter, we analyse how Bourn sought to expand the remit of the NAO, the NAO's encounters with war and peace especially through the analysis of the Iraq War and the NAO's accommodations to the public sector reforms of the Blair era. The chapter explains how Bourn left office in 2008 as well and the appointment of Tim Burr as C&AG.

Chapter 6 covers the term of Amyas Morse as C&AG from 2009 to 2019. Whereas Bourn had presided over a period in which the NAO sat within a UK whose economic position was continually improving, Morse's tenure was punctuated by crises. The first was the financial crisis of 2007–2009. The UK adapted a policy of spending cuts to respond to the crisis called austerity: Morse's NAO joined government in those spending cuts, reversing over 20 years of steady expansion. The NAO was faced with three individual challenges in Morse's period: how to audit the reduction in spending after the financial crisis, how to audit the UK's exit from the EU and how to cope with a loss of trust in UK institutions, displayed in the context of audit by the abolition of the NAO's sister organisation, the Audit Commission in 2015, and criticisms of government accounting.

Chapter 7 covers Gareth Davies' time as C&AG since 2019. Davies's period in office like that of Morse has been consumed with crisis; particularly the COVID-19 pandemic since 2020. Davies has pushed the NAO rhetorically to be more committed to finding auditing approaches to the climate crisis as well.

In Chapter 8, we provide an analysis of the impacts and implications of this history. We provide a summary of what we have found and discuss some of the impacts and implications of that for the meaning of democracy in the UK during this era and beyond it, stretching into the future. We discuss some of the limitations of the system that has evolved over the past 40 years since the early 1980s and some of its strengths, plus suggest potential questions for the future that scholars and legislators may wish to take up.

1.7 Chapter summary

The chapter has provided a summary of how we will address public sector auditing in the UK through a critical examination of the evolution of the NAO over 40 years, from its creation in 1984 to 2024, drawing upon the theorisation of regulatory space.

However, before we do that, in the next chapter we will analyse how UK public sector audit developed over more than a century between 1866 and 1984 before the NAO was established, by looking at the E&AD. This is the context for how the NAO came about and the world that it inherited.

Notes

1 The UK was created by a series of unions. England had imperial possessions in both Ireland and Wales during the Middle Ages, and several wars were fought between England and Scotland. In the 16th century, Wales and England were brought together into a union. In 1603, the King of Scotland, James I, succeeded to the throne of England and Wales. However, it was not until 1707 that an enduring union of the English and Scottish Parliaments was constructed. In 1801, Great Britain was united with Ireland through another act of union. In 1922, Eire became an independent country. The UK now includes England, Scotland, Wales and the six counties in the north of Ireland that remain part of the UK after the independence of Eire.

2 The Crichel Down affair was a British political scandal of 1954, which led to the adoption of the Crichel Down Rules, guidelines applying to compulsory purchase. The case centred on 725 acres of agricultural land at Crichel Down, Dorset, which was purchased compulsorily in 1938 by the Air Ministry for use by the Royal Air Force. In 1941, Winston Churchill promised Parliament that the land would be returned to its owners after the war. Instead, it was handed over to the Ministry of Agriculture. In 1949, the owners began a campaign for the government's promise to be kept. They gained a public inquiry which was damning about actions of those acting for the government. In 1954, the minister responsible, Sir Thomas Dugdale, announced that the owner could buy the

land back and told the House of Commons he was resigning. The resignation has been taken as a precedent on ministerial responsibility, even though only partially supported by the details of the case.

3 Christian van Stolk, various posts at RAND Europe including Executive Vice President 2008–ongoing.

4 Many of the key personalities within the NAO's history changed their names, often by acquiring titles. In this volume, we have given them the name which they held when they held the responsibilities we are describing. For example, until 2014, Amyas Morse is Amyas Morse; after he was knighted, he becomes Sir Amyas Morse if we are describing events until he was given a peerage in 2021. Consequently, when describing his interview, we would list him as Lord Morse, but for events in his tenure, he is Sir Amyas Morse or Amyas Morse.

References

Ahrens, T. and Chapman, C. S. (2006). Doing qualitative field research in management accounting: Positioning data to contribute to theory. *Accounting, Organizations and Society, 31*(8), 819–841.

Andon, P., Free, C. and O'Dwyer, B. (2015). Annexing new audit spaces: Challenges and adaptations. *Accounting, Auditing and Accountability Journal, 28*(8), 1400–1430.

Bailyn, B. (2017). *The ideological origins of the American revolution, fiftieth anniversary edition.* Cambridge, MA: Harvard University Press.

Bevan, G. (2023). *How did Britain come to this: a century of systematic failures of governance.* London: London School of Economics Press.

Bogdanor, V. (2001). *Devolution in the United Kingdom.* Oxford: Oxford University Press.

Bovens, M. (2010). Two concepts of accountability: accountability as a virtue and a mechanism. *Western European Politics, 33*(5), 946–967.

Bringselius, L. (2018). Efficiency, economy and effectiveness—but what about ethics? Supreme audit institutions at a critical juncture. *Public Money & Management, 38*(2), 105–110.

Buggeln, M. Daunton, M. and Nützenadel, A. (2017). The political economy of public finance since the 1970s: questioning Leviathan. In M. Buggeln, M. Daunton and A. Nützenadel (eds.) *The political economy of public finance: taxation, state spending and debt since the 1970s.* Cambridge: Cambridge University Press, 1–31.

Burke, J. (1854). *The speeches of the Right Hon. Edmund Burke with memoir and historical introductions.* Dublin: James Duffy.

Clark, D. (2023). *Defence expenditure as a share of GDP in the United Kingdom from 1980 to 2021.* Available at https://www.statista.com/statistics/298527/defense-spending-as-share-of-gdp-united-kingdom-uk/ accessed on 10 October 2023.

Clark, T. and Dilnot, A. (2001). *Long-term trends in British taxation and spending.* London: Institute for Fiscal Studies.

Constitutional Reform Act (2005). *Constitutional Reform Act, 2005.* Available at https://www.legislation.gov.uk/ukpga/2005/4 accessed on 23 February 2024.

Cooper, C., Tweedie, J., Andrew, J. and Baker, M. (2023). The new "corporate state": The meshing of corporate and political power and the erosion of democratic accountability in the UK. *Financial Accountability & Management, 39*(2), 268–285.

Cordery, C. and Hay, D. (2020). *Public sector audit.* Abingdon: Routledge.

Council of the Army (1652). *To the supreme authoritie the parliament of the commonwealth of England. The humble petition of the officers of the army….* London: Giles Calvert.
Davis, A. (2022). *Bankruptcy, bubbles and bailouts: The inside history of the Treasury since 1976*. Manchester: Manchester University Press.
Dewar, D. and Funnell, W. (2016). *A history of British National Audit: The pursuit of accountability*. Oxford: Oxford University Press.
Edgerton, D. (2018). *The rise and fall of the British nation*. London: Allen Lane.
Evans, A. (2015). Back to the Future? Warnings from history for a future UK constitutional convention. *Political Quarterly, 86*(1), 24–32.
Evans, A. (2019). Inter-parliamentary relations in the United Kingdom: Devolution's undiscovered country? *Parliaments, Estates and Representation, 39*(1), 98–112.
Evans, A. (2020). A tale as old as (devolved) time? Sewel, Stormont and the legislative consent convention. *Political Quarterly, 91*(1), 165–172.
Ferry, L. (2019). *Audit and inspection of local authorities in England; five years after the Local Audit and Accountability Act. Parliamentary academic fellowship report by Professor Laurence Ferry to Housing, Communities and Local Government select committee*. London: House of Commons.
Ferry, L. and Ahrens, T. (2021). The future of the regulatory space in local government audit: A comparative study of the four countries of the United Kingdom. *Financial Accountability & Management, 38*(3), 376–393.
Ferry, L., Eckersley, P. and Zakaria, Z. (2015). Accountability and transparency in English local government: Moving from 'matching parts' to 'awkward couple'? *Financial Accountability & Management, 31*(3), 345–361.
Ferry, L., Hamid, K. and Hebling Dutra, P. (2023). An international comparative study of the audit and accountability arrangements of supreme audit institutions. *Journal of Public Budgeting, Accounting and Financial Management, 35*(4), 431–450.
Ferry, L. and Midgley, H. (2022). Democracy, accountability and audit: The creation of the UK NAO as a defence of liberty. *Accounting, Auditing and Accountability Journal, 35*(2), 413–438.
Ferry, L. and Midgley, H. (2023). Institutional entrepreneurship in a supreme audit institution: The National Audit Office and the use of data in financial audit. In T. Rana and L. Parker (eds.) *The Routledge Handbook of Public Sector Accounting*. Abingdon: Routledge.
Ferry, L. and Midgley, H. (2024). Are public sector accounts trusted? Exploring the verdict of the Public Administration and Constitutional Affairs Committee in the United Kingdom. *Public Administration*. https://doi.org/10.1111/padm.12983.
Ferry, L., Midgley, H. and Green, S. (2024). Accountability, emergency and liberty during COVID-19 in the UK 2020–22. *Accounting, Auditing and Accountability Journal, 37*(1), 176–197.
Ferry, L., Midgley, H. and Ruggiero, P. (2023). Regulatory space in local government audit: An international comparative study of 20 countries. *Public Money and Management, 43*(3), 233–241.
Ferry, L., Oldroyd, D. and Funnell, W. (2023). A genealogical and archaeological examination of the development of corporate governance and disciplinary power in English local government c.1970–2010. *Accounting, Organizations and Society, 109*, 1–16.
Ferry, L., Radcliffe, V. S. and Steccolini, I. (2022). The future of public audit. *Financial Accountability & Management, 38*(3), 325–336.
Ferry, L. and Ruggiero, P. (2022). *Auditing practices in local governments: An international comparison*. Emerald: Leeds.

Ferry, L. and Sandford, M. (2022). Developing "place leadership" when hierarchical accountability is omnipresent: The case of English sub-national government. *Journal of Public Budgeting, Accounting and Financial Management, 34*(4), 557–565.
Foster, H. and Knox, C. (2022). The 'eyes and ears of parliament': Devolved public accounts committees in the UK. *Journal of Legislative Studies.* https://doi.org/10.1080/13572334.2022.2079860
Foster, H. and Knox, C. (2023). Variegated accountability: Devolved public accounts committees in the UK. *Parliamentary Affairs, 76*(3), 641–661.
Free, C., Radcliffe, V., Spence, C. and Stein, M. (2020). Auditing and the development of the modern state. *Contemporary Accounting Research, 37*(1), 485–513.
Funnell, W. (1994). Independence and the state auditor in Britain: A constitutional keystone or a case of reified imagery? *Abacus, 30*(2), 175–195.
Funnell, W. (2004). Victorian parsimony and the early champions of modern public sector audit. *Accounting History, 9*(1), 25–60.
Funnell, W. (2007). The reason why: The English constitution and the latent promise of liberty in the history of accounting. *Accounting, Business and Financial History, 17*(2), 265–283.
Funnell, W. (2008). The "Proper Trust of Liberty": Economical reform, the English constitution and the protections of accounting during the American War of Independence. *Accounting History, 13*(1), 7–32.
Funnell, W. (2011). Keeping secrets? Or what government performance auditors might not need to know. *Critical Perspectives on Accounting, 22*(7), 714–721.
Givens-Wilson, C. (2016). *Henry IV.* New Haven: Yale University Press.
Goodare, J. (1989). Parliamentary taxation in Scotland, 1560–1603. *Scottish Historical Review, 68*(1), 23–52.
Heald, D. and Steel, D. (1981). Nationalised industries: The search for control. *Chartered Institute of Public Finance and Accountancy, Public Money, 1*(1), 13–19.
Hobbes, T. (1996). *Leviathan* (R. Tuck, ed.). Cambridge: Cambridge University Press.
Hoppit, J. (2021). *The dreadful monster and its poor relations: Taxing, spending and the United Kingdom, 1707–2021.* London: Penguin.
Hopwood, A. (1983). On trying to study accounting in the contexts in which it operates. *Accounting, Organizations and Society, 8*(2–3), 287–305.
Hopwood, A. (1984). Accounting and the pursuit of efficiency. In A. Hopwood and C. Tomkins (eds.) *Issues in public sector accounting.* London: Philip Allan Publishers, 145–159.
Human Rights Act (1998). *Human Rights Act 1998.* Available at https://www.legislation.gov.uk/ukpga/1998/42/contents accessed on 23 February 2024.
Innes, A. (2023). *Late Soviet Britain: Why materialist utopias fail?* Cambridge: Cambridge University Press.
International Monetary Fund (2023). *GDP based on PPP % of World.* Available at https://www.imf.org/external/datamapper/PPPSH@WEO/GBR?zoom=GBR&highlight=GBR accessed on 13 November 2023.
International Organisation of Supreme Audit Institutions (INTOSAI) (2022). *Rio Declaration, XXIV International Congress of Supreme Audit Institutions (INCOSAI), 11 November, Brazil.* Available at: https://www.intosai.org/fileadmin/downloads/about_us/Organs/Congresses/2022_Rio_Declaration/EN_Rio_Declaration_2022.pdf accessed on 20 April 2023.

Jackson, B. (2012). The thinktank archipelago: Thatcherism and neo-liberalism. In B. Jackson and R. Saunders (eds.) *Making thatcher's Britain*. Cambridge: Cambridge University Press, 43–61.
Johnsen, A. (2005). What does 25 years of experience tell us about the state of performance measurement in public policy and management? *Public Money and Management, 25*(1), 9–17.
Kelsey, T. (2023). The retreat from high technology in twentieth century Britain. *English Historical Review*. https://doi.org/10.1093/ehr/cead183.
Leach, S., Stewart, J. and Jones, G. (2017). *Centralisation, devolution and the future of local government in England*. Abingdon: Routledge.
Locke, J. (1988). *Two treatises of government* (P. Laslett, ed.). Cambridge: Cambridge University Press.
Maddicott, J. R. (2010). *The origins of the English Parliament*. Oxford: Oxford University Press.
Mair, P. (2013). *Ruling the void: The hollowing of Western democracy*. New York: Verso.
Midgley, H. (2016). Payment by results in nineteenth-century British education: A study in how priorities change. *Journal of Policy History, 28*(4), 680–706.
Millward, R. (2014) The growth of the public sector. In R. Floud, J. Humphries and P. Johnson (eds.) *The Cambridge economic history of modern Britain*. Cambridge: Cambridge University Press, 387–416.
Mir, M., Fan, H. and Maclean, I. (2018). Public sector audit in the absence of political competition. *Managerial Auditing Journal, 32*(9), 899–923.
Mitchell, T. N. (2019). *Athens: A history of the world's first democracy*. New Haven: Yale University Press.
Mueller, J. W. (2011). *Contesting democracy: Political ideas in twentieth century Europe*. New Haven: Yale University Press.
Mulgan, R. (2000). Accountability: An ever expanding concept. *Public Administration, 78*(3), 555–573.
Murphy, A. (2023). *Virtuous bankers: A day in the life of the eighteenth century Bank of England*. Princeton, NJ: Princeton University Press.
Normanton, E. (1966). *The accountability and audit of governments*. Manchester: Manchester University Press.
Norton, P. (2007). Tony Blair and the constitution. *British Politics, 2*, 269–281.
O'Dwyer, B., Owen, D. and Unerman, J. (2011). Seeking legitimacy for new assurance forms: The case of assurance on sustainability reporting. *Accounting, Organizations and Society, 36*(1), 31–52.
O'Hara, G. (2011). Parties, people, and Parliament: Britain's "Ombudsman" and the politics of the 1960s. *Journal of British Studies, 50*(3), 690–714.
Otia, J. and Bracci, E. (2022). Digital transformation and the public sector auditing: The SAI perspective. *Financial Accountability and Management, 38*(2), 252–280.
Pallot, J. (2003). A wider accountability? The audit office and New Zealand's bureaucratic revolution. *Critical Perspectives on Accounting, 14*(1–2), 133–155.
Parker, D. (2009). Debate: History of privatization. *Public Money & Management, 29*(3), 140–142.
Power, M. (1999). *The Audit Society*. Oxford: Oxford University Press.
Radcliffe, V. (1998). Efficiency audit: An assembly of rationalities and programmes. *Accounting, Organizations and Society, 23*(4), 377–410.
Radcliffe, V. (1999). Knowing efficiency: The enactment of efficiency in efficiency auditing. *Accounting, Organizations and Society, 24*(4), 333–362.
Radcliffe, V. (2008). Public secrecy in auditing: What government auditors cannot know. *Critical Perspectives on Accounting, 19*(1), 99–126

Radcliffe, V. (2011). Public secrecy in government auditing revisited. *Critical Perspectives on Accounting, 22*(7), 722–732.
Richards, S. (2023). *Turning points: Crisis and change in modern Britain, from 1945 to truss.* London: Macmillan.
Roberts, A. (2011). *The logic of discipline: Global capitalism and the architecture of government.* Oxford: Oxford University Press.
Russell, C. (1973). *The origins of the English civil war.* London: Macmillan.
Sinclair, A. (1995). The chameleon of accountability. *Accounting, Organizations and Society, 20*(2–3), 219–237.
Sloman, P. (2021). Welfare in a neo-liberal age: the politics of redistributive market liberalism. In A. Davies, B. Jackson and F. Sutcliffe Braithwaite (eds.) *The neoliberal age? Britain since the 1970s*,. London: UCL Press, 75–93.
Stolk, Christian van, Interview
Sturgess, G. (2018). Public service commissioning: Origins, influences, and characteristics. *Policy Design and Practice, 1*(3), 155–168.
Taylor, D. (1991). A Big Idea for the nineties? The rise of the citizens' charters. *Critical Social Policy, 11*(33), 87–94.
Thompson, H. (2016). Inevitability and contingency: The political economy of Brexit. *The British Journal of Politics and International Relations,* 19(3), 434–449.
Thompson, H. (2017). How the City of London lost at Brexit: A historical perspective. *Economy and Society, 46*(2), 211–228.
Tocqueville, A. de (1856) *The old regime and the revolution.* Available at https://oll.libertyfund.org/titles/tocqueville-the-old-regime-and-the-revolution–1856 accessed on 14 April 2024.
Turnbull, T. (2022). 'No solution to the immediate crisis': The uncertain political economy of energy conservation in 1970s Britain. *Contemporary European History, 31*(4), 570–592.
White, H. (2022) *Held in contempt: What's wrong with the House of Commons.* Manchester: Manchester University Press.
Wickham Jones, M. (2021). Neoliberalism and the Labour Party. In A. Davies, B. Jackson and F. Sutcliffe Braithwaite (eds.) *The neoliberal age? Britain since the 1970s.* London: UCL Press, 226–253.

2

LEGACIES AND ARGUMENTS

2.1 Introduction

In 1992, the *Economist* magazine published a critical article about the National Audit Office (NAO). It compared the NAO to its sister organisation, the Audit Commission. After running through the two organisations' records and arguing the Audit Commission had made much more of an impact on Whitehall, especially because it was not tied to Parliament unlike the NAO, the *Economist* moved on to note the different origins of the two organisations. John Banville[1] and Howard Davies,[2] the first two controllers, 'set up [the Commission] virtually from scratch', whereas the NAO was established as a '1984 revamp of the Exchequer and Audit Department (E&AD), which had few new ideas since it was set up in 1866. The name changed, but most of the staff remained the same' (*Economist*, 1992). Leaving aside the comparison to the Audit Commission, which had a different function and played a different role, the *Economist*'s argument was brutal and, as we shall we see in our subsequent chapters, inaccurate, but their claim of continuity between the old E&AD and the new NAO does have a ring of truth.[3]

To understand the modern history of the NAO, we need to examine what it retained from the E&AD. Where the *Economist* erred was to stress the NAO inherited its staff from the E&AD as its only inheritance from its predecessor. As this chapter will show, there are other legacies from the E&AD. As Lord Macpherson[4] said, 'the changes in the 19th century which in a sense form the basis, I know there have been further acts and adaptations, but the Gladstone settlement in the mid-19th century

DOI: 10.4324/9781003520085-2

has really informed the way that public expenditure has been controlled and audited ever since' (Macpherson, interview). Robert Sheldon[5] agreed: when he was chair of the PAC, he said that his 'sceptical attitude to the Permanent Secretary that comes before us [is] largely based on the tradition of Gladstone' (Procedure Committee, 1990, Q244).

In this chapter, we describe those legacies. Firstly, we review the E&AD as established by Gladstone and the constitutional arguments which were advanced to support it, analysing a constitutional legacy of the auditor as the instrument of Parliamentary and Treasury control over expenditure. This analysis encompasses the E&AD's constitutional role within the Gladstonian system, its relationship with the Treasury and the initial development of value-for-money audit as a device to prevent waste.

Secondly, we take account of the changing nature of the state and the emergence of the 1983 Act via changes to the constitutional position of the E&AD and the state demand for value for money; political concerns about the civil service leaked into worries about the capacity of the civil service's auditor, which in turn led to an E&AD response. Indeed, the UK state changed dramatically during the 20th century: it fought two world wars, lost an empire and gained a welfare state. These changes reshaped the E&AD's work.

We show how debates around them reshaped the way that audit was conceived of in two ways. From the 1870s onwards, British elites conceived that the British state was declining. This trend intensified under the influence of the two great political communicators of decline in the latter half of the 20th century: Harold Wilson[6] and Margaret Thatcher (Tomlinson, 2009). Both advanced changes to the civil service to make it more efficient and to fit a reformed British economy. Their supporters saw reframed value-for-money audit as a central plank of these changes.

Thirdly, we look at other factors which affected the legacies inherited by the NAO. In particular, the changing nature of the state and its greater control over individuals inspired a counter-movement to strengthen the institutions of democratic scrutiny. This led to the development of select committees in Parliament. At the same time, politicians and others started to reconsider the E&AD's relationship with the executive, arguing it required more formal independence and better coverage of the public sector. In addition, the E&AD itself was professionalising during this period. These factors, along with the constitutional legacy of the auditor and changing nature of the state including an increased demand for value for money, came together to form the context for the NAO as it began in 1984.

Finally, in the concluding part of this chapter, we highlight the DNA of the E&AD within the NAO. As the *Economist* argued, the NAO of 1984 owed a lot to the E&AD, but the legacy was a complicated one of interlocking constitutional, political and human dimensions. As subsequent chapters will show, the new NAO's trajectory over the next 40 years was shaped by these legacies.

2.2 The Gladstonian system

2.2.1 The E&AD's constitutional role

Public sector financial control, accounting and audit in the UK have medieval and early modern roots in both political reality and argument (Oldroyd, 1997; O'Regan, 2003; Givens-Wilson, 2016; Midgley, 2016a; Dewar and Funnell, 2017), but its modern history begins with the 1866 Exchequer and Audit Department Act, which created the E&AD. The Act built on decades of pressure within Parliament for improvements to accounting and audit within government (Dewar and Funnell, 2017, pp. 80–106). According to Gladstone, the bill was intended to 'close the circle of [parliamentary] control' over public finances (Dewar and Funnell, 2017, p. 106). The bill's two key concepts were control and the reduction of expenditure (Funnell, 2004). The centre of the bill was the plan to unite two offices, the Comptroller of the Exchequer and the Board of Audit, into one office: the Comptroller and Auditor General (Funnell, 1996). The argument for this was to make controlling public expenditure simpler. The Comptroller would become more independent, and the auditor's work would cover more of the government's activity. The Comptroller had one 'function of the greatest importance and dignity' that was, in Gladstone's words, 'to note all the issues of public money that were authorized to take place under warrants from the Treasury, and to see that those issues were within the amounts voted by Parliament' (House of Commons, 1865, col. 286). Gladstone and other proponents of the bill wanted to unite the two offices because between them they could enable better financial control of expenditure. As Lord Welby[7] (permanent secretary to the Treasury 1885–94 and a close ally of Gladstone) explained, 'so far from regarding the two functions as different in their nature . . . they are both functions of check' (Committee on National Expenditure, 1902, p. 177). Whereas the Comptroller prevented unauthorised expenditure, the auditor would be able to detect it and bring the offending department before the Committee for Public Accounts.

Gladstonian MPs were the heirs of a long tradition of thinking concerned about the exploitation by the executive of military power to overawe the legislature (Bill of Rights, 1689; Schwoerer, 2019). The initial reforms to public sector audit in the UK were partly inspired by a sense that Parliament had lost control of military expenditure (Funnell, 1997). By the 19th century, these constitutional concerns fused with a fear that the state was increasingly consuming more and more of the country's resources and raising more and more debt to do so (Hilton, 2006). Growing public expenditure in areas such as education motivated reformers to attempt to restrain it and direct it to the ends that Parliament envisaged (Midgley, 2016). The political community was anxious that debt should only have been incurred for expenditure that Parliament had authorised (and therefore that was acceptable to the wider political community) (Daunton, 2007). Dicey[8] summarised the constitutional orthodoxy on spending thus:

> What may it be asked, is the real security that the moneys paid by the taxpayers are expended by the government in accordance with the intention of Parliament? The answer is that this security is provided by an elaborate system of control and audit. Under this system not a penny of public money can be obtained by the Government without the authority or sanction of persons (quite independent, be it remarked, of the Cabinet) whose duty it is to see that no money is paid out of the Exchequer except under legal authority. To the same official ultimately comes the knowledge of the way in which the money thus paid out is actually expended, and they are bound to report to Parliament upon any expenditure which is or may appear to be not authorised by the law. The centre of this system of Parliamentary control is the Comptroller and Auditor General.
>
> *(Dicey, 1982, p. 205)*

The *Times* obituarist of Sir Frank Tribe[9] agreed, describing the 'essential function' of the C&AG being 'to see that the money voted by Parliament was spent as Parliament decided it should be' (*The Times*, 1958). In 1962, a Treasury civil servant summarised the constitutional position of the accounting officer (the most senior official in a department, charged with responding to the C&AG's reports) as being the official 'who will have to answer after the event to the Public Accounts Committee of the House of Commons for the financial propriety of his department's actions' (Caulcott, 1962, p. 273). As late as 1982, Sir Douglas Henley[10] would describe the 'constitutionally . . . fundamental' function of appropriation accounts as 'to show, in some detail, that Government departments have spent the funds voted to them by Parliament for the purposes and within the amounts prescribed by law' (Henley, 1982, p. 170). The task therefore for the E&AD was one of discerning judgement against a body of law which made the 'Talmud a mere monograph' (Robinson, 1924, p. 146). The Victorian emphasis therefore was on the offices of Auditor General and Comptroller together as a mechanism for control over public spending, backed by the PAC and by the creation of Accounting Officers who were personally accountable for any breaches of control. Gladstone himself put this emphatically when he spoke of the 1866 Act establishing the Comptroller and Auditor General as 'closing the circle of control' (quoted in Einzig, 1959, preface).

2.2.2 Gladstone's constitutional auditor and the Treasury

The focus on control explains a second legacy from the Gladstonian origins of the E&AD: the department's relationship with the UK's Finance Ministry, HM Treasury and its independence. Whilst the Treasury now sees itself as an economics and finance ministry, responsible for the fluctuations of the UK economy as well as managing the public finances, its medieval and early modern origins were as a finance ministry, concerned purely with managing how much and where the government spent.

The Treasury began the 19th century with very limited powers over other departments (Roseveare, 1969, p. 138). The Treasury, prior to the act, in the words of Lord Welby theoretically controlled public spending but 'could not exercise that control even beneficially because it did not know what the other departments were doing' (Committee on National Expenditure, 1902, p. 177).

Treasury civil servants saw the arrival of the E&AD as a mechanism to assist in cementing control. Sir Francis Mowatt[11] (Treasury Permanent Secretary 1894–1903), in his evidence to the Expenditure Committee, said his department viewed the C&AG as an ally: 'we do not regard ourselves as the criminals for whom he is the police, but that we are branches of the same police force, and therefore we support him in every way in our power' (Committee of National Expenditure, 1902, p. 93). Mowatt's reference to criminals and police was deliberate: early PAC reports focus on the legality of public spending and whether departments had broken the law.

The policing could be intense: Sir Richard Awdry,[12] Accountant General in the Navy, explained in 1902 that the auditors 'live with us and they watch the appropriation of money day by day' (Committee on National Expenditure, 1902, p. 42). In 1873, Welby, then principal clerk for financial business at the Treasury, described the impact of the audit: he told the Select Committee for reducing civil service expenditure 'that the Post Office had been in the habit for years of granting small allowances and gratuitous and small items of expenditure of that kind without any Treasury authority and in fact it is only the check of the audit office that has made the Treasury aware of what has been going on' (Select Committee on reductions in expenditure for civil servants not under Treasury control, 1873, p. 13). In the same year, Ralph Lingen[13] proposed that the C&AG should authorise sick pay, administering a general rule established by the Treasury, so as to ensure that the Treasury and auditor could reduce the amount paid out and force departments to align to a central policy (Select Committee on reductions in expenditure for civil servants not under Treasury control, 1873, p. 145). This alliance worked to inhibit the auditor too. A long-established maxim in the civil service held that 'show the auditor a Treasury letter and he shuts up like an oyster' (Robinson, 1924, p. 148). Treasury culture as late as the 1980s was informed by the presence of auditors: Lord O'Donnell[14] told us in his early days at the Treasury that the presence of the E&AD was 'something you grew up with in the Treasury' (Lord O'Donnell, interview).

Spending ministers perceived an association between the accountants in the Treasury and the E&AD and were frustrated by their exerting control. Some departmental histories were defined by battles with the auditor and the Treasury operating in a sort of alliance (Hamilton, 1917, p. 309; Sutherland, 1973, 2004). These criticisms came from the highest levels in government. Lord Salisbury,[15] speaking as prime minister in the debate on the Queen's speech in 1900, blamed the Treasury system (including the E&AD) for British failures in war during the 19th century, suggesting that

> I feel I am laying my hand on the sacred feature of the Constitution when I say there is the Treasury. . . . I say that the exercise of its powers in governing every department of the Government is not for the public benefit. The Treasury has obtained a position in regard to the rest of the departments of the Government that the House of Commons obtained in the time of the Stuart dynasty. It has the power of the purse, and by exercising the power of the purse it claims a voice in all decisions of administrative authority and policy. I think that much delay and many doubtful resolutions have been the result of the peculiar position which, through many generations, the Treasury has occupied.
>
> *(House of Lords, 1900, col. 32)*

The fact that the Prime Minister felt ready to criticise publicly one of his own departments for possessing too much power over policy demonstrates how profound the frustrations felt by spending ministers were about the Treasury's role. Salisbury never served as a Treasury minister, even when the prime minister's focus was on the UK's position in global affairs: for him, Treasury and audit control flowed through as reasons for British failures in war through the 19th century (from Walcheren, the Crimea to the Boer War).[16]

Nevertheless, the E&AD's close relationship with the Treasury endured, although often challenged. For example, Sir Henry Campbell Bannerman[17] (Prime Minister 1905–8) was forced to reassure the Commons that the C&AG, the enforcer of Treasury control, was really an independent official (House of Commons, 1906, col. 1696). Even after the 1921 Exchequer and Audit Departments Act rendered the E&AD's audit less all encompassing (the Act enabled the C&AG to audit all accounts on a 'test' basis rather than evaluating every single voucher to prove an amount), there was still a strong sense in Whitehall of a link between the two organisations. Outsiders and insiders often referred to the E&AD as part of the machinery of the state. The *Telegraph* wrote, in an obituary of Sir John Bromley,[18] a longtime official at the E&AD, that he 'was for many years connected with the financial departments of the government' and later correctly described E&AD employees as civil servants (*The Telegraph*, 1915, 1938, 1964). Sir Douglas Henley (C&AG 1976–81) agreed with the Treasury about the C&AG's wider role, telling the Expenditure Committee that 'the department is independent of all other public departments including the Treasury but at the same time it is an important instrument of the Treasury, since it is responsible for ascertaining that their directions relating to expenditure are duly observed' (Expenditure Committee, 1978, p. 30). Henley argued that 'Parliament presupposes a unity of purpose between the Treasury and the Exchequer and Audit Department' (Expenditure Committee, 1978, p. 30). These close links explain why the E&AD was only semi-independent of the executive. Pay rates for its staff were set by the Treasury. The Treasury appointed new staff to the E&AD. The Treasury appointed the C&AG. As Funnell (1994) shows, the E&AD worked hand in hand with the Treasury.

The alliance flowed, however, from a sense that Parliament and Treasury shared an interest in curbing and controlling public spending. There was a long-standing issue as to whether the C&AG was an officer of the House: despite the fact that he had never formally been designated as such, numerous official sources including the Speaker in 1913 (House of Commons, 1913, col. 898), Sergeant at Arms in 1935 (Butcher, 1935) and numerous ministers gave him that designation. The E&AD was conscious of its special relationship with Parliament. In 1931, for example, Sir Malcolm Ramsey[19] wrote to the Revenue department confirming that

> you cannot expect me to accept the implication that I, as Comptroller and Auditor General, am in any way bound by assurances or understandings given to ministers. As an Officer of the House of Commons I am entirely independent of the executive and am given a complete discretion to report to the House on such matters as in my judgement require their attention.
>
> *(Ramsay, 1931)*

The C&AG's close link to the PAC reinforced this impression: for example, when Sir Frank Tribe (C&AG 1946–58) died, George Benson,[20] the chair of the Committee said that the C&AG had been the Committee's 'guide, philosopher and friend' (Benson, 1958). Sir Douglas Henley gave evidence to the Expenditure Committee and reiterated that he reported 'for the benefit of Parliament' (Expenditure Committee, 1977a, p. 595). There were close links between some parts of Parliament and the E&AD: two E&AD specialists were seconded to the defence sub-committee of the Expenditure Committee in the 1970s (Procedure Committee, 1978a, p. 152). In this sense, the E&AD was the ultimate embodiment of the efficient secret of the British constitution: that legislature and executive were fused and that the parliamentary state 'was designed and intended to be a power-hoarding rather than a power-sharing polity' (Flinders and Kelso, 2011, p. 254).

When during the debates about the E&AD's constitutional status, John Garrett[21] spoke of how 'a supine House of Commons has allowed this great instrument, fashioned by Parliament in 1866 for parliamentary control, to be taken over by the Treasury and blunted' (House of Commons, 1983, col. 1165), Garrett drew on this rhetoric about the E&AD's links to Parliament but missed the point that parliamentary allegiance and Treasury alliance were not necessarily alternatives (Flinders and Kelso, 2011). In Gladstone's system, 'the Treasury, the Comptroller and Auditor General's department and the Public Accounts Committee are natural allies, they seek after all the same objectives' (Procedure Committee, 1978a, p. 137).

The C&AG's role in this alliance of the Treasury, PAC and the E&AD was as an arbiter over the legality of government spending. Frequently, the C&AG was described as a kind of judge. Sir Francis Mowatt commented in 1902 that Parliament had assured the independent judgement of the C&AG as it had 'followed the lines of appointment and tenure of the judges, which has always been regarded as the best possible tenure for ensuring absolute impartiality' (Committee of National Expenditure, 1902, p. 93). For Dicey, the role of the C&AG was to enforce the legal control of Parliament. The C&AG 'like a Judge in a Court . . . may be called upon not merely to place an interpretation on the words written in the Act, but also [to] determine what must be deemed to have been in the minds of the Commons when making the grant to the Crown and whether the Crown has faithfully observed that intention in its expenditure' (Robinson, 1924, p. 148). C&AGs might find themselves opposing civil servants: they functioned in this unique role 'very much as a lone wolf' (Sir Frank Tribe cited in Chubb, 1949, p. 347). They were praised for providing examples of judicial qualities: Ralph Assheton[22] (PAC chair 1948–50) wrote on Sir Frank Tribe's death about how much he valued Tribe's 'vigilance for the public purse and absolute fairness in approaching a problem' (Assheton, 1958). This judicial analogy persisted as an image for the C&AG right down into the 1970s and the discussion of a new replacement NAO (E&AD, 1895; Tribe, 1954; *The Times*, 1958; Expenditure Committee, 1977a, p. 596). The C&AG, in the 1866 system, was in place to ensure that the Common's authority (and the Treasury's) proved true across the whole of Whitehall by making quasi-judicial rulings on each account and audited item of expenditure.

2.2.3 First steps towards value for money

E&AD's audit evolved in the first half of the 20th century, partly because of changes made to the financial accounts, for example, the introduction of accrual accounting in the aftermath of the First World War. Accrual accounting was introduced on a trial basis in the War Office, and it ran from 1919–20 to the mid-1920s. Whilst there were advocates in the War Office, concerns were raised about the cost of this reform, whether the accounts complied with the Gladstonian legislation and there were technical difficulties in implementation (Dewar and Funnell, 2017, pp. 161–4). Technical changes to the C&AG's audit arose out of the 1921 Act: the Act enabled the C&AG to audit all accounts on a 'test' basis rather than evaluating every single voucher to prove an amount (Dewar and Funnell, 2017, pp. 156–7). These changes were the result of the increasing size of the state: the Acland Committee (under the chairmanship of the veteran Liberal MP Sir Francis Acland[23]) recommended this flexibility because audit had become 'impracticable and uneconomical' (Acland, 1921, p. 3). Sir Robert Horne[24] (Chancellor of the Exchequer 1921–2) explained in a covering minute to the cabinet that 'with the large increase of public accounts this is essential unless considerably greater expense is to be incurred' (Horne, 1921). However, Acland restated the importance of appropriation audit: 'we should be the last to suggest or support any attempt to alter its [the Exchequer and Audit Department's Act 1866] main lines' (Acland, 1921, p. 3).

In the early 20th century, E&AD's remit was also already expanding into analysing and reporting on government waste. This was not Gladstone's view of audit which focussed on the question of control: had Parliament controlled government expenditure and had the government submitted to that control? Gladstone had ruled out examinations of waste and inefficiency reporting to Parliament, seeing the identification of these as a matter for the executive (Dewar and Funnell, 2017, p. 127). Lord Welby (Permanent Secretary to the Treasury 1885–94) concurred: 'I think it is very important that the Committee of Public Accounts should deal with the audited accounts only and should not mix itself up with administration' (Committee on National Expenditure, 1902, p. 176). This orthodoxy could be summed up thus, 'it is not the auditor's business to exceed the directions of his principal [Parliament] or to raise objections on any action he has ratified' (Robinson, 1924, p. 147). Gladstonian reluctance to audit waste though was overcome early in the 20th century.

The expansion of audit into waste depended upon the E&AD assuming that Parliament would never mean to authorise waste and extravagance: consequently, waste could be envisaged as a failure of control and placed within the Gladstonian system of vigilance about control. D. C. Richmond[25] (C&AG, 1900-1904) told the Committee on National Expenditure that he had a 'free hand' to report to Parliament and considered that he would 'report anything which in my judgement . . . it concerns the House of Commons to know' especially including 'anything which has occurred in the course of my audit during the year which indicates loss or waste' (Committee of National Expenditure, 1902, p. 48). Richmond was not acting on his own authority: he was under pressure from MPs who wanted the auditor to examine waste including younger MPs such as Austen Chamberlain[26] and Winston Churchill,[27] who led the questioning. Secondly, he also established crucial guard rails around this duty, commenting, 'it is not for me to criticise administrative action as such' but merely to report instances of waste (Committee of National Expenditure, 1902, p. 495). This qualification is important: when the PAC suggested a general review of fraud in government by the E&AD, the Treasury stated that this would be 'an administrative duty which my Lords consider inconsistent with the critical and quasi-judicial role of an auditor' (E&AD, 1895).[28] Richmond's extension of the C&AG's role into waste and extravagance became the orthodoxy: in 1930, Sir Malcolm Ramsey said the C&AG did not merely report on whether money was spent in accordance with law, but also that he had a duty to report anything,

> which in his judgement it concerns the House of Commons to know, including any action of an Accounting Department which appears to involve improper expenditure or waste of public money or stores and he is not debarred from so doing by the fact the accounts themselves may be in order and that no obvious irregularity has occurred.
>
> *(Ramsay, 1930, p. 1192)*

The E&AD believed that this expansion of audit was the result of encouragement from 'successive Parliamentary committees' (Tribe, 1954, p. 372). Conceptually, therefore, a shift had taken place from an exclusively Gladstonian audit focussed on control to an audit which focussed on both control and waste, as described first by Richmond and then by Ramsay.

C&AGs were mildly conservative: appearing to stay strictly within the remit set by Parliament (Armstrong, 2004). Sir Leo Pliatzky[29] (Second Permanent Secretary, Treasury 1976–7) commented in 1976 that 'it is value for money with which they [the E&AD] are primarily concerned', but it was an examination of waste to which Pliatzky referred (Procedure Committee, 1978a, p. 174). In the same year as Pliatzky made his statement, Sir David Pitblado[30] (C&AG 1971–6) defined the terms of his job in words that Malcolm Ramsey could have agreed with in the 1930s:

> In his examination, a Comptroller and Auditor General is required to ensure that the fundamental framework of regularity is maintained and to watch over efficiency and economy in the use of resources and the avoidance of waste. I have continued to bring to the attention of Parliament matters on which the Public Accounts Committee, after their examination of accounting officers can make constructive comments and recommendations.
>
> *(C&AG, 1976, p. liii)*

Pitblado's evidence describes value for money in the 1970s very well. It was intrinsically linked to financial audit and arose out of the audit of the accounts. An auditor would, after questioning the department about any payments in which they detected waste, put together an inter-departmental reference sheet, initiating an inquiry (Chubb, 1949, p. 350). This would then become a case to be investigated and could be reported to the PAC. Like Pitblado, Sir Douglas Henley (C&AG 1974–81), in his evidence to the committee, said the E&AD 'put a great deal of weight on a fully documented case' emerging from a financial audit. Henley explained that 'we have found over the years that if the Audit Department tries to make a more generalised analysis of criticism, it is often very difficult to pin it' (Expenditure Committee, 1977, p. 590). The E&AD, in part led by the PAC, focussed on a traditional menu of issues such as defence and contracting (Flegmann, 1980, p. 168). Advance was slow: 'if you look at the process, people pushed at the boundary and work was allowed' (David Clarke,[31] interview). Clarke was right to note its slowness and comparative obscurity, but it also had an impact. Governments changed their behaviour under threat from the E&AD and PAC. Fear of the scrutiny of the E&AD and PAC blocked some privatisations (such as the sale of the Wytch Farm oil field) and established other features of privatisation in the UK, such as the appointment of an independent advisor, initially designed as 'an extra line of defence against a possible investigation' by the E&AD and PAC (Lawson, 2011, pp. 182, 191).

2.3 The changing nature of the state and the coming of the NAO Act, 1983

2.3.1 Changes to the constitutional position of the E&AD

Gladstone's Parliament had worked together with the Treasury to constrain departmental expenditure during the 19th century, but this function was not so important in the 20th century. The focus of British politics changed following the advent of the new welfare state under Asquith and Lloyd George, the two world wars and the rise of the Labour Party. The Treasury's task shifted: it became the manager of the economy especially during the Second World War (Fright, 2021). During the late 20th century, the British state became less military: defence spending fell from a 1950s peacetime level of 7% of GDP to around 2% of GDP by 2020. Governments of all parties increased other departmental spending in response to new demands most notably in areas like health. The Commons thus became even more what Bagehot described as an electoral college: providing and supporting a new government to carry out its agenda.

Harold Wilson recognised this change and suggested it could and should lead to a different role for accountability for expenditure. This is the role which Harold Wilson mapped out for the E&AD in a series of speeches in the Commons as chair of the PAC in the early 1960s. Wilson told the Commons that the Gladstonian tradition of using public sector accountability to restrain spending was obsolete: for Wilson, 'expenditure depends on policy', and policy was set by the House of Commons: consequently public sector accountability was about how the government should spend money, not whether (House of Commons, 1961, col. 640). For Wilson, the Committee and the E&AD remained a 'powerful weapon in the hands of the Treasury' but one drafted in for a particular purpose: to promote the efficiency of government (House of Commons, 1960, col. 899).

This point was echoed by other MPs. Robert Sheldon, during the Procedure Committee's inquiry into the select committee system, underlined this point: he opposed what he described as 'what is fairly simple, which is calling attention to waste and extravagance and the other aspect, control of expenditure' and questioned whether it was really possible to control expenditure when 'the executive grows from our Parliament' (Procedure Committee, 1978a, p. 140). Enoch Powell[32] made the same point, arguing that if 'the minister is responsible to the House of Commons for the collective decision of the Government' about priorities for spending, no select committee or auditor could take that power away (Procedure Committee, 1978a, p. 143). Wilson, Sheldon and Powell all recognised that the constitutional reality behind the audit settlement in the 1860s had fundamentally changed, and in Wilson's view, that meant a change in the role of the auditor as well. This was recognised internally too. Sir Douglas Henley, in a minute he wrote to the Treasury in 1980, said that 'Parliament can learn nothing about the efficiency or success of public sector operations from Appropriation Accounts. V[alue] F[or] M[oney] auditing is therefore very important in the public sector' (Henley,

1980b). Henley's words describe a Wilsonian concept of what the auditor was there to do. The auditor ceased to superintend a relationship between Treasury and Parliament, on one side, and departments, on the other, enforcing economy and legal spending, and became a body devoted to scrutiny of whether a Parliamentary majority's wishes had been carried out appropriately.

2.3.2 The state demand for value for money

Accompanying the changing shape of the state and therefore the changing nature of control was a change in ideological sentiment towards the state. Starting in the Labour Party in the 1950s, a strong argument emerged that the subject matter of British politics should be the decline of the UK as a world power; not merely a (possibly expected) proportionate decline but an absolute decline. This analysis received its initial impetus from the left in the 1950s and early 1960s before becoming a theme taken up and extended by the right in the late 1970s and 1980s (Tomlinson, 2009; Edgerton, 2018). These narratives of decline had a crucial impact on the role of audit through narratives about civil service incapacity and incompetence at two key points. The first of these was the critique advanced by Harold Wilson and colleagues in the 1960s culminating in the Fulton report of 1968 and the second was Margaret Thatcher's criticisms of the civil service which were contemporaneous with the passage of the National Audit Act, 1983.

Wilson and his advisors were sceptical about the quality of the civil service (Balogh, 1959), culminating the 1968 Fulton Report. Fulton's[33] team involved several figures who would become key to the future of the NAO including John Garrett, Robert Sheldon and John Bourn.[34] Fulton concluded that the 'structure and practices of the service have not kept up with the changing tasks' it faced (Fulton, 1968, p. 11). The report targeted generalist civil servants and specifically noted that they lacked both specialist abilities and managerial skills (Fulton, 1968, p. 12). Wilson described Fulton's report as an 'essential contribution to the modernisation of the basic institutions of this country' (House of Commons, 1968, col. 455) and the report's conclusions as a route to 'efficient management and economy' (House of Commons, 1968, col. 457). Fulton's recommendations sought to change accountability by creating accountable units within the civil service. Sir Burke Trend[35] (Cabinet Secretary 1963–73) recognised in a minute to the Cabinet that this would require 'necessary changes in the system of government accounting' (Trend, 1968, p. 2).

In the late 1970s, a second tradition of thinking came out of Thatcherite views of civil service reform. Thatcher and her allies came from a tradition that saw deprivileging the civil service (a phrase promoted by her advisor

John Hoskyns[36]) as one of the keys to getting Britain moving (Hennessy, 1990, pp. 591, 628). In her first Cabinet meeting in May 1979, she instructed ministers to freeze all civil service recruitment, conduct 'urgent examination[s] of functions to secure reductions in civil service manpower' and 'make it their personal responsibility to pursue the promotion of efficiency and elimination of waste in their department[s]' (Cabinet Office, 1979, pp. 2–3). Thatcher blamed poor leadership and the absence of private sector discipline for the civil service's wastefulness (Thatcher, 1993, pp. 46, 48). In 1979, the new Conservative government wanted desperately to reduce public expenditure and do so quickly (Lawson, 2011, p. 50).

Both of these changes in sentiment led to arguments about how value-for-money audit should be extended. Fulton did not discuss the E&AD but did recommend each department should regularly conduct efficiency audits of its own practices (Fulton, 1968, p. 54). In evidence to the Expenditure Committee in 1976, Garrett suggested that the committee should push forward with this, and that whilst 'the Fulton Committee did not consider the question of public accountability at any length', an investigation into civil service reform should consider the 'system of state audit' (Expenditure Committee, 1977a, p. 847). Thatcher too began to see reformed audit as part of a system that could support her newly efficient civil service. During the 1979 election campaign, Thatcher was advised by Leslie Chapman[37] about civil service reform who had already published work arguing for strengthening the E&AD so that audit could be a weapon against civil service waste and extravagance (Chapman, 1979). He saw the E&AD and PAC's examinations as being full of 'superficiality and ineffectuality' (Chapman, 1979, p. 89), arguing that the E&AD were engaged in a 'stately minuet' with departments in which they asked questions and then waited over a year to publish any answers (Chapman, 1979, p. 143). His proposals for a new audit department, like Garrett's for an NAO, were therefore for a far more assertive institution which would 'as a matter of course inquire into management decisions or the lack of them' (Chapman, 1979, pp. 148–9). As Clive Priestley,[38] a close associate of Thatcher's in her civil service reforms, put it, the new audit department would be

> staffed up with detectives, forensic analysts, barristers, inquisitors and others, who would go round and find out where the bodies were buried. They would then bring the offending bureaucrats before a Committee of the House of Commons which would sit in judgement while these offenders were grilled by the high-powered inquisitors.
>
> *(quoted in Hennessy, 1990, p. 592)*

The tone of Thatcher and Wilson and their envisaged function for the civil service were hugely different, but the diagnosis of lack of specialist skills, especially management, and a requirement for audit to perform a role in correcting the decline of the institutions of the state was similar.

Unsurprisingly, parliamentarians shared this language and in the 1970s criticised the E&AD for its conservative approach to value-for-money audit. Giles Radice,[39] a Labour MP, mocked the E&AD's obsession with minutiae, asking the C&AG whether he would agree that his department 'is extremely good at discovering that other Government departments have bought too many left hand boots, but is not so well equipped at securing long term improvements in efficiency' (Expenditure Committee, 1977a, p. 591). Sir Edward Du Cann[40] (Conservative MP and PAC Chair 1974–9) argued that 'the PAC was established by an Act of Parliament in 1866, amended in a minor way in 1921, and the work of the PAC has endured in roughly speaking its old style ever since' (Procedure Committee, 1978a, p. 135). The Expenditure Committee's 1977 report deepened this critique: it said that the E&AD still devoted 'most of its resources to financial audit, although it has gone beyond this limited role to some extent in recent years'; however, compared to the General Accounting Office (GAO) (the US equivalent of the E&AD at that time),[41] the committee argued that this represented an over emphasis on financial audit (Expenditure Committee, 1977, p. lxviii). The committee recommended that the E&AD should be 'empowered to conduct audits of the management efficiency and effectiveness of all that it audits financially' (Expenditure Committee, 1977, lxviii).

The E&AD responded to these critiques. Henley wrote that he was 'developing rather wider audit studies than some of those we have done in the past' (Henley, 1982, p. 174): he was seen as an advocate for 'the bigger picture and . . . more insightful reports' (*The Times*, 2003). Lord Armstrong[42] (cabinet secretary, 1979–87) recognised this in his short biographical note of Henley, stating that 'he took the initiative in encouraging a broader approach than that of merely looking for faults and failures in the control of public expenditure, with the development of more progressive reviews and reports on value for money in public spending' (Armstrong, 2011). Henley even went so far as to suggest that there should not be 'any rigid line between what are regarded as matters of policy and those that are not' (Henley, 1982, p. 173). Crucially, the PAC argued strongly for extending the C&AG's role too: they argued that the 'dividing line between an examination of the department's procedures . . . and an examination of the effectiveness of the policy itself is in our opinion impossible to maintain' (PAC, 1981, p. xvii). Audit would therefore have to be extended, and it was.

The National Audit Act 1983 established value-for-money audit for the first time and defined it as the audit of economy, efficiency and effectiveness. This new legal definition thus put the new NAO in a very different position to that enjoyed by the E&AD even after D. C. Richmond's advance towards value for money. Peter Riddell[43] told us that as an external observer, he had discussed the Act with Joel Barnett (a key influence) and Barnett told him that 'the key change was recognising that audit should go beyond a traditional numbers adding up propriety function to looking at value for money', and for Barnett it was vital that it was 'legally enshrined' (Riddell, interview). As Lord Butler (Principal Private Secretary to the Prime Minister 1982–5, Cabinet Secretary 1988–98) put it in his interview with us, the creation of the NAO was part of the 'modernisation' of the British state: a move towards a more efficient and managerial civil service.

2.4 Other factors

2.4.1 Select committees and independence

Wilson was at the heart of another development in scrutiny which later impinged directly upon the NAO in 1984: the role of (select) committees and their independence. As the new leader of the opposition after the death of Hugh Gaitskell in 1963, Wilson decided that Labour would endorse reforms to Parliament, which would attempt to rebalance the power of the executive. As early as the aftermath of the First World War, the Haldane Committee commented that 'a more efficient public service may expose the state to the evils of bureaucracy unless the reality of Parliamentary control is so enforced as to keep pace with any improvement in departmental methods' (Machinery of Government Committee, 1918, p. 16). For those on the political left, parliamentary control represented a way to live with the welfare state without compromising on freedom: Richard Crossman, for example, in the 1950s suggested that the next Labour government should balance the welfare state, created by Attlee in the 1940s, with select committees to supervise it (Crossman, 1956). Crossman was not alone: a disquiet about the size and extent of the state lay behind numerous campaigns to strengthen Parliament's infrastructure of scrutiny (Downs, 1982; Drewry, 1984; Flegmann, 1986). Wilson developed these ideas in a speech at Stowmarket in 1964 where he endorsed the creation of a public sector ombudsman, comparable to those in Denmark and New Zealand and the creation of new select committees.

After the general election of 1966, Wilson appointed Richard Crossman as Leader of the House of Commons and developed a new set of departmental committees, which became the predecessors to the current departmental select committees (Aylett, 2019). Wilson was not alone in thinking that the Commons needed bolstering in the early 1960s. An influential group of House of Commons clerks, most notably Michael Ryle, felt similarly and had developed proposals before the committees of the late 1960s were set up (Ryle, 1965). Whilst Wilson and Crossman's committees were quietly abandoned in the 1970s, the idea of a select committee structure was not. A series of influential reports in the late 1970s called for departmental select committees to shadow the main departments of state (Expenditure Committee, 1977; Procedure Committee, 1978). In 1979, Norman St John Stevas, appointed leader of the Commons by Margaret Thatcher, announced the creation of new select committees in the Commons, trumpeting them as the most important constitutional reform of the previous century (Norton, 2019; Midgley, 2019).

Agitation for parliamentary reform, and the view that Parliament was underpowered compared with the executive, were bound to have an impact upon the status of E&AD. As Ferry and Midgley (2022) demonstrate, over the next 20 years, the argument that the E&AD should be much more closely tied to Parliament became more and more powerful. Similarly to select committee reform, the pressure for change began with an account from an insider. E. L. Normanton had been at the E&AD and, whilst on secondment at Manchester University, published a comparative study of audit across different countries including the UK. He argued that 'the real situation of state audit in Britain remains that of a subordinate body influenced in various practical ways by the executive' (Normanton, 1966, p. 373). Normanton's target was the relationship between the E&AD and the Treasury: in particular, rules on appointment of officials and the way that audit was carried out. The significant fact about Normanton's analysis was that it was taken up by a group of MPs. In 1973, John Garrett and Robert Sheldon published their own analysis of the constitutional position of the E&AD in a Fabian pamphlet that largely echoed Normanton's concerns (Garrett and Sheldon, 1973).

Garrett forced the issue to the forefront in Parliament through a series of select committee reports in the 1970s. Firstly, the Expenditure Committee, in their 1976–7 inquiry into the civil service, focussed their attention on the E&AD and its position. They were adamant that the C&AG and his staff were 'properly part of the staff of Parliament' and 'should initiate enquiries if requested to do so by the House or its Committees' (Expenditure Committee, 1977, p. lxix). The Procedure Committee were next to focus on this question. Their 1978 report endorsed the creation of a new set of departmental spending committees but also suggested fundamental reforms to the E&AD, linking constitutional control and audit reform. Edward Du Cann (chair of PAC 1974–9) made this linkage explicit in his evidence:

> We have it seems to me, in a phrase which Lord Hailsham used in his Dimbleby lecture, increasingly an elective dictatorship. I believe that

> the surest way through which an increased control of the executive can be established is through control of the purse strings.
>
> *(Procedure Committee, 1978a, p. 134)*

Du Cann's argument reflects the anxieties that Crossman and others were discussing in the 1950s. Under pressure, the C&AG had to restate his commitment to Parliament. For example, Henley, confronted by sceptics on the Expenditure Committee, insisted that

> I am, in fact, consulted by the Treasury on every matter connected with the form of accounts and if it happened that I felt strongly that a particular form was inadequate or that some different form ought to be adopted, I should say so in no uncertain terms and if it appeared I could not get my way on such an important issue, I might well consider it necessary to report to Parliament.
>
> *(Expenditure Committee, 1977a, p. 595)*

Similarly, he stressed to the PAC that he now disagreed with the view that he was an instrument of the Treasury, though he emphasised he 'worked very closely with them' (PAC, 1979, p. 11). Privately, Henley dismissed concerns about independence as 'over-emphasizing the practical effects of what may seem, at any rate in modern circumstances to be outdated provisions' and argued parliamentary control of the C&AG's 'day to day work' would be 'a very real limitation on his independence of action' (Henley, 1980a).

In 1981, the PAC devoted a full report to the C&AG's status and powers, unlike other select committees. PAC contextualised its report saying that 'in the 115 years since the 1866 Act public expenditure has expanded enormously and Government has assumed a much wider function' (PAC, 1981, p. vi). Importantly, one way to improve the C&AG's ability to serve Parliament was, in their view, to ensure that he might 'be authorised to report to Parliament the results of his examinations from time to time' instead of alongside the accounts (PAC, 1981, p. xvii). Sir Gordon Downey, then C&AG, deemed this to be an important change, describing it as having 'significant advantages' and even proposed to the PAC a way forward, if legislation proposing a new NAO did not pass (Downey, 1982). The committee argued that the 'present position seems to us to be equivocal' and suggested appointment by the House of Commons and that the head of the NAO should be an officer of the House (PAC, 1981, lv).

This suggestion, we were told by Helen Irwin,[44] arose out of a conversation between herself and Michael Ryle[45] (Helen Irwin, interview). She thought that the C&AG had to be an officer of the House because that was where he should fit (Helen Irwin, interview). In 1982, Norman St John Stevas won the private members' ballot and was able to propose a bill. Three years before, in 1979, as leader of the House, he had proposed the creation of the departmental select committees, fulfilling Crossman's and Wilson's reform. It was natural that he then turned to reform of the E&AD. However, the intellectual impulse behind his bill did not come from Stevas himself. Peter Riddell, a journalist at the time, told us that

> The bill was largely Joel Barnett's. Barnett was Chairman of the PAC, had been Chief Secretary to the Treasury and was an ex-accountant. He understood you needed to reorientate the E&AD. He worked with the Treasury and C&AG of the time and was the key person in shifting the bill through. It had little to do with St John Stevas at all bar the fact that he put the bill formally forward. It was one of those rare interventions by Parliament which has been totally benign.
>
> *(Peter Riddell, interview)*

Barnett, according to Riddell, linked this to the expansion of the C&AG's remit: he 'felt that the whole process was far too narrow and even though your predecessors wanted to move in a different direction, they needed a new legal framework to do it with' (Riddell, interview).

Helen Irwin, who as PAC clerk in 1981 drafted the PAC report, was handed the bill to draft, assisted by others within the clerk's office (interview with Helen Irwin). Sir Gordon Downey gave detailed comments assisting Stevas as well (Downey, 1982a). Therefore, the bill that St John Stevas presented was based on the PAC report of 1981 and included many of its key points: making the C&AG an officer of the House and changing his appointment conditions (so that the Chair of the PAC and the Prime Minister together appointed a new C&AG) (Ferry and Midgley, 2022). In the Commons, John Garrett, Sir Edward Du Cann, Robert Sheldon and Michael English[46] all spoke in support of the bill (Ferry and Midgley, 2022). These measures might look superficially similar to comments in the 1930s by Ramsey and others, but the key difference was the climate. As Norton (2019) argues, the 1979–83 Parliament included a generation of MPs who thought, as Haldane[47] and Crossman[48] had before, that Parliament should be a control on rather than a collaborator with the executive. Civil servants were also much more accustomed to appearing before Parliament: Lord Butler said that 'after 1979 when there were departmental select committees, all civil servants were very much more used to doing these things' (interview, Lord Butler). The new NAO therefore took shape within this new rhetoric of parliamentary empowerment (Ferry and Midgley, 2022). Peter Riddell said to us that this advance was crucial, 'the fact that the NAO is statutorily independent is so significant'

(Peter Riddell, interview). Richard Bacon,[49] a later MP and PAC member, told us that he thought that this change was 'tectonic'.

2.4.2 Coverage of state audit

The parliamentary critique of the E&AD was also concerned about gaps in the system of accountability in the way that public money was audited. They identified four principal gaps: public bodies, the nationalised industries, local government and defence spending on major projects which E&AD did not audit.

PAC said in 1981 that 'it is extremely difficult to establish a clear pattern of which accounts the C&AG does audit and which he does not, and why he does not audit a particular body or have a right of access to its papers' (PAC, 1981, p. xviii). The first principle that PAC stated was that where a body was 'mainly supported from public funds' the C&AG should be the auditor (PAC, 1981, p. xx). The second two issues though were more controversial at the time and were raised frequently both inside and outside of Parliament.

PAC made it clear why they wanted the C&AG to audit nationalised industries, arguing that 'the real issue with which we are concerned in this review, is the extent to which the nationalised industries are or ought to be accountable to Parliament for their efficient use of what by any standards are vast sums of public money' (PAC, 1981, p. xxiii). The PAC therefore recommended that the C&AG should have access to all nationalised industries (PAC, 1981, p. xxxi). This recommendation was blocked by the government of the day.

The third area where PAC wanted change was local authority audit. The PAC set out the position in 1981 that local authorities could 'choose either to be audited by the District Auditor or by a private firm of accountants approved by the Secretary of State for the Environment' (PAC, 1981, p. xxxii). The District Audit Service had largely audited local government since the 19th century. In the 1970s, various official commissions including the Layfield Commission and the Advisory Committee on Local Government Audit (established in 1979) proposed reform. PAC (1981, p. xlii) argued that 'the present arrangements for local authority audit need to be improved' with 'greater attention . . . paid to value for money audit' (PAC, 1981, p. xlii). Some witnesses to the committee, including the Advisory Committee on local government audit, suggested the amalgamation of the E&AD and district audit service (PAC, 1981, p. xxxvi). PAC (1981, p. xliii) did not go quite so far, recommending the development of close links between the district auditors and E&AD. All this discussion, however, was rendered obsolete by the creation of a new high-powered auditor for local government: the Audit Commission (Campbell-Smith, 2008).

The fourth area that the PAC was concerned about was defence. In 1981, they reported on the Chevaline project, a project to improve the effectiveness of the UK's nuclear deterrent. The committee complained that in the case of Chevaline, a 'major project costing £1,000 million continued for over ten years without Parliament being properly informed of its existence and escalating costs' (PAC, 1982, p. viii). Whilst the C&AG had had access to the relevant papers, he had decided not to review the way that the project functioned. The committee noted that there was a difference between civil projects where 'it is customary to require the separate costs to be shown of at least the major projects' in the relevant estimates but that in the case of the Ministry of Defence, the 'costs of even major projects are not shown separately either in the estimates or the Appropriation Accounts and the Department does not keep PAC or the Defence Committee informed of significant changes in costs' (PAC, 1982, p. ix). The C&AG promised extra cooperation with PAC about defence projects, and the report led to the NAO doing a regular review of major projects in defence which still continues; however, the PAC's concerns about defence spending and its accountability were a factor in the debates of the early 1980s.

In all four of these cases, the gaps that PAC had identified in the UK's system of accountability were not solved solely through the 1983 Act, but they formed part of the context within which the Act was developed. Parliament's inability to hold nationalised companies, local councils or the Ministry of Defence to account helped MPs see the need for reform of the E&AD.

2.4.3 The professionalisation of auditing

Professionalisation of auditing within the E&AD had been an ongoing effort since the Tenney Committee at the end of the First World War (Dewar and Funnell, 2017, p. 159). Early on in the history of the E&AD, outside commentators believed that audit was a function which required 'not intellectual accomplishments but a peculiar acuteness and a very strict sense of duty' (*Telegraph*, 1870). The E&AD 'dragged its history along with it' and had a 'very strong identity' (David Clarke, interview). However, the 1983 National Audit Act was preceded by an immediate set of crises focussing on E&AD's audit.

There were three immediate causes for concern in the 1970s just before the creation of new NAO: the resourcing of the E&AD; the Crown Agents case and its implications for financial audit; and concerns expressed in Parliament about the skills underpinning the value-for-money work conducted by E&AD.

Resourcing for the E&AD was decided by the Treasury and had been since the 1860s. Normanton (1966) argued that the Treasury were unwilling to give the auditors the resources they needed to be effective. The government, in their initial response to calls from the PAC and Procedure Committee to let the Commons control the C&AG's budget, said the 'present administrative arrangements work' and pointed out that 'the E&AD have been exempted from recent cuts in civil service numbers' (Treasury, 1981, p. 7). In private, Sir Douglas Henley wrote that he had always found the Civil Service Department's management of his budget to be 'reasonable' (Henley, 1980). Despite public denials, an internal minute to the C&AG pointed out that the Treasury (and latterly the Civil Service Department) had forced staff reductions on the E&AD in 1951–2 and 1974–5 (E&AD, 1980). PAC itself had been very critical of the Treasury's willingness to cut the E&AD's staff in the 1950s:

> Your committee are surprised to learn that the figure of total staff in the Exchequer and Audit Department, fixed at 546 following the report of the Committee of 1945-6, has never been approached in practice owing to periodic limits imposed by the Treasury and that, in spite of additional work falling on the Department, the numbers in post have actually reduced this year with the prospect of additional cuts to come. . . .. They are satisfied that the Comptroller and Auditor General has maintained only an essential minimum standard of audit in recent years and they would deprecate any further cuts in his staff without prior consultation with the Committee of Public Accounts.
>
> *(PAC, 1952, p. 10)*

The 1952 PAC report demonstrates the powerlessness the MPs felt: even when they had set staff numbers for E&AD, the Treasury could and did ignore their request. Sir David Pitblado informed the House of Commons, through a minute attached to the 1974–5 Appropriation accounts, that his staffing was 'at present subject to limitation as a contribution towards the general policies of restraint on the growth in public expenditure' (C&AG, 1976, liii). Despite Treasury assurances, the fact that such cuts had happened twice suggested to reformers that change was required.

The rationale for change went further than Treasury control over E&AD budgets, with particular concerns having arisen about the audit of the Crown Agents in the mid- to late 1970s. The E&AD conducted their audit, but their position was, as Judith Hart[50] (the then Minister for Overseas Development) said, 'somewhat constitutionally obscure'. E&AD's audit of the Crown Agents arose because the Treasury had, under powers granted to it in the 1921 Exchequer and Audit Departments

Act, ordered the E&AD to carry out the audit (House of Commons, 1974 col. 1583; Fay, 1977, p. 35). The Crown Agents were initially a group who managed financial transactions on behalf of British colonies, including grants to the colonies from the Treasury and purchases by the colonies. After the end of empire, the Crown Agents diversified into other financial and business operations and became involved in the secondary banking crisis of the mid-1970s. In 1974, Crown Agents made a formal request for assistance to the UK government and were provided with a grant of £85 million. A committee for inquiry under Justice Fay and with Sir Edmund Compton[51] (C&AG 1958–66) as one of its members, was appointed to examine why the Crown Agents had to come to the government for assistance.

One of the reasons that the government had not managed Crown Agents well was, according to the committee, that ministers and others relied on the E&AD's work, presuming 'the fact that the accounts were audited by the Exchequer and Audit Department was evidence that little could go wrong in this field' (Fay, 1977, p. 189).

However, the committee found that this confidence was misplaced as the E&AD's audit was poor. Because the Crown Agents were not part of the civil service, and their audit was one ordered by the Treasury, delays to their audited accounts being published did not breach the 1866 Exchequer and Audit Departments Act (Fay, 1977, p. 121). Consequently, the committee found that the E&AD did not prioritise the audit: it audited the accounts in a 'leisurely way'. The inquiry committee said that they considered 'that the C&AG should have applied a greater sense of urgency to this assignment' and that they 'are surprised that he did not report to the Treasury on the delays' to accounts (Fay, 1977, p. 121). The E&AD's failure to prioritise the Crown Agents audit did not just produce delays: it 'materially understaffed the audit team', leading to the minimal output from the accounts team being still 'sufficient to keep the Exchequer and Audit team fully occupied' (Fay, 1977, p.120). Questions were raised in the House of Commons linking the failure of the E&AD to audit Crown Agents well with the assertion that it was the 'weakest system of audit in the Western world' (House of Commons, 1978, col. 1354). Michael English in a Commons debate specifically pointed out the failure of the E&AD:

> The recent incident with the Crown Agents, where for the whole of its existence the Exchequer and Audit Department had not realised that expenditure by the Crown Agents was totally illegal – illegal for more than a century, surely shows the need for lawyers independent of the Crown to serve any competent audit department.
>
> *(House of Commons, 1978a, col. 1104)*

In effect, English's argument was that the E&AD had completely failed to carry out its function by being the auditor of appropriation accounts. This created a 'trauma' within the E&AD and had a long-term effect on the development of the E&AD and subsequently the NAO (David Clarke, interview; Michael Whitehouse, interview). The Fay Committee's report and the questions in the Commons raised the issue of whether the C&AG and the E&AD were sufficiently skilled to carry out the task that Parliament had given to them and whether numbers audited by them could be trusted.

Whilst there wasn't an immediate crisis in the same way in value-for-money work, general concerns about civil service competence narrowed into a question about the abilities of the E&AD to audit government spending effectively. John Garrett, in his evidence to the Expenditure Committee, said that the E&AD was 'less expert than any other [Supreme Audit Institution] in the Western world' (Expenditure Committee, 1977a, p. 847). In the committee, Garrett asked Sir Douglas Henley the question directly 'could you explain how a body of executive officers mostly recruited as A level school leavers, some of whom are studying part-time for an accounting qualification, are competent to carry out studies of the management of these bodies [in government]' (Expenditure Committee, 1977a, p. 588). The Expenditure Committee shared this analysis: comparing the E&AD to the GAO (the USA's Supreme Audit Institution at that time), it stated that of the GAO's staff, four-fifths were qualified in some way, but whilst more than half of them were accountants, the remainder were economists, statisticians or had other specialisms (Expenditure Committee, 1977, p. lxviii). The Expenditure Committee were not alone in their verdict: Sir Edward Du Cann said that 'the American equivalent is very much better fitted to the contemporary age, very much better fitted to give advice to Members of Parliament by qualification, to survey, to cross-examine, to question, the activities of technical departments' (Procedure Committee, 1978a, p. 136). These criticisms did not only come from within Parliament: Leslie Chapman, one of Margaret Thatcher's advisors, aimed his attacks on the E&AD's failure to spot waste during its audits that he was aware of (Chapman, 1979, p. 82). Privately, civil servants acknowledged that value-for-money audit was weak in the 1970s: Richard Wilson[52] first came across the NAO in the late 1970s when he was in charge of nuclear power policy in the Department for Energy:

> I had responsibility for the Atomic Energy vote and the E&AD used to turn up and you had reference sheets. Our budget at that time was some hundreds of millions of pounds and we had a huge programme of research and building reactors. I can remember reference sheets[53] [E&AD questionnaires about departmental spending] coming in to me

> and being hugely relieved that they were so narrow and the questions that the auditors asked were easy to deal with because they were never on the main points like how did we determine how we spent the money, was it good value for money and all sorts of difficult questions. You could answer the questions that were asked narrowly. I cannot tell you the relief I felt when I discovered how unthreatening reference sheets were. At that time, the E&AD were number crunchers looking for trivial or numerical errors [and] not asking the right questions in terms of holding us to account.
>
> *(Richard Wilson, interview)*

Wilson said that he was summoned before the PAC: 'they didn't get anywhere near what I as a taxpayer would have wanted them to ask me' in contrast to the Science and Technology Committee, whose chair, Arthur Palmer, was 'much more knowledgeable and effective' than the PAC backed by the E&AD (Richard Wilson, interview). There were civil servants who found more issues with the E&AD: David Omand[54] told us that 'the only time I ever saw my old mentor, Sir Frank Cooper,[55] on the run was before the Public Accounts Committee after an audit report on the Ministry of Defence'. The E&AD acknowledged though that it often lacked the staff to perform its role. In 1979, Henley acknowledged himself that he lacked capacity, facing a 'physical shortage' of qualified staff to assist select committees in their investigations into the efficiency of departments (PAC, 1979, p. 2).

The E&AD's response to this was a series of reforms beginning in the early 1970s. To meet the initial concerns about financial audit and the Crown Agents, E&AD shifted resources to financial audit. By 1981, the C&AG was investing 60% of his staff's effort into financial audit (PAC, 1981, p. xi).

The E&AD decided at the same time to improve the skills of the organisation. They began with the E&AD moving its trainees from the London School of Economics and Political Science (LSE), where they had been trained since the 1920s, to train with the Chartered Institute of Public Finance and Accountancy (CIPFA). They also started to recruit graduates as well.

The most profound reforms followed from the management review of 1978–9, which started from the assumption that 'the pressures on the work and staff of the department (the E&AD) had been mounting for a number of years as a result of the rapid growth in the size and variety of public expenditure and of the introduction of increasingly complicated financial and management accounting systems' (E&AD, 1979). Sir

Douglas Henley, in private, was more critical: acknowledging the E&AD as a 'worthy organisation' but criticising it as applying 'traditional, virtually sacrosanct methods verging on the arcane' to its work (Dewar and Funnell, 2017, p. 206). Significantly, the review team included representatives of the accounting firms, and they interviewed permanent secretaries; former, current and future chairs of the PAC; the District Audit Service and representatives of the accounting bodies (Dewar and Funnell, 2017, pp. 207–8). As David Dewar, one of the review's authors, reported years later, the review was 'not an open minded exercise' (Dewar and Funnell, 2017, p. 209). The review team found a great amount of informality in the practice of audit and recommended change: for example, few audit plans were produced and monitoring was ad hoc. In both cases, formalisation was recommended (E&AD, 1979, p. 26). Similarly, the review team recommended moving towards a systems-based approach which 'concentrates examination on the systems for controlling and accounting for the activities and transactions of the audited organisation' even though the review authors acknowledged that the value of this approach to value-for-money audit would need to be 'assessed' (E&AD, 1979, pp. 27–8). The review made numerous recommendations to improve both career management and staff forecasting and training (E&AD, 1979, pp. 33–4). Again, there were specific recommendations in these areas, for example, that a centralised computer audit unit (established in 1973) should be combined with training in computing to enable 'auditors in line divisions with sufficient computer expertise to carry out most of the review and analysis of computerised systems' (E&AD, 1979, p. 36). For Henley, this was always the first stage of reform: he imagined that once the E&AD's financial audit had improved, 'certification work should account for no more than 40% of the E&AD's work as it did until fairly recently' (Henley, 1980b).

The effort to improve the capacity of the E&AD was recognised externally: the PAC wrote that the 'E&AD has been bringing its working practices up to date and has changed its method of recruitment' in ways that its critics did not recognise (PAC, 1981, p. vi). They recognised that by 1981, most of the new entrants to the E&AD were 'honours graduates' and that they were required to obtain professional qualifications (PAC, 1981, p. l). However, the committee also argued that the new NAO 'would not be cheap' (PAC, 1981, p. xlix). Consequently, those who passed the new Act envisaged one of its strengths would be to enable Parliament to give the new NAO the resources it required to thrive. This, though, built upon the progress that had already been made. David Clarke, who had been a trainee in the E&AD, described the change through the 1980s as 'more evolution than revolution' (David Clarke, interview).

2.5 Chapter summary

The *Economist* magazine was right to point out that the post-1983 NAO had been founded on the E&AD. Their comparison to the Audit Commission was not entirely just, however: the Audit Commission was created for a different role within the constitution from the NAO. As this chapter has made clear, democratic auditors can have very different remits because they have different functions. However, the *Economist* was right to say that the DNA of the E&AD ran through the NAO's history.

Many of the key figures in the new NAO had been key within the old E&AD: the C&AG, Sir Gordon Downey, for example, stayed in post from 1981 to 1983 as head of the E&AD and from 1984 to 1988 as head of the new NAO.

In addition, there are three aspects of the E&AD's legacy from the 19th and 20th century that still affect the NAO's work today. Firstly, the E&AD had a unique relationship with government. On the one hand, as Mowatt said, it was another constable alongside the Treasury on the police force which sought to restrain departmental spending. On the other, as Ramsey stated in the 1930s (echoing Speaker Lowther[56] from 1913), the C&AG was an officer of the House and should support the Commons in their work. This way of thinking about the C&AG and E&AD became more important after the passage of the National Audit Act 1983, because the Act was part of a series of reforms intended to strengthen Parliament against the executive (Ferry and Midgley, 2022). Consequently, the acknowledgement of the C&AG's dual role, by Ramsey, had by Garrett's time become a crucial part of a reassertion of powers by the Commons against the executive. Framed within the context of the newly developed select committee system, an assertion in legislation of the C&AG's position was a crucial reframing of the purpose of state audit in the UK, enabling the C&AG to operate and report more effectively.

Secondly, the scope of the E&AD's audit had begun with financial control. The executive and Parliament wanted to know whether departments were behaving in line with their constitutional accountability to Parliament. During the 20th century, E&AD evolved so that its audit considered questions of waste and extravagance as well as accurate accounting. By the 1960s, Harold Wilson had led auditors to a wider vision of their role. The Expenditure Committee pushed this further and the 1983 Act recognised this with the inclusion of effectiveness and efficiency alongside economy as key parts of value for money. This evolution though should not mask an underlying continuity: the Epitome (the official collection) of PAC reports contains reports from the committee in the 1890s, which are very similar to reports on the topics in the 1990s.

The E&AD's core definition of the auditor, set out in 1866, and its developments across the 20th century formed the basis for the NAO's exploration of its new mandate set out in 1983.

Thirdly, the staff who worked for the E&AD transferred across to the NAO on 1 January 1984. Many of them continued to work in the NAO long after E&AD had been forgotten by almost everyone at Westminster. Senior figures from the E&AD continued in their posts or were promoted under both Sir Gordon Downey and Sir John Bourn. People like David Dewar and John Higgins, both later Assistant Auditors General, whose careers stretched back into the 1950s and 1960s, stayed at the new NAO into the 1990s and beyond. The last members of staff who had started with the old E&AD did not leave the NAO until the early 2020s. The work begun by Sir Douglas Henley, to professionalise the E&AD, formed the basis of the work conducted by later C&AGs in the NAO. The trauma of the failure of the Crown Agents' audit and the debates over the NAO's creation in the 1970s and 1980s continued to have an effect on the organisation long after they had been forgotten in Westminster. As Neil Sayers put it, 'the NAO's history did not start in 1983, it was a progression' (Neil Sayers, interview).

The *Economist* therefore was more right than they understood when they wrote that the NAO was a child of the pre-1983 E&AD: the two organisations were linked together because of their shared role, remit and the personal histories of their staff. This legacy though was not, as the *Economist* argued, a source of weakness but rather left the new NAO with a sense of its constitutional role, its links to Parliament and government, and an enduring cultural continuity with the practices and patterns of work developed by the old E&AD.

Notes

1 John Banham, 1940–2022, Foreign Office 1962–4, private sector posts including McKinsey 1965–83, Controller Audit Commission 1983–7, Director General CBI 1987–92 and other posts. Knighted 1992.

2 Howard Davies, 1951–, Foreign Office 1973–6, HM Treasury 1976–82, McKinsey and Co. 1982–7, Special Advisor to the Chancellor of the Exchequer 1985–6, Controller Audit Commission 1986–92, Director General CBI 1992–5, Deputy Governor Bank of England 1995–7, Chairman of the Financial Services Authority 1997–2003, Director LSE 2003–11 and other posts. Knighted 2000.

3 This was pointed out in letters to the *Economist* at the time by Robert Sheldon, the then chair of the Public Accounts and C. N. Bilsnand on behalf of Somerset Council. Bilsnand argued that whilst the NAO's work was 'original', the Commission's was based on what was 'already best practice in local government', in a sector which was more open and democratic than central government at the time, and Sheldon added the point that the Commission

identified best practice rather than having to survey one instance of a programme (Sheldon and Bilsnand, 1992).

4 Nicholas Macpherson, 1959–, CBI 1982–3, private sector posts 1983–5, HM Treasury 1985–2016 including Principal Private Secretary to the Chancellor of the Exchequer 1993–7, Head of Work Incentives Programme 1997–8, Deputy Director, then Director (Welfare Reform) Budget and Public Finances 1998–2001, Managing Director Public Services 2001–4, Budget and Public Finances 2004–5, Permanent Secretary 2005–16 and other posts. Knighted 2009, created Lord Macpherson 2016.

5 Robert Sheldon, 1923–2020, MP for Ashton under Lyme 1964–2001, Member of the Fulton Committee on the Civil Service 1966–8, Chair Public Accounts Committee 1983–97, Standards and Privileges Committee 1997–2001, Liaison Committee 1997–2001. Created Lord Sheldon 2001.

6 Harold Wilson, 1916–95, MP for Ormskirk and Huyton 1945–83, President of the Board of Trade 1947–51, Shadow Chancellor of the Exchequer 1955–61, Chair of the Public Accounts Committee 1959–63, Shadow Foreign Secretary 1961–3, Leader of the Opposition 1963–4, 1970–4, Leader of the Labour Party 1963–76, Prime Minister 1964–70 and 1974–6. Knighted 1976, created Lord Wilson 1983.

7 Reginald Welby, 1832–1915, Treasury 1856–94, Permanent Secretary of the Treasury 1885–94. Knighted 1874, created Lord Welby 1894.

8 Albert Dicey, 1834–1915, Vinerian Professor of English, Oxford University 1882–1909.

9 Frank Tribe, 1893–1958, Ministry of Labour 1920–38 including Private Secretary to Ministers for Labour 1923–8, Treasury 1938–40, Ministry for Labour 1940–2, Permanent Secretary Ministry of Fuel and Power 1942–5, Permanent Secretary Ministry of Aircraft Production 1945, Permanent Secretary Ministry of Food 1945–6, Comptroller and Auditor General 1946–58. Knighted 1945.

10 Douglas Henley, 1919–2003, Treasury and other civil service positions 1946–76, Second Permanent Secretary Treasury 1972–6, Comptroller and Auditor General 1976–81. Knighted 1970.

11 Francis Mowatt, 1837–1919, Treasury 1856–1903, Permanent Secretary 1894–1903. Knighted 1884.

12 Richard Awdry, 1843–1916, Accountant General of the Royal Navy 1896–1904.

13 Ralph Lingen, 1819–1905, Secretary to the Committee of Council on Education 1849–69, Permanent Secretary Treasury 1869–85, Knighted 1878, created Lord Lingen 1885.

14 Gus O'Donnell 1952–, Lecturer University of Glasgow 1974–9, Treasury 1979–90, Press Secretary to the Prime Minister 1990–4, Treasury 1994–2005 including Permanent Secretary 2002–5, Cabinet Secretary 2005–11 and other posts 2011–. Knighted 2005, created Lord O'Donnell 2011.

15 Robert Cecil, 1830–1903, MP for Stamford 1853–68, Secretary of State for India 1866–7, 1874–8, Foreign Secretary 1878–80, 1885–6, 1887–92, 1895–1900, Prime Minister 1885–6, 1886–92, 1895–1902, Lord Privy Seal 1900–1902, succeeded as Lord Salisbury 1868.

16 The Walcheren expedition was an unsuccessful attempt by the UK to invade the Netherlands in 1809. The Crimean War was fought from 1852 to 1855 between an alliance of the French and the UK against Russia. The Boer War was fought between the UK and the South African Republic and Orange Free State between 1899 and 1902.

17 Henry Campbell Bannerman 1836–1908, MP for Stirling 1868–1908, Chief Secretary for Ireland 1884–5, Secretary of State for War 1886, 1892–5, Leader of the Liberal Party 1899–1908, Prime Minister 1906–8. Knighted 1885.
18 John Bromley, 1849–1915, Exchequer and Audit Department 1869–1903, Accountant General to the Board of Education 1903–9. Knighted 1908.
19 Malcolm Ramsey, Foreign Office 1896–7, Treasury 1897–1902, Private Secretary to the Prime Minister 1902–5, Treasury 1905–21, Comptroller and Auditor General 1921–31. Knighted 1915.
20 George Benson, 1889–1973, MP for Chesterfield 1929–31, 1935–64, Chair of the Public Accounts Committee 1952–9. Knighted 1948.
21 John Garrett, 1931–2007, Consultant to the Fulton Committee 1966–8, MP, Norwich South 1974–83, 1987–97.
22 Ralph Assheton, 1901–84, MP for Rushcliffe 1934–45, City of London 1945–50, Blackburn West 1950–5, Chair Public Accounts Committee 1948–50. Created Lord Assheton 1955.
23 Francis Acland, 1874–1939, MP for Richmond, North West Cornwall and Tiverton, 1906–22, 1923–4. Created Baronet 1926.
24 Robert Horne, 1871–1940, academic posts at University College, North Wales and Aberdeen University, MP for Hillhead, Glasgow, 1918–37, Minister for Labour 1919–20, President of the Board of Trade 1920–21, Chancellor of the Exchequer 1921–2. Knighted 1920, created Lord Horne 1937.
25 Douglas Richmond, 1839–1930, Charity Commission 1875–96, Assistant Comptroller and Auditor General 1896-1900, Comptroller and Auditor General 1900–1904.
26 Austen Chamberlain 1863–1937, MP for East Worcestershire and Birmingham West 1892–1937, Chancellor of the Exchequer 1903–5, 1919–21, Secretary of State for India 1915–17, Minister without Portfolio, 1918–19, Lord Privy Seal and Leader of the House of Commons 1921–2, Leader of the Conservative Party 1921–2, Foreign Secretary 1924–9, First Lord of the Admiralty 1931. Knighted 1925.
27 Winston Churchill, MP for Oldham, Manchester North West, Dundee, Epping and Woodford 1902–22, 1924–64. President of the Board of Trade 1908–10, Home Secretary 1910–11, First Lord of the Admiralty 1911–15, Chancellor of the Duchy of Lancaster 1915, Minister of Munitions 1917–19, Secretary of State for War 1919–21, Secretary of State for Air 1919–21, Secretary of State for the Colonies 1921–2, Chancellor of the Exchequer 1924–9, First Lord of the Admiralty 1939–40, Prime Minister 1940–45, 1951–5, Minister for Defence 1940–5, 1951–2, Leader of the Conservative Party 1940–55, Leader of the Opposition 1945–51. Knighted 1953.
28 For over a hundred years, the Treasury's responses to PAC reports (Treasury Minutes) were signed off by the Lords of the Treasury. The First Lord of the Treasury is normally the prime minister. During the last 200 years, the only First Lords not to have been prime minister were W. H. Smith, the Earl of Iddlesleigh and A. J. Balfour under the premiership of Lord Salisbury. The Second Lord of the Treasury is always the Chancellor of the Exchequer.
29 Leo Pliatzky, 1919–99, Ministry of Food 1947–50, Treasury 1950–77 including Second Permanent Secretary 1976–7, Permanent Secretary Department for Trade 1977–9. Knighted 1977.
30 David Pitblado, 1912–97, Dominions Office 1937–42, Treasury 1942–51, Private Secretary to the Prime Minister 1951–6, Treasury 1956–69, Permanent Secretary Ministry of Technology 1969–70, Permanent Secretary Civil Service Department 1970–1, Comptroller and Auditor General 1971–6. Knighted 1967.

31 David Clarke, E&AD 1980–3, NAO 1983–2012, including Directorate posts.
32 Enoch Powell, 1912–98, MP for Wolverhampton South West, Down South and South Down 1950–87, Minister for Health 1960–3, Shadow Defence Secretary 1965–8.
33 John Fulton 1902–19, Chaired Committee on the Civil Service 1966–8, created Baron Fulton of Falmer in January 1966.
34 Sir John Bourn, KCB, 1934–2022, Air Ministry 1956–63, Treasury 1963–4, Ministry of Defence 1964–74, 1977–82, 1985–8, Northern Ireland Office 1974–7, 1982–4, Comptroller and Auditor General 1988–2008, Auditor General for Wales 1999–2005, Advisor to the Prime Minister on Ministerial Interests 2006–8. Knighted 1991.
35 Burke Trend, 1914–87, Ministry of Education 1936–7, HM Treasury 1937–62, Cabinet Secretary 1963–73, Knighted 1962, created Lord Trend 1973.
36 John Hoskyns, 1927–2014, Head of the Prime Minister's Policy Unit 1979–82, Director General of the Institute of Directors 1984–9. Knighted 1982.
37 Leslie Chapman, 1919–2013, Civil Service 1939 and 1945–74.
38 Clive Priestley, 1935–2012, Ministry of Education 1960–7, Civil Service Department 1969–79, Prime Minister's Office 1979–83.
39 Giles Radice, 1936–2022, MP for Chester Le Street and Durham North 1973–2001, Chairman Public Service Select Committee 1996–7, Chairman Treasury Select Committee 1997–2001, created Lord Radice 2001.
40 Edward Du Cann, 1924–2017, MP for Taunton 1957–87, Chair Select Committee Public Expenditure 1971–3, Chair Public Accounts Committee 1974–9, Chair Liaison Committee 1974–83, Chair Treasury and Civil Service Committee 1979–83, Chair Public Accounts Commission 1984–7. Knighted 1985.
41 Initially it was called the General Accounting Office. Its name was changed in 2004 to the Government Accountability Office. §022.09 (GAO) History of the GAO – Budget Counsel.
42 Robert Armstrong, 1927–2020, Principal Private Secretary to the Prime Minister 1970–5, Permanent Secretary Home Office 1977–9, Cabinet Secretary 1979–87, Head of the Home Civil Service 1981–7. Knighted 1978, created Lord Armstrong 1988.
43 Peter Riddell, 1948–, *Financial Times* 1970–91, *The Times* 1991–2010, Senior Fellow Institute for Government 2010–12, Director, Institute for Government 2012–16, Commissioner for Public Appointments 2016–21.
44 Helen Irwin, 1948–, House of Commons Clerk 1970–2, 1977–2008, including Clerk of Committee for Public Accounts 1977–81, Table Office 1981–5, Clerk of Committees 2005–8.
45 Michael Ryle, 1927–2013, House of Commons Clerk 1951–89, including Clerk of Committees 1987–9.
46 Michael English, 1930–2019, MP for Nottingham West 1964–83.
47 Richard Haldane, 1856–1928, MP for Haddingtonshire 1885–1911, Secretary of State for War 1905–12, Lord Chancellor 1912–15, 1924, Created Lord Haldane 1911.
48 Richard Crossman, 1907–74, MP for Coventry East 1945–1974, Minister of Housing and Local Government 1964–6, Leader of the House and Lord President of the Council 1966–8, Secretary of State for Social Services 1968–70.
49 Richard Bacon, 1962–, MP for South Norfolk 2001–, Member Public Accounts Committee 2001–17, Chair Public Accounts Commission 2017–.
50 Judith Hart, 1924–91, MP for Lanark 1959–83 and Clydesdale 1983–7, Parliamentary Under-Secretary of State for Scotland 1964–6, Minister of

State, Commonwealth Office, 1966–7, Minister of Social Security 1967–8, Paymaster General 1968–9, Minister of Overseas Development 1969–70, 1974–5 and 1977–9. Created Baroness 1988.

51 Edmund Compton, 1906–94, 1929–66 UK Civil Service, Third Permanent Secretary Treasury 1949–59, Comptroller and Auditor General 1959–66 Parliamentary Commissioner for Administration 1967–71. Knighted 1955.

52 Richard Wilson, 1942–, 1966–2002 UK Civil Service, Permanent Secretary, Department for the Environment 1992–4, Permanent Secretary Home Office 1994–7, Cabinet Secretary and Head of the Home Civil Service 1998–2002. Created Lord Wilson 2002.

53 Inter-departmental reference sheets were sent by E&AD auditors to senior officials in departments and contained questions about spending on particular programmes and projects. Questions all had a monetary aspect but could pertain to value for money in selected areas according to the judgement of the auditor.

54 David Omand, 1947–, GCHQ 1969–70, Ministry of Defence 1970–96, Director of GCHQ 1996–7, Permanent Secretary Home Office 1998–2001, Cabinet Office 2001–5, including Permanent Secretary Cabinet Office and Security and Intelligence Coordinator 2002–5, Visiting Professor Kings College London 2006–. Knighted 2000.

55 Frank Cooper, 1922–2002, Air Ministry 1948–64, Ministry of Defence 1964–70, Civil Service Department 1970–3, Permanent Secretary Northern Ireland Office 1973–6, Permanent Secretary Ministry of Defence 1976–82, Honorary Fellow, Pembroke College, Oxford University 1976–. Knighted 1974.

56 James Lowther, 1855–1949, MP for Rutland, Penrith, Penrith and Cockermouth 1883–5, 1886–1921, Speaker 1905–21, Created Viscount Ullswater 1921.

References

Acland, Sir F. (1921). *Report of the committee appointed to consider the provisions of the exchequer and audit departments act 1866*, Cmd 1383. London: HMSO.

Armstrong, R. (2004). Sir Edmund Compton. *Oxford New Dictionary of National Biography.*

Armstrong, R. (2011). Sir Douglas Henley. *Oxford New Dictionary of National Biography.*

Assheton, R. (Lord Clitheroe) (1958). Sir Frank Tribe. *The Times*, 28 June.

Aylett, P. (2019). Reform and consolidation: A new perspective on Commons select committees 1960–1980. *Parliamentary Affairs*, 72(4), 742–760.

Balogh, T. (1959). The apotheosis of the dilettante. In H. Thomas (ed.) *The establishment.* London: Anthony Blond.

Benson, Sir G. (1958). Sir Frank Tribe. *The Times*, 2 July 1958.

Bill of Rights (1689). *Bill of Rights 1689.* Available at https://www.legislation.gov.uk/aep/WillandMarSess2/1/2/introduction accessed on 7 June 2023.

Butcher, R. (1935). R. Butcher 9 May 1935. In *Comptroller and Auditor General: Status*, AO29/92, unpublished MSS, National Archives, London.

Butler, Robin, interview

Cabinet Office (1979). Conclusions of a meeting of the Cabinet held at 10 Downing Street on Thursday 10 May 1979 at 10.30 am. In *Cabinet Conclusions*, CAB128/66/1, unpublished MSS, National Archives, London.

Campbell-Smith, D. (2008). *Follow the money: The Audit Commission, public money and the management of public services, 1983 – 2008.* London: Penguin.
Caulcott, M. (1962). The control of public expenditure. *Public Administration, 40*(3), 267–288.
Chapman, L. (1979). *Your disobedient servant: The continuing story of Whitehall's overspending.* Harmondsworth: Penguin.
Chubb, B. (1949). Parliamentary control of the public accounts. *Parliamentary Affairs, 3*(2), 344–351.
Clarke, David, interview
Committee on National Expenditure (1902). *Report of the select committee on national expenditure together with the proceedings, minutes of evidence, appendix and index.* Session 1902, HC387. London: House of Commons.
C&AG (1976). Report of the Comptroller and Auditor General. In *Appropriation accounts: Volume 3: Classes x-xv and xvii, 1974-5. Appropriation accounts of the sums granted by parliament for classes X-XV and XVII for the year ended 31 March 1975 together with the report of the Comptroller and Auditor General thereon and upon certain revenue and store accounts*, Session 1975-7, HC79. London: House of Commons.
Crossman, R. (1956). *Socialism and the new despotism, Fabian Tract No. 298.* London: Fabian Society.
Daunton, M. (2007). *Trusting leviathan: The politics of taxation in Britain.* Cambridge: Cambridge University Press.
Dewar, D. and Funnell, W. (2017). *A history of British National Audit: the pursuit of accountability.* Oxford: Oxford University Press.
Dicey, A. V. V. (1982). *Introduction to the study of the law of the constitution.* Indianapolis: Liberty Fund. (Reprint of 1915 edition).
Downey, G. (1982). Gordon Downey to Joel Barnett, 13 July 1982. In *Government's reply to the Public Accounts Committee (PAC) report on the Role of the Comptroller and Auditor General (C&AG)* AO38/11, unpublished MSS, National Archives, London.
Downey, G. (1982a). Sir Gordon Downey to Norman St John Stevas, 21 December 1982. In *National Audit Office (NAO) Act 1983: Draft Bills and notes on clauses; includes arrangement of sections* AO39/11, unpublished MSS, National Archives, London.
Downs, S. J. (1982). *Select committees in the House of Commons: An ineluctable development, Hull papers in politics, No. 32.* Hull: Hull University.
Drewry, G. (1984). The new select committees; a constitutional non-event. In D. M Hill (ed.) *Committees in action: A symposium, Strathclyde papers on government and politics 24.* Hull: Hull University, 30–56.
Economist (1992). Watching the watchdogs. *The Economist, 324*(7766), 33.
Edgerton, D. (2018). *The rise and fall of the British Nation.* London: Allen Lane.
Einzig, P. (1959). *The control of the purse: Progress and decline of Parliament's financial control.* London: Secker and Warburg.
Exchequer and Audit Department (1895). Jurisdiction and functions of the Comptroller and Auditor General in regard to the public accounts. In *Comptroller and Auditor General: Functions* AO29/91, unpublished MSS, National Archives, London.
Exchequer and Audit Department (1979). Appendix 1: Management review of the Exchequer and Audit Department: Report of the steering committee. In *Public Accounts Committee second special report from the Committee of Public Accounts, the work of the Committee of Public Accounts and the status and functions of the Comptroller and Auditor General*, Session 1978-9, HC330. London: House of Commons, 21–41.

Exchequer and Audit Department (1980). The Treasury, the CSD and the Exchequer and Audit Department. In *Status of the Comptroller and Auditor General (C&AG) and his staff: Paper for the Public Accounts Committee (PAC)*, AO38/6, unpublished MSS, National Archives, London.

Exchequer and Audit Departments Act (1921). *Exchequer and Audit Departments Act 1921*. Available at https://www.legislation.gov.uk/ukpga/Geo5/11-12/52/ contents accessed on 10 March 2024.

Expenditure Committee (1977a). *Eleventh report from the Expenditure Committee: Together with the minutes of evidence taken before the general sub-committee in Sessions 1975-6 and 1976-7 and appendices: the civil service. Vol. III. Appendices*. Session 1976-7, HC535-II. London: House of Commons.

Expenditure Committee (1977). *Eleventh report from the Expenditure Committeetogether with the minutes of evidence taken before the general sub-committee in Sessions 1975-6 and 1976-7 and appendices: The civil service*, Session 1976-7, HC535-I. London: House of Commons.

Expenditure Committee (1978). *Twelfth report from the Expenditure committee: Together with the minutes of evidence taken before the general sub-committee in session 1978 and appendices, Response to the Government's observations on the committee's report on the civil service*. Session 1977-8, HC576. London: House of Commons.

Fay, E. S. (1977). Report by the Committee of Inquiry appointed by the Minister of Overseas Development into the circumstances which led to the Crown Agents requesting financial assistance from the government in 1974, Session 1977-8, HC48. London: House of Commons.

Ferry, L. and Midgley, H. (2022). Democracy, accountability and audit: the creation of the UK NAO as a defence of liberty. *Auditing, Accounting and Accountability Journal, 35*(2), 413–438.

Flegmann, V. (1980). The Public Accounts Committee: A successful select committee? *Parliamentary Affairs, 33*(1), 166–172.

Flegmann, V. (1986). *Public expenditure and the select committees of the Commons*. Aldershot: Gower.

Flinders, M. and Kelso, A. (2011). Mind the gap: Political analysis, public expectations and the parliamentary decline thesis. *The British Journal of Politics and International Relations, 13*, 249–268.

Fright, M. (2021). *The moments of and movements for national accounts: Contextualising changes to British national accounting from the 1930s to the 1950s*. Unpublished doctoral dissertation, Cambridge University.

Fulton, J. (1968). *The Civil Service*, Cmnd 3638, Session 1967-8. London: HMSO.

Funnell, W. (1994). Independence and the state auditor in Britain: A constitutional keystone or a case of reified imagery. *Abacus, 30*(2), 175–195.

Funnell, W. (1996). Why 1866? Historical notes on the passage of the Exchequer and Audit Departments Act. *Abacus, 32*(1), 102–110.

Funnell, W. (1997). Military influences on the evolution of public sector accounting and audit. *Accounting History, 2*(2), 10–29.

Funnell, W. (2004). Victorian parsimony and the early champions of modern public sector audit. *Accounting History, 9*(1), 25–60.

Garrett, J. and Sheldon, R. (1973). *Administrative reform: The next step, Fabian Tract No. 426*. London: Fabian Society.

Givens-Wilson, C. (2016). *Henry IV*. New Haven: Yale University Press.

Hamilton, Lord G. (1917). *Parliamentary reminiscences and reflections: 1868 to 1885*. London: John Murray.

Henley, Sir D. (1980). Status of the Comptroller and Auditor General and his staff: Note by the Comptroller and Auditor General. In *Status of the Comptroller and Auditor General (C&AG) and his staff: Paper for the Public Accounts Committee (PAC)* AO38/6, unpublished MSS, National Archives, London.

Henley, Sir D. (1980a). Sir Douglas Henley to Michael English, 2 May 1980. In *Government's reply to the Public Accounts Committee (PAC) report on the Role of the Comptroller and Auditor General (C&AG)* AO38/11, Unpublished MSS, National Archives, London.

Henley, Sir D. (1980b). The C&AG's audit of Appropriation Accounts, 29 September 1980. In *The nature of the Comptroller and Auditor General's (C&AG) audit,* AO39/6, unpublished MSS, National Archives, London.

Henley, Sir D. (1982). Current issues in public sector auditing. In M. Bromwich, A. Hopwood and J. Shaw (eds.) *Auditing research: Issues and Opportunities.* London: Deloitte, Hoskins & Sells, 167–179.

Hennessy, P. (1990). *Whitehall.* London: Fontana Press.

Hilton, B. (2006). *A mad, bad and dangerous people: England 1783-1846.* Oxford: Oxford University Press.

Horne, Sir R. (1921). Exchequer and Audit Bill, 18 July 1921. In *Exchequer and Audit Bill. Committee of Home Affairs*, CAB24/126/42, unpublished MSS, National Archives, London.

House of Commons (1865). *Hansard*, Vol. 180, 15 June 1865.

House of Commons (1906). *Hansard*, Vol. 167, 20 December 1906.

House of Commons (1913). *Hansard*, Vol. 48, 11 February 1913.

House of Commons(1960). *Hansard*, Vol. 632, 19 December 1960.

House of Commons (1961). *Hansard*, Vol. 650, 30 November 1961.

House of Commons (1968). *Hansard*, Vol. 767, 28 June 1968.

House of Commons (1974). *Hansard*, Vol. 883, 18 December 1974.

House of Commons (1978). *Hansard* Vol. 957, 10 November 1978.,

House of Commons (1978a). *Hansard*, Vol. 959, 4 December 1978.

House of Commons (1983). *Hansard*, Vol. 35, 28 January 1983.

House of Lords (1900). *Hansard*, Vol. 78, 30 January 1900.

Irwin, Helen interview

Lawson, N. (2011). *Memoirs of a Tory radical.* London: Biteback Publishing.

Macpherson, Nicholas, Interview

Machinery of Government Committee (1918). *Report of the machinery of government committee.* London: HMSO.

Midgley, H. (2016). Payment by results in nineteenth century British education: A study in how priorities change. *Journal of Policy History*, *28*(4), 680–706.

Midgley, H. (2016a). Political thinking and the creation of the assembly of 1653. *Seventeenth Century*, *31*(1), 37–56.

Midgley, H. (2019). The National Audit Office and the Select Committee system 1979–2019. *Parliamentary Affairs*, 72(4), 779–798.

National Audit Act (1983). *National Audit Act, 1983.* Available at https://www.legislation.gov.uk/ukpga/1983/44/contents accessed on 10 March 2024.

Normanton, E. L. (1966). *The accountability and audit of government.* Manchester: Manchester University Press.

Norton, P. (2019). Departmental select committees: The reform of the century? *Parliamentary Affairs*, 72(4), 727–741.

O'Donnell, Gus, Interview

O'Regan, P. (2003). Accountability and financial control as patriotic strategies: Accomptants and the Public Accounts Committee in late 17 and early 18 century Ireland. *Accountants Historian Journal*, *30*(2), 105–131.

Oldroyd, D. (1997). Accounting in Anglo-Saxon England: context and evidence. *Accounting History*, 2(1), 7–34.
Procedure Committee (1978). *First report from the select committee on procedure together with the proceedings of the committee, minutes of evidence and appendices. Volume 1. The report.* Session 1977-8, HC588-I. London: House of Commons.
Procedure Committee (1978a). *First Report from the select committee on procedure together with the proceedings of the committee, minutes of evidence and appendices. Volume II.* Minutes of evidence. Session 1977-8, HC588-II. London: House of Commons.
Procedure Committee (1990). *Second report from the select committee on procedure. Session 1989-90. The working of the select committee system. together with the proceedings of the Committee relating to the report, minutes of evidence, and appendices*, Session 1989-90, HC19. London: House of Commons.
Public Accounts Committee (1952). *Third report from the Committee of Public Accounts*, Session 1951-2, HC253. London: House of Commons.
Public Accounts Committee (1979). *Second special report from the Committee of Public Accounts, the work of the Committee of Public Accounts and the status and functions of the Comptroller and Auditor General*, Session 1978-9, HC330. London: House of Commons.
Public Accounts Committee (1981). *First Special Report of the Committee of Public Accounts together with the proceedings of the committee, minutes of evidence and appendices session 1980–1: The Role of the Comptroller and Auditor General Vol III, appendices to the minutes of evidence*, Session 1980-1, HC115-III. London: House of Commons.
Public Accounts Committee (1982). *Ninth report from the Committee of Public Accounts, session 1981–2, Ministry of Defence Chevaline improvement to the Polaris missile system, together with the proceedings of the committee, minutes of evidence and appendices*, Session 1981-2, HC269. London: House of Commons.
Ramsay, M. G. (1930). Statement submitted by the Comptroller and Auditor General. In *Royal Commission on the Civil Service, minutes of evidence taken before the Royal Commission on the Civil Service 1929-30*. London: HMSO.
Ramsay, M. G. (1931). M.G. Ramsey to E.R. Forbes, 5 January 1931. In *Comptroller and Auditor General: Status* AO29/92, unpublished MSS, National Archives, London.
Riddell, Peter, interview
Robinson, A. T. (1924). The Exchequer and Audit Department. *Public Administration*, 2(2), 142–152.
Roseveare, H. (1969). *Treasury: The evolution of a British institution*. London: Allen Lane.
Ryle, M. (1965). Committees of the House of Commons. *The Political Quarterly*, *36*, 295–308.
Sayers, Neil, interview
Schwoerer, L.G. (2019). *No standing armies: The anti-army ideology in seventeenth century England*. Baltimore: Johns Hopkins University Press.
Select Committee on Reductions in expenditure for civil service departments not under Treasury control (1873). *Third report, minutes of evidence, appendix and index*, 1873 Session, HC352. London: House of Commons.
Sheldon, R. and Bilsnand, C. N. (1992). Called to account. *The Economist*, *324*(7774), 4.

Sutherland, G. (1973). *Policy making in elementary education 1870–95*. Oxford: Oxford University Press.
Sutherland, G. (2004). Ralph Robert Wheeler Lingen, Baron Lingen. *Oxford New Dictionary of National Biography.*
Thatcher, M. (1993). *The Downing Street Years*. London: Harper Collins.
The Telegraph (1870). Our civil service at home. *The Telegraph*, 15 November 1870.
The Telegraph (1915). Sir John Bromley. *The Telegraph*, 18 January 1915.
The Telegraph (1938). A post likely for Sir D. Banks. *The Telegraph*, 9 March 1938.
The Telegraph (1964). and his followers. *The Telegraph*, August 17 1964.
The Times (1958). Sir Frank Tribe: A watch on public spending. *The Times*, 23 June 1958.
The Times (2003). Sir Douglas Henley: Auditor General who breathed new life into feudal and inward looking department. *The Times,* 16 October 2003.
Tomlinson, J. (2009). Thrice Denied: 'Declinism' as a recurrent theme in British history in the long twentieth century. *Twentieth Century British History, 20*(2), 227–251.
Treasury (1981). *The role of the Comptroller and Auditor General*, Session 1980-1, Cmnd 8323. London: HMSO.
Trend, Sir B. (1968). The Fulton Committee report on the civil service: A note by the Prime Minister. In *Cabinet Memoranda, 71(68)-80(68)*, CAB 129/137/9, Unpublished MSS, National Archives, London.
Tribe, Sir F. (1954). Parliamentary control of public expenditure, *Public Administration, 32*(4), 363–382.
Whitehouse, Michael, interview
Wilson, Richard, interview

3

THE ESTABLISHMENT OF THE NAO UNDER SIR GORDON DOWNEY 1984–8

3.1 Introduction

The 1983 Act was purposefully vague about the NAO in several ways. Whilst it granted powers to conduct audits of the economy, efficiency and effectiveness of public spending, those words were not defined in the Act (and have never been 'legally' defined since). The Act was vague about the NAO's relationship with Parliament: the C&AG was made an officer of the House – a status which lacks clarity – and was told to 'take account' of the opinions of the PAC in coming up with his work programme but did not have to agree it with them. Oversight of the budget for the new NAO did move from the Treasury to the Public Accounts Commission[1] (TPAC), a new statutory body established by the Act, but the Treasury still retained the right to comment on it. The Act established that the appointment of the C&AG was a joint decision by the Prime Minister and the chair of PAC, but the process was kept vague. The Act did not alter the fact that there was no limit to the time a C&AG could serve. Nor did the Act say anything about the capacity with which the office would deliver its new responsibilities.

Sir Gordon Downey had been appointed in 1981 as C&AG and had been involved as discussed previously in the drafting of the Act. Downey was a Whitehall veteran having served at the Treasury since 1951. He and his staff had to negotiate their way through Treasury, Whitehall and PAC to create the new NAO, and this chapter chronicles that process.

Downey was well aware of the multiple ambiguities in the task that Parliament had set him. For example, in 1983 as the Act went through, he corresponded with the Treasury Solicitor, Sir Michael Kerry, about

DOI: 10.4324/9781003520085-3

his new status as an officer of the House and what, in practice, it meant (Downey, 1983). Kerry responded that the C&AG was 'a rather unusual officer of the House', and therefore, 'it is difficult for me to give you any very firm advice as to the implications of your appointment' (Kerry, 1983). The NAO itself was forming its image: as a minute of a senior board meeting said in November 1984, 'at present, the NAO lacked an independent corporate image with most people regarding it as allied to a government department' (Senior Management Group, 1984). The Act was vague, and the NAO did not exist in the public imagination in 1984. All the new organisation had to work with was the legacy of the E&AD and the calls by MPs for change and improvement. As Peter Hennessy[2] put it, in an article for the *Times*, 'the job of turning the new powers into achievement falls on Mr Sheldon [chair of the PAC 1983–97] and Mr Gordon Downey' (Hennessy, 1983). This chapter considers the early attempts by Downey and others to, using Hennessy's phrase, turn the powers granted by the Act into achievement.

The purpose of this chapter is to examine the period of Downey's term as C&AG from 1984 to 1988. To do so the chapter sets out the political context of the period and then considers the categories of regulatory space: organisational context (including independence), capacities and audit scope. This enables us to show how Downey and his senior colleagues interpreted the new mandate of the NAO and how they operated within the context of the Thatcherite revolution. Choices made in this period especially about the NAO's relationship to Thatcherite reform initiatives would provide precedents for later NAO work.

3.2 The political context

The NAO came into being on 1 January 1984, and Sir Gordon Downey continued to be C&AG until he was succeeded by John Bourn in 1988.

Downey's period in office therefore overlapped with the Conservative government of Margaret Thatcher, one of the more radical governments in British history which helped set the pattern for over 40 years of UK politics and policy that still continues. Thatcher had been elected in 1979 and then re-elected with large majorities in 1983 and 1987. The Thatcher government, influenced by a set of political ideas about promoting markets and moving away from planning, carried out a large programme of reform to the UK's political economy and its governmental structures. These reforms included confrontation with the trade union movement, especially during the miners' strike of 1984. She also brought forward legislation to move many of the nationalised industries into the private sector which started before the creation of the NAO and would continue post Downey's resignation. Thatcher furthermore carried out important reforms to the civil service's operations: she empowered Lord Rayner to carry out reviews of the operations of Whitehall departments looking for efficiencies in administration and opportunities to divest some of their activities. Finally, it was under Thatcher that the E&AD ceased to exist and the NAO was created.

3.3 Organisational context

Most of the changes that arose from the Act related to the NAO's relationship to Parliament. The Act made it clear that the NAO was now part of Parliament's orbit: as Helen Irwin, the clerk who drafted it, told us, it 'absolutely' put the C&AG on the legislature's side. The NAO immediately saw itself as a parliamentary institution. David Myland as deputy C&AG wrote in 1987 to William Knighton,[3] a senior official at the Department for Trade and Industry, that 'the central purpose of our V[alue] F[or] M[oney] work is not directly to improve V[alue] F[or] M[oney] but to provide a basis for departmental accountability to Parliament on major areas of public expenditure or revenue on which we aim to provide information, advice, and assurance to PAC' (Myland, 1987). Myland was not alone in taking this view.

Sir Gordon Downey agreed: he argued in public in 1984 that 'the main objectives of our value-for-money audit are accordingly to provide information, advice and assurance to Parliament' and that the NAO 'is not a management consultancy providing Department's with expert advice about efficiency' (Downey et al., 1984, pp. 11–12). The Public Accounts Commission[4] set out this new remit in its first report on the NAO's activities: the NAO was the 'most important instrument' to support the Commons in bringing 'the ever growing activities of Government under more careful and continuous scrutiny' (Public Accounts Commission, 1984, p. 6). The partnership between Robert Sheldon as chair of the PAC and Gordon Downey as C&AG was key.

The new purpose emboldened officials within the new NAO. David Clarke, who joined E&AD in 1980, told us that the Act brought with it a sense of excitement and a belief that Parliament had 'endorsed the NAO with a big tick for its role' (David Clarke, interview). Senior managers shared this sentiment: during a meeting between the NAO and the principal finance officers (generally the senior official responsible for financial matters) of departments, when responding to a query about the NAO's budget, David Dewar 'asked if departments were suggesting that a price should be placed on the need for public accountability' (NAO, 1987). Dewar's assertiveness stressed the NAO's role as an 'independent' advisor to Parliament (NAO, 1985). The NAO's fixation on this role was not purely altruistic: senior managers were also aware that 'ensuring a high and favourable profile with Parliament must be a principal consideration as they control our funding and the legislation defining our role' (Head of Communications, 1986). Prior to 1984, the E&AD's budget was controlled by the Treasury: after 1984 it was controlled by a committee of the Commons. This illuminates the subtext to David Dewar's outburst about public accountability as the discussion was in the context of the NAO budget. The new Public Accounts Commission decided to continue increasing the NAO's budget after 1983 (as will be discussed later) (Public Accounts Commission, 1984). The impact of this can be seen in discussions of the new building that the NAO began to look for after 1983. Until 1983, the auditors had been spread out in their client buildings as well as in the central Audit House; now they would have a place of their own. Initially, Treasury civil servants wrote that the case for the building was 'none too strong' and said they had only given way due to parliamentary pressure (Rayner, 1984; Bailey, 1984).

Despite its key role in working for Parliament, early on, the NAO was keen to stress its independence from the House of Commons. Senior management were concerned that the House of Commons as a whole did not treat them as a resource due to the pressure this would place on the NAO's finite capacity were it to become a source of advice for all MPs as well as the PAC. Senior management suggested in a memorandum that the NAO should have 'a rather more arm's length relationship with ordinary MPs, even though our closer position [since the 1983 Act] vis-a-vis Parliament may encourage them to see the C&AG as someone acting on their behalf' (AAG/B, 1985). Downey was also concerned that the NAO did not get dragged into partisan argument: he made a sharp distinction between the chamber of the House of Commons (where legislation, for example, is voted upon), within which policy debate happened, and the PAC which dealt solely with matters for which civil servants were accountable (Downey et al., 1984).

The meaning of independence with respect to Parliament was contested, and so was its meaning with regards to the executive. There is evidence that the NAO in 1984 was behaving more assertively. This was noticed inside government where at a meeting of permanent secretaries in 1984, the attending civil servants complained that 'as a result of the greater independence afforded to the NAO' in the Act, the auditors were focusing more on their performance audit work than on financial audit (Cabinet Office, 1984). It was also noted outside: for example, the *Financial Times* reported on the 'increasing stern line' that Downey was taking on nationalised industries in August 1984 (Pauley, 1984).

The NAO itself was aware of the risks involved in a more combative approach with departments, and in 1984 David Myland considered whether the NAO should issue pointed press notices of its own when it published its reports. This was after noting that arguments between the NAO and department(s) in public would be 'very interesting preludes to particular PAC enquiries'. He suggested that the office should 'avoid confrontation and seek a higher profile by gradually raising the quality and interest to Parliament of our reports and ensuring in a non-provocative way that the press is aware of them and helped to understand their significance' (Myland, 1984).

Myland's caution was based on an awareness of what departments could do if they chose. Relationships could easily sour. Indeed, even with this knowledge and caution, in January 1986, Downey and Sir David Hancock, permanent secretary at the Department for Education, disagreed publicly in a PAC session about what had been agreed by the department and NAO during discussions of an NAO report. The committee decided to pause its consideration of the NAO report: as Robert Sheldon put it, 'we have had our time wasted up to now. We cannot proceed without an agreed report' (PAC, 1986, p. 10). The committee largely backed the NAO, with the exception of Fred Silvester, Conservative MP for Manchester Withington, who suggested that it was the C&AG's comments in the report that had caused problems for clearance (PAC, 1986, p. 9). Sheldon told Hancock that "I must ask you not to do this again to this committee but to let us know if there is a disagreeement that cannot be resolved so we can be prepared to deal with it" (PAC, 1986, p. 6). Sheldon ensured it was the department who took responsibility for the issues involved, but it was a warning that the NAO could not afford too many disputes in front of MPs without risking more MPs (especially of the governing party) deciding it was the auditor being unfair, rather than the department obfuscating. Relations between departments and Parliament created threats for the NAO: for example, in 1986, the NAO was caught between departments who requested that the auditors supply them with the detailed questions that the PAC would ask in its sessions and Sheldon, who thought the NAO should not share this information (NAO, 1986).

Tensions between the NAO and departments emerged more often in private. Whilst the Act gave the NAO the right to access information, in practice, that right was conditional on departmental cooperation. Departments could restrict access to material or slow down studies with multiple objections if they wanted to. The NAO was aware of these constraints: in October 1984, the Senior Management Group was informed that the NAO's access rights could be defended so long as they were not 'abused' (Senior Management Group, 1984a). The press alleged that departments hid things from the auditor by keeping documents unnumbered in files, so it would be unclear whether any documents had been removed. They also alleged some documents to be hidden from the auditor were stamped as 'not for NAO eyes' (Norton-Taylor, 1985). The government argued that these files were predominantly those concerned with preparing for the PAC and dealing with the NAO itself (House of Commons, 1985). Further papers were withheld from the NAO at times: in 1987, Sir Peter Middleton, then permanent secretary at the Treasury, explained to Downey that he could not access

> Internal Treasury papers which concern other departments' accountability at ministerial or accounting officer levels. In most cases these will be expenditure divisions' papers. There the accepted and established practice has always been that your access is to the accountable departments' papers. These will naturally include all of its exchanges with the Treasury.
>
> *(Middleton, 1987)*

Middleton undermined his own point by immediately stating that these documents would not contain the full record held by the Treasury: he said he would not share Treasury papers as it would be 'wrong to introduce material into your reports or into the evidence upon which they are based, of which Accounting Officers are unaware' (Middleton, 1987). Senior NAO officials thought they had a legitimate case for access as the Treasury's role 'in the appraisal and approval of departments' capital projects over a certain value . . . seems to be a legitimate subject for an NAO investigation under the Act' (Le Marechal, 1986). Note though the reference to 'established practice' from Middleton: the government's case for restricting NAO access relied on precedent prior to the Act and relied heavily on a ministerial statement in committee stage that the Act had not been intended to change pre-existing practice (Le Marechal, 1986).

The government's approach was based on the Act as well as precedent. The NAO believed that the Treasury had attempted to control the C&AG's access to documents by inserting a reasonableness condition into the Act, limiting the auditor's access (NAO, 1985a). Sir Peter Middleton in the controversy referenced above referred Downey to the 'reasonable' condition in the Act (Middleton, 1987). In its own guidance to departments, published shortly after the NAO was established, the Treasury made it clear that the C&AG required 'adequate access but not totally free access' (Treasury, 1984). This opened up a potentially more politically controversial case: that of Cabinet papers or minutes which were relevant to a study. Downey's position was that Cabinet papers could conceivably be part of a reasonable set of document requests:

> We have been advised that the 'reasonableness' of any request for documents depends on the circumstances of the case rather than on the

> nature of the document, which suggests that we may have a statutory right of access to cabinet papers in appropriate cases.
>
> *(Downey, 1986)*

Downey explained circumstances in which he felt that the auditors were entitled to see Cabinet papers in a note he wrote to PAC in 1987: he said firstly that he would only seek such papers in the context of a project that had been approved by the Cabinet. In such a case,

> Although I need to see satisfactory evidence of any Cabinet decision relating to the approval of substantial projects or programmes of expenditure, I still think it unnecessary to seek access to cabinet minutes. However, it seems to me that, in order to ensure departments have provided ministers with accurate and relevant information upon which to base their decision, it would be reasonable under the N[ational] A[udit] Act for me to have a right of access to copies of departmental submissions to the Cabinet . . . and in those very rare circumstances where there is prima facie evidence on departmental files that raises doubts about the accuracy and relevancy of the information put before ministers it would be reasonable for me to request access to those Cabinet papers.
>
> *(Downey, 1987)*

Downey's point hinged upon the nature of the decisions that he was charged to examine. He was not charged to examine decisions about policy so Cabinet discussions on policy were normally excluded from his view. However, he needed to know the results of those discussions as the starting point for his audit: a point that the Treasury solicitor agreed with. Furthermore, he argued that if civil servants advised ministers using faulty information, as his role was to hold the civil servants to account before the PAC on the basis of the Act, he did have a right to see the papers to ascertain if they had done so.

The arguments put forth by Downey did not always find a receptive audience in government: in 1985, for example, defence ministers decided that papers on the department's efficiency were 'personal reports to them rather than departmental papers' (NAO, 1985b). If access was governed by reasonableness, the Act had set out no way of reconciling those differences save through compromise or appeal to the House of Commons through the PAC (Hosker, 1984).

Concern about access was not the only way that departments could seek to restrict the NAO's impact. Another argument between departments and the NAO focussed on the timeliness of departmental feedback about studies. In 1987, the NAO complained that they had an agreed target of twenty-five weeks for departmental clearance but on average agreeing a report took forty-two weeks. Departments responded that the NAO's expansion of the scope of its work and the increased sensitivity of the reports caused the delay (NAO, 1987a). Consequently, staff within the NAO realised that departmental fears had to be allayed: as one auditor put it, 'if we were seen to be acting in an unreasonable way sources of information would become much more difficult to tap and . . . the work of the Office would become in a large measure impossible' (Birch, 1985). Theoretically, the NAO might be independent, but its effective function 'will turn on mutual trust and goodwill' between it and the departments it audited (Birch, 1985).

Timeliness was especially a challenging issue for the new NAO to circumnavigate in the world of national security. Under previous auditing arrangements, both the Attlee government in the 1940s and the Wilson government in the 1970s had hidden defence projects, such as the development of the British nuclear deterrent and the Chevaline project (a project to equip the UK's nuclear deterrent better) from the House of Commons (Aldrich, 2010, p. 414). Concerns had been raised in Parliament during the discussions of the 1983 Act about the E&AD's ability to scrutinise expenditure in these areas. Downey quickly established the NAO's independence on defence. Firstly, the fifth report that the new NAO published focussed on the new Trident programme (the UK's new nuclear weapons programme beginning in the 1980s). The report, however, examined purely administrative aspects of the programme such as its 'project management and financial control' and tempered any criticism through recognition that the project was at an 'early stage' (C&AG, 1984a, p. 1). A follow-up report in 1987 (C&AG, 1987g) took a similar line. The NAO's role was divided: on the one hand, to subject these programmes to Parliamentary scrutiny and, on the other, to ensure national security was not compromised.

The C&AG's willingness to be open about government defence projects and stand up for Parliament's rights was called into question a few years later, however. A journalist working with the *New Statesman*, Duncan Campbell, discovered the existence of a British spy satellite project called Zircon. By interviewing Robert Sheldon, he also identified that the chair of the PAC and hence Parliament knew nothing about the project (Aldrich, 2010, p. 432). There was anger in Parliament: Graham Allen (MP for Nottingham North 1987–2017) described the incident as one of 'the two most notorious breaches of financial accountability' in recent history[5] (House of Commons, 1987, col. 1198). Downey responded by pointing out, both in a press statement and through Sir Edward Du Cann as Chair of TPAC, that the Zircon project did not, in 1987, yet meet the threshold which required reporting to Sheldon (House of Commons, 1987a, col.

594). He could have also pointed out that the NAO in the past had shared information with MPs when required: for example, in his report on the defence of the Falkland Islands in 1984, Downey pointed out that

> I intend to provide the Committee of Public Accounts with some further details to supplement the report, on a confidential basis.
>
> *(C&AG, 1984d, p. 1)*

The Zircon affair caused issues for the BBC including the resignation of the then Director General, but Downey was not forced out. It illustrated, however, the difficulties that the NAO faced in maintaining both good relations and trust with departments needed to perform its role and together with the trust of Parliament as their sentinel in government.

3.4 Capacities

Apart from considering how to navigate the mandate within the organisational context of government, the new NAO needed to consider its capacity to do so. This included establishing a new corporate identity and corporate purpose, as described above. A high-profile organisation also needed more and better trained staff to perform its role. The E&AD did not have appropriate premises for all its staff. Instead, as The Public Accounts Commission noted, staff were spread across two main buildings and 26 other smaller offices (Public Accounts Commission, 1984, p. 5). NAO officials from the 1980s talked about how important establishing a new headquarters building was to create and strengthen a new NAO corporate culture was, although the E&AD had always had a strong culture thanks to its nature as a 'cuckoo in the governmental nest' (David Clarke, interview).

Capacity was always a constraint for the newly established NAO. The E&AD had to set up its successor organisation, but the outside observers were not impressed. Embarrassingly, the Treasury even questioned the E&AD's understanding of parliamentary financial accounting, describing its first attempt at an estimate for the newly created NAO as 'meaningless' (Rayner, 1983). The new NAO realised it needed to improve its management systems, including adopting accepted good managerial practices such as business planning, activity recording, divisional accountability reviews, computerising personnel and resource management and improving the professionalism of training (Michael Whitehouse, interview, NAO, 1986). In 1983, a Treasury official pointedly remarked 'it hardly encourages confidence in the government's audit service if it cannot even get its own figures straight and you may like to point this out gently to Mr Downey' (Rayner, 1983). The NAO addressed this too by adopting a new corporate planning process, allowing for enhanced accountability to Parliament (Michael Whitehouse, interview).

As we mentioned in the previous chapter, the Crown Agents affair suggested that the E&AD was experiencing serious problems in satisfying Parliament that it could perform financial audit to an appropriate standard. Before its creation, Downey was concerned that the newly created Audit Commission would be able to pay more than the NAO (Bailey, 1984). In 1984, the Senior Management Group decided against auditing the United Nations (UN) as 'experienced good quality staff [were] in short supply' (Senior Management Group, 1984a). In particular, the NAO were concerned about the difference between their staff and those of the private sector (audit) firms: 'at the moment NAO staff did not have anything like the same exposure to certification audit approach and methods as staff in private sector firms' (Senior Management Group, 1984b).

The first major challenge to confront was the E&AD/NAO budget. Even before 1983, the Treasury had acknowledged the problem: the government and the E&AD had agreed in 1978 to increase the number of staff that the E&AD employed by 5% a year to bolster the E&AD's financial audit work (Public Accounts Commission, 1984, p. 5). However, once control switched to TPAC, the new NAO was positioned to make a stronger argument for further increased funds, albeit the Treasury would still be consulted on the NAO budget.

Others also marked the change between the two regimes. Sir Edward Du Cann, for example, claimed one of his achievements as chair of TPAC was to provide more funding to the NAO (Du Cann, 1995). David Clarke, who entered the NAO in 1980 as a graduate trainee, said that he thought the change to funding was 'really important' (David Clarke, interview). Difficulties in keeping pace with private sector pay rates in the wider economy were reducing the number of qualified accountants the NAO had (Public Accounts Commission, 1986). At the NAO, senior managers were aware that accounting salaries were going up by 10% a year in the mid-1980s and that the NAO had to keep pace to keep its staff (Senior Management Group, 1986). Whilst these difficulties were easing by the end of Downey's time in power, the commission said that it retained a 'keen interest' in ensuring NAO staff were paid sufficiently to make them stay (Public Accounts Commission, 1988).

NAO weaknesses went beyond the budget, with numerous interviewees who joined during the early 1980s telling us that there was a cultural clash between the CIPFA qualified trainees and older members of staff who had not had to pursue a professional qualification (Jeremy Lonsdale, Steve Corbishley, interviews). Even towards the end of Downey's period, junior staff thought that the office was still stuck in the 'Edwardian era'

(Martin Sinclair, interview). The E&AD culture had been based upon a traditional hierarchy: then a junior member of staff, David Clarke, recalled:

> When I joined in 1980, I was in the office with a senior auditor who was supposed to be my boss and he had a list of people with their birthdays and marked it with anyone younger than him who was senior. He was pre-CIPFA and he was going to be passed over whereas previously his expectation would have been that he would have progressed up the ladder.
>
> *(David Clarke, interview)*

This was out of step with the reality that CIPFA qualified staff would be promoted more quickly, as well as out of step with the reality that the NAO had to some extent become a standard accountancy recruiter. For example, in 1984, the Senior Management Group concluded that qualified staff would want more flexible careers, moving in and out of the NAO over time: 'it was no longer realistic to assume that they [graduate recruits] would all remain with the NAO for the rest of their careers. The trend was for increasing numbers of qualified staff – particularly the most able – to find alternative employment' (Senior Management Group, 1984). Significantly, in 1986, the NAO invited one of those professional audit firms, Grant Thornton, to review its capacity on financial audit, and one of their recommendations was that the NAO should 'create an environment in which staff accept the possibility of leaving the NAO as a natural part of their career development' (Grant Thornton, 1986). Grant Thornton also argued that professional firms could come in and assist the NAO with its work (Grant Thornton, 1986). These changes, which meant the NAO becoming more flexible, would move it culturally some way towards the professional accountancy firms.

Change was needed to culture and to pay to keep these new highly trained staff. Downey did make significant changes to the culture of the NAO, but even at the end of Downey's period in charge though, a strengths and weaknesses analysis compiled for his successor, John Bourn, identified 'hierarchy, prescription, closed culture, slow translation of best practice, poor development of leaders, pioneers, lateral thinkers, and conflict between qualified and non-qualified staff' and an 'unthinking approach' to financial audit as weaknesses (Policy Unit, 1988). The changes suggested by the Management Review of 1979 and accelerated by the NAO Act 1983 had further to go.

Thirdly, the NAO was also concerned about the training it offered its staff. An internal review from 1984 of NAO financial audits found that there was a

> need for re-examining certification audit training more widely for staff at all levels: directors generally have endorsed this view. Certainly the large professional firms invest more heavily in basic training than we do and the content of their courses is more directed towards establishing a sound approach to auditing basics with heavy use of case studies to simulate actual work.
>
> *(NAO, 1984)*

The review noted that the average trainee received 10 and a half days of training during their contract, whereas their private sector equivalents received 30–40 (NAO, 1984).

Fourthly, there were concerns about pay in the private sector and the rest of the public sector (including the Audit Commission) outpacing pay at the NAO. TPAC noted this in their own reports: because the NAO had been experiencing difficulties with both recruitment and retention, the commission found that 'a key factor in most moves had been pay and prospects' as both private sector firms and the Audit Commission paid more (Public Accounts Commission, 1984a, p. 3). Whilst the Treasury were inevitably sceptical, a team of management consultants advising the commission stated that the NAO would still be in the bottom 15% of payers for finance firms (Public Accounts Commission, 1984a, p. 5). The result of these factors was to suggest, as a gloomy minute to the Senior Management Board stated in December 1984, that by 1990 the NAO would face 'a serious mismatch of available resources' to their tasks (NAO, 1984a).

Fifthly, the E&AD and subsequently then the NAO had focussed on building up the financial audit capacity of the organisation post the Management Review of 1979. By 1984, when TPAC reported, it found that 'although this programme has been successful, one result of the implementation of a revised approach to certification audit has been to decrease to an unacceptable degree the amount of staff effort available for economy, efficiency and effectiveness examinations'. They endorsed Downey's ambition to 'devote 50% of his resources to value for money work' and approved an increase in the NAO's number of staff by 5% a year to obtain this objective (Public Accounts Commission, 1984, p. 6). The Public Accounts Commission viewed achieving this balance between financial and value-for-money audit as a 'prime aim' of the NAO (Public Accounts Commission, 1986, p. 5). The NAO still perceived gaps in skills on value-for-money studies through the expectation that one in three staff on a value-for-money study would be a qualified accountant (NAO, 1984a). The NAO began an analyst scheme in 1983 for non-accountants, but entrants were limited to 15, with 3 economists and recruits supposed to remain in the office for two years at the most (NAO, 1984b).

What was crucial is that this entire process of strengthening the organisation was underpinned by the Public Accounts Commission.

3.5 Audit scope

Finally, having considered the organisational context and capacities, we need to look at audit scope during Downey's period as C&AG at the newly established NAO.

The 1983 Act both did and did not alter the scope of the NAO's audit. On 13 January 1984, the Treasury circulated a minute to the heads of expenditure divisions within departments: in it, they wrote that the NAO had produced a 'clear explanation of what the new office does' and added a point 'though that is not in substance different from what the E&AD used to do' (Judd, 1984). The Treasury's perception was accurate in terms of what the NAO would do with its financial audit where the Act made no changes. However, in value-for-money audit, the Act for the first time set out that the NAO would report on economy, efficiency and effectiveness. To some extent, this formalised, as discussed in Chapter 2, existing practice; however, a move into auditing the effectiveness of government policy was novel. The NAO did not initially exploit the new part of its remit. Garrett (1986) wrote that in his view the pre- and post-1983 C&AG tended to confine his reports to the first of those three e's: economy. Studies stressed the continuity between the E&AD's work before the Act and NAO's work after the Act (C&AG, 1984b, p1, 1986f, p. 1, 1986h, p. 1). Lord Wilson remembered the reaction in the civil service when the Act passed:

> When the Act was going through, Principal Finance Officers used to get together under Treasury leadership. We all were slightly alarmed and fascinated by what this new bill was going to do and what looking at value for money was going to do to the way that the new NAO were going to do their role. We were divided, no one knew. Some people were of the view that though it went into policy and value for money, the auditors were not up to it, they were trained to be narrow specialists looking at the numbers and we didn't have much to fear. Some people said if you look at the wording of the bill literally, it is sweeping and gives them huge authority and allows them to go anywhere. We all waited to see what happened. Then, my memory is that the NAO's remit did not expand quickly.
>
> *(Lord Wilson, interview)*

Wilson's recollections, placed alongside Garrett's comments and the NAO's existing commitment to maintaining its scope, suggest that whilst the Act was radical, the auditors themselves were conservative in how they interpreted it.

Methodologies remained conservative too: when NAO examined efficiency, it would do so by analysing either departmental documents such as the department's own records of outcomes or estimates by external consultants provided to the department (examples include C&AG, 1984c, p. 9, 1986d, pp. 11–12). There were examples of methodological innovation, but these came at the end of Downey's period in charge: a study on prison farms involved visits to a number of prisons to see what was happening, and a study on customer service in the Department of Health and Social Security made use of a poll conducted by Gallup for the NAO (C&AG, 1987h, 1988b). This is not surprising. As Downey made clear: the initial studies published after the Act were actually based on work that had been going on before (Downey et al., 1984). Furthermore, methodological conservatism could lead to positive results: in 1986, the NAO republished analysis from the Department for Health about the failure of the UK's cervical cancer screening programme which led to reforms in the programme (C&AG, 1986j).

The NAO itself was adjusting administratively to being its own organisation. Consequently, it was only in 1985 that David Myland, deputy C&AG, wrote to all directors announcing the establishment of a policy unit within the NAO, one of whose responsibilities was to be the 'focal point for clear definitions of the NAO's objectives and means of achieving them' (Myland, 1985). Any extension of the NAO's role had to confront Treasury scepticism: as late as October 1987, the NAO thought that the 'Treasury's lack of interest [in the NAO's work] and poor participation was because they were far more interested in containing expenditure than in considering value for money and . . . suggested the Treasury had a narrow view of the NAO's role and responsibilities' (Director of Policy and Planning, 1987). Note that the NAO argued that the Treasury had adopted a Gladstonian view of public sector audit, whereas NAO had moved beyond that into incorporating value for money.

If little changed initially because of the Act, what can we say did change? The first major change concerned value-for-money audit. The Act gave the C&AG the right to report directly to the House of Commons on value for money. Previously, reports had to be attached to the Appropriation Accounts (see the previous chapter) and came bundled together in a very long document, which few would ever read or discuss. A stand-alone value-for-money report had a higher profile, and because the C&AG was granted the right to report to the Commons, NAO reports retained parliamentary privilege, meaning that the NAO could report on the facts without fear of any legal consequences. Allowing the C&AG to report on efficiency and effectiveness had a major impact on value-for-money audit, liberating the auditor from the confines of the accounts. Reports no longer had to relate directly to the accounts, which meant value-for-money reports could address different subjects within the remit set by the Act, reports could be much wider in scope and, perhaps most importantly, the C&AG could report directly to Parliament throughout the year while Parliament was sitting.

The effect of this can be seen in early reports. The NAO was very careful about how it exercised this responsibility, so, for example, in one of the first reports to touch on effectiveness on housing in 1984, the C&AG carefully outlined both where he had obtained his understanding of the government's objectives for policy and what the NAO defined as those objectives (C&AG, 1984c, pp. 2–3). At times, this kind of commentary could cross over into an implicit criticism of the audited programme: in 1986, the NAO noted of the government's spending on legal aid that 'the broad aims of the Legal Aid Scheme introduced in 1960 . . . had not been defined in more specific terms against which achievement could be monitored' (C&AG, 1986c, p. 1). Secondly, as noted above, reports could be published throughout the parliamentary year, therefore making an immediate impact and putting pressure on senior civil servants and ministers since criticism of departments could be coming regularly. The NAO itself had to set up new functions including a press office (after the Zircon affair (Private Information)) and consider explicitly its own external relations with the press, MPs and public.

NAO reports still remained fairly drab documents without much illustration: the first map appeared in a report on New Towns only in 1986 and the first pie chart in a report on postgraduate education funding in 1987 (C&AG, 1986k, 1987e, p.2).

The development of value-for-money audit created more subtle changes too. In 1986, David Dewar, a senior official at the NAO, briefed officials from Whitehall that value-for-money reports were changing: as Dewar argued, 'the facts were no longer left to speak for themselves and conclusions and interpretation were becoming a more significant feature' (NAO, 1986). Departments definitely noticed: principal finance officers complaining at a meeting with the NAO that reports were becoming 'much more judgemental' (NAO, 1986a). This change in the NAO's reports was conscious: a review of value-for-money work in 1984 suggested that whilst the NAO intended to provide a 'mixed diet' of reports to the PAC, the C&AG thought that they should move from 'selective criticism and small scale value for money investigations towards broader-based and larger-scale investigations' (NAO, 1984c). The government noticed: the Treasury commented cautiously in 1984 that the PAC was 'extending much more into the "effectiveness" field than in the past' (Treasury, 1984). Departments were scared of these developments: Sir

Kenneth Couzens (Permanent Secretary, Department of Energy) had to be reassured in 1985 that the NAO were not planning to launch a value-for-money study of the coal industry in the midst of the miners' strike (Birch, 1985). If departments were fearful, then the Commons anticipated a more activist auditor. They pushed the NAO to embrace the extension to its remit, especially towards examining the effectiveness of government spending (Public Accounts Commission, 1986, p. 6).

However, the NAO's approach to value-for-money audit in the 1980s was not radical. We can see this if we look at two examples: its approach to auditing the government's efficiency programmes and its approach to the audit of privatisation. Thatcher's agenda for increasing efficiency in public services led to the Financial Management Initiative and the Rayner Reviews.[6] The NAO's reviews of Thatcher's efficiency initiatives demonstrated how far it thought it could press its mandate.

In its report on the Financial Management Initiative, the NAO accepted the principle of the initiative and discussed 'progress with the development of these arrangements across 12 government departments' (C&AG, 1986a, p. 1). The NAO did not attempt to evaluate whether, if implemented, the programme itself would actually deliver its claimed objectives.

The NAO reviewed the Rayner scrutiny process and stated that the C&AG 'endorses the continuing usefulness of the scrutiny process as a high level management technique to improve value for money' (C&AG, 1986b, p. 1). The report focussed on whether departments had chosen the right subjects for Rayner's team to review and whether the savings identified had actually been delivered. The C&AG recognised that these initiatives were not alone: 'departments are increasingly making use of the range of consultancy, inspection and review techniques' (C&AG, 1986b, p. 6). There is no evidence in these reports that the C&AG challenged any of these developments, however, or examined their underlying premise, and in fact, the C&AG seemed to push the government to extend them if anything into effectiveness and policy work (C&AG, 1986, p. 6).

The NAO would often instead criticise government's variable implementation of reform, commenting on the 'varying quality' in the NHS of hospital plans for savings (C&AG, 1986e, p. 2). The reports on Thatcher's efficiency programme monitored the extent to which Whitehall had complied with them rather than questioning the value for money of the central programme (e.g. C&AG, 1987c). To some extent, the NAO's willingness to stand behind the Thatcher programme might have matched its own instincts: the first line of the report about charity regulation, for example, asserted that 'charities are big business': a contentious statement (C&AG, 1987f, p. 1). It indicates, however, that the NAO may have been a willing promoter of neo-liberal reform. In this sense, the C&AG retained his traditional position as an agent for Treasury control in the public sector.

The NAO's involvement with the Thatcherite programme of government reform was not purely focussed on government efficiency. The C&AG also examined, through his reports, several of the large privatisations of the 1980s (C&AG, 1985, 1987, 1987a, 1988). Downey carefully emphasised the continuity of the subject matter: the NAO were building on work by the E&AD. As the report on the privatisation of British Telecom set out clearly, the NAO were checking that the government had responded to recommendations made by the PAC in 1981 and 1982 (C&AG, 1985, p. 1). By 1987–8, Downey had established a clear format for these reports on privatisation. Each report would set out the government's objectives for the sale, the arrangements for the sale, results of the sale and then a set of conclusions. Commentary focussed on the precise mechanisms that the department used to establish a price and ensure they maximised their revenue from the sale as well as minimising their own costs, for example, in the cases of British Gas and Rolls Royce (C&AG, 1987, pp. 15–16, 1988a, pp. 12–13). The reports accepted the government's objectives for the sale as read and measured progress against those objectives. As with the Thatcher reforms to the civil service, this approach to accountability for value for money for the privatised industries might have been uncomfortable for the departments questioned in the Commons but was designed to ensure that the NAO did not cross the line on examining policy. However, by limiting his consideration of the sales to analysing the economy of the deals, the C&AG implicitly accepted the government's contention that they were not responsible for the effectiveness of the operation of these services post-privatisation or for meeting wider government objectives such as widening share ownership.

NAO staff were aware that changes to value for money appeared over time. Jeremy Lonsdale, who spent his career at the NAO, starting in the late 1980s, and completed a PhD examining the conduct of value-for-money work (Lonsdale, 2000), suggested that the NAO took at least 10 years from its creation to work out what value-for-money audit activity could actually entail and to start to make the most of its remit (Jeremy Lonsdale, interview).[7] Glynn (1985) concurs and argues that at this point the UK needed to look overseas to identify successful examples of value-for-money auditing. There were examples of more expansive value-for-money audit though they were few and radicalism was unusual; an exception to this in the 1990s was Sweden. The NAO was a part of a system, so changes in its behaviour had knock-on effects elsewhere in the system of accountability. Departments complained of 'more aggressive' questioning at the PAC, focussed on the minutiae of what had been identified by the auditor (NAO, 1988). This cycle conditioned what the NAO's value-for-money audit looked like as well.

From 1982 onwards, the Audit Commission had become another source of value-for-money expertise within government, with a remit for local government that would later also include the National Health Service. The NAO felt under pressure from its more adventurous sister organisation (Campbell-Smith, 2008,). But the Audit Commission's work was crucially different because of its different constitutional position. An internal NAO memorandum compared the approaches of the two audit organisations in 1986:

> both organisations are developing value for money audit techniques and there is probably much to be gained by exchanges of experience. The Commission appears to use consultants and other specialists to a greater degree than the NAO and local government officers are sometimes seconded to the Commission for the duration of studies. Although both organisations may gather information using interview and questionnaire approaches, NAO attaches much more importance to direct evidence in order to avoid unnecessary disputes over facts. We also place great store on producing agreed reports and in presenting our conclusions in a balanced and objective way. The Commission seeks publicity and tends to sensationalise its findings, apparently as a means of attracting attention and influencing public opinion in the absence of the kind of pressure which PAC can exert. It also makes great use in its reports of tables, graphs, pie and bar charts.
>
> *(NAO, 1986b)*

The note's emphasis on the shaping effects of both departmental clearance and parliamentary involvement on the way that the NAO audited is important. Firstly, the pressure of departmental clearance led the NAO to take a restrictive attitude to evidence, preferring 'direct' to 'indirect' evidence (i.e. evidence from the department rather than that produced by others such as those who used departmental services) which the department would find more difficult to contradict. Secondly, the NAO even in its new independent state, under the pressure of clearance and reporting to PAC, preferred not to 'sensationalise' its findings but rather focussed on reporting to PAC because it had no need for an external audience to make an impact. The memorandum was not purely an academic exercise: officials were worried that the Audit Commission occasionally 'appeared to go outside their statutory functions in commenting on the effectiveness of provisions or directions in achieving the objectives of central government and not simply their impact on local authorities', a fact that 'is of course of interest to us as their auditors' (Director of Policy and Planning, 1986). The Audit Commission's approach did influence the NAO: in 1986, Myland anxiously reported that the TPAC was interested in whether the

NAO could publish how much its value-for-money work had saved the public. The Audit Commission already were publishing a figure, and it was 'apparently impressing the government' (Myland, 1986). There were examples of working together as well: the NAO's 1985 report on local tax collection noted that it 'drew upon the findings of a study of the Audit Commission' and was so integrated with the commission's work that it contained appendices which summarised their investigation (C&AG, 1985c). Influence therefore came through both competition and collaboration between the two organisations. Whatever the Audit Commission's approach to its remit, its presence meant that the NAO alone did not get to decide what the words of the Act meant: instead, the NAO, Parliament, departments and the commission were together engaged in a process of defining exactly what value for money in the public sector would mean.

If the NAO's value-for-money audit was slowly becoming more assertive, the NAO's coverage of value for money was set by the Act. There was no real push in the 1980s to expand the coverage of public sector audit. With regard to the BBC, for example, the NAO audited the funds going to the BBC from the Foreign Office to fund the BBC World Service and in this was accused of being a tool of government policy. John Tusa, who worked for the BBC as a broadcaster and later administrator, arguing against the presence of the auditors, suggested that if the BBC World Service 'lose management independence as well as editorial independence then the whole credibility of the external services will be threatened' (Fiddick, 1986). The NAO could come close to examining the BBC, for example, examining the collection of licence fees by the Home Office, but under Downey, it did not expand into the actual audit of the corporation (C&AG, 1985b). Similarly, in local government, the NAO's influence was constrained because of the creation of the Audit Commission, but it took its responsibility to examine central government's interactions with local government seriously. In a report on urban regeneration, for example, the NAO noted that

> some of the problems [in the programme] were due to the division of responsibility between DOE [the Department for the Environment then responsible for local government] and local authorities, the NAO could not satisfy itself from DoE records that appraisal and monitoring by the department was adequate for it to be certain that the authorities gave sufficient attention to strategies for dealing with local problems.
>
> *(C&AG, 1985d, p. 1)*

The NAO concluded similarly about gaps in the accountability of the Metropolitan Police (C&AG, 1986g). The NAO also clearly positioned itself as able to audit the central funding of local government when they assessed, with the Audit Commission, the Department for Environment's funding of local authority capital spending. It examined the way that the department controlled local authority spending as well as whether the system of funding 'promote[s] a good match between the availability of resources and the incidence of need' (C&AG, 1986i, p. 2). The NAO argued that departments had a responsibility to oversee the financial management of organisations, even those to whom the department had delegated powers, and especially in circumstances such as community care where key policy objectives depended upon local government (C&AG, 1987d, p. 10, 1987i, p. 2). In some ways, these conclusions anticipate work the NAO was to do 30 years later under Amyas Morse, when he stressed departmental responsibility for the system of local government, though here, as in Morse's time, the NAO commented solely on central government's responsibilities for local government. Not all innovations from the 1980s had successors: the NAO evaluated the value for money of the European Communities' Common Agricultural policy in 1985, a report that had few successors (C&AG, 1985e).

Again with respect to nationalised industries, the NAO respected the limits imposed by the 1983 Act. In 1985, the NAO looked at the government's monitoring of nationalised industries but was clear that it was not looking at the management of the industries, in line with the 1983 Act, which did not grant it this role and emphasised that this work was a continuation of work that the E&AD had started in 1983 (C&AG, 1984, p. 1, 1985a, p. 1).

NAO's interactions with Parliament outside PAC were relatively reserved in this period. Similarly, despite the intentions of the framers of the 1983 Act, the NAO's interaction with the new select committee system was very limited (Midgley, 2019, pp. 784–785). Arguably, the post-1983 NAO was more cautious about select committees than the E&AD had been: there was no repeat of Sir Douglas Henley's report to the Environment Select Committee on the sale of council housing (Dewar and Funnell, 2017, p. 205; Midgley, 2019, p. 785). In one regard, the C&AG did advance beyond his normal mandate, however: in 1987, a House of Lords judgement about the Trustee Savings Bank raised the question of whether Parliament had been sufficiently informed when passing an Act in 1985. The C&AG reported to the House that he believed that the Treasury had endeavoured to 'disclose the position fully to Parliament both at the outset and as matters developed' (C&AG, 1987b, p. 5). Despite his reassuring judgement, Downey established a precedent that the NAO could question the information that government departments presented to Parliament during the consideration of an Act. It is a precedent that otherwise remains unused though. Downey was in general, apart from the example of the Trustee Savings Bank, cautious about further involvement with the House of Commons other than through the PAC.

Turning to financial audit, the Act did not comment directly on the audit of the financial accounts. Legally, the NAO enforced (as had the E&AD) the 1866 and 1921 Exchequer and Audit Departments Acts. According to Michael Whitehouse, then a trainee, the NAO remained 'scared stiff' of a repetition of the Crown Agents affair (see the previous chapter).[8]

The professionalisation of staff, proposed by the Management Review of 1979 in the aftermath of the Crown Agents affair, drove changes to the E&AD's and NAO's approach to financial audit, most of which continued throughout this period. New entrants to the NAO began to be trained by CIPFA. Secondly, financial audit was resourced much more, with increases in expenditure of 5% a year flowing to financial audit, so much so that an office where money was mostly spent on examinations of value for money in 1979 (value for money at this time meant reports attached to the accounts exploring points of waste and inefficiency) transitioned to one in which the majority of the budget went on financial audit (a situation that has remained largely true ever since; see subsequent chapters) (E&AD, 1979, p. 24). For Steve Corbishley,[9] that decision 'changed the culture of financial audit, albeit slowly'. Improvement in quality was slow: in 1984, an internal review of 21 financial audits found that only 5 were 'sound in all respects', in 12 'a defensible standard was being reached', but in 4 audits, the reviewers found that 'the audit was not considered as reaching a minimum professional standard' (NAO, 1984).

The NAO was conscious, however, that the system of accounting and audit did not provide Parliament with what it required in terms of financial information. PAC (1987) referred to the 'doubtful effectiveness' of parliamentary control over expenditure. John Garrett criticised accounts from the parliamentary viewpoint, describing the 'inadequacy of the data provided by departmental accounts', criticising both the ways in which financial data was presented and the lack of performance data (Garrett, 1986, p. 427).

The C&AG agreed: his diagnosis was that while Parliament should get more accountability from the executive, 'MPs in general . . . did not seem to think this was an important issue. One of the problems was apathy' (Norton-Taylor, 1987). In 1984, the NAO decided to carry out its own report into financial accounting and estimates within government. The report was recognised internally as 'an important exercise as far as the NAO was concerned and one on which the office's credibility would depend' (NAO, 1984d). The pre-occupation of the NAO's report was that accounting had a constitutional purpose. The NAO analysed what Parliament received and needed. Based upon that analysis, the NAO recommended that new principles should be adopted for government financial reporting across estimates, accounts and other sources of evidence. These new principles are set out below:

> To provide Parliament and departmental select committees in particular with information which is reliable and sufficient as the basis for the examination of departments' performance in carrying out policies, functions, programmes and projects;
>
> To provide Parliament with information which is reliable and sufficient as the basis for its consideration and approval of the levels of finance voted to services in the Appropriation Act;
>
> To ensure Department's accountability by demonstrating their stewardship of the money voted by Parliament; and
>
> To provide Parliament systematically with information on performance which is reliable as an assurance of the economy, efficiency and effectiveness with which departments are operating services and as the basis for selective enquiries.
>
> *(C&AG, 1986, p. 12)*

As the report noted, given that 'Parliament authorises supply on the basis of assumptions about levels of services, it is arguable that it should also receive systematic outturn information on the levels actually achieved' (C&AG, 1986, p. 14). Interestingly, despite identifying asset valuation as an issue, the report was conservative about the need for accruals accounting, backing the 'great depth' of the analysis of the Crick report in 1950 in suggesting there was no need to abandon the cash basis for accounts (C&AG, 1986, p. 6). This report was not alone in stressing the constitutional importance of the accounting and estimates process (C&AG, 1986g). Despite the constitutional basis that it provided for financial accounting, and contemporary interest in the report (Treasury and Civil Service Committee, 1988), none of our interviewees viewed it as a landmark. Indeed, many who served in financial audit at the NAO at the time and shortly afterwards could not recall it at all.

As has been shown, in both value-for-money and financial audit, the new organisation led by Downey adopted a conservative posture. It emphasised the continuity between post- and pre-1983 practice in auditing. Flashes of reforming zeal such as the report to Parliament on the constitutional place of financial accounting could easily be forgotten if not taken up more widely. Equally, the NAO were careful to use their new statutory powers, positioning themselves as Parliament's independent adviser and providing advice, information and assurance on the value for money of public services.

3.6 Chapter summary

The chapter examined the period of Downey's time as C&AG from 1984 to 1988 including the establishment of the NAO, through considering both the political context and categories of regulatory space concerning organisational context, capacities and audit scope.

As Peter Hennessy commented in 1983, Downey's job was to establish the NAO as a new organisation. In 1988, when the NAO moved into its new building, one might think that Downey's work had been completed. The new institution had been established and guided through its first five years. Downey's NAO was cognisant of its new constitutional role. Its independence was cemented, and Parliament demonstrated that through allocating the new organisation more money and significantly a new building, bolstering the new organisational context and its mandate with increased capacity. The NAO began to consider exactly what its new powers meant in terms of audit scope: how far did its access rights run? What did financial audit now mean? What should value for money involve?

It was also a cautious organisation though: its analysis of both the efficiency reforms and privatisation policy of the Thatcher government were cautious. Yet even this cautious approach was seen by departments as strident. The NAO tried to stick to its remit as defined by the Act and interpreted it narrowly. It did not engage significantly with other select committees and saw itself as a supplier to PAC of studies of economy, efficiency and effectiveness. There were paths not taken, particularly the NAO's work on financial reporting which appears to have been broadly welcomed and even more broadly forgotten.

Downey, on his resignation in 1988, could reflect on an NAO which was now an established part of the constitution, with its own new building, but there was plenty for his successors to build upon.

Notes

1 The Commission consists of nine members of the House of Commons: two are ex officio (leader of the House of Commons and chair of the Public Accounts Committee) and seven are appointed by the House, none of whom may be ministers of the Crown. The secretary of the commission is a senior member of the Clerk's Department. The commission publishes a report, from time to time. As a statutory body, not a Committee of the House, its proceedings enjoy qualified, not absolute, privilege.

2 Peter Hennessy, 1947–, Academic and Journalist, 1974–82 Whitehall Correspondent *The Times*, 1992–2000 Professor of Contemporary History, Queen Mary and Westfield College University of London, 2001– Attlee Professor of Contemporary British History, Queen Mary, University of London, Created Lord Hennessy 2010.

3 Knighton served as Principal Finance and Establishments Officer at the Department for Trade and Industry between 1986 and 1991.

4 The role of the Public Accounts Commission is defined by the National Audit Act 1983 and the Budget Responsibility and National Audit Act 2011. The Commission's principal duties under the Acts are to examine the NAO Estimate and lay it before the House, to consider reports from the appointed auditor of the NAO and to appoint non-executive members of the NAO Board.
5 The other being the Chevaline affair.
6 Some have argued that this agenda of efficiency was what really underlay the growth in prestige of value-for-money auditing in this period (Glynn, 1985).
7 Jeremy Lonsdale was a senior official in the NAO, including being Director General, value for money, leading the NAO's value-for-money work and staff (2006–13) together with publishing widely on audit.
8 Michael Whitehouse was a career NAO official, latterly Assistant Auditor General and then Chief Operating Officer.
9 Steve Corbishley is a long-standing financial audit director in the NAO.
10 The letter was misdated by its author to 13 January 1983, but as it mentions that the National Audit Office came into being on 1 January, it clearly must have been written in 1984 rather than 1983.

References

AAG/B, 1985. Handling of correspondence from MPs and members of the public. In *NAO Senior Management Group Minutes of Meetings*, AO36/2/4, unpublished MSS, National Archives, London.

Aldrich, R.J. (2010). GCHQ. New York, Harperpress.

Bailey, A. M. (1984). A.M. Bailey to P.M. Rayner, 4 July 1984. *New headquarters for the National Audit Office (NAO)*, T524/39, Unpublished MSS, National Archives, London.

Birch, R. A. (1985). R.A. Birch to D. Myland, 10 January 1985. *National Audit Office (NAO) Act 1983: interpretation,* AO39/13, Unpublished MSS, National Archives, London.

Cabinet Office (1984). Meeting of permanent secretaries: Minutes of a meeting held in conference Room C, Cabinet Office, on Wednesday 23 March 1984. In *Status and Functions of the C&AG*, CAB164/1810/1, Unpublished manuscript, National Archives, London.

Campbell Smith, D. (2008). *Follow the money: The Audit Commission, public money and the management of public services.* London: Penguin Allen Lane.

Clarke, David, interview

C&AG (1984). *Departments of Energy, Trade and Industry and Transport: Monitoring and control of nationalised industries*, Session 1983-4, HC553. London: National Audit Office.

C&AG (1984a). *Ministry of Defence: Trident project*, Session 1983-4, HC287. London, National Audit Office.

C&AG (1984b). *Export Credits Guarantee Department: Claims and recoveries*, Session 1983-4, HC632. London: National Audit Office.

C&AG (1984c). *Department of Health and Social Security: Housing benefits scheme*, Session 1983-4, HC638. London: National Audit Office.

C&AG (1984d). *Property Services Agency: Defence works on the Falkland Islands*, Session 1984-5, HC31. London: National Audit Office.

C&AG (1985). *Department for Trade and Industry: Sale of government shareholding in British Telecommunications PLC*, Session 1984-5, HC495. London: National Audit Office.

C&AG (1985a). *Departments of Transport, Trade and Industry and Energy: monitoring and control of investment by the Nationalised industries in fixed assets*, Session 1984-5, HC284. London: National Audit Office.
C&AG (1985b). *Home Office: Control of broadcast receiving licence revenue*, Session 1984-5, HC223. London: National Audit Office.
C&AG (1985c). *Department of the Environment: Operation of the rate support grant system*, Session 1984-5, HC313. London: National Audit Office.
C&AG (1985d). *Department for the Environment: Urban programme*, Session 1984-5, HC513. London: National Audit Office.
C&AG (1985e). *Achievements and costs of the Common Agricultural Policy in the United Kingdom,* Session 1984-5, HC578. London: National Audit Office.
C&AG (1986). *Financial reporting to Parliament*, Session 1985-6, HC576. London: National Audit Office.
C&AG (1986a). *The Financial Management Initiative*, Session 1985-6, HC588. London, National Audit Office.
C&AG (1986b). *The Rayner scrutiny programmes, 1979-1983*, Session 1985-6, HC322. London: National Audit Office.
C&AG (1986c). *Lord Chancellor's Department: Provision of legal aid in England and Wales,* Session 1985-1986, HC182. London: National Audit Office.
C&AG (1986d). *Department of the Environment, Scottish Office and Welsh Office – Enterprise Zones*, Session 1985-86, HC209. London: National Audit Office.
C&AG (1986e). *Value for money developments in the National Health Service*, Session 1985-6, HC212. London: National Audit Office.
C&AG (1986f). *Department of Trade and Industry: Assistance to British shipbuilders*, Session 1985-6, HC304. London: National Audit Office.
C&AG (1986g). *Financial control and accountability of the Metropolitan Police*, Session 1985-6, HC347. London: National Audit Office.
C&AG (1986h). *Ministry of Defence – Financial arrangements for the provision of meteorological services*, Session 1985-6, HC360. London: National Audit Office.
C&AG (1986i). *Department of the Environment – Control of local authorities' capital expenditure*, Session 1985-6, HC395. London: National Audit Office.
C&AG (1986j). *National Health Service – Preventive medicine*, Session 1985-6, HC432. London: National Audit Office.
C&AG (1986k). *Department of the Environment – Disposal of New Town assets*, Session 1986-7, HC76. London: National Audit Office.
C&AG (1987). *Department for Energy, Sale of government shareholding in British Gas*, Session 1987-8, HC22. London: National Audit Office.
C&AG (1987a). *Department for Transport, Sale of government shareholding in British Airways*, Session 1987-8, HC37. London: National Audit Office.
C&AG (1987b). *Trustee Savings Banks – Rights of ownership*, Session 1986-7, HC237. London: National Audit Office.
C&AG (1987c). *Competitive tendering for support services in the National Health Service*, Session 1986-7, HC318. London: National Audit Office.
C&AG (1987d). *Department of the Environment – Financial reconstruction of New Towns in England*, Session 1986-7, HC339. London: National Audit Office.
C&AG (1987e). *Department of Education and Science – Postgraduate awards*, Session 1986-7, HC368. London: National Audit Office.
C&AG (1987f). *Monitoring and control of charities in England and Wales*, Session 1986-7, HC380. London: National Audit Office.

C&AG (1987g). *Ministry of Defence and Property Services Agency – Control and management of the Trident programme*, Session 1987-8, HC27. London: National Audit Office.

C&AG (1987h). *Home Office Prison Department – Objectives, organisation and management of the Prison Service industries and farms*, Session 1987-8, HC93. London: National Audit Office.

C&AG (1987i). *Community care developments*, Session 1987-8, HC108. London: National Audit Office.

C&AG (1988). *Report by Comptroller and Auditor General. Department of Transport: Sale of government shareholding in BAA Plc*, Session 1987-8, HC312. London: National Audit Office.

C&AG (1988a). *Report of Comptroller and Auditor General. Department of Trade and Industry: Sale of government shareholding in Rolls-Royce Plc*, Session 1987-8, HC243. London: National Audit Office.

C&AG (1988b). *Department of Health and Social Security – Quality of service to the public at local offices*, Session 1987-8, HC451. London: National Audit Office.

Corbishley, Steven, interview

Dewar, D. and Funnell, W. (2017). *The pursuit of accountability: A history of British National Audit*. Oxford: Oxford University Press.

Director of Policy and Planning (1986). Relations with the Audit Commission. In *Senior management board, minutes and papers*, AO36/3/3, Unpublished MSS, National Archives, London.

Director of Policy and Planning (1987). Director of Policy and Planning to David Myland, October 1987. In *National Audit Office (NAO) relations with Treasury expenditure divisions*, AO39/17, Unpublished MSS, National Archives, London.

Downey, Sir G. (1983). Sir Gordon Downey to Sir Michael Kerry, 28 June 1983. In *National Audit Office (NAO) Act 1983: Interpretation*, AO39/13, Unpublished MSS, National Archives, London.

Downey, Sir G. (1986). Sir Gordon Downey to Sir Edward Du Cann, 10 January 1986. In *National Audit Office (NAO) Act 1983: Interpretation* AO39/13, Unpublished MSS, National Archives, London.

Downey, Sir G. (1987). Access by the National Audit Office to Cabinet Office and Treasury documents for the purposes of economy, efficiency and effectiveness examinations: Note by the Comptroller and Auditor General, 23 December 1987. In *National Audit Office (NAO) access for value for money activity*, AO39/9, Unpublished MSS, National Archives, London.

Downey, Sir G., Leech, J., Norris, G., Williams, R. and Wise, D. (1984). Debate: National Audit Office Reports, Commonwealth Development Corporation, high spending cities, pay review bodies, the British experiment with the unemployed. *Public Money*, *4*(3), 10–14.

Du Cann, E. (1995). *Two lives: the political and business careers of Edward Du Cann*. Upton upon Severn: Images.

Exchequer and Audit Department (1979). "Appendix 1: Management review of the Exchequer and Audit Department: Report of the steering committee" in Public Accounts Committee *Second special report from the Committee of Public Accounts, the work of the Committee of Public Accounts and the status and functions of the Comptroller and Auditor General*, Session 1978-9, HC330. London: House of Commons, 21–41.

Fiddick, P. (1986). BBC senses 'back door' move for state role. *The Guardian*, 3 December 1986.

Garrett, J. (1986). Developing state audit in Britain. *Public Administration*, *64*(6), 421–433.

Glynn, J. J. (1985). Value for money auditing: An international review and comparison. *Financial Accountability & Management*, *1*(2), 113–128.

Grant Thornton (1986). Review of the NAO's certification audit grading. In *The National Audit Office's Benchmark/Matrix system: Includes report entitled 'review of the National Audit Office's certification audit grading' and appendices to report*, AO39/29, unpublished MSS, National Archives, London.

Head of Communications (1986). NAO external relations. In *National Audit Office senior management group minutes of meetings and papers*, AO36/3/5, Unpublished MSS, National Archives, London.

Hennessy, P. (1983). Backbench power poised for renaissance. *The Times*, 16 August 1983.

Hosker, G. (1984). G.A. Hosker to R. Le Marechal, 28 November 1984. In *National Audit Office (NAO) Act 1983: Interpretation* AO39/13, Unpublished MSS, National Archives, London.

House of Commons (1985). *Written Answers*, Vol. 81, 20 June 1985.

House of Commons (1987). *Hansard*, Vol. 124, 16 December 1987.

House of Commons (1987a). *Hansard*, Vo1. 108, 19 January 1987.

Judd, C. H. A. (1984). C.H.A. Judd to heads of expenditure divisions, 13 January 1984[10]. In *Establishment and future development of the National Audit Office (NAO)*, T632/21, Unpublished MSS, National Archives, London.

Kerry, Sir M. (1983). Sir Michael Kerry to Gordon Downey, 12 July 1983. In *National Audit Office (NAO) Act 1983: Interpretation* AO39/13, Unpublished MSS, National Archives, London.

Le Marechal, R. (1986). R. Le Marechal to G.A. Hosker, 12 August 1986. *National Audit Office (NAO) Act 1983: Interpretation,* AO39/13, unpublished MSS, National Archives, London.

Lonsdale, J. (2000). *Advancing beyond regularity: Developments in value for money methods at the National Audit Office 1984-1999.* Unpublished PhD Thesis, Brunel University.

Lonsdale, Jeremy, interview

Middleton, Sir P. (1987). Sir Peter Middleton to Sir Gordon Downey, 18 February 1987. In *National Audit Office (NAO) Act 1983: Interpretation,* AO39/13, Unpublished MSS, National Archives, London.

Midgley, H. (2019). The National Audit Office and the select committee system 1979–2019. *Parliamentary History*, 72(4), 779–798.

Myland, D. (1984). NAO Press notices 26 March 1984. In *National Audit Office senior management group minutes of meetings and papers*, AO36/1/2, Unpublished MSS, National Archives, London.

Myland, D. (1985). The formation of a central policy unit on PP division, 19 November 1985. In *National Audit Office (NAO) Policy Unit,* AO39/26, Unpublished MSS, National Archives, London.

Myland, D. (1986). Financial and other benefits arising from NAO work. In *National Audit Office senior management group minutes of meetings and papers*, AO36/3/4, Unpublished MSS, National Archives, London.

Myland, D. (1987). David Myland to William Knighton, 30 June 1987. In *National Audit Office (NAO) relations with principal finance officers (collectively)* AO39/16, unpublished MSS, National Archives, London.

National Audit Office (1984). Review of certification audit, 26 March 1984. In *National Audit Office senior management group minutes of meetings and papers,* AO36/1/2, Unpublished MSS, National Archives, London.

National Audit Office (1984a). Numbers of qualified and unqualified staff, 20 December 1984. In *National Audit Office senior management group minutes of meetings and papers,* AO36/1/3, unpublished MSS, National Archives, London.

National Audit Office (1984b). Recruitment of non-accounting staff 21 August 1984. In *National Audit Office senior management group minutes of meetings and papers,* AO36/1/3, unpublished MSS, National Archives, London.

National Audit Office (1984c). VFM investigations intended to lead to C&AG's reports, April 1984. In *National Audit Office senior management group minutes of meetings and papers,* AO36/1/2, unpublished MSS, National Archives, London.

National Audit Office (1984d). Minutes of senior management group meeting 31 July 1984. In *National Audit Office senior management group minutes of meetings and papers,* AO36/1/1, unpublished MSS, National Archives, London.

National Audit Office (1985). NAO/Principal finance officers meeting on NAO VFM investigations 21 May 1986. In *National Audit Office (NAO) relations with principal finance officers (collectively)*, AO 39/16, unpublished MSS, National Archives, London.

National Audit Office (1985a). Access to documents for VFM purposes, undated but from file position September 1985. In *National Audit Office senior management group minutes of meetings and papers,* AO36/2/4, unpublished MSS, National Archives, London.

National Audit Office (1985b). Access problems reported by divisions. In *National Audit Office (NAO) Act 1983: Interpretation* AO39/13, unpublished MSS, National Archives, London.

National Audit Office (1986). NAO/Principal finance officers meeting on NAO VFM investigations 3 June 1986. In *National Audit Office (NAO) relations with principal finance officers (collectively)*, AO39/16, Unpublished MSS, National Archives, London.

National Audit Office (1986a). NAO/Principal finance officers meeting on NAO VFM investigations 4 June 1986. In *National Audit Office (NAO) relations with principal finance officers (collectively)*, AO 39/16, Unpublished MSS, National Archives, London.

National Audit Office (1986b). Relations with the Audit Commission. In *National Audit Office senior management group minutes of meetings and papers* AO36/3/5, unpublished MSS, National Archives, London.

National Audit Office (1987). NAO/Principal finance officers meeting on NAO VFM investigations 3 June 1987. In *National Audit Office (NAO) relations with principal finance officers (collectively),* AO39/16, unpublished MSS, National Archives, London.

National Audit Office (1987a). NAO/Principal finance officers meeting on NAO VFM investigations 2 June 1987. In *National Audit Office (NAO) relations with principal finance officers (collectively)*, AO39/16, unpublished MSS, National Archives, London.

National Audit Office (1988). Minutes of NAO meeting with departmental principal finance officers, 22 September 1988. In *National Audit Office (NAO) relations with principal finance officers (collectively)*, AO39/16, unpublished MSS, National Archives, London.

Norton-Taylor, R. (1985). Audit office kept in the dark. *The Guardian*, 31 May 1985.

Norton-Taylor, R. (1987). MPs 'apathetic' on Whitehall finances. *The Guardian*, 13 October 1987.

Pauley, R. (1984). What the figures fail to tell. *Financial Times*, 17 August 1984.

Policy Unit (1988). SWOT analysis of the NAO. In *Monitoring the National Audit Office (NAO) environment; overtaken by policy development review*, AO39/34, unpublished MSS, National Archives, London.
Public Accounts Commission (1984). *First Report*, Session 1983-4, HC290. London: House of Commons.
Public Accounts Commission (1984a). *Second Report pay of professional audit staff &c.*, Session 1983-4, HC455. London: House of Commons.
Public Accounts Commission (1986). *Third Report*, Session 1985-6, HC450. London: House of Commons.
Public Accounts Commission (1988). *Fourth Report*, Session 1987-8, HC604. London: House of Commons.
Public Accounts Committee (1986). *Redundancy compensation payments to university staff*, Session 1985-6, HC179. London: House of Commons.
Public Accounts Committee (1987). *Eighth report from the Committee for Public Accounts*, Session 1986-7, HC98. London: House of Commons.
Rayner, P. M. (1983). P.M. Rayner to A.M. Bailey, 20 July 1983. In *HM Treasury relationship with the National Audit Office (NAO)*, T632/23, unpublished MSS, National Archives, London.
Rayner, P. M (1984). P.M. Rayner to A.M. Bailey, 9 May 1984. In, *New headquarters for the National Audit Office (NAO)*, T524/39, unpublished MSS, National Archives, London.
Senior Management Group (1984). Minutes of meeting held on 6 November 1984. In *National Audit Office senior management group minutes of meetings and papers,* AO36/1/1, unpublished MSS, National Archives, London.
Senior Management Group (1984a). Minutes of meeting held on 18 October 1984. In *National Audit Office senior management group minutes of meetings and papers,* AO36/1/1, unpublished MSS, National Archives, London.
Senior Management Group (1984b). Minutes of meeting held on 12 April 1984. In *National Audit Office senior management group minutes of meetings and papers,* AO36/1/1, unpublished MSS, National Archives, London.
Senior Management Group (1986). Minutes of meeting held on 14 November 1986. In *National Audit Office senior management group minutes of meetings and papers,* AO36/3/1, unpublished MSS, National Archives, London.
Sinclair, Martin, interview
Treasury (1984). C&AG's access to departmental files and papers, November 1984. In *National Audit Office (NAO) Act 1983: Interpretation* AO39/13, unpublished MSS, National Archives, London.
Treasury and Civil Service Committee (1988). *Sixth report: Financial reporting to Parliament, together with the proceedings of the Committee*, Session 1987-8, HC614. London: House of Commons.
Whitehouse, Michael, interview
Wilson, Richard, interview

4

SIR JOHN BOURN 1988–97 – NAVIGATING A WORLD OF MANY SUBTLE SHADES OF GREY

4.1 Introduction

In 1985, a senior civil servant – John Bourn – privately wrote down his thoughts on the development of British public administration in the years running up until the millennium, arguing that

> the most important development in British public administration over the next ten to fifteen years is likely to be an increasing attention to management: in particular to setting objectives, to specifying programmes to achieve them, allocating resources accordingly; measuring performance and pressing at all times for value for money.
>
> *(Bourn, 1985)*

Bourn's note, written three years before he would become C&AG, significantly does not mention the National Audit Office (NAO) at all despite its focus on management, although it is indicative in saying much about the NAO in Bourn's first era in post. Bourn understood that the focus of the Conservative government of Margaret Thatcher (and of her eventual successor John Major) was firmly on reforms to public administration and frequently those reforms deployed terms like 'value for money': a concept central to the purpose of the NAO. Bourn (1985) reflects upon the fact that 'the interest, activity and commitment of members of Parliament . . . will continue to increase', and this would drive public administration.

For Bourn, the NAO sat at the right point in the political system to impact upon what he saw as the driving pre-occupation of politics in the

DOI: 10.4324/9781003520085-4

late 1980s and early 1990s, but that made the NAO vulnerable as well as potentially influential. He believed that the NAO's role stood at the centre of politics in the 1980s, but the organisation itself was peripheral to politics. There was both an opportunity to shape the politics and public administration of the UK and the risk that the NAO would find itself politically isolated, its audit too limited, narrow or inexpert to fulfil its role on history's stage.

The purpose of this chapter is to examine the first period of Bourn's time in office as C&AG from 1988 to 1997, during the Conservative governments of Margaret Thatcher and John Major. The chapter sets out the political context of the period and then considers the NAO within the categories of regulatory space: organisational context (including independence), capacities and audit scope. Through doing this, we analyse the history of the NAO between 1988 and 1997.

4.2 Political context

Bourn took over the NAO in 1988. Margaret Thatcher had been Prime Minister since 1979 and had just triumphed in the 1987 general election. However, within three years, Thatcher would resign and be succeeded by John Major, who was prime minister until 1997, when he was defeated by New Labour under Tony Blair.

Thatcher remained in power for the first two years of Bourn's time as C&AG before being ousted by her party in 1990 following the resignation of senior cabinet ministers largely over the UK's policy on Europe. She was challenged for the leadership of her party by Michael Heseltine[1] in 1990 and replaced by John Major. Major won the 1992 general election with a small majority. However, in the autumn of 1992, the UK was forced out of the European Exchange Rate Mechanism (ERM), a fixed currency system that it had entered in 1989 on Major's urging and against Thatcher's wishes. The UK's decision to remove sterling from the ERM destroyed the economic credibility of John Major's government. After 1992, Major struggled to maintain discipline within the Conservative Party, and in 1995, he invited a leadership challenge from the right of the party. Despite defeating John Redwood in the ensuing leadership election, Major's government remained unpopular. This unpopularity had three main causes: the government's loss of its battle to defend sterling's rate in the Exchange Rate Mechanism in 1992, the Conservative Party's splits over the European issue and a series of scandals affecting Conservative MPs. Whilst the Conservatives struggled to maintain their grip on power, the Labour Party elected a succession of credible contenders to succeed Major: in 1992 they elected John Smith and, after Smith's death, Tony Blair. In 1997, Blair won a landslide victory over John Major.

This period saw a substantial programme of reform driven by the failure of Thatcher's governments to reduce public spending. Consequently, sympathetic writers in the press argued that 'improving public sector efficiency may be the main political task of the 1990s' (*Economist*, 1988). Both Thatcher and Major promoted new public management reforms and privatisation. Major's governments attempted to extend the reform agenda of Margaret Thatcher: in 1991, the government announced the Citizen's Charter, designed to give citizens the right to interrogate the quality of public services. Further privatisations including British Rail (1994–7) were also carried out. The Major government carried out other domestic reforms including the creation of an internal market in the NHS. Alongside these, the Thatcher government began, and the Major government continued, major reforms to the structure of the civil service: new executive agencies were formed to carry out the executive tasks of government, moving them away from the policy-focussed departmental civil service structure. Lord Butler described this change as follows:

> One of the common misunderstandings about Next Steps is that the agencies were hived off, they weren't. They were still accountable to Parliament. They had someone to run them who was concerned with the execution and not the policy, their focus was looking downwards on the operation rather than upwards to the minister. This was to introduce an element of effective management.
>
> *(Lord Butler, interview)*

Significantly, these new agencies had accounting officers who reported to the Public Accounts Committee (PAC), compiled their own annual reports and could be subjected to value-for-money studies. Lastly, the scandals affecting the Conservative government led to the creation of the Committee on Standards in Public Life chaired by Lord Nolan[2] in 1994. In 1995, the Nolan Committee produced seven principles for public life that have endured as a core statement of the ethics of government service ever since (Committee on Standards in Public Life, 1995; Bew, 2015). Taken together with the domestic reform agenda, the 1990s were as significant as the 1980s in embedding the approach scholars have described as New Public Management in the government of the UK.

4.3 Organisational context

In 1988, John Bourn attended a presentation by a PR agency about the NAO and wrote in his diary:

> At the present, the NAO's strongest point may be its mystery, the fact that it is seen to be part of the constitution – 'something we have to have' and that it is 'the medium not the message' so there may be no need for P[ublic] R[elations]? But the world is changing unless the NAO is known, who will join it? And how will it protect itself against future onslaughts, as people realise it is in the world of politics?
>
> *(Bourn, 1988)*

There are two insights in this passage: one is about the purpose of public relations, but the other more crucial point is about the vulnerability of the NAO to external critique and even to abolition. Bourn and his senior management were very aware that regardless of what audit staff believed, the NAO was 'in the world of politics' and its defence of its independence had to be rooted in politics. Senior managers agreed with Bourn: a note prepared for discussion in 1987 argued that if the NAO was not to be privatised then 'we perhaps will need to take steps to be so indispensable and highly regarded that our position is impregnable' (AAG/B, 1987). Bourn did not find all members of NAO staff shared his appreciation of the political: one particular senior manager was described by Bourn as 'unable and/or unwilling to appreciate the political aspects of studies' (Bourn, 1988b). It was not only in the NAO that these political skills were seen as valuable: when Bourn was appointed in 1988, he was summoned to a meeting with the Cabinet Secretary, Sir Robert Armstrong. Armstrong told Bourn that he was being appointed due to his possession of the 'necessary qualities of knowing Whitehall and political feel' (Bourn, 1987).[3] Armstrong may not have shared Bourn's or the NAO's existential anxiety, but he could see as clearly as Bourn that the NAO might be independent of partisan politics, but it still had to exist within a political world.

An analysis of the NAO's external environment, prepared internally in 1988, set out the different groups to whom the NAO might appeal. Included were groups that Downey might well have identified too: PAC, the Public Accounts Commission, professional accounting bodies and government departments. The note also identified other links which 'need fostering' including with academics, other select committees, local authorities, nationalised industries, the private sector and government agencies (Policy Unit, 1988).

Of all these actual or potential relationships, the key ones for the NAO were two: its relationship with government departments and its relationship with PAC. This created a political dilemma and a problem for the NAO. As Bourn noted in a memorandum sent to directors, this meant that the NAO was dealing with customers whose interests were 'diametrically opposed' (Bourn, 1988a). Bourn identified the dichotomy in the vision for the NAO relating to the civil service and PAC which we have already described in the debates about the 1983 Act. Should the NAO act as a consultant for government or as an independent scrutineer for Parliament?

In the 1990s, Bourn adopted various strategies for dealing with this ambiguity. His rhetoric occasionally described a world in which ministers were attempting to deliver and the civil service was preventing them from doing so. For example, the *Guardian* in 1989 reported that the C&AG had stated that

> He [Bourn] identified a gap between ministers' statements on government policy and what happens in practice after the statements are made. Money then trickles through the gap, he said.
>
> *(Gunn, 1989)*

Positioning the NAO with ministers as oppositional to departments was not the strategy that Bourn adopted long-term. We can see how he managed departments both from his own recollections and from comments by permanent secretaries about his NAO. Bourn, as a civil servant, had pre-existing relationships with permanent secretaries: he got the job in part because of the lobbying by Sir Peter Levene,[4] who spoke on his behalf to Robert Sheldon (Bourn, 1990). Bourn's deep history in the civil service supported him as C&AG and hence the NAO's relationships with senior civil servants. Lord Butler, then Cabinet Secretary and head of the Home Civil Service, told us that Bourn

> had grown up in the Ministry of Defence, I'd grown up in the Treasury, we'd known each other reasonably well for years: he had been a colleague and the relationship between us was a personal relationship.
>
> *(Lord Butler, interview)*

Former colleagues in the Ministry of Defence like Sir David Omand recalled Bourn too (Sir David Omand, interview). Butler was not alone in seeing Bourn frequently. Lord Wilson recalled that he regularly saw Bourn for lunch when he was Permanent Secretary at the Department for the Environment and at the Home Office. Wilson described their relationship as follows:

> I became friends with John Bourn and I would talk to him about forthcoming appearances [at PAC] and his views, I didn't try and stop him doing something but John was incorruptible but helpful. I would talk to him honestly about what I thought we'd done right and done wrong.
>
> *(Lord Wilson, interview)*

Sir Richard Packer[5] also spoke of regular meetings with John Bourn (Sir Richard Packer, interview). Indeed, Butler said in his view that the civil service thought 'we knew him [Bourn] well and he understood the job that Permanent Secretaries were doing' (Lord Butler, interview). The relationship with the NAO was important for civil servants as well because of the link between the NAO and the PAC: Sir Michael Quinlan[6] commented that the PAC was a body of which he was 'continually conscious' (quoted in Scott, 1996, p. 1084).

In other words, within government, Bourn was seen as an insider: in 1991, he was even invited to a seminar at Chequers, the Prime Minister's country retreat, on ideas for Major's signature policy programme, the Citizen's Charter (Bourn, 1991b). Michael Jack[7] said that ministers sought NAO advice too (House of Commons, 1996, col. 901). Bourn built legitimacy for the NAO by demonstrating its worth to these insiders. From early on in his tenure, the NAO published statistics showing that its work had a financial impact. In 1991, the NAO were able to tell the Public Accounts Committee that changes already made by departments in 1988 and 1989 had saved £215 million (PAC, 1991, p. vi). Often the savings made were presented as a multiple of the NAO's running costs, starting at a ratio of 7 to 1. This is probably an underestimate, as the NAO's impacts were increasingly rigorously checked and audited so were cautious rather than confident.

Bourn was keen to ensure that unnecessary conflict was not created: in 1988, he wrote about one report where the NAO were critical of a department and said 'it was madness for the NAO to put the PAC up to call officials liars. This could lead only to them finding something to prove their case. I could not see why people could not see this so I had to alter the report on my own initiative' (Bourn, 1988b). There was agitation in the PAC and a sense in the civil service that the NAO was friendly to them. In 1994, the *Economist* reported that

> members of the PAC complain that the audit office works too closely with government departments and that its style is too consensual. They note that the NAO appears to avoid politically sensitive subjects, such as the reform of the National Health Service, preferring safer issues such as hospital catering. There appears to be some truth in this charge. One former senior civil servant says the NAO tries hard 'not to rock too many government boats'.
>
> *(Economist, 1994)*

The most controversial example of the NAO's caution was, as with Gordon Downey, its approach to secret material. This was exemplified by the NAO's report into the Al Yamamah arms contract. In 1985, Michael Heseltine as Secretary of State for Defence agreed to a contract between BAE Systems and Saudi Arabia for the provision of aircraft and other weapons systems (*Daily Telegraph*, 2008). There were allegations of bribery, and in 1989 the NAO began an investigation (*Daily Telegraph*, 2008). The NAO produced its report in 1992, but it was not circulated widely due to concern about damaging relationships with Saudi Arabia (Sikka and Lehman, 2015), a position endorsed by ministers later (House of Commons, 2007, col. 879). The report was published but only to the Chair of the PAC, Robert Sheldon. Sheldon said, 'we found no evidence of fraud or wrongdoing in the MoD or government departments' and did not, according to reports, share the NAO report on Al Yamamah with committee members (Burrows, 2003). This position was repeated in 2007 by Sheldon's successor, Edward Leigh. Leigh told the Commons that

> My predecessor as Chairman of the Committee – who was, of course, in the minority Labour party – had a private hearing with the senior Conservative member and the Comptroller and Auditor General. The Comptroller and Auditor General has told me that during that private hearing no evidence whatsoever of corruption on the part of the Ministry of Defence was found.
>
> *(House of Commons, 2007, col. 863)*

Bourn and Sheldon, despite public pressure on the NAO to release its findings, appear to have decided that the UK's diplomatic and commercial interests required the NAO not to publish the report widely.

More broadly, as under Downey, the NAO's attitude to the accountability of the intelligence services in this period was very much based on Bourn's own experience as an MOD insider. Lord Butler spoke to us about the intelligence of the security services in this period: he said,

> I remember sitting with Robert Sheldon and John Bourn high up in the House of Commons and I remember it being a rather perfunctory, chummy occasion and I don't remember it being very testing at all.
>
> *(Lord Butler, interview)*

Bourn's keenness to ensure departments and the NAO did not come into conflict did not mean that the scope of audit had reduced (see later sections), but it did mean the NAO continued on the path set out by Gordon Downey for clearing reports. Bourn would note if departments were not happy with the NAO: for example, Bourn addressed the MOD in 1988 and got back the message from senior staff there that 'we are studied to death' (Bourn, 1988c). Some civil servants sought to manipulate the NAO's willingness to compromise to ensure there was an absence of conflict at the PAC. Sir Richard Packer wrote that 'bitter experience taught me it was essential to fight like a tiger over the wording of the original NAO report. The NAO often threatened to say what they thought whether I liked it or not, but in practice they preferred to have an agreed document which gave one some leverage' (Packer, 2015, p. 217). The NAO was swayed by evidence and argument: Packer said, 'If you could produce decent arguments, the NAO gave ground. One of the BSE schemes they said was impressive in the circumstances. This is a scheme that had been absolutely crucified in public and they didn't go along with that' (Packer, 2015, p. 217).

Packer wasn't alone: an ethnographical study of the NAO's audit of Welsh employment schemes revealed that the report went through nine redrafts following comments from the Welsh Office and its agencies (Roberts and Pollitt, 1994, p. 534). Clearance issues, for Bourn, reinforced the point that the NAO was political:

> When the government accepts the results of an NAO study, it is because it is on balance in its political interests to do so. And this means that, since we work on the basis of an agreed report, the work that the NAO does will never be published unless it is politically agreeable to the government of the day; so much it seems to me for the myth of our independence from government.
>
> *(Bourn, 1989a)*

Whether Bourn actually thought the NAO's independence from government was a complete myth (there is plenty of evidence to suggest he often endorsed this 'myth' himself), clearance definitely had an impact on what the NAO did. James Robertson,[8] who arrived in 1995 at the NAO, said that he thought that the effect of the open-ended clearance process on NAO reports was 'deadening' and 'clearance could keep going for far longer than might seem reasonable' (James Robertson, interview). It is clear that Bourn's NAO was definitely heavily influenced by departments' approach to clearing reports in the 1990s and 2000s.

Issues about independence were particularly difficult when it came to the extension of audit into effectiveness. In a survey conducted in 1990, NAO auditors expressed concerns about departments effectively vetoing the audit of effectiveness due to concerns it would involve the auditor in commenting about policy (Pendlebury and Shreim, 1990). The NAO were cautious too in other areas: Lord Butler, for example, 'did not recall the NAO responded to Next Steps' (Lord Butler, interview).

Bourn and the other senior officials of the 1990s had a strong sense of what civil servants should be held to account for. Bourn was concerned about the employment of outsiders in the civil service as he feared its consequences of potentially sending the civil service 'back to the nineteenth or even the eighteenth century' (Bourn, 1994). He had particular concerns about what it meant for accountability: he told the Treasury select committee in 1994 that 'sometimes they have been rather surprised to find that I am reporting on them and criticising them. I remember one of them saying to me "Why are you doing this to me?"' (Treasury and Civil Service Committee, 1994, Q1602).

Relations with the civil service were crucial to the operation of Bourn's (and Downey's) NAO, but the NAO was involved in other organisational relationships in Bourn's period of office too. Perhaps the most important was with the Audit Commission. The Audit Commission, established as covered in previous chapters in 1983, had a history which overlapped with that of the NAO. In the late 1980s and early 1990s, the NAO began to collaborate with the Audit Commission, but there were concerns within the civil service about this. Sir Terence Heiser,[9] for example, wrote to Bourn in 1988 raising concerns that Audit Commission auditors should not be allowed to see papers collected by the NAO for the purpose of their studies (Heiser, 1988). Nevertheless, the NAO's relationship with the Audit Commission developed in this period: from 1987, the NAO's archives contain records of regular liaison meetings with the Audit Commission where details of upcoming studies, the potential to conduct joint training and potential collaboration were discussed (NAO, 1987, 1988a, 1989, 1989a, 1990, 1991, 1992, 1992a). These meetings evidence a complex relationship. The two organisations were keen to ensure that when they worked on the same topic, their reports should 'present different perspectives' but should share 'a consistent overall picture' (NAO, 1988a). A set of guidelines for future work emphasised their 'partnership of equals' and set out that when parallel investigations happened, neither organisation should compromise its independence (Audit Commission and NAO, 1989). This relationship could strengthen the NAO: for example, an NAO report on probation conducted in 1989 drew on a parallel Audit Commission study for evidence of how the system was functioning at a local level (C&AG, 1989).

Despite evidence of strength and collaboration, there were rumours of tensions between the two organisations, and outsiders noted that there were some areas of activity such as policing where the Audit Commission and the NAO both audited different bodies within the policing landscape but did not produce joint studies (*The Economist*, 1994). The two organisations were explicitly compared. Bowerman (1994) pointed out that while the NAO and the Commission coordinated their activities to ensure that they did not examine the same aspect of a topic at the same time, the two bodies did not actively plan together to ensure rounded coverage of topics across the public sector, which she regarded as a missed opportunity. The

Economist in 1992 compared the NAO's report on probation with the Audit Commission's and argued that the former was too focussed on the central department, whilst the latter (more usefully in their opinion) looked at the service on the ground. This conclusion points out the difficulty of making comparisons. The NAO's remit was limited to auditing the central management of probation, whereas the Audit Commission audited local probation services on the ground (*Economist*, 1992). Definitely, there was a sense in the 1980s and 1990s that the NAO's value-for-money audit was 'almost Ruritanian by comparison with the Commission's and a rapid catch up was required' (Campbell-Smith, 2008).

Building and maintaining relations with departments had to be balanced with the NAO's relationship with the House of Commons. Robert Sheldon continued to chair the PAC throughout this period. Lord Wilson told us that the standard of sessions at the PAC was entirely different in the 1990s to how it had been in the early 1980s or 1970s. He thought that this came down to the fact that the NAO's briefing was far more extensive for MPs (Lord Wilson, interview). Sir Richard Packer told us that PAC's 'system of being unreasonable the whole time is surprisingly effective', describing PAC in operation (Sir Richard Packer, interview). The NAO had to show political judgement in its interactions with PAC: for example, it might choose to look at a politically sensitive subject but in such a way that Labour MPs could focus on attacking the policy and Conservative MPs on seeing the issue in terms of administration, for example, its scrutiny of Welsh Employment programmes (Roberts and Pollitt, 1994). Bourn was very conscious of the requirements of the Act not to interfere in policy: he told the Procedure Committee that 'I think it would be considered a failure on the part of the Comptroller and Auditor General if he were seen to be crossing that line' to criticise policy objectives (Procedure Committee, 1990, Q682). Robert Sheldon agreed with him, seeing that the committee's unanimity was crucial to its success (Procedure Committee, 1990, Q229).

The NAO was responsive to the requirements of PAC. Reports were framed around parliamentary interest: a 1996 study of UK government aid to Indonesia explained that the NAO had selected seven projects to investigate but confessed this selection was based on 'public and parliamentary interest' and was 'not therefore a representative sample' (C&AG, 1996, p. 3). A study of the governance of courses at the Swansea Institute of Higher Education likewise only took place because 'a member of the Public Accounts Committee drew to the attention of the National Audit Office allegations concerning the financial management and governance' at the institute (C&AG, 1997, p. 1).

In various areas, Bourn and the PAC formed an alliance: Bourn noted in his diaries in 2002 after changes were made to the NAO's remit (covered in the next chapter) that he had been pressing for these changes from the 1990s: 'I remember going with Robert Sheldon and Peter Hordern[10] to Kenneth Clarke to argue for these things in 1994' (Bourn, 2002). The reference to Hordern is important: the Public Accounts Commission also protected the NAO. For example, the Commission stated, that whilst the Treasury had the right to comment on the NAO's budget when it came before the Commission, the Commission saw the 'independence of the NAO . . . as an important constitutional principle which it is the duty of the Commission to protect' and warned the Treasury repeatedly it would do so (Public Accounts Commission, 1994, p. 2).

It was the PAC though who were often the NAO's main focus. We will return to changes in the system of ministerial directions in our discussion of scope: but the PAC only supported Bourn in getting these rights as 'I [Bourn] got the PAC to ask for this in the context of a report on the Pergau dam in Malaysia . . . and I know that I got it only in the context of a particular case – you cannot win on matters of principle but on particular cases' (Bourn, 1994a). This was not the only example of Bourn and the NAO asking PAC members to lobby for them: as early as 1988, an NAO memorandum notes that PAC members offered to lobby the government on the NAO's behalf and also offered advice about the NAO's strategy in its relationships with the civil service (NAO, 1988). The partnership between Sheldon and Bourn was incredibly powerful and important to the NAO. Sheldon 'was very proper and very conscious of the constitutional conventions governing his role as PAC chair' (Gabrielle Cohen,[11] interview). Sheldon saw himself both as a protector of the NAO and as a supporter of its constitutional role, a role he had performed since 1983.

As a protector of the NAO's constitutional role, Sheldon also saw himself as a shield between the NAO and other select committees in the House of Commons, but other select committees resented the privileged relationship that the PAC had with the NAO. This was particularly given the NAO's rights to access government documents. These concerns had arisen under Downey, but they were brought to further attention under Bourn (Midgley, 2019).

A particular case arose with the sale of Rover to BAE Systems. Sir Kenneth Warren,[12] the chair of the Trade and Industry Committee, was upset to discover that after his committee had held an inquiry, including evidence from Lord Young,[13] the secretary of state, and completed its work, they discovered that Bourn had shared a memorandum on the same subject, with the PAC outlining government concessions to BAE Systems, which they had not been made aware of (Negrine, 1992; Midgley, 2019).

Michael Mates,[14] the chair of the Defence Committee, was also unhappy that the NAO reported to PAC in confidence on defence topics so that they could not be seen or used by his committee (Midgley, 2019). In Mates's case, he had requested documents from the NAO and the NAO had sought advice from Sheldon, who rejected the request and the NAO had therefore followed Sheldon's instruction (Procedure Committee, 1990, lv). This problem had deepened because, as the Procedure Committee concluded in 1990, the NAO's scope had evolved: 'the old distinction between the supposed concentration on value for money by the PAC and the greater emphasis on policy matters by the departmentally related select committees has become increasingly hard to sustain' (Procedure Committee, 1990, p. lvii).

For Bourn's NAO, the Procedure Committee's judgement represented two different threats: how could the NAO remain trusted by the government to access information if it worked with other select committees? Secondly, how could it work with other select committees yet avoid policy issues? Within the civil service it was clear that the other select committees were different at this point. Lord Butler said,

> I don't think we saw the NAO working with other select committees at all. Departmental Select Committees focussed on policy. With the PAC, you were the accounting officer and so there was a much more personal accountability than there would be with a departmental select committee.
>
> *(Lord Butler, interview)*

Civil servants, as Butler suggested, saw the PAC and the NAO as fundamentally different creatures to the other select committees. Both Bourn and Sheldon saw risks to the NAO becoming more involved with select committees for precisely this reason. Sheldon told them that giving other select committees access to the NAO's research would 'put at risk the . . . [C&AG's] access to Government papers' (Procedure Committee, 1990, p. 58). (A potential exception supports Sheldon's judgement: Sir David Omand told us that the Intelligence and Security Committee's 'remit was essentially the administration and value for money obtained from the secret vote' but that everyone on that committee was security cleared and it reported in private[15]).

Sheldon explained to the Procedure Committee why the NAO should not report to the other committees. He argued that the C&AG's 'position is quite neutral. We are looking at finance and arguing on the basis of economy and efficiency. It would be very difficult for a departmental select committee to rule out the main purpose they are there for, which is to improve the way in which the government is run, the way policies are decided and the choice of policies' (Procedure Committee, 1990, p. 62). Sheldon's response guarded the NAO against interference from the other select committees: it was based though on Sheldon and Bourn's assessment that the NAO's independence had to be safeguarded by ensuring it could not be dragged into political argument.

4.4 Capacity

The NAO in 1988 was stronger than it had been in 1983, but there were still challenges. In one of Bourn's first meetings with his old colleagues at the Ministry of Defence, he was told that 'NAO people know nothing' (Bourn, 1988c). In both financial and value for money, the 1990s saw the NAO prioritise the technical knowledge that would give the organisation more credibility in Whitehall and fortify its position politically. There are three ways that Bourn sought to do this: firstly, by raising the overall level of resources that the NAO had available to it; secondly, by professionalising value-for-money audit by bringing in more expertise from outside; and lastly, by changing the NAO's training relationships in financial audit. We will cover each in turn.

In terms of the overall level of resources available to Bourn's NAO, expenditure clearly increased during the period from 1988 to 1997. In 1987–8, the NAO spent £26 million pounds: by 1996–7, the NAO had grown financially by a third, now spending £43 million (NAO, 1988b, 1997). Much of this expansion took place in the early years of Bourn's period as C&AG: the NAO's budget rose by 10% in 1988–9, 9% in 1989–90, 11% in 1990–1 and 12% in 1991–2 before the pace of growth slowed over the last few years of the Conservative government (NAO, 1989b, 1990a, 1991a, 1992b). In the mid-1990s, the Treasury pressed the NAO to slow its spending to match central government departments whose spending was restricted: Bourn, however, successfully argued that his budgets should remain high (Public Accounts Commission, 1996).

Expanded resources were matched by developments in the NAO's internal structure, which included putting extra resources into value for money to enhance its expertise. Indeed, from 1990 onwards, the NAO split its work into two separate streams: internally people could opt to be value-for-money auditors or financial auditors. This meant that staff could actively choose to become value-for-money practitioners and increased the level of specialisation in value-for-money audit. This also enabled the NAO to build on the experiment of recruiting staff directly to value-for-money audit begun under Downey. It was necessary to do this both to ensure the development of value-for-money methodologies and intellectual rigour and to ensure a sufficient pipeline of staff into the workstream.

Michael Whitehouse detected that Bourn 'wanted to professionalise the value for money discipline', and he did so in two ways. Firstly, Bourn wanted the NAO to be more open to outsiders. At times, this might mean recruiting specialists to perform specialist roles. The NAO built capacity when it audited in new areas: for example, when under Bourn, it decided the audit of human resources was important, it appointed a specialist director and recruited specialists from outside to assist (Easteal, 1992). The NAO also built capacity in existing areas of study as it expanded its traditional audit focus from a narrow financial perspective to the assessment of the efficiency and effectiveness. The NAO's work in the NHS provides a good example. Auditors wanted to understand better the ways in which they could audit the efficiency and effectiveness of clinical areas of the NHS. In fact, the first external adviser, Irene Gordon,[16] to be appointed to the NAO was a health professional of many years' standing. She helped build networks with many professional bodies within the NHS and with key individuals, increased the understanding and expertise of auditors re the NHS, including its array of clinical statistics and performance indicators. She was a precursor to many other external appointments and helped improve the credibility of the NAO's reports (interview, Irene Gordon).

She was not alone: the NAO also brought in retired defence officials to work on reports (Bourn, 1991). In addition, Bourn also pointed the organisation to focus on thinking about external perspectives on its work. NAO reports at this time were insular and never made any acknowledgement of others' work on a subject and did not reference other reports. Bourn wanted the NAO to be 'rather more self-conscious' about its audit, which meant, in his view, putting reading lists filled with academic material at the end of its training courses for staff to take away with them; indeed, he could not work out why they were not there to begin with (Bourn, 1989a). Being more self-conscious and more open to academic and expert opinion of effectiveness and value for money was for Bourn, not just words. In 1991, Bourn wrote an article for the *Royal United Services Institute Journal* appealing for them to give the NAO ideas for the NAO's work (Bourn, 1991). This principle did not just apply to defence reports: increasingly, teams conducting value-for-money studies would consult experts from the outside to inform their conclusions (Pollitt and Summa, 1997; Lonsdale, 1999, p. 130). Keen (1998) examined a sample of 81 NAO reports published between 1994 and 1997 and found that in 22 cases the NAO cited the work of experts in the report. Justin Keen was an example himself of this trend in the NAO to use the skills of outsiders to support its audit: a health economist from Brunel University, he was the first NAO research fellow, a post organised by Professor Christopher Pollitt, who had been invited in by Bourn to study the NAO as an organisation. The setting up of this fellowship is another aspect of Bourn's openness to the outside world. The research fellowship, which lasted until 2010, was filled by five others subsequently. Bourn, according to Michael Whitehouse, was always seeking to 'expose the NAO to more challenge'.

Secondly, NAO reports in the 1990s were much more methodologically diverse than they were in the 1980s. Lonsdale (1999, 2000) documented this change. He compared a three-year period in the 1980s and a three-year period in the 1990s and examined how studies covered their methods. Whilst he found that the NAO still relied heavily on interviews and document reviews in the 1990s, the number of mentions of surveys as a method went up seven times; case studies tripled, and mentions of observations or site visits and international comparisons doubled (Lonsdale, 1999, p. 130). The NAO increasingly and uniquely amongst Supreme Audit Institutions used focus groups to ascertain the public's view of services (Lonsdale, 1999, pp. 137–138). At one point, Michael Whitehouse recalled that Bourn told him 'I'd love to do a study where we could get an anthropological perspective on government and value for money' (Michael Whitehouse, interview). These methodologies went far beyond the standard audit work under Downey, and this methodological diversity continued right up to the 2000s.

These developments in value-for-money audit were matched on the financial audit side of the NAO. Financial audit was becoming more demanding with the setting up of the Next Steps Agencies (see below), and auditors could not easily keep up with the demands of both value-for-money audit and financial audit as both work streams were developing. The key change in terms of financial audit was that in 1991 the NAO decided to move its trainees from the Chartered Institute of Public Finance and Accountancy (CIPFA) to the Institute of Chartered Accountants for England and Wales (ICAEW). This had consequences as we will see below for the scope of the NAO's financial audit.

Just as important for the development of capability on financial audit was the creation of the Next Steps Agencies from 1988 onwards. These agencies all had their own accounts (on an income and expenditure basis as opposed to vote accounts, which were still cash based) and consequently required their own audit reports. This meant that under Bourn there were pressures for the NAO to move resources into financial audit to enable the NAO to perform the increased number of audits at the same time as more resources were shifted to value for money as a priority for professionalisation. In 1990, Bourn told the Procedure Committee that 'certification . . . takes up half the resources of the Office' (Procedure Committee, 1990, Q690).[17] However, the minutes of the Public Accounts Commission reflect the fact that whilst the NAO's number of value-for-money reports remained static, the number of accounts the NAO was auditing did not. These reports suggested a continuing increase in the number of government accounts to be audited: an increase by 11% between 1993–4 and 1995–6 and a further 20% from 1995–6 to 1998–9 (Public Accounts Commission, 1994, 1996, 1998). The NAO used private sector auditors to perform some of this work: by 1996, 10% of the NAO's financial audits were contracted out (Treasury, 1996, p. 48). Similarly, the TPAC saw the development of resource accounting as a justification for further funding to the NAO. The growing volume of financial audit became a reason for further increases in NAO spending over the forthcoming decade, but also meant that resources had to go into financial audit.

These developments in capacity boosted the reputation of the NAO. In 1996, Robert Sheldon told the House of Commons that the NAO's collective effort had created an audit organisation which was incredibly different to the E&AD:

> Now, we have auditors and professionally qualified accountants, who are in great demand in the City of London and accounting firms. They now have a level of professionalism that we never saw before – certainly not up until the early 1980s.
>
> *(House of Commons, 1996, col. 863)*

Jeremy Lonsdale recalled that many professionally qualified staff left during this period as the economy improved. Sheldon's comment couples the new professionalism on value for money and increased emphasis on the importance of financial audit with the increased capacity of qualified staff to present a picture of an organisation capable of performing its role more powerfully for Parliament.

4.5 Scope

The NAO's role under Bourn changed radically. Bourn presented himself as a continuation of a long history of public sector audit in the UK, going back 'over 600 years' (Bourn, 1989, p. 60). He argued in public that whilst the 1983 National Audit Act gave the NAO an 'expanded role', it 'accelerated' changes that were already happening (Bourn, 1989). His view was that state audit was an old and enduring institution. But that does not match what people on the outside saw. Pollitt and Roberts (1994, p. 545) pointed out that academics had been largely oblivious to the evolution of the NAO, and yet 'during the last decade and a half it has evolved from exercising a dominant concern with regularity audits and the identification of waste into a body which also conducts value for money analyses into often politically sensitive programmes'.

Lord Wilson told us that when he returned to PAC facing jobs in the early 1990s, he was told that the NAO and PAC had changed:

> When I became a Permanent Secretary in 1992, I discovered what a fantastic leap had happened between 85-6 and 92. When I was PFO

> we were not that bothered by Value for Money reports. When I was appointed as Permanent Secretary in the Department for Environment, I was told by all my mates in the civil service, 'Watch out the PAC are different now'. They warned me that 'this is not the NAO you used to know, this is not the PAC you used to know. There was a sea change between 86 and 1992'.
>
> *(Lord Wilson, interview)*

Wilson commented further that for permanent secretaries, 'instead of being a peripheral thing, the PAC and NAO became central' (Lord Wilson, interview).

Wilson was not wrong: the increased visibility of NAO's work led to the Prime Minister himself requesting a weekly briefing on all significant NAO or PAC reports before he went to Prime Minister's Questions (Burr, 1994). The change that Wilson referred to was mostly confined to the value-for-money practice; however, financial audit also went through a sea change of its own in the mid-1990s. This increased scope was matched by an increase in activity: Robert Sheldon told the Procedure Committee that whereas in 1977–8 there were 10 sessions of the PAC, in 1988–9, there were 52 (Procedure Committee, 1990, p. 57). Wilson's comments were not just about the scale of audit; they were also concerned with the content of the audits. Something had changed between 1986 and 1992: so, what did Bourn change about NAO audit in the 1990s?

4.5.1 Value-for-money audit

Wilson's comments on the increasing importance of value-for-money audit reflected a real change, as the first thing that Bourn did when he arrived at the NAO in 1988 was to challenge whether the organisation was actually carrying out the remit granted to it by the 1983 Act. In September 1988, Bourn told an audience of Northern Irish civil servants that 'most studies are economic [or] efficiency' based (Bourn, 1988d). In a paper he prepared for senior management in 1988, Bourn commented that the NAO was charged to do effectiveness audit, but 'we hardly ever do it' (Bourn, 1988a). Bourn was so concerned by the issue of effectiveness that he produced a separate paper for his senior management criticising the NAO's approach. He pointed out that on the NAO's training course on value for money they offered nine examples of effectiveness studies, but Bourn criticised them for providing examples only of the NAO's assessment of 'whether the department has criteria for assessing effectiveness' a 'perfectly legitimate' approach but one that 'does represent something of a watering down of our original objective' (Bourn, 1989a). He asked his readers to reflect what the NAO 'would make of an organisation which defined an objective in one way and then unilaterally watered it down to suit their convenience' (Bourn, 1989a).

Bourn offered in his paper critiques of a series of NAO reports offered to him as good examples of effectiveness audit: two of the reports he read used the word 'effectiveness' as a synonym for economy and efficiency or efficiency alone, one discussed 'issues of output rather than impact' and a third category 'contains no discussion of what impact is being assessed' (Bourn, 1989a). Bourn identified only one case in which impact had clearly been studied, and in that report on the Forestry Commission, the NAO had contracted out the analysis to a firm of economic consultants (Bourn, 1989a). Bourn did not want the NAO to reinterpret its mandate abruptly on the basis of his analysis, but rather to 'negotiate our progress successfully' through recognising that they were 'not moving through a world of blacks and whites here but in a world of many subtle shades of grey' (Bourn, 1989a).

Bourn's words landed in an organisation that was ready to listen: a survey of NAO auditors conducted in 1990 suggested that 90% of them believed that value-for-money audit could not just consist of examinations of economy and efficiency. However, a majority of the auditors surveyed believed that in practice, audit focussed on economy and efficiency (Pendlebury and Shreim, 1990). The impetus towards effectiveness was fuelled by other developments. Michael Whitehouse told us that 'there was a general move internationally amongst audit offices to do more effectiveness work' and particularly singled out the US Government Performance and Reporting Act (signed by Bill Clinton in 1993) as an influence on the NAO's attitudes (Michael Whitehouse, interview). Dewar (1991) noted that a feature of the contemporary NAO was 'more examinations dealing with effectiveness issues'.

As discussed above, there was a vast change in methods in the NAO in this period which contributed to much increased discussion of effectiveness and also 'quality of service', which interested value-for-money staff greatly, especially around the time of the introduction of the Citizen's Charter. New methods meant that the NAO no longer examined the department's own data about a programme but was willing to produce data about outcomes itself. This evidence generated conclusions that Downey's NAO would not have reached. In a 1992 report on the Probate Service's grants of representations to solicitors and applicants dealing with the affairs of deceased persons, the NAO found that the service 'did not meet all their own targets for the speed of dealing with applications for grants submitted to them', but despite that, surveys of applicants and solicitors 'showed overwhelmingly that both private citizens and solicitors were very pleased with the service provided' (C&AG, 1992, p. 1). Focus groups could be used as a way to give those running public services instructions as to what the public wanted: for example, in a study on the Metropolitan Police Force's telephone service, the NAO developed 'twelve golden rules for communications officers when dealing with calls from the public' from their focus group (C&AG, 1995, p. 38). Collaboration with other organisations enabled the NAO to extend its work on effectiveness further: in 1996, the NAO, together with the Northern District Audit and the University of Strathclyde, were able to create their own estimates for levels of accidents in NHS trusts in the entire UK (C&AG, 1996a, p. 3). All these examples demonstrate how new methods extended the remit of audit to cover effectiveness for the first time.

The 1990s brought greater self-reflection about the process of value-for-money audit. This did not just involve the expansion of reporting into areas like effectiveness, but it also embraced thinking more clearly about the epistemology of value-for-money reports. The NAO evolved an approach called issue analysis, described by Keen (1998) as an established process. He described the NAO's conceptualisation of a study:

> A study is represented as involving the decomposition of a problem into two or three issues for which decisive (yes/no) answers can be obtained. The main issues (termed here macro-issues) are decomposed into micro issues which can be tackled during a study.
>
> *(Keen, 1998, p. 515)*

The idea behind this approach to studies was that every main question (macro-issue) within the study could be broken down into micro-issues which could then either be further broken down or answered empirically. As Keen (1998) argues, this approach was designed to demonstrate a correspondence between the report's findings and the world as it existed. Studies using this methodology became 'strings of micro-issues' bound together to present a macro-picture, which relied 'on the accumulation of evidence rather than on argument' (Keen, 1998, pp. 521, 522). Issue analysis combined with methodological innovation produced NAO reports that were far more focussed on outcomes and effectiveness than they had been in the 1980s.

However, not all NAO studies followed these new approaches or focused on new issues; for example, the NAO reported on the procurement of routine items in MOD in 1997 purely examining the MOD's successful implementation of best practice in procurement processes (C&AG, 1997a). Such reports had value but did not match Bourn's more expansive vision for value for money.

Value for money also extended in the 1990s to cover subjects that the NAO and E&AD had never tackled before. Dewar argued, as a senior manager at the NAO, for increased attention to the environment: he posited that the public needed 'reliable information' about environment issues to engage in democratic debate (Dewar, 1991a). He suggested that the NAO as an independent body reporting to Parliament was the right body to conduct this work and suggested that the environment might even be a 'fourth e' alongside economy, efficiency and effectiveness (Dewar, 1991a). The NAO began to conduct audits of environmental policy. Audits went further than just auditing the effectiveness of government in reducing its own environmental impact: they assessed the effectiveness of government policy. For example, in 1994, an NAO report on the environmental impact of buildings examined government regulation of the construction industry from an environmental viewpoint, government communications about the environmental risks of different building techniques and, lastly, government's own approach to construction but only to see whether it was 'leading by example' (C&AG, 1994, p. 1). Similarly, the NAO carried out reviews of the government's approach to reducing and enforcing laws against pollution at sea and in English rivers (C&AG, 1991, 1995a).

4.5.2 Financial audit

The scope of financial audit changed also during these years, as we highlighted above. Financial audit retained its constitutional purpose but with two significant changes: firstly, the introduction of accruals accounting from the mid-1990s, and secondly, from the early 1990s, the NAO decided to train its trainees under the ICAEW, ushering in a process of cultural change in the financial audit community, which continued for the next 30 years and substantially affected what financial auditors thought they were doing.

4.5.2.1 Appropriation audit and the proper conduct of public business

The NAO's audit had been established on the Gladstonian basis that the auditor's role was to check that money had been spent on what Parliament had originally intended. This continued in the early years of John Bourn. For example, Neil Sayers, who in 1988 started working on the audit of benefits, highlighted the NAO's audit at that point was 'very precise and very procedural, very focussed on regularity but not much else' (Neil Sayers, interview).

Two cases illustrate the way that the NAO conducted its financial audit in this period, both of which are important for the future of the office. The first case was that of Norman Lamont,[18] Chancellor of the Exchequer during the early 1990s. On 13 April 1991, the News of the World contacted the Treasury press office to say that they were going to run a story that Lamont was renting out his private house to 'a prostitute who is using it as a kinky sex parlour' (C&AG, 1993, p. i). The Treasury ended up paying for the use of a PR firm to assist Lamont with the press coverage. Lord Butler explained the justification to us:

> Norman Lamont thought that his expenses for dealing with this could legitimately come from public funds and the distinction that was made in this was that he could have public funds for the public relations firm to deal with the media and not the legal costs to evict his tenant and this was because we judged rightly or wrongly that if he had not been Chancellor of the Exchequer he would not have had to hire a PR firm to deal with the press interest. This approach was agreed between me and Peter Middleton.
>
> *(Lord Butler, interview)*

The C&AG argued in a memorandum in 1993 that the rules were unclear and recommended a review be set up to judge what they should be (C&AG, 1993, p. v). Lord Butler said,

> John Bourn was the C&AG and I think he understood the distinction we had drawn and I remember him as being reasonable and sympathetic and he allowed us to comment on the way that he was drafting his memorandum and we were able to get across the distinction between what we thought Lamont could claim back and what we thought he could not.
>
> *(Lord Butler, interview)*

In response, PAC reiterated the principle that 'there must always be the clearest possible distinction between the use of public funds or resources used to meet expenses incurred by ministers and civil servants in the direct conduct of their official duties . . . and the use of such funds for other expenses incurred in relation to the activities of ministers' and agreed that there should be a review along the lines the C&AG suggested (PAC, 1993, p. viii). What was crucial here was not the case but the principle that Butler, the C&AG and the PAC all worked to: that the central objective of public expenditure accountability was to ensure that the line between regular and irregular spending remained clear.

The second case related to the Pergau Dam. The dam was constructed in Malaysia with funding from the UK. The question was whether the UK should have funded the dam. The head of the Overseas Development Administration (ODA), Tim Lankester,[19] advised his ministers that 'providing aid funds for Pergau would not be consistent' with his duty to 'ensure that aid funds were administered in a prudent and economical manner' (C&AG, 1993a, p. 7). In 1993, the NAO published a report about the affair revealing the existence of the direction (C&AG, 1993a, p. 11). When the NAO published its report, according to Lankester, the 'storm broke' (Lankester, 2013, p. 98). The NAO's report caused an avalanche of press and parliamentary interest. As Lankester himself said,

> Between then [the NAO's publication of their report] and April 1994, there was rarely a week when Pergau wasn't in the news and much of this centred on Parliament. There were formal inquiries by two select committees of the House of Commons, two House of Commons debates and numerous Parliamentary questions.
>
> *(Lankester, 2013, p. 98)*

Of these subsequent inquiries, including one by the High Court (1994) which found the expenditure unlawful, the PAC report set out the most important precedent for the NAO. The committee recommended that as it was 'particularly important for us to conduct enquiries in those cases where the Accounting Officer's advice is overruled', the 'Accounting Officer should communicate to the Comptroller and Auditor General without undue delay the papers relating to all cases where Ministers have issued directions on matters involving prudent and economical administration, efficiency and effectiveness', ensuring that the C&AG 'would then be in a position to report on such cases to this Committee' (PAC, 1994a, xiv). Despite concerns about it in government, the prime minister, following the advice of the chancellor, decided that the government were unable to block the recommendations of the committee (Newton, 1994; Clarke, 1994; Allan, 1994). In addition to changing the way that ministerial directions were given, the ODA and the NAO reviewed together ODA's current spend against the High Court's judgement (House of Commons, 1995, col. 291). This had a real impact inside the civil service; as Lord Wilson told us,

> Directions became far more important after Tim Lankester and the Pergau Dam in Malaysia and we suddenly discovered [their importance]. As Permanent Secretary at the Home Office, I thought that something which Ministers wanted to do was of doubtful propriety because it was too close to an election. I said you can do it but you will have to give me a direction which I will publish. I told John Bourn that he didn't have to do anything but I was going to ask for a direction. I won the argument but it was the power to ask for a direction and for that to become public which was the deciding factor.
>
> *(Lord Wilson, interview)*

The Pergau Dam affair, as Wilson argued, enhanced civil servants' power to ensure that politicians kept to the constitutional boundaries, but this relied upon the NAO seeing its role as primarily constitutional.

The Lamont and Pergau cases, as Sayers implies above, revealed that the NAO's audit continued to focus on the investigation and reporting of failures in the regularity regime, as Gladstone had intended 120 years previously when framing the E&AD Act. For David Dewar, it was an 'important element in the audit of central government' and took the concept further, suggesting that regularity 'merges into propriety and the broader concerns surrounding the proper conduct of public business' (Dewar, 1991).

PAC brought these ideas together in its report on the 'Proper Conduct of Public Business'. Using examples taken mostly from the NAO's audit of the accounts, the committee called for action after 'a number of serious failures in administrative and financial systems and controls within departments and other public bodies, which have led to money being wasted or otherwise improperly spent' (PAC, 1994, p. v). Issues identified by the PAC flowing out of the audit of the accounts included a 'climate [within the Foreign Office] that was conducive to fraud and theft' (PAC, 1994, p. viii), failures of financial controls in the Insolvency Service and Department of the Environment (PAC, 1994, p. ix), failure by the Ministry of Defence and Department for Employment to control irregular payments (PAC, 1994, p. x) and a decision by the Welsh Office to grant a redundancy payment which was not within the rules set by Treasury (PAC, 1994, p. xi). These examples, and others, were used to support an argument that the government needed to improve the conduct of public business. The government viewed the PAC's report as sitting within the wider context of the Nolan Committee. Consequently, the government responded to the PAC via a white paper in 1996, which reaffirmed the principle that 'public audit should go wider than statutory audit in the private sector, placing greater emphasis on regularity, including compliance with any Financial Memorandum or other document governing the financial arrangements of the organisation and how well and properly public funds are used' (Treasury, 1996, p. 26).

4.5.2.2 The changing culture of financial audit

However, financial audit was changing in this period, becoming more akin to the audit of a company. This was underpinned by two developments in this period: firstly, changes in government accounting and, secondly, changes in the training provided to the NAO's junior staff.

Changes to financial accounting in government came in two stages during this period. Firstly, at the beginning of the period, the government switched from a cash accounting process (focussed on cash alone) to accounting for income and expenditure. Here, the shift from cash accounting to accruals began with the setting up of Next Steps Agencies, which were required to produce annual reports and accounts and had their own accounting officers appointed by HM Treasury to ensure the personal accountability of the accounting officer to Parliament for the performance of the agency. The new executive agencies accounted on an income and expenditure basis because many were engaged in semi-commercial or commercial operations for which they charged fees and needed to be able to show debtors, creditors and work in progress at the year end. Existing non-departmental bodies of various kinds also began to make the shift to accruals accounting, although central departments stayed on a cash basis for longer.

Secondly, the government announced in the 1993 budget that it would move to full resource accounting by 2000. This involved a move from accounting in cash terms to accounting for accruals. In his budget statement, the then Chancellor, Ken Clarke, described government accounting as 'archaic' and said he would be publishing a paper on accounting for the way that resources were used in the public sector (House of Commons, 1993, col. 933). The Treasury published a green paper following up on this commitment in 1994: in it, Clarke said that his proposals were 'firmly based on improvements in accounting practice and financial control that have taken place decades ago in most other large organisations' and would help make the public sector more 'businesslike' (Treasury, 1994, p. iii). Interestingly, amongst the stated benefits for resource accounting from the Treasury were more accurate management information for departments, better informed decisions about capital and current expenditure within departments, improvements in government public expenditure planning, facilitating better cash control, contributing to a more strategic approach to managing the civil service, better information for formulating economic policy and producing national statistics, reducing the public sector's expenditure of funds but nothing about accountability (Treasury, 1994, pp. vii–viii).

The NAO were not involved in this set of decisions. Martin Sinclair[20] said that the announcement came 'out of the blue' as far as the NAO was concerned (Martin Sinclair, interview). However, once the decision was made, the NAO assisted in the process. Sir Andrew Likierman[21] said that the NAO was instrumental in helping to secure the change:

> It was broadly supportive of the change, which was very helpful. Getting anything to change in public finance is difficult and there were an awful lot of people who felt that everything was fine. They asked

> 'What's the problem? Why should we do anything?' So having the NAO as an advocate for change was really useful.
>
> *(Sir Andrew Likierman, interview)*

Sinclair said that the NAO (and before it the E&AD) had traditionally supported accrual accounting and consequently welcomed the Treasury's move (Martin Sinclair, interview). Interestingly, this was not true in the 1980s when Downey's NAO had published a report endorsing earlier criticisms of implementing accrual accounting in the public sector. Likierman particularly highlighted the influence of John Bourn, who was 'enthusiastic' and particularly important in 'briefing the Public Accounts Committee' about the change so that they endorsed it (Andrew Likierman, interview). Sinclair said though that this acceptance of the new type of accounting was based on the fact that the

> new form of accounting reconciled with what was the fundamental original purpose of the accounts to Parliament which derives from the Bill of Rights of 1689 which states that raising taxes without the consent of Parliament is illegal and spending money on topics that Parliament has not approved is illegal. The original purpose of the House of Commons was to control the finance of the Crown to fight wars and the vehicle for discharging that from the audit office's perspective was twofold: the Comptroller function and then it was the Appropriation Account so the question was how did you integrate that with the concept of accrual accounting?
>
> *(Martin Sinclair, interview)*

Sinclair's perspective was not the perspective of all in the NAO. Bourn privately was more cautious than he appeared to Likierman: at a meeting of the International Federation of Accountants,[22] Bourn detected what he described as 'cultural imperialists, trying in the manner of 19th century missionaries to spread new ways of thinking that will bend the world into American accounting categories' (Bourn, 1991a). Bourn opposed this as to what he saw as the key principle that 'politics rules not accounting' (Bourn, 1991a). This is not too far from the perspective of Sinclair, who said that the new accounting system had to be justified within the existing constitutional requirements for accounts within the UK.

The NAO initially considered resource accounting as a constitutional change, rather than seeing it through a technical lens. It tried to preserve the constitutional role of the auditor within this new system of accounting. The Treasury's White Paper envisaged the NAO's audit being conducted on a 'presents fairly basis' (Treasury, 1995, p. 9). This basis was used in local authorities or in some non-departmental public bodies where the accounts were compiled on a different set of principles. The NAO in response argued that they should not perform their audit on this basis as 'in some eyes, a "presents fairly" opinion could be seen as a second class of opinion which could wrongly imply that the audit and opinion fell short of a true and fair view' (C&AG, 1996b, p. 11). But the NAO also went further: it stressed that resource accounting meant that 'the focus of [the reader's] attention is to shift from inputs to the outputs and achievements of programmes' (C&AG, 1996b, p. 12). The NAO argued on this basis for 'an external scrutiny and validation of the performance data published with the accounts' and suggested that this could be done during the period that resource accounting was implemented (C&AG, 1996b, p. 1). They suggested furthermore that this was part of the responsibility of the NAO itself. They further argued that if 'performance data are so unreliable that they cannot withstand scrutiny, it is questionable whether they are worth disclosing unless they are subject to a suitable health warning for the benefit of those who might overwise rely on them' (C&AG, 1996b, p. 12). As with Sinclair, the official NAO position was that resource accounting should be used to open up parliamentary accountability: the change to accounting practice had to be done for a constitutional purpose to be successful.

The history of audit in this period was affected not just by accounting changes but also by changes to its staffing. Prior to 1991, the NAO's new audit staff were trained by the Chartered Institute of Public Finance and Accountancy (CIPFA), as they had been since the 1970s. Bourn reported to the PAC that the first entrants to the private sector Institute for Chartered Accountants in England and Wales (ICAEW) programme started in the autumn of 1991 (PAC, 1992, p. 24). Bourn's decision to opt to change training provider was based on a political judgement. Michael Whitehouse told us that

> You have to see that decision in the light of the backdrop of the Thatcher/Major era when they were privatising all these utilities and the whole ethos in government was a more commercial one. John Bourn didn't feel CIPFA, rightly or wrongly, gave the right image. He wanted to show that we were as good as the commercial firms and that's what drove him in going for the ICAEW. He thought there were lots of potential audit clients out there for which an ICAEW qualification would be required like the BBC or government owned companies. Lastly, Bourn felt it would attract recruits to the NAO. The decision reflected the post-Thatcher philosophical drive to a more commercial public sector and Bourn saw it as part of the NAO's ability to respond to that.
>
> *(Michael Whitehouse, interview)*

In addition, the NAO had been criticised by PAC member Tim Smith, who had been a partner in a Big Four firm. John Bourn later told Neil Sayers a slightly different story, that 'because of various historical issues the Treasury were not sure the NAO was competent to audit accruals accounting and Bourn had to persuade them it was and one of the ways that he could do this was to move professional training from CIPFA to ICAEW' (Neil Sayers, interview). Whilst these accounts are slightly different, the common thread is that both Whitehouse and Sayers saw the NAO's move to training its staff with ICAEW as part of the organisation's evolution in a Whitehall world enthralled by a commercial view of accountability, audit and accounting.

Moving the NAO's training regime to the ICAEW had a long-term effect on the approach that new trainees took to audit. Khalid Hamid,[23] who joined in the penultimate cohort of CIPFA, described the 'new cohorts coming from ICAEW as a culture shift with the NAO believing that it needed to be more in line with commercial practice, increasing the technical accounting aspects of professional accounting' (Khalid Hamid, interview). For Neil Sayers, the training that NAO trainees received at the ICAEW was too technical: he argued that the ICAEW mindset was formed by 'their training at the institute which is all about the accounting standards and how to apply them but misses a vast amount of the stuff which is important in the government context'; for these staff, 'regularity no longer mattered' (Neil Sayers, interview). From 1991, the NAO's staff were increasingly trained in a methodology which assumed a set of private sector accounting standards, and hence, culturally the organisation moved away from the presuppositions of the E&AD's audit, focussed on regularity and propriety. This combined with the new accounting approach refocussed, over the long term, the NAO's audit away from regularity and towards technical compliance.

Whilst the NAO accepted the new accounting regime on constitutional grounds, the changes that were made to accounting shifted the government towards a more commercial version of accounting. Clarke and the Treasury's rhetoric on accruals accounting saw it as part of a shift to make the government more business-like. The NAO might have endorsed this change on the basis of the constitution, but the rhetorical shift from the Treasury was important for the future. This was particularly true for the NAO because of the shift in the training provider: moving to the ICAEW meant in the long run, as Hamid and Sayers argued, moving away from the constitutional perspective of Sinclair and towards the perspective embodied in Clarke's 1995 comments. The 1990s did not see this change happen, but it laid the foundations for changes to come in the 2000s and 2010s.

4.5.3 What the NAO's audit covered

As the last point suggests, one of the big issues facing Bourn and the NAO was the question of what the NAO should audit. The NAO and the House of Commons both approached this as a constitutional issue. The National Audit Act 1983 had set out that the NAO's audit covered government departments. However, at the time, MPs had suggested that the NAO should support public sector accountability by other bodies: nationalised industries, for example. Under Downey, the NAO's remit remained stable. The 1990s saw more instability over its remit. There were two principal areas in which expansion to the NAO's remit was discussed during the 1990s. These were the executive agencies and other semi-autonomous parts of government, and the Royal Household. We shall discuss each in turn.

From 1988, the government increasingly delivered services through the newly created executive agencies and through new government wholly owned companies (Cooper et al., 2021). Robert Sheldon complained that the NAO 'does not audit other non-departmental public bodies' and told the government that in these cases,

> the Executive, rather than Parliament, appoint their own auditors. Where public money is involved, it must be Parliament, not the Executive, that appoints the auditors. Something is fundamentally wrong there.
>
> *(House of Commons, 1996, col. 869)*

Sheldon made an argument in public that he and Bourn were pursuing in private with the government of the day (Bourn, 2002). The pressure to increase the NAO's audit scope was one of the factors which lay behind the adoption of the ICAEW qualification because it would give the NAO the ability to conduct Companies Act financial audits (Michael Whitehouse, interview). The fundamental point that Sheldon and the PAC were making though was constitutional. They were entitled to access these records through the NAO because Parliament, not the executive, should have the right to appoint the auditors of any public body.

One way to define a public body was to define it, as in the 1983 Act, as a body subject to the direction of ministers, but there were particular issues relating to the Royal Household. Scandals about the Royal Household led to demands for the NAO to become involved in their audit. In 1992, Bourn noted that 'politically I could not avoid agreeing' to investigate expenditure on castles and palaces in occupation by the Royal Family (Bourn, 1992a). The demand for change was phrased in exactly the same way as when it was made about non-departmental public bodies. In 1994, the PAC reported on the management of the Royal estate: they concluded that while since 1990 the estate had been funded by a grant from the Department for the Environment, the Royal Household still did not publish annual reports and accounts and was not subject to an NAO audit. The PAC argued that the NAO should have access 'to enable the Royal Household and the Department to demonstrate effectively their stewardship of public money' (PAC, 1994b, p. ix). The point the committee were making, again, was a constitutional one: that the NAO's remit should stretch to wherever public money was spent.

In both areas, therefore, where the PAC and NAO were pressing for the scope of the NAO's audit to be widened, the auditor was seen as a constitutional rather than a technocratic authority. This is important because it reflects the discussion with regard to both value-for-money and financial audit. Bourn's NAO in the 1990s was an extension of Downey's in the 1980s: its key purpose was constitutional, and extensions to its authority therefore rested on the argument that the executive should be subject to parliamentary accountability.

4.6 Chapter summary

The chapter examined the first decade of Bourn's period as C&AG from 1988 to 1997 under Conservative governments of Thatcher and Major. This considered the political context and categories of regulatory space concerning organisational context, capacities and audit scope.

In 1991, Bourn had reflected on the auditor as 'Sherlock Holmes manqué'. In a speech, he reflected on the role of a detective: they 'investigated the way that the hinge that links motive to circumstance can result in crime or waste' (Bourn, 1991c).

It is tempting to see this as a one-off metaphor that Bourn developed, but actually it encapsulates a wider truth about the way that he saw the NAO in the 1990s and the way that the NAO developed. Bourn, like Downey, knew the civil service well and through his alliance with Robert Sheldon sought to improve and strengthen the NAO's powers.

The NAO became a much more highly skilled organisation than the one that Downey had left in 1988. This meant that the type of studies it carried out and analyses it executed were increasingly sophisticated, advancing as Bourn had argued it should, into the realm of effectiveness audit. The NAO still preserved in key ways the appropriation audit that the E&AD and Downey had bequeathed, though, as we have noted, eroded by tactical decisions to concede to the Treasury's approach on changing financial audit. From the point of view of a civil servant, Sir Richard Packer said the NAO in the 1990s and 2000s, 'were a respected set up and there was no point in trying to reject them or fight them and you had to work with them and they were part of the constitution and were not under the control of government but reported to Parliament' (Sir Richard Packer, interview).

When Bourn spoke about the 'auditor as detective', he could see a police force that had significantly developed its capability, but crucially also a force that looked at single incidents. In his detective speech, Bourn discussed a particular set of poor decisions regarding a building built for HMRC which was 'never occupied by Customs for whom it was obtained' (Bourn, 1991c). However, he could draw no implication from this case for his audience. The pressure from Whitehall and Parliament was to try and draw lessons from the analysis that the NAO provided. PAC itself had done this with relation to the better conduct of public business.

Bourn knew the power of the individual case to make a wider point, but he was already thinking beyond this: he spoke to an audience of academics in 1992 and confessed that he and the NAO knew that truth 'does not lie simply in records and accounts' and could not be found 'in the Audit Office, in Buckingham Palace Road, in London SW1' he sought some other account of a truth that audit could find within the world of scholarship and asked his audience to supply him with it (Bourn, 1992). This broadening of the auditor's insight is what Bourn and his colleagues devoted themselves to from the 2000s onwards. His successors dropped his expansive vision of the evidence base from which auditors could draw but retained his ambition for the influence of the NAO.

Notes

1 Michael Heseltine, 1933–, MP for Tavistock and Henley 1966–2001, Secretary of State for the Environment 1979–83, 1990–2, Defence Secretary 1983–5, Secretary of State for Trade and Industry and President of the Board of Trade 1992–5, First Secretary of State and Deputy Prime Minister 1995–7, created Lord Heseltine 2001.

2 Michael Nolan, 1927–2007, Judge High Court 1982–91, Lord Justice of the Court of Appeal 1991–3, Lord of Appeal in Ordinary 1994–8, Chair Committee on Standards in Public Life 1994–7. Knighted 1982, created Lord Nolan 1994

3 John Bourn's diaries are referenced here by their date, and the volume is included in the list of references. The diaries themselves are unpaginated.

4 Peter Levene, 1941–, Various commercial posts, Chief of Defence Procurement, Ministry of Defence 1985–91, Advisor to Defence Secretary 1984, Secretary of State for the Environment 1991–2, Chancellor of the Exchequer 1992, President of the Board of Trade 1992–5, Prime Minister 1992–7. Knighted 1989, created Lord Levene 1997.

5 Richard Packer, 1944–, Ministry of Agriculture, Fisheries and Food 1967–2000, Permanent Secretary, Ministry of Agriculture, Fisheries and Food 1993–2000. Knighted 2000.

6 Michael Quinlan, 1930–2009, Air Ministry and Ministry of Defence 1954–83, Permanent Secretary Department for Employment 1983–8, Permanent Secretary Ministry of Defence 1988–92. Knighted 1985.
7 Michael Jack, 1946–, MP for Fylde 1987–2010, Financial Secretary to the Treasury 1995–7, Shadow Agriculture Minister 1997–8, Chairman of the Environment, Food and Rural Affairs Select Committee 2003–10.
8 James Robertson, Chief Economist/Head of Economics and Statistics Practice Area, NAO, 2006–10, Director, NAO, 1995–6, Chief Economic Adviser, Employment Department then Department for Education and Employment/Head of Profession 1993–5, other civil services roles in departments including DTI, DfT and Department of Energy.
9 Terence Heiser, 1932–, Colonial Office, Ministry of Works, Ministry of Housing and Local Government and Department for the Environment 1949–92, Permanent Secretary Department for the Environment 1985–92. Knighted 1987.
10 Peter Hordern, 1929–, MP for Horsham and Horsham and Crawley 1964–97, Chairman Public Accounts Commission 1988–97.
11 Gabrielle Cohen, National Audit Office 1987–2015, Head of Press Office 1996–2000, Director of Communication and Corporate Affairs 2000–2005, Assistant Auditor General 2005–15.
12 Kenneth Warren, 1926–2019, MP for Hastings and Hastings and Rye, 1970–92, Chairman Select Committee on Trade and Industry 1983–92.
13 David Young, 1932–2022, Minister without Portfolio 1984–5, Secretary of State for Employment 1985–7, Secretary of State for Trade and Industry and President of the Board of Trade 1987–9, created Lord Young 1984.
14 Michael Mates, 1934–, MP for Petersfield and East Hampshire 1974–2010, Chair Select Committee on Defence 1987–92, Northern Ireland Committee 2001–5.
15 Due to the private nature of their deliberations, it is impossible to say from the outside how much interaction there was between the Intelligence and Security Committee and the NAO. The ISC was set up in 1994.
16 Miss Irene I Gordon, RGN, DipN, RM, MBA, had a long career in the NHS, culminating in being appointed as Deputy Chief Nursing Officer for Scotland in 1982. She also worked at senior levels in the Scottish Office. In 1988, she was appointed specialist adviser to NAO specialising in the health sector.
17 Certification audit is financial audit.
18 Norman Lamont, 1942–, MP for Kingston on Thames 1972–97, Chief Secretary to the Treasury 1989–90, Chancellor of the Exchequer 1990–3, created Lord Lamont 1998.
19 Tim Lankester, 1942–, Private Secretary to the Prime Minister 1978–81, Permanent Secretary Overseas Development Agency, 1989–94, Permanent Secretary Department for Education 1994–5. Knighted 1994.
20 Martin Sinclair, 1957–, Exchequer and Audit Department 1981–3, National Audit Office 1983–2015, Assistant Auditor General and Executive Leader, NAO 1999–2015.
21 Sir Andrew Likierman, 1943–, various academic posts 1968–, Head of Government Accountancy Service and Chief Accountancy Advisor, HM Treasury 1993–2003, Chair, National Audit Office 2009–15. Knighted 2001.
22 The International Federation of Accountants is the global voice for the accountancy profession, serving the public interest through advocacy, development and support for member organisations and accountants around the world. https://www.ifac.org/

23 Khalid Hamid, Director of International, CIPFA, 2020–, currently Chair, Financial Audit and Accounting Subcommittee of INTOSAI, Director, UAE State Audit Institution, 2001–20, other posts including NAO since qualifying with CIPFA in 1990.

References

AAG/B (1987). NAO in the 1990s. In *Monitoring the National Audit Office (NAO) environment; overtaken by policy development review*, AO39/34, unpublished MSS, National Archives, London.

Allan, A. (1994). A. Allan to N. Macpherson, 23 May 1994. In *Parliament. Accounting Officer issues: Public Accounts Committee; National Audit Office; part 1* PREM 19/4874, unpublished MSS, National Archives, London.

Audit Commission and NAO (1989). Guidelines for cooperation between the Audit Commission and the National Audit Office on examinations of economy, efficiency and effectiveness, June 1989. In *National Audit Office (NAO) relations with the Audit Commission*, AO39/25, unpublished MSS, National Archives, London.

Bew, P. (2015). The Committee on Standards in Public Life: Twenty years of the Nolan principles 1995–2015. *Political Quarterly*, 86(3), 411–418.

Bourn, J. (1985). *The most important likely development in or for British public administration over the next 10–15 years.* Unpublished MSS, John Bourn Private Archive.

Bourn, J. (1987). Wednesday 2 December. In *Diary of Sir John Bourn*, Unpublished MSS. John Bourn Private Archive.

Bourn, J. (1988). Friday 9 September 1988. In *Diary of Sir John Bourn,* Unpublished MSS. John Bourn Private Archive.

Bourn, J. (1988a). Problems of the NAO. In *Monitoring the National Audit Office (NAO) environment; overtaken by policy development review*, AO39/34, unpublished MSS, National Archives, London.

Bourn, J. (1988b). Thursday 29 September 1988. In *Diary of Sir John Bourn,* Unpublished MSS. John Bourn Private Archive.

Bourn, J. (1988c). Wednesday 19 October 1988. In *Diary of Sir John Bourn,* Unpublished MSS. John Bourn Private Archive.

Bourn, J. (1988d). *N. Ireland seminar*, Unpublished MSS, John Bourn Private Archive.

Bourn, J. (1989). National Audit Office: Force for change. *Public Money & Management,* 9(1), 60–63.

Bourn, J. (1989a). Effectiveness audit. In *Effectiveness audit* AO39/30, unpublished MSS, National Archives, London.

Bourn, J. (1990). 9 December 1990. In *Diary of Sir John Bourn,* Unpublished MSS. John Bourn Private Archive.

Bourn, J. (1991). Auditing defence. *The RUSI Journal, 136*(1), 79–82.

Bourn, J. (1991a). 24 February 1991. In *Diary of Sir John Bourn,* Unpublished MSS. John Bourn Private Archive.

Bourn, J. (1991b). 3 June 1991. In *Diary of Sir John Bourn,* Unpublished MSS. John Bourn Private Archive.

Bourn J. (1991c). 23 April 1991. In *Diary of Sir John Bourn,* Unpublished MSS. John Bourn Private Archive.

Bourn, J. (1992). *Truth and History.* Unpublished manuscript, John Bourn Private Archive.

Bourn, J. (1992a). 6 December 1992. In *Diary of Sir John Bourn,* Unpublished MSS. John Bourn Private Archive.

Bourn, J. (1994). 1 January 1994. In *Diary of Sir John Bourn*, Unpublished MSS. John Bourn Private Archive.
Bourn, J. (1994a). 7 July 1994. In *Diary of Sir John Bourn*, Unpublished MSS. John Bourn Private Archive.
Bourn, J. (2002). 29 March 2002. In *Diary of Sir John Bourn*, Unpublished MSS. John Bourn Private Archive.
Bowerman, M. (1994). The National Audit Office and the Audit Commission: Co-operation in areas where their VFM responsibilities interface. *Financial Accountancy & Management*, *10*(1), 47–63.
Burr, T. (1994). Briefing for the Prime Minister's Office on PAC and NAO reports, 3/3/1994. In *Parliament. Accounting Officer issues: Public Accounts Committee; National Audit Office; part 1* PREM 19/4874, unpublished MSS, National Archives, London.
Burrows, G. (2003). Out of arms way. *The Guardian*, 8 August 2003.
Butler, Robin, interview
Campbell-Smith, D. (2008). *Follow the money: The Audit Commission, public money and the management of public services 1983–2008*. London: Allen Lane.
Clarke, K. (1994). K. Clarke to J. Major, 19 May 1994. In *Parliament Accounting Officer issues: Public accounts committee; National Audit Office; part 1* PREM 19/4874, unpublished MSS, National Archives, London.
Committee on Standards in Public Life (1995). *Standards in public life*, Cm. 2850. London: HMSO.
C&AG (1989). *Home Office: Control and management of probation services in England and Wales*, Session 1988–9, HC377. London: National Audit Office.
C&AG (1991). *Department for Transport: Oil and chemical pollution at sea*, Session 1990–1, HC225. London: National Audit Office.
C&AG (1992). *Lord Chancellor's Department: Probate- service to the public.* Session 1991–2, HC290, London: National Audit Office.
C&AG (1993). *Memoranda submitted by the Comptroller and Auditor General to the Committee for Public Accounts*, Session 1992–3, HC386-i. London: National Audit Office.
C&AG (1993a). *Pergau hydro-electric project*, Session 1992–3, HC908. London: National Audit Office.
C&AG (1994). *Buildings and the environment*, Session 1993–4, HC365. London: National Audit Office.
C&AG (1995). *Metropolitan Police Service: Responding to calls from the public*, Session 1994–5, HC753. London: National Audit Office.
C&AG (1995a). *National Rivers Authority: River pollution from farms in England*. Session 1994–5, HC235. London: National Audit Office.
C&AG (1996). *Aid to Indonesia*, Session 1996–7, HC101. London: National Audit Office.
C&AG (1996a). *Health and safety in NHS acute trusts*, Session 1996–7, HC82. London: National Audit Office.
C&AG (1996b). *Resource accounting and budgeting in government: The White Paper proposals*, Session 1995–6, HC334. London: National Audit Office.
C&AG (1997). *Governance and the management of overseas courses at the Swansea Institute of Higher Education*, Session 1996–7, HC222. London: National Audit Office.
C&AG (1997a). *Ministry of Defence: Improving the efficiency of the procurement of routine items*, Session 1997–8, HC31. London: National Audit Office.
Cooper, C., Tweedie, J., Andrew, J. and Baker, M. (2021). From "business-like" to businesses: Agencification, corporatization, and civil service reform under the Thatcher administration. *Public Administration*, *100*(2), 193–215.

Cohen, Gabrielle, interview

Daily Telegraph (2008). BAE Arms deal with Saudi Arabia, timeline. *Daily Telegraph*, 30 June 2008.

Dewar, D. (1991). The audit of central government. In M. Scherer and S. Turley (eds.) *Current issues in auditing*, London: SAGE Publications Ltd.

Dewar, D. (1991a). Environmental auditing: The fourth 'E'. *Managerial Auditing Journal*, 6(5), 7–13.

Easteal, M. (1992). The audit of human resources. *International Journal of Government Auditing*, *19*(1), 10–11.

Economist (1988). How to make public money go further. *The Economist*, *306*(7532), 21.

Economist (1992). Watching the watchdogs. *The Economist*, *324*(7766), 33.

Economist (1994). Fierce watchdog or soft poodle: Public auditing, *The Economist*, *332*(7880), 30.

Gordon, Irene, interview

Gunn, S. (1989). National Audit Office: Scrutiny to be stepped up. *The Guardian*, 14 December 1989.

Heiser, T. (1988). Cooperation between the NAO and the Audit Commission, Letter to John Bourn, 14/7/1988. In *National Audit Office (NAO) relations with the Audit Commission*, AO39/25, unpublished MSS, National Archives, London.

High Court (1994). *R v. Secretary of State for Foreign Affairs ex parte the world development movement.* Available at https://www.bailii.org/ew/cases/EWHC/Admin/1994/1.html accessed on 14 December 2023.

House of Commons (1993). *Hansard*, Vol. 233, 30 November 1993.

House of Commons (1995). *Hansard*, Vol. 253, 25 January 1995.

House of Commons (1996). *Hansard*, vol. 282 16 October 1996.

House of Commons (2007). *Hansard*, Vol. 456 7 February 2007.

Keen, J. (1998). On the nature of audit judgements: The case of value for money studies. *Public Administration*, 77(3), 509–525.

Lankester, T. (2013). *The politics and economics of Britain's foreign aid: The Pergau Dam affair.* Abingdon: Routledge.

Likierman, Andrew, interview

Lonsdale, J. (1999). Methods. In C. Pollitt, X. Girre, J. Lonsdale, R. Mul, H. Summa and M. Waerness (eds.) *Performance or compliance? Performance audit and public management in five countries.* Oxford: Oxford University Press.

Lonsdale, J. (2000). *Advancing beyond regularity: Developments in value for money methods at the National Audit Office 1984–1999.* Unpublished PhD Thesis, Brunel University.

Midgley, H. (2019). The National Audit Office and the select committee system 1979–2019. *Parliamentary Affairs*, 72(4), 779–798.

National Audit Office (1987). Note of the National Audit Office/Audit Commission liaison meeting, 30 July 1987. In *National Audit Office (NAO) relations with the Audit Commission*, AO39/25, unpublished MSS, National Archives, London.

National Audit Office (1988). Public Accounts Committee deliberative meeting, 8 February 1988. In *National Audit Office (NAO) access for value for money activity*, AO39/9, unpublished MSS, National Archives, London.

National Audit Office (1988a). Note of the National Audit Office/Audit Commission liaison meeting, 11 May 1988. In *National Audit Office (NAO) relations with the Audit Commission*, AO39/25, unpublished MSS, National Archives, London.

National Audit Office (1988b). Class VIIIB National Audit Office. In *Appropriation Accounts 1987–8, Vol. 18 classes XVIII, XVIIIA and XVIIIB...* London: House of Commons.

National Audit Office (1989). Note of the National Audit Office/Audit Commission liaison meeting 14 March 1989. In *National Audit Office (NAO) relations with the Audit Commission*, AO39/25, unpublished MSS, National Archives, London.
National Audit Office (1989a). Note of the National Audit Office/Audit Commission liaison meeting, 14 December 1989. In *National Audit Office (NAO) relations with the Audit Commission*, AO39/25, unpublished MSS, National Archives, London.
National Audit Office (1989b). Class VIIIB National Audit Office. In *Appropriation Accounts 1988–9, Vol. 18 classes XVIII, XVIIIA and XVIIIB...* London: House of Commons.
National Audit Office (1990). Note of the National Audit Office/Audit Commission liaison meeting, 26 July 1990. In *National Audit Office (NAO) relations with the Audit Commission*, AO39/25, unpublished MSS, National Archives, London.
National Audit Office (1990a). Class VIIIB National Audit Office. In *Appropriation Accounts 1989–90, Vol. 18 classes XVIII, XVIIIA and XVIIIB...* London: House of Commons.
National Audit Office (1991). Note of the National Audit Office/Audit Commission liaison meeting, 22 February 1991. In *National Audit Office (NAO) relations with the Audit Commission*, AO39/25, unpublished MSS, National Archives, London.
National Audit Office (1991a). Class VIIIB National Audit Office. In *Appropriation Accounts 1990–91, Vol. 18 classes XVIII, XVIIIA and XVIIIB...* London: House of Commons.
National Audit Office (1992). Note of the National Audit Office/Audit Commission liaison meeting, 30 March 1992. In *National Audit Office (NAO) relations with the Audit Commission*, AO39/25, unpublished MSS, National Archives, London.
National Audit Office (1992a). Note of the National Audit Office/Audit Commission liaison meeting, 26 November 1992. In *National Audit Office (NAO) relations with the Audit Commission*, AO39/25, unpublished MSS, National Archives, London.
National Audit Office (1992b). Class VIIIB National Audit Office. In *Appropriation Accounts 1989–90, Vol. 18 classes XVIII, XVIIIA and XVIIIB...* London: House of Commons.
National Audit Office (1997). Class VIIIB National Audit Office. In *Appropriation Accounts 1996–7, Vol. 18 classes XVIII, XVIIIA and XVIIIB...* London: House of Commons.
Negrine R. (1992). Reporting parliamentary committees: The investigation of the Rover Group sale to British Airways . *Parliamentary Affairs*, 45, 399–408.
Newton, T. (1994). T. Newton to K. Clarke, 13 May 1994. In *Parliament. Accounting Officer issues: Public Accounts Committee; National Audit Office; part 1* PREM 19/4874, unpublished MSS, National Archives, London.
Omand, David, interview
Packer, Richard, interview
Packer, R. (2015). *Life to Seventy*. London: Grosvenor House Publishing Ltd.
Pendlebury, M. and Shreim, O. (1990). UK auditors' attitudes to effectiveness audit. *Financial Accountability and Management*, 6(3), 177–189.
Policy Unit (1988). SWOT analysis of the NAO. In *Monitoring the National Audit Office (NAO) environment; overtaken by policy development review*, AO39/34, unpublished MSS, National Archives, London.
Pollitt, C. and Roberts, S. (1994). Audit or evaluation: A National Audit Office VFM study. *Public Administration*, 72(4), 527–549.

Pollitt, C. and Summa, H. (1997). Performance auditing: Traveller's tales. In E. Chelimsky and W. Shadish (eds.) *Evaluation for the 20th century: A handbook*. Newbury Park, CA: SAGE, 86–106.

Procedure Committee (1990). *Second report from the select committee on procedure. Session 1989–90. The working of the select committee system. together with the proceedings of the committee relating to the report, minutes of evidence, and appendices*, Session 1989–90, HC19. London: House of Commons.

Public Accounts Commission (1994). *Seventh Report*, Session 1993–4, HC567. London: House of Commons.

Public Accounts Commission (1996). *Eighth Report*, Session 1995–6, HC658. London: House of Commons.

Public Accounts Commission (1998). *Ninth Report*, Session 1997–8, HC921. London: House of Commons.

Public Accounts Committee (1991). *Twenty-ninth report: National Audit Office corporate plan 1991–2 to 1995–6 and estimates for 1991–2*, Session 1991–2, HC413. London: House of Commons.

Public Accounts Committee (1992). *Tenth report: National Audit estimates 1992–3*, Session 1991–2, HC207. London: House of Commons.

Public Accounts Committee (1993). *Twenty fifth report: Payment of legal expenses incurred by the Chancellor of the Exchequer*, Session 1992–3, HC386. London: House of Commons.

Public Accounts Committee (1994). *Eighth report: The proper conduct of public business*, Session 1993–4, HC154. London: House of Commons.

Public Accounts Committee (1994a). *Seventeenth report: Pergau hydro-electric project*, Session 1993–4, HC155. London: House of Commons.

Public Accounts Committee (1994b). *Fortieth Report: Property services in English occupied royal palaces*, Session 1993–4, HC316. London: House of Commons.

Roberts, S. and Pollitt, C. (1994). Audit or evaluation? A National Audit Office VFM study. *Public Administration*, 72(4), 527–549.

Sayers, Neil, interview

Scott, Sir R. (1996). *Return to an address of the Honourable the House of Commons dated 15th February 1996 for the report of the inquiry into the export of defence equipment and dual-use goods to Iraq and related prosecutions*, Session 1995–6, HC115. London: House of Commons.

Sikka, P. and Lehman, G. (2015). The supply-side of corruption and limits to preventing corruption within government procurement and constructing ethical subjects. *Critical Perspectives on Accounting*, 28, 62–70.

Sinclair, Martin, interview

Treasury (1994). *Better accounting for taxpayer's money: Resource accounting and budgeting in government*, Cm. 2626. London: HMSO.

Treasury (1995). *Better accounting for taxpayer's money: The government's proposals. Resource accounting and budgeting in government*, Cm. 2929. London: HMSO.

Treasury (1996). *Spending public money: Governance and audit issues*. Cm. 3179. London: HMSO.

Treasury and Civil Service Committee (1994). *The role of the civil service, Minutes of Evidence 1 February 1994*. London: House of Commons.

Whitehouse, Michael, interview

Wilson, Richard, interview

COMPTROLLERS AND AUDITORS GENERAL, 1981–2024

FIGURE 1 Sir Gordon Downey, Comptroller and Auditor General, 1981–8. He founded the National Audit Office and professionalised it. He began modern-day value-for-money work following the passing of the National Audit Act, 1983.

National Audit Office, London.

FIGURE 2 Sir John Bourn, Comptroller and Auditor General, 1988–2008. He built on Sir Gordon Downey's solid foundations to create a world leading audit institution. His 'dignified, regal presence' suffused the National Audit Office.

National Audit Office, London.

FIGURE 3 Tim Burr, Comptroller and Auditor General, 2008–9. He 'steadied the ship' readying the National Audit Office to be passed to his successor.

National Audit Office, London.

FIGURE 4 Sir Amyas Morse, Comptroller and Auditor General, 2009–19. The first qualified Comptroller and Auditor General, 'light hearted but with a mind of steel', who led the National Audit Office through Brexit and austerity, focusing on the National Audit Office's purpose as national auditor.

National Audit Office, London.

FIGURE 5 Gareth Davies, Comptroller and Auditor General, 2009–19, the C&AG who put the NAO on an emergency footing, to provide accountability through the COVID-19 pandemic when others 'simply didn't have the tools' to scrutinise and focussed auditors on the long-term challenge of environmental change.

National Audit Office, London.

5

JOHN BOURN AND THE NEW LABOUR ERA 1997–2008

5.1 Introduction

John Bourn recognised that the challenges facing the NAO after 1997 were different from those the NAO faced at its creation in 1983. Bourn wrote, in a letter to Peter Hennessy, about what he saw as the main challenges for the UK in the 21st century. Apologising for sounding negative, he picked out what he described as the

> hobbled state. By this I mean the present state, caught half way between the public provision of Old Labour and the private provision of the 'New Public Management' of Reagan and Thatcher, under which many services are now provided by bewilderingly complicated compromise arrangements with elements of public and private provision yoked together, with instructions and programmes that are hard for citizens to understand; confusing for staff to work in with blurred accountability to UK parliaments and assemblies and the elected members of local authorities and consequently difficult for anyone to analyse and appraise their performance.
>
> *(Bourn, 2001c)*

This hobbled state was a consequence of the political settlement reached in the UK by 2001. The Thatcher and Major governments had carried out major reforms to the way that public services and the state operated; after 1997, the trajectory of reform continued. But whereas Thatcher and Major established areas of the postwar state, which would move into the

DOI: 10.4324/9781003520085-5

private sector (the nationalised industries especially), the Blair governments of the 2000s retained, for the most part, the public sector that they inherited. Privatisations that did happen followed the precedent of the 1980s and 1990s, but the state retained responsibility for central public services. Blair, as did Thatcher and Major, attempted to reform those services. This left the UK, as Bourn argued, with a state that was at once social democrat in many of its ambitions and Thatcherite in many of its means; a complex web of accountability had to be developed which could encompass this, including practices brought in from the private sector such as resource accounting.

Bourn's NAO had developed substantially in the 1990s: it was much more methodologically innovative and attuned to the needs of the users of services. Bourn was fixated on ensuring that the NAO fulfilled every part of the NAO Act. However, as the hobbled state matured, the NAO's approach to accountability also changed.

The purpose of this chapter is to examine the second period of Bourn's time in office as C&AG from 1997 to 2008. To do so, the chapter sets out the political context of the period and then considers the categories of regulatory space: organisational context (including independence), capacities and audit scope. This allows us to show how the change in political climate led to the NAO being more assertive and more supportive of Parliament but also led to it becoming more interested in advising government as well as holding it to account. The NAO interpreted this role as being focused on insights from audit work and best practice guidance. The NAO increased its capacity massively during the 2000s but as an organisation became increasingly dependent on Bourn as an individual, which contributed partly to his eventual fall. Also, it allows us to show the continued expansion of the scope of NAO's work and, at the same time, Bourn increasingly seeking lessons from the NAO's work for government. In particular, Bourn's vision of government accounting was only partially realised in his years of office. Furthermore, it enables an examination of how the NAO under Tim Burr[1] responded to Bourn's resignation after 20 years as C&AG, setting the stage for the arrival of Amyas Morse, who had a very different sense of how accountability and public sector audit should function.

5.2 The political context

In the 2000s, the NAO faced a New Labour government elected on two occasions with vast majorities. The dominance of Labour created potential issues for the NAO: Bourn himself wrote during the 1997 election that he thought that the NAO acquired powers when governments conceded them as 'one aspect of propitiating public opinion' (Bourn, 1997a). Given Labour were in such a strong position politically, Bourn was not confident Labour would give the NAO more powers if the question arose (Bourn, 1997a).

Because Labour presided over an economy which grew until the financial crisis in 2008–9, they were able to increase public expenditure. This changed political climate meant that the NAO faced very different problems in public services from those of the 1990s. Labour wanted to renew the asset base of the public sector in particular, and did so using the Private Finance Initiative in health, education and other services. After the 2001 election, Labour began to increase spending on the main public services, especially health and education, alongside reforms, many of which followed thinking that had originally been developed under Major and Thatcher.

Labour did not only focus on renewing public services but also had an extensive constitutional reform agenda. Unlike the previous pulse of constitutional reform in the 1980s which created the select committees and the NAO, Labour's interest focussed on constitutional questions outside Parliament. In particular, Labour devolved power away from Westminster and to the four nations and, in some cases, the local areas of the UK. In September 1997, Scottish voters voted for devolution, and an Act was passed in 1998 creating a Scottish Parliament. Similarly, in Wales, a narrow victory for devolution in the 1997 referendum resulted in the creation of a Welsh assembly in 1999. Lastly, as part of the peace process to resolve the troubles in Northern Ireland, an assembly was set up there too in 1998 (although in the case of Northern Ireland, there have been several periods in which, due to difficulties in the peace process, the assembly has not sat). These constitutional changes were piecemeal: different assemblies and Parliaments were granted different powers. Blair himself and his colleagues were often uninterested and unenthusiastic about devolution despite the scale of the constitutional revolution that it promised (Evans, 2023). Constitutional reforms also included local government: for example, the creation of the office of Mayor of London and extending the role of the Audit Commission.

Labour's years in power from 1997 to 2010 therefore presented the NAO with different challenges. On one level, like Thatcher and Major, Blair particularly and Brown were interested in public service reform and performance. However, on another level, Labour's decisions to reform the constitution would change the powers of Parliament and hence affect the rights and interests of Parliament's auditor.

5.3 Organisational context

5.3.1 Politics

The previous chapter set out how John Bourn viewed the NAO in a much more political way than many staff did in the 1980s and 1990s.[2] Bourn's political nous continued to be important in guiding the NAO through the New Labour years. Speaking to a conference of NAO financial auditors in 2001, he put it in his own words, 'our objective is that we shall still be on the field at the end of the game and not be carried off before half time, like poor Elizabeth Filkin[3]! Or even at full-time like Sir David Ramsbotham'[4] (Bourn, 2001a). It is notable that in both examples, Bourn had identified public servants who like him were there to regulate government but were dismissed because of the way that they put those criticisms (*Economist*, 2001; *Telegraph*, 2022). Bourn told the Directors' Conference at the NAO in the same year that he thought about organisations in evolutionary terms:

> every morning in Africa a gazelle wakes up. It knows it must run faster than the fastest lion or it will be killed. Every morning in Africa a lion wakes up, it knows it must run faster than the slowest gazelle or it will starve. It doesn't matter whether you are a gazelle or a lion, when the sun comes up you had better be running.
>
> *(Bourn, 2001b)*

In another speech, Bourn compared the NAO to the dinosaurs, who 'had had one hundred and fifty million years of success' but vanished in 'a blink of time's eye and we need to make sure that we did not go the same way' (Bourn, 1999). His staff understood this: 'the boss's view was always expand, you have to move forward, make yourself more relevant, if you stand still, you are dead' (Neil Sayers, interview).

Bourn was not alone in seeing political threats. James Robertson concurred: 'you did pick-up, you know, the street gossip about the political pressures. And if you can pass an Act in 1983 to create an NAO, you could pass an Act to reverse it' (James Robertson, interview). Jeremy Lonsdale noted a particular anxiety in the late 1990s and continuing into the early 2000s related to discussion of audit and inspection acting as a barrier to innovation (to the extent that NAO published a press notice on the subject) and the publication of Power (1999), a volume describing and critiquing the "audit society" (Jeremy Lonsdale, interview).

Bourn's sense of the vulnerability of the NAO permeated his view of the relationships between the NAO and Parliament and the NAO and government.

5.3.2 Parliament

The first key relationship of the NAO that changed in 1997 was that Robert Sheldon had to stand down as the chair of the Public Accounts

Committee (PAC).[5] He was replaced by David Davis.[6] Sheldon's attitude to the press had been very conservative: David Davis commented that Sheldon 'didn't do a great deal in public'. This was symbolised for Davis by the fact that the BBC did not understand that he was not appearing as a Conservative politician but as a chair of the PAC when they invited him on to programmes: 'I had to keep telling the media, particularly the BBC, that when I appear as Chair of PAC, I am not appearing as a member of the opposition. This is not my take or the Tory view on this issue but the view of the committee' (David Davis, interview). This lack of visibility of the PAC even extended to a lack of profile within Parliament itself. Gabrielle Cohen said that 'I remember David telling me that when he told other parliamentarians about his intention to become the chair of PAC, they were baffled by his decision as the Committee was perceived as something of a backwater' (Gabrielle Cohen, interview). Davis, like Sheldon, understood the unique nature of the role but wanted it to be much more public facing:

> I tried to get all the members of PAC to pick up a role regionally so because the press want to come to me for the national things but they could hit their regional newspapers. But I think I slightly surprised all the Labour members by saying to them 'you can take every report and push it forward in your area'.
>
> *(David Davis, interview)*

Gabrielle Cohen said that Davis 'came to the PAC with a purpose. He was ambitious, the Tories were likely to be out of power for at least two Parliaments and he saw the potential platform the committee would offer. I don't think we went very far into the 1997 parliament before everybody knew what the PAC was' (Gabrielle Cohen, interview). Davis was the first PAC chair who actively engaged with NAO teams on reports, being briefed directly, and clearly knew the reports well. It was the first time staff had had this kind of exposure and challenge on their own to the chair of the committee. Cohen wasn't alone in appreciating the change. Sir Edward Leigh,[7] Davis's successor as chair, saw it too: 'David Davis was the first modern chairman of the PAC who really got loads of publicity for the PAC's reports: he raised the bar for the role' (Sir Edward Leigh, interview). Richard Bacon thought that 'he did a lot in that four years' (Richard Bacon, interview). Bourn was also concerned that over time, parliamentarians had less understanding of how to run an organisation: there were fewer businessmen and trade unionists on either side of the House (Public Administration Committee, 2009, Ev. 5).

This new dynamism from the chair continued in a more muted form by Leigh. Leigh was 'much more consensual' (Richard Bacon, interview). Leigh was rigid about the PAC's remit though; Mark Etherton,[8] clerk to the committee, told us 'Edward Leigh was very strong on, "we're not doing policy at PAC. We don't get ministers in front of the Committee"' (Mark Etherton, interview).

The impetus given by Davis and Leigh was followed by the younger MPs elected in 2001 who joined the committee in his wake including ambitious new MPs such as George Osborne[9] or Richard Bacon or experienced former ministers like Frank Field[10] (Gabrielle Cohen, interview); (Neil Sayers, interview). These MPs used NAO reports to make a political impact. For example, in July 2005, the NAO reported on foreign national offenders held in the UK's prisons: the C&AG noted in his report that the Home Office 'has not kept records of the number of people detained on immigration grounds following the end of their criminal sentence who have been released from detention and not removed' (C&AG, 2005, p. 3). The Home Office supplied data to the PAC about the numbers of these offenders but later had to correct the record before the committee in response to pressure from Richard Bacon, after the department realised the situation was 'much more serious than initially presented' (PAC, 2006, p. 10). The political impact of this discovery was considerable: Charles Clarke,[11] then Home Secretary, subsequently left the Cabinet and his successor, John Reid,[12] described the Home Office as 'not fit for purpose' (BBC, 2006; Mulholland and Tempest, 2006).

Taken together, these developments put pressure on the NAO to devote more time to its relationship with PAC. Consequently, after David Davis's election as chair in 1997, and his clear intention to operate a more muscular approach to the role, the NAO saw the need to set up a dedicated team to manage its interactions with the committee and smooth relations between the committee and Whitehall (Gabrielle Cohen, interview).

Despite these efforts on relationship building, there were significant clashes between the NAO and committee members, especially after 2001. In 2003, the PAC took evidence on the NAO's examination of the UK's acquisition of the Heart Hospital (C&AG, 2002). Jon Trickett,[13] then a member of the committee, asked Robert Naylor, Chief Executive of University College London NHS Trust, whether some information was commercially confidential. Trickett explained that he had asked the question as 'I asked for this information from the NAO, and they refused to give it to me on the grounds of commercial confidentiality. I think it has been a waste of the committee's time' (PAC, 2003, Ev. 7). When Bourn said he had no record of the call and Trickett should have called him, Trickett replied that 'I just hope the point is established that if members [of the PAC] ring the NAO we should not have to speak to Sir John to get the information needed to prepare questions for meetings of this Committee' (PAC, 2003, Ev. 7). Trickett's truculence was not something that Sheldon would have indulged when he was chair.

MPs were not only concerned with the NAO's support for them: they also raised awkward questions for the NAO about the quality of its reports. In a PAC hearing about NHS Local Improvement Finance Trusts, MPs challenged the NAO's use of figures. Trickett announced when he was given the opportunity to question the department that 'I am going to put all my questions to Sir John or his assistant' (PAC, 2006, Ev. 9). Trickett complained that the NAO had used two contractors to perform analysis for them, and that one was also a student and the other had a conflict of interest as they had advised the companies involved in several of the PFI projects under scrutiny: as Trickett put it to Sir John, 'the Committee for Public Accounts has to be beyond reproach and the advice we receive which is to Parliament and therefore the taxpayer has to be absolutely unimpeachable' (PAC, 2006, Ev. 9–10). Edward Leigh told Bourn that 'it is very important that it is taken very seriously (PAC, 2006, Ev. 10). Both Richard Bacon and Greg Clark[14], in less obvious ways, criticised the report for the same reasons that Trickett did (PAC, 2006, Ev. 11).

The criticism from Jon Trickett was not an isolated example. Bourn wrote in 2001 about "PAC's attack" on an NAO report on PFI, describing hostile comments from Trickett in particular (Bourn, 2001). Richard Bacon said that the NAO report on the National Programme for IT was a "disaster" (Richard Bacon, Interview). Bacon said he realised "after only about five minutes" that the senior manager at the NAO tasked with briefing him when the report was published "hadn't got a clue" because he himself had access to a couple of very highly-placed sources within the programme (Richard Bacon, Interview). These individuals submitted evidence to the Committee which included a list of issues that the NAO report had missed and a recommendation that the "NAO should review its methods of investigating large IT projects" (Kwo, Shackman and anonymous others, 2007, Ev. 113). Bacon rewrote the draft report that was provided to the PAC to ensure that it matched this supplementary evidence and reflected what he and the other MPs saw as the truth of the programme (Richard Bacon, Interview, PAC, 2007). This kind of challenge was completely new to the NAO and had not been seen under Sheldon: MPs often were keen to state that they were not attacking the NAO directly, but they were no longer willing merely to defer to the expertise of the auditor.

More assertive MPs changed the nature of the NAO's work. Richard Bacon recalled for example that "The NAO reports were a little ho hum on the Private Finance Initiative (PFI), until Alan Williams[15] pushed the NAO to do more on refinancing and that showed how particularly in the world of falling interest rates you could get very high returns." Bacon suggested that both studies on the Norfolk and Norwich PFI scheme and on capability reviews of departments only originated because of his interest (C&AG, 2009). In the latter case, he had pointed out to Tim Burr that there were no studies which allowed members to question the Cabinet Secretary (Richard Bacon, interview). Other MPs also pressed for the NAO's remit to be extended. Alan Williams, for example, had "decade long campaigns" to get the NAO's remit extended to the BBC and Bank of England, campaigns that came to full fruition only after he had left the committee (Richard Bacon, Interview).

However, the increased assertiveness of MPs did not mean the Committee had lost respect for the NAO or indeed the C&AG. Sir Edward Leigh recalled that John Bourn "helped me along. I mean, I couldn't have done anything at the PAC without him" (Sir Edward Leigh, interview). MPs were in awe of Bourn. Richard Bacon told us that when he joined the Committee as a young MP, he had an immense respect for John Bourn: "he was like the Pope and when he said something it was like a papal bull" (Richard Bacon, interview). Bacon further commented that in opposition, through the NAO, "I had sources of information that our frontbench spokesmen didn't have; they could have had if they had made themselves aware of the process but mostly they didn't" (Richard Bacon, interview). Nick Wright[16] said that he thought the relationship was so close that at times "I wondered at the extent to which the Committee had actually been captured by the NAO at that point" (Nick Wright, interview). Bourn was very pleased in 1997 that Robert Sheldon became Chair of The Public Accounts Commission and in 2001, when Sheldon went to the House of Lords, he was replaced by Alan Williams. Williams had been a veteran of the PAC, sitting on it since 1987, and was yet another connection to the world of Harold Wilson and John Garrett. Williams was, according to Gabrielle Cohen, "the NAO's biggest supporter" in Parliament (Gabrielle Cohen, interview) and more widely was seen as an MP with a "real interest" in the NAO (Neil Sayers, interview).

The changes to the NAO's work were permissive too. Sir Edward Leigh and Alan Williams were much more relaxed about the NAO taking on further work for other select committees (Midgley, 2019). Williams, as Chair of The Public Accounts Commission, encouraged it by allocating the NAO specific funding for this work (Midgley, 2019). Gabrielle Cohen recalled the change in approach from Sheldon to Davis and, with the support of Alan Williams as Chair of TPAC, argued that this allowed the NAO to broaden the support it was able to offer to Parliament more generally, for example, supporting the work of other select committees. Bourn welcomed this: his basic attitude was that "if someone in Parliament asked the NAO to do something, we should do it and become part of their trusted advisor network" (Neil Sayers, interview). The NAO's work for select committees expanded in three ways. Firstly, NAO teams began to do more ad hoc work for select committees when they needed assistance (Midgley, 2019). Some of this role on accounts was duplicated by the Scrutiny Unit, created in 2001, to which the NAO also seconded staff (Ferry et al., 2021). Secondly, the NAO provided briefings to individual committees about the departmental accounts they had to analyse, beginning with the Defence, Business Enterprise and Regulatory Reform and Communities and Local Government Departments (Liaison Committee, 2009, p. 85). Thirdly, from 2003, the NAO developed a special relationship with the Environmental Audit Committee: its work on the environment was often discussed in this committee and the NAO supported them with a secondee (Liaison Committee, 2007, pp. 62–63).

The NAO though was concerned to ensure that the PAC remained the supreme select committee; for example, when it came to reporting on the war in Iraq, the NAO ensured that it got its report out before the official review was completed. Their logic was that the Defence Select Committee would hold hearings on the official report, but the NAO report would enable the PAC to report first. Consequently, the NAO and PAC version would be the "first official response" to the war (David Clarke, interview).

A more assertive PAC potentially threatened the NAO's other key relationships, namely the NAO's relationship with the government itself which is analysed below. However, Bourn's skills as a politician are revealed by the NAO's positioning in this period. PAC often wanted the NAO to do things that other stakeholders would not welcome. For example, on NAO access to the royal household, Michael Whitehouse said that,

> we were under considerable pressure to get access to the Royal Household at the time which was really irritating the Royal Household but Bourn could not let go of that because that was what Parliament wanted, so on the other side when the Prince of Wales, the current King, started all this initiative about accountability for sustainability and phoned up John Bourn, he saw this as an opportunity to demonstrate the added value which audit could provide.
>
> *(Michael Whitehouse, interview).*

Whilst Bourn was told by HM Queen when he was knighted, "Oh you're the man who made me pay tax!" [17], he was publicly thanked by the Prince of Wales for his support (Jonathan Bourn, interview, Bourn, 2006). He also tried to play down the risks of accountability to the Palace: at a lunch where he and David Davis represented the NAO and the PAC, he told officials from the Royal Household that,

> The Palace should do an annual report drawing attention to its financial successes. I said it would not stop the bad stories the Palace gets but it would be a weight on the other side of the scale.
>
> *(Bourn, 1998b).*

Bourn had to keep reconciling the ambitions of an assertive Parliament with the need for the NAO to maintain alliances with other institutions.

5.3.3 Constitutional reform and the NAO

Parliament might be becoming more assertive, but its role was changing within the UK territorial constitution. Northern Ireland acquired a legislature for the first time since 1972. In 1999, a Scottish Parliament sat for the first time since the Act of Union in 1707; Scotland now had a Parliament solely concerned with its affairs after a gap of nearly 300 years. The Welsh Assembly became the first Welsh legislature since the Welsh Act of Union with England in the 16th Century. Donald Dewar[18], the first First Minister of Scotland, put the story of devolution into a romantic nationalist context when he spoke in 1999:

> we reach back through the long haul to win this Parliament, through the struggles of those who brought democracy to Scotland, to that other Parliament dissolved in controversy nearly three centuries ago.
>
> *(Dewar, 1999).*

Dewar's words demonstrate the deep commitment to the Scottish Parliament as the embodiment of a Scottish democratic tradition amongst those who were unionists like him but also nationalists. The entire devolution settlement in both countries rested upon, what Peter Hain[19], then a junior minister at the Welsh office, suggested was its opposite: the previous situation in which "Wales [was] trapped in the past—weak, divided, and cowering before power centralised in London" (House of Commons, 1997, col. 816). However lukewarm in private (Evans, 2023), the rhetoric from government and supporters of the new devolved systems was clear: they needed their own institutions.

The question therefore raised by all three new devolved systems was: did they require their own auditors? Initially, the NAO thought it could remain the auditor of the Welsh and Scottish governments. There were two issues with this conceptually. Firstly, there was a technical issue: could the C&AG audit the Scottish and Welsh Parliaments if this were an appointment by a minister? The Speaker's Counsel, the leading advisor to the Speaker of the House of Commons on legal issues, suggested this was possible so long as it was clear that any appointment would not compromise the C&AG's loyalty to the House of Commons as opposed to the executive (Speaker's Counsel, 1997). The NAO had prepared for the 1997 election in 1996 with a paper put to the senior management team setting out that their "prime concern is the safeguarding of strong, independent and high-quality audit on behalf of Parliament and the taxpayer" (Mawhood, 1996). Beyond the legal issue, the NAO ran into obstacles in seeking to do this work: at a meeting between the NAO, the Treasury and the Scottish Office, the NAO argued that the C&AG becoming the auditor of the devolved nations would be the best solution "on cost effectiveness grounds and experience" (NAO, 1997). A letter from the NAO set out their view that if the government were to set up two devolved audit offices, they would discover that this would not be "cost effective" costing perhaps £1 million a year more than the NAO's arm in Scotland for example, and furthermore "neither office would be viable. Because of their limited size, they would be unable to offer staff the prospect of a reasonable career and would be unable to develop a cadre of high quality, professional staff experienced in the specialism of public sector audit" (Mawhood, 1997).

The Scottish Office and the Treasury objected on "political grounds": referencing the desire within Scotland to have its own democratic institutions as opposed to using Westminster's (National Audit Office, 1997). This perspective dominated in Scotland.

When Bourn visited Scotland in October 1997, he showed a video about the NAO to his staff in Scotland and then asked them if they needed a new audit office in Edinburgh and received a discouraging answer:

> They say they do. The video is too London based though the only image of London is of Parliament which is supposed to concern us all and they ask for Sean Connery[20] and Kirsty Wark[21] to be presenters as opposed to the English sounding John Humphries.[22]
>
> *(Bourn, 1997b).*

It was not just NAO staff that had objections; there were more senior objections to the NAO becoming the auditor in Scotland. In a meeting with Gordon Brown, Bourn learnt that the Chancellor had strong views: Brown said, "in effect, that the C&AG could not be the AG [Auditor General for Scotland]; that inspection of books and records [by the C&AG] was out" (Bourn, 1998c).

The Scotland Act (1998) provided for the appointment of an Auditor General in Scotland. The first incumbent was Robert Black[23]. The NAO published a report summarising progress against its previous reports with a Scottish dimension for the new Scottish Parliament and Auditor General to start from (Comptroller and Auditor General, 1999a). The new organisation Audit Scotland took on many staff from the NAO: for Bourn, who delivered a valedictory speech to them in 2000, these staff "had the chance to define the nation, and build on Scottish history" (Bourn, 2000).

Wales followed Scotland. Bourn initially took the role in Wales as Auditor General between 2000 and 2005. Jeremy Colman[24] replaced Bourn in 2005: Colman was a former senior NAO official. Colman's successor in 2010 was Huw Vaughan Thomas[25], whose career resembled that of Robert Black. In Northern Ireland, these considerations did not apply because there had been a Comptroller and Auditor General of Northern Ireland from the 1920s: this official resumed their previous relationship with the Assembly (though in Northern Ireland, periods when the Assembly did not sit created difficulties for both the C&AG of Northern Ireland and the C&AG of the UK Parliament).

The evolution of a devolved system of public sector accountability had consequences both for the NAO and accountability in the UK. It meant that NAO reports from 2000 onwards only covered reserved matters (that is, those which had not been devolved), or where matters had been devolved, the NAO covered the English or English and Welsh service rather than the entire UK.[26] Scholars argued that the political community in Scotland, Wales and Northern Ireland were better able to hold their governments to account than Westminster was (Foster and Knox, 2022, 2023).

So, from this point, the NAO faced another dynamic in its organisational context: it had to negotiate, particularly as regards those services shared between the UK government and devolved governments, as to what it could audit. It now shared responsibility for defining public sector audit in the UK with four bodies, not only the Audit Commission. In 1998, the Public Audit Forum was created to link together the UK's five public sector audit bodies. There were attempts at cooperation: for example, in 2001, the NAO, the Audit Commission and Welsh Audit Office jointly published reports on the training of medical staff in England and Wales (C&AG, 2001c). However, joint reporting and the creation of the Public Audit Forum could not mask the possibility that the different public sector auditors could find themselves competing as the Audit Commission and the NAO did for example over access to housing associations (Bowerman et al., 2003, p. 6).

5.3.4 Ministers and civil servants

Ministers appear to have been fairly uninterested in the operations of the NAO. Lord Wilson told us that Blair and those around him were "not interested" in the NAO during the period that they pursued public sector reform (Lord Wilson, Interview). Wilson said that "Blair would never have regarded the NAO as being relevant, he hadn't got that experience to see it as important". He contrasted that to other ministers like Jack Straw[27], who he thought "regarded the NAO as an ally in getting the department to do well and [deliver] value for money". Lord Turnbull agreed with Lord Wilson about the lack of interest in the NAO from Blair and Gordon Brown. Turnbull and Wilson thought that ministers did not see the NAO as particularly relevant or having much to offer with regard to the Blair government's reforms of public services during that period. In Lord Turnbull's view, they should have paid more attention to the NAO as the office did good work although he thought that the NAO would increase its usefulness if, in addition to distilling lessons to be learned from spending that has gone wrong in the past, it did more to highlight lessons from current best practice (Lord Turnbull, Interview).

David Davis told us that Robert Sheldon advised him as soon as he was appointed to ask the new government to end the document classification "Not for NAO Eyes" (generally used for files predominantly concerned with preparing for the PAC and dealing with the NAO itself) and that due to the "naivety" of the new administration they accepted this point (David Davis, Interview).

This lack of interest at senior political levels in government was not reflected inside the civil service. Permanent secretaries still considered that the PAC and NAO dominated their world. Richard Bacon remembered Sir David Bell[28] saying that "I am always very aware as a Permanent Secretary that whatever I am working on might come up before the Public Accounts Committee" (Richard Bacon, interview). Sir David Omand described his relationship with the NAO during his time as Home Office Permanent Secretary as "always very rational" but said when in that role, the PAC handling of NAO reports could nevertheless get very confrontational (Sir David Omand, interview). The NAO were open to initiatives that Omand took such as trying to get the PAC to hold him, along with the Permanent Under-Secretary at the Lord Chancellor's Department (the predecessor of the Ministry of Justice), and the Director of Public Prosecutions as jointly and severally accountable for the criminal justice system as a system, and attempting to get MPs to accept a portfolio approach to managing innovative criminal justice initiatives not all of which could be expected to succeed to the same extent (Sir David Omand, interview).

The next section sets out the sizeable issues which created the potential for dispute between the auditor and government in this period. The NAO and the government fought over what the NAO should audit, culminating with the government accepting the proposals of the Sharman Review (2001). The NAO in its response to Sharman (2001) also accepted that it would take a new role as advisor to government, by sharing insights from audit and best practice guidance, as well as holding it to account. Lastly, at the end of Bourn's time, a crisis over data and HMRC brought the police into the NAO headquarters.

5.3.5 Government vs Parliament

The NAO's organisational context was reshaped in this period by a battle between government and Parliament over the NAO's access to government bodies and material relating to government contracts. Parliament turned its hand to campaigning for the NAO's powers to be extended. After 1995, when the government announced resource accounting (see previous chapter), the PAC in particular advanced the case that the NAO's audit rights should extend to new bodies and the C&AG's access rights be written into government contracts meaning that auditors of government departments could ask questions of major contractors with that department and request relevant documentation. In 1999, the government proposed legislation to change the form of accounts that should be presented to Parliament. The Committee struck at that point, arguing that as part of the legislation the range of the C&AG's audit should be extended. Robert Sheldon supported the Committee, saying that the Government should recognise the original intention of the 1983 Act by extending access for the NAO to all public sector organisations (House of Commons, 2000, col. 833). The Committee stated that,

> the framework established by Gladstone provided for the Comptroller and Auditor General to give assurance through his audit of departments' accounts that funds approved by Parliament had been spent in accordance with the principles of appropriation. It gave the Comptroller and Auditor General access to documents and information within Departments which at that time spent voted funds. But Government has changed out of all recognition since the 19th century. Funds are now spent through a range of bodies which help to deliver Departmental programmes.
>
> *(PAC, 1999, p. v).*

The Committee campaigned on this issue. Later that same year, the Committee returned to the subject:

> The Committee is concerned about the number of bodies, voted funds by Parliament, whose finances are audited by auditors appointed by and reporting to Ministers, rather than Parliament's own officer, the Comptroller and Auditor General.... The Committee believes that Parliamentary accountability will be enhanced if the Comptroller and Auditor General is able to audit on behalf of Parliament all public bodies

> carrying out central government functions and has statutory access to bodies and contractors delivering services on behalf of Government departments.
>
> *(PAC, 2000, p. vi).*

The PAC continued to agitate on this issue. In debate, its members reiterated the constitutional points made by the Committee. Alan Williams for example said that the House should set out that NDPBs should be made responsible to the NAO's (and in particular the C&AG's as an officer of the House) audit:

> I do not believe that anyone outside this House should have the right to determine what powers it needs. It is effrontery for the Executive to tell Parliament that we should not have the right to inspect them.
>
> *(House of Commons, 2000, col. 843).*

PAC's attitude to the NAO was decisive. The NAO definitely felt at the time that "we were lucky that we had PAC on our side in the late (19)90s fighting our corner" (Jeremy Lonsdale, interview). It is in this context that Michael Whitehouse referred to David Davis as a "a champion for the NAO" (Michael Whitehouse, interview). Other MPs agreed with PAC. William Cash[29] described the question of the NAO's access as "the essence of parliamentary democracy and parliamentary accountability" (House of Commons, 2000, col. 844).

The Treasury were less inclined to support the NAO to gain these rights of access, arguing they were unnecessary and a distraction at a time when they had more important matters to deal with. David Davis told us that he saw it as one of the Treasury's attempts to "curb" the power of the C&AG and the NAO. Jeremy Lonsdale spoke of the Treasury appearing to want to "clip the NAO's wings" a bit (Jeremy Lonsdale, interview).

Under pressure from the Committee and without much appetite for reform, the Treasury suggested a review led by Lord Sharman[30]. They selected Sharman who was a senior figure at KPMG. Jeremy Lonsdale, who was seconded along with a representative from the Treasury, to work for Lord Sharman on the review in 2000-01, said the presumption within the Treasury appeared to be that they should engage a senior private sector partner from a firm who would take one look at NAO and consider they were miles behind the pace (Jeremy Lonsdale, interview).

The choice proved unwise. Sharman and Bourn had known each other for years (Bourn, 2002). Furthermore, as Lonsdale noted, Sharman was an auditor himself so "instinctively sympathetic" to the NAO case (Jeremy Lonsdale, Interview) and could not understand why NAO should be constrained in its role and not have all the access it needed. The Sharman report resolved the conflict about NDPBs in favour of the NAO. Sharman concluded that "it is recommended that, as a matter of principle, the Comptroller and Auditor General (C&AG) be appointed as the auditor, on behalf of Parliament, of all NDPBs, including those where the relevant minister currently appoints the auditor" (Sharman, 2001, p. 2).

5.3.6 The HMRC Discs and the NAO

The NAO's work could involve risks which materialised in 2007 with the loss of child benefit data sent to the NAO by HMRC. The NAO initially requested this data, justifying it because of new International Auditing Standards, "which are more exacting on auditors than previous standards" (Second Director, HMRC Audit, 2007[31]). HMRC sent 2 compact discs to the NAO containing 25 million records including dates of birth, addresses, national insurance numbers and banking details for 7.25 million child benefit claimants, 15.5 million children, 2.25 million alternative payees such as partners or carers and 15,000 appointees or agents who received child benefit under court instruction or on behalf of third parties (BBC, 2007). These discs were never recorded as arriving at the NAO. The Chancellor of the Exchequer had to make a statement to the House of Commons about the data loss. The loss of the child benefit data discs was a matter of significant public and political concern and the NAO agreed to allow the Metropolitan police to search their premises. Given the sensitive nature of the information held by the NAO, the search was closely supervised.

The C&AG committed to the Chancellor that he would review why the NAO made the request. The NAO was forced to apologise to HMRC: writing that "there are lessons to be learnt on all sides" (Mawhood, 2007). Alistair Darling[32], then Chancellor, was understandably furious: he described the entire incident as "the stuff of a Whitehall farce had it not been so serious" and was incredulous that the NAO had requested the data from HMRC in the first place (Darling, 2011). Darling though reserved most of the blame for HMRC and senior officials at HMRC resigned (Darling, 2011). The incident had long term implications for the way that the NAO managed data but did not affect the relationship between the NAO and government much.

5.3.7 International relations

John Bourn saw the NAO as an established, democratic auditor as countries around the world were developing democracies and democratic institutions of their own. He believed that the NAO could help other audit institutions establish themselves. He was aware that "many auditor generals face a different reality – few staff; hostile politicians; difficult PACs;

inability to publish reports and underneath all this, it is said, massive corruption" (Bourn, 2003). Bourn thought that the NAO had an opportunity to both help countries address these problems and to increase UK influence by providing advice to supreme audit institutions internationally. For him, this was particularly true in the aftermath of the Cold War, the expansion of the European Union and NATO and the general confidence in liberal democracy as a governing paradigm (Private information).

5.4 Capacity

In terms of capacity the NAO looked to and did increase their resources during this period. They used this additional budget in new ways. Nevertheless, there remained weaknesses alongside strengths, explored below.

5.4.1 Securing increased resources

Securing increased capacity so that the NAO could perform its tasks well was one of Bourn's principal tasks. He thought that it was important that the NAO was able to perform the role that Parliament had granted it and felt that continuous expansion was one route to do that. Consequently, Bourn devoted a lot of effort to ensuring the NAO's budget increased each year. He "delegated the running of the NAO to others" (David Clarke, interview). Discussions about capacity were also strategic. In the early 2000s, the NAO opened an office in Newcastle, with around 100 staff and including senior management so that it would have a sizeable and substantial presence outside London (Michael Whitehouse, interview). Bourn's NAO grew in this period, and he was committed to seeing the NAO connected to consultancies and academics doing the same kind of work; consequently, the NAO often contracted out parts of studies or whole reports and also involved academics in scrutinising its reports for quality.

The NAO's budget grew continuously from 1997 to 2009. It grew faster than in the previous decade when Bourn had already increased the scale of the NAO significantly. In 1996-7, the NAO spent a gross amount of £43.4 million and a net amount of £36.6 million. By 2007-8, Bourn's last year, the NAO spent £98.3 million gross and £80.6 million net. To put that growth in context, over Bourn's first nine years as C&AG, the NAO's budget had grown by 64% and in the following eleven years, it grew by 118%. This partly matched the growth in public expenditure happening at the same time. The number of staff employed rose too: 765 staff were employed by the NAO in 2003-4 and by 2006-7 (at which point the method of counting staff members changed) the number of staff were 873. There was resistance to the NAO's continued growth: in 1999,

Alan Milburn[33], then Chief Secretary to the Treasury "was concerned at the size of the increase requested" by Sir John Bourn (Public Accounts Commission, 2000, p. iii). The Commission, demonstrating yet again the effectiveness of the 1983 Act in defending the NAO's budget, swept objections aside, noting that the NAO's workload had increased during the 1990s and would continue to do so in the 2000s (Public Accounts Commission, 2000, p. iii). The pressures on the NAO's spending were also continuous: the NAO complained to the PAC that it faced rising pressures on wages for staff in a "very competitive market" where "it can be difficult to compete with the schemes and benefits available in the private sector for qualified staff" (PAC, 2001, p. 3).

5.4.2 How the increased resources were employed

From 2001 onwards, it is possible to see how this additional spending flowed through into the NAO's activities as the annual report and accounts break down expenditure by purpose. From 2001 to 2008, the NAO devoted on average 44% of its funding to financial audit: this ranged between 43% in 2004 and 47% in 2007 but generally fluctuated within this narrow band (NAO, 2004a, 2007). Conversely, spending on non-financial audit, which includes value for money work, varied between 57% and 53% of the NAO's spending and averaged at 56%. This meant that the increases to funding during the 2000s led to increases in both of the NAO's main budgets. Spending on certifying accounts rose from £29 million in 2003 to £38 million in 2008 and for value for money the amount spent rose too, from £16.8 million in 2003 to £22.3 million in 2008 (NAO, 2003a, 2008).[34]

As regards how the NAO spent its money, as budgets for the NAO increased, so too did the number of staff but much more slowly. So, for example, between 2003 and 2008, the NAO's spending increased by 39% but its number of staff only rose from 765 to 873 (a rise of 14%) (NAO, 2003, 2008). The reason for this is that the NAO enhanced its capacity during this period through spending on consultants to assist in delivering projects, especially on value for money. Christian van Stolk told us that when he joined RAND in the 2000s, his role was to "manage the strategic partnership that RAND had with the National Audit Office at that time and that strategic partnership was all about outsourcing parts of studies or components of studies or even in due course whole studies. We were involved in the hot review process about which studies would be taken forward" (Christian van Stolk, interview). Jeremy Lonsdale noted that an increasingly diverse range of consultants were used more often as Bourn's tenure advanced (Jeremy Lonsdale, interview). Academics were involved in working with the NAO too: Patrick Dunleavy described his engagement with the NAO as beginning under Bourn and focussing on the presentation and argument of reports (Patrick Dunleavy, interview). The reviews described by Christian van Stolk above brought academic and external scrutiny to NAO reports. Jeremy Lonsdale said that they "introduced ideas which we wouldn't have thought about and helped with training" (Jeremy Lonsdale, interview).

Bourn's interest in these advisers was partly defensive, alongside his desire for the NAO to be less insular and more outward facing. He wanted to ensure that the NAO was the most effective commentator on value for money in the public realm so that no one could suggest replacement or competition. Specific consultants, as in the 1990s, were brought in to help with specific reports: for example, on the NAO's report into the invasion of Iraq, Sir John Bourn recruited "quite expensive military people" and Admiral Sir Peter Abbott[35] to provide the NAO with additional expertise (David Clarke, interview; C&AG, 2003). Clarke described seeing the "impact of that when he came to a clearance meeting and all the MOD people stood up when he [Sir Peter Abbott] came in" (David Clarke, interview).

Not all of this spending on consultancy generated as much in terms of outcomes and impacts as might have been expected. NAO staff were often searching for ways to augment studies methodologically in order to spend their budgets for external support rather than being driven by the needs of the subject under examination (Private information). Bourn regarded the size of the NAO's budget as a metric of success. There was therefore potential later on to cut the office's spending without impacting the quality of its work.

Some of this spending was also politically strategic. The NAO opened a new office in Newcastle during the 2000s. Since 1983, the NAO had consolidated its workforce into its own offices; before 1983, auditors were usually based in the departments they audited. A relic of this was that the NAO retained into the 1990s out stations in Blackpool and Newcastle which focused on DWP claims process functions. Bourn decided that he wanted to close the Blackpool office down but retained the Newcastle office and moved it into its own building to demonstrate that the NAO was "completely independent." Michael Whitehouse, who was involved in the decision, explained his rationale: "he was always worried that we would be criticised because we were a London based office and he wanted to show that the NAO was not just London based" (Michael Whitehouse, interview). Whitehouse said that whilst earlier in the NAO's history, faced with the pressure to move out of London, the organisation had envisaged offices in Leeds or Sheffield, they decided on Newcastle because "there were more satellite departments up there and his thinking was that he could show those departments that he was listening to them" (Michael Whitehouse, interview).

5.4.3 Enduring strengths and weaknesses

Despite this expansion, the NAO did have weaknesses. By 2008, Bourn had been in position for twenty years. As he ran through his second decade as C&AG, senior managers increasingly became people whose careers had been formed by Bourn himself, whilst many of those who were now permanent secretaries were from a younger generation who did not know him so well. Dunleavy et al. (2009, p. 8) reported that within the NAO, Bourn was known as "the boss." Senior officials within the NAO talked about how difficult it was to challenge Bourn at the time and how his "dignified, regal presence" suffused the organisation (Ed Humpherson, Interview). Perhaps this is most revealed by the problems that the NAO encountered with Bourn's expenses. In 2007, the Guardian reported that Bourn, his wife and private secretary had run up a travel bill of £365,000 and of £27,000 on lunches over the previous three years (Hencke, 2007). MPs including members of the PAC, criticised Bourn and welcomed his resignation in 2007 (Hencke, 2007; Summers, 2007). The disclosure of Bourn's expenses also created problems for NAO staff who were challenged by departments about it at the time (Private Information). The next chapter covers Bourn's resignation, but it reveals issues about the NAO's capability to run itself in this period: the NAO's governance clearly had failed in the 2000s and, as an organisation, it proved unable to challenge its head when he made unwise decisions.

Parliamentarians marked the improvements to the NAO's ability to conduct audits, despite the conflicts in PAC discussed above. Richard Bacon told us, for example, that "I remember David Davis saying to me that membership of the Public Accounts Committee is the best postgraduate degree in government you could ask for" (Richard Bacon, interview). Davis himself had a high opinion of the capacity of the NAO to carry out the work it was designed to perform: he said that "in all my time in dealing with government institutions, the NAO was the best: better than the Treasury, better than the Foreign Office and certainly, better than the Department for Exiting the European Union" (David Davis, interview). Bacon did add that while the NAO's work was normally of an admirably high and even academic quality, the Office often seemed to operate at "a rather stately or even sedate pace" (Richard Bacon, interview).

5.5 Scope

These changes in organisational context and capacity brought with them changes in the scope of the NAO's audit, affecting both value for money and financial audit during the New Labour era.

5.5.1 Changes to scope in value for money

There were three main changes to the scope of value for money during this period. The first was the growing confidence with which the NAO pursued its value for money responsibilities. Secondly, there was a continual deepening of the NAO's methodological diversity. The NAO expanded what it meant by value for money through its work on service users and the costs they were bearing from of failed government policy: essentially the audit of the effectiveness of politics fed back into consideration of its efficiency and economy. Thirdly, the NAO became much more interested in a more systematic examination of what drove government performance, led by Bourn's interest in how government could stop repeating its mistakes.

Firstly, the NAO became more confident in the late 1990s and 2000s than it had been previously. The NAO in the 1980s had been cautious about how it exercised its responsibilities and some of that caution survived into the 1990s. However, a series of reports illustrated the fact that the organisation was tackling increasingly difficult political issues. John Bourn, as David Clarke put it "was much braver than we imagined at the time and was willing to tackle very tricky subjects" (David Clarke, interview). Clarke thought he was the "bravest of the C&AGs" that he served under during his NAO career which lasted from the 1980s to 2012 (David Clarke, interview). Clarke identified the report on Operation Telic (the official name for the invasion of Iraq in 2003),

> given the politics that was going on around that, given the stuff that was going on with Blair, the views of the Chair, he had all of that but yet we reported on it. We built up to it but that was quite a brave thing and that was the only NAO report that's been debated on the floor of the House of Commons and it landed in the middle of all of this controversy and people from both sides of the debate used it. He had to have a certain amount of confidence in the NAO to deliver it and get the messaging right.

Clarke believed that the NAO could deliver this report because of a series of other projects that they had done which had gained the Ministry of Defence's (MOD) trust. The NAO had audited the financial management of the Kosovo campaign for example (C&AG, 2000). Clarke described how previous reports had set up the Iraq report:

> we had a track record on this and had done a huge amount of work behind the scenes. I knew everybody who was involved, and we had a strategy to do this. We had got to the point where the military were comfortable that we could review a military event
>
> *(David Clarke, interview).*

Clarke said that there,

> was a certain amount of scepticism about it and John Bourn was a huge champion and when we got some push back within the NAO, Bourn highlighted that a big step forward for NAO was hiring Sir Peter Abbott which stopped the internal criticism (David Clarke, interview).

Bourn's intervention helped quieten criticism of the report, but it demonstrated as well how high profile this piece of work was to the NAO.

Confidence from the NAO and confidence in the NAO extended the role of the organisation. There were two short run developments in the late 1990s which demonstrated how far the NAO had developed into a credible organisation. Firstly, the NAO was asked to conduct an audit of the underlying assumptions used by the Treasury in developing in the Budget (but not Treasury forecasts). Gordon Brown set this up in the aftermath of the 1997 election because during the campaign there had been controversy over the figures produced by the Conservative Chancellor, Ken Clarke. Brown wanted his figures to be "vetted as being reasonable and cautious" (James Robertson, interview). John Bourn thought the NAO acquired this work because it had the reputation for being "helpful and independent" and because it had hired ex-Treasury civil servants like Tim Burr and ex-Whitehall economists like James Robertson (Bourn, 1997). The audit of budget assumptions proceeded on an annual basis from then on. In 2010, just after Bourn left, the Office for Budget Responsibility (OBR) took over the function. Robertson argued that "I would say that a major reason why the OBR exists is because we did that work" (James Robertson, interview). Confidence in the NAO transferred to confidence in a mechanism which has underpinned the scrutiny of the budget process ever since (so much so that when it did not happen in 2022, it caused, in part, the fall of a Prime Minister, Liz Truss).

The second of these developments was Bourn's appointment as Advisor to the Prime Minister on ministerial interests. Blair said in the Commons that he appointed Bourn due to his "impartiality and integrity" which were "beyond reproach" (House of Commons, 2006). Bourn conducted no investigations in this role; he was replaced when Blair resigned in 2007 but his appointment demonstrated the confidence that others had in the credibility of the NAO and the C&AG (Armstrong and Rhodes, 2023, p. 39). However, this appointment had the potential to involve Bourn directly in political controversy about ministerial conduct, something that might have called into question the NAO's relationship with the government or its perceived independence. Nor did Bourn consult the Public Accounts Commission as to whether he should accept this role, despite TPAC's role in the scrutiny of C&AGs (David Heald, interview).

Secondly, as in the 1990s, the NAO continued to innovate its methods for value for money studies in the New Labour years. The NAO through the 2000s was trying, as in the 1990s, to improve coverage of the perspective of the users of public services. The NAO continued to use focus groups and study visits when looking at services in which members of the public engaged with government: examples included the audits of children's centres (C&AG, 2006), of end-of-life care (C&AG, 2008) and of mothers' experiences of neo-natal care (C&AG, 2007). Sometimes, as in the case of the NAO's study on the complexity of the benefits system, focus groups might be directed at those who advised the benefit claimant through the system rather than the claimant themselves (C&AG, 2005b).

The NAO also used surveys: sometimes as in the case of the Indian Ocean Tsunami these were confined to those actually involved in a disaster or crisis (NAO, 2006) but at other times, as in the NAO's study of blood donations, the NAO would commission a survey of the general public (C&AG, 2000d). The NAO's reports show engagement with other literatures: for example, citing academic journals to prove that the benefits system was overly complex (C&AG, 2005b, p. 9) or comparing systems for compensating victims of crime to those developed in insurance companies for payment of claims for personal injuries (C&AG, 2000c). The NAO also published more international comparative work: for example, in education, from 2003, the NAO published its analysis of the UK's performance against nine other comparable countries (NAO, 2003, 2006a).

The NAO sponsored international conferences on methodology, and Bourn proudly proclaimed that 'when V[alue] F[or] M[oney] started, methodologies came from economics, statistics or/and management. Methodologies now come from psychology, political science, and many other subjects including for us, biology and botany' (Bourn, 1998a). The NAO began to cooperate with external organisations more: for example, developing the use of operational research methods in value-for-money studies alongside RAND Europe and academics at the LSE (Bechberger et al., 2011). These techniques were directed at trying to assess effectiveness. A lot of these developments came from the staff within the NAO rather than from Bourn himself, but Bourn gave permission for value for money to develop (Neil Sayers, interview). Many reports though continued to examine traditional topics in traditional ways; for example, a 2005 report on working with the third sector did involve the NAO cooperating with external organisations but purely focused on internal government processes and departmental working practices (C&AG, 2005f).

Michael Whitehouse said that Bourn was a 'neo-liberal' who was fascinated by Hayek and his criticisms of big, centralised, bureaucracies and consequently saw his role at the NAO as 'constantly bringing new challenges to the state' about how it delivered its services. A new focus on public services can be seen in the NAO's reporting: under Downey, 19% of the NAO's value-for-money reports concerned defence, but in Blair's first term, only 12% of the NAO's reports focussed on defence. (By 2019–23, this had dropped to 7%.) This shift to examining domestic government was held back by Bourn's natural interest in defence, but it was something that those inside the NAO especially the defence team were aware of (David Clarke, interview). It also made the drive to assess effectiveness better more urgent.

The changes to methodology had consequences for the NAO's reports which often, due to this focus on the user, could be very influential. For example, the NAO's 2005 report on stroke care used a variety of different methods to argue that stroke should be taken much more seriously by the NHS (C&AG, 2005a). The report included an economic analysis of the costs of stroke care to the entire UK health and social care system, a survey of GPs about the importance they accorded to stroke care and an analysis of the Department of Health data. The NAO report had a huge effect. As Alex Scharaschkin[36] said:

> the 'Act Fast' campaign which was about recognising the signs of a stroke, face, arms, speech came from the recommendations of that study. One of the biggest things you could do to reduce harms from stroke was to get it treated as the same emergency as a heart attack. For stroke, it's the equivalent thing to a heart attack for a brain, and some of the treatments work very well but you have to get to patients quickly enough.
>
> *(Alex Scharaschkin, interview)*

The NAO had successfully raised the profile of a condition that affected millions of people within the NHS using a multi-method approach to show both that intervention could be justified and that government action could achieve value for money. Significantly, this focus on effectiveness meant that the NAO was extending the way in which value for money itself could be seen: no longer a pure economical approach, value for money could be used to justify extending spending or government action. Other reports shared this wider sense of value for money: for example, the NAO's report on benefit complexity stressed the cost to the citizen rather than the gain for the government from the complexity that successive governments had designed into benefits (C&AG, 2005b, pp. 9–10).

The new approach to value for money spread into the study of regulation. Regulation had been part of the NAO's remit since the government in the 1980s and 1990s privatised the regulated industries. The first real studies which examined regulation came before the 1997 election, but it was still not seen as significant within the NAO itself (C&AG, 1993, 1996,

1996a). When Ed Humpherson[37] initially applied for a managerial role on the regulation team, he was told that 'I must be mad to do regulation and that it was a backwater' (Ed Humpherson, interview). Over time, the team rose in prestige and covered more areas. Alex Scharaschkin pointed out that the audit of the regulated industries expanded: the NAO continued looking at the regulated industries which focussed on the recently privatised industries, but it also broadened out, examining the regulation of industries which were not privatised such as banking (Alex Scharaschkin, interview). This trend started in the late 1990s and early 2000s when the regulated utilities 'were kind of encountering the first wave of competition' (Ed Humpherson, interview).

Emphasis on users and improving the quality of regulation allowed further innovation in what value for money actually meant. As Alex Scharaschkin recalled, the emphasis on regulation to achieve value for money led the NAO to think of the economy of services in terms of not just their cost to the government but also the cost to taxpayers as service users (Alex Scharaschkin, interview). As Ed Humpherson suggested, the NAO were concerned with 'how does regulation protect the interests of consumers' (Ed Humpherson, interview). The audit of regulation therefore represented a move conceptually in what value for money meant: regulation, as it involved minimal spending of public money, was an area that could only be justified through examining its impact and also through examining the cost of the policy to consumers rather than to just the cost to the Exchequer. NAO studies on regulation argued that the regulators needed to understand effectiveness properly to achieve value for money. In 2002, a report on the regulation of postal services in the UK argued that without 'information on what really matters to customers', it would be hard for the postal regulator, POSTCOMM to effectively regulate (C&AG, 2002a, p. 9). A follow-up report told the House of Commons that the regulator still was not regulating what customers were interested in: 'The current system does not, however, measure all the aspects of quality that are important to consumers. For example, the highest number of complaints to Royal Mail concern loss of mail. Yet this is not measured' (C&AG, 2006a, p. 4). The NAO drily noted that the regulator of the postal services excluded Christmas deliveries from its consideration of customer issues with the mail (C&AG, 2006a, p. 4). However, they also went further: NAO studies suggested that government should be looking to minimise the costs to consumers as well as to itself. Hence, for example, a 2006 study looking at the regulation of markets in which target prices had been removed, focussed on whether citizens were actually able to choose between different tariffs (C&AG, 2008a).

Thirdly, the last major development in value for money's scope in this period related to the NAO's ambition for this form of audit. Michael Whitehouse said that

> the second stage of Bourn's development [after 1997] as C&AG was that he began to ask the question that I keep writing these reports that identify failure but how can the NAO respond to systemic issues which explain those failures.
>
> *(Michael Whitehouse, interview)*

Whitehouse argued that this was a response to the way that government itself was developing then and to Lord Sharman's recommendation that a public sector auditor should be an advisor as well as a scrutineer of public policy.

Therefore, the NAO started producing reports which identified good practice in the public sector. These reports were framed explicitly with the thought that they were 'not about the failures of the past' but were 'about the opportunities of the present' (C&AG, 1999, p.1). Examples of this trend included reports on issues like procurement and risk management which sought to learn from good practice in both the public and private sectors (C&AG, 1999b, 2000b). This was followed by other similar pieces of work that sought to identify lessons about systemic issues in the public sector (C&AG, 2002c, 2006c). In 2001, the NAO published a report on joined-up government which drew on academic work to suggest that

> many of the most difficult issues faced by society – drug abuse, social deprivation, juvenile crime and inner-city decline cut across traditional departmental responsibilities. They require a co-ordinated and combined response by departments, local authorities and other bodies in delivering public services.
>
> *(C&AG, 2001a, p. 1)*

The point of these reports was to highlight lessons that departments could learn from each other. A 2006 report on digital projects in the public sector put this best: the NAO wrote that its report was 'about success; how IT-enabled change can be got right' and highlighted 24 case studies from within the public and private sectors of when this had happened (C&AG, 2006c, p. 4). These reports would identify international comparisons as well to try and stimulate change: an NAO report in 2002 on e-government identified that whereas in the UK 52% of government services were online, in Germany the comparable figure was 59% (C&AG, 2002c, p. 3). The NAO's reports on PFI that we discussed above fit into this category too. The NAO followed up on this work: providing assessments and recommendations which flowed from report to report. For example, the NAO's 2004 study on risk management in government drew on and identified progress from the position they had described in 2000 whilst providing further case studies for improvement (C&AG, 2004).

The NAO's growing confidence in itself and political pressures (described in our section on the organisational context of the office) provide the impetus for value for money to continue to evolve. As we have seen, it did this in three directions. Firstly, the NAO grew in confidence and reported on controversial issues such as the Iraq War. Secondly, it continued to innovate methodologically and to focus on the effectiveness of public services and in regulation even began to include costs to the consumer as part of its assessment of their economy. Thirdly and lastly, it took on Sharman's point and began to try and identify broader lessons from its work. Cumulatively, in his two periods as C&AG, Bourn, according to those who served at the NAO, 'didn't invent value for money audit but he pushed it forward' (Neil Sayers, interview).

5.5.2 Financial audit

The NAO's financial audit during the latter part of John Bourn's time as C&AG continued in many ways from where it had been in the 1990s. The NAO had to respond to the implementation of resource accounting from 2000 onwards which caused issues both for itself and for departments. The implementation of resource accounting was supposed to be accompanied by innovation in how departmental performance was reported to Parliament. This began to take place under Bourn but as we shall see did not evolve in the ways that Bourn and Sharman had envisaged. Resource accounting was therefore only ever partially implemented and remained from the viewpoint of Bourn an incomplete project.

The transition to resource accounting was complex. The Treasury launched resource accounting in 1994, but full implementation waited several years. In 1997–8, departments produced resource accounts parallel to their appropriation accounts for the first time, but these were not audited. In 1998–9, departments again produced resource accounts, and this time they were audited but unpublished. In 1999–2000 and 2000–2001, departments produced two sets of accounts, both of which were audited and published, and in 2001–2 resource accounts were produced for the first time alone (Heald, 2005, p. 165). The NAO reported to Parliament about its review of the first audited (but unpublished) accounts and the first year of published resource accounting. In this report, Bourn declared that he remained 'concerned at an over reliance on too few key personnel and a lack of technically competent supporting staff in departments to prepare accounts' (C&AG, 2001b, p. 1).

The NAO received 52 accounts for 1998–9 (audited but not published): the C&AG qualified his opinion on 30 of them including three where he gave a 'nil opinion', where the 'accounts were insufficiently developed to offer an audit opinion' (C&AG, 2001b, p. 25). Due to changes in departmental boundaries, 49 accounts were eventually laid for the first year of resource accounts: of these only 12 were qualified (C&AG, 2001b, p. 26, 2002, p. 13). The following year, Bourn noted that the accounts submitted to him were improving but was concerned about 'the time taken to prepare and render accounts for audit' (C&AG, 2002, p. 1).

Resource accounting exposed problems in departments which did not keep good records. Richard Bacon referred to 'explosive' findings from PAC sessions involving resource accounts such as the discovery of fraud in the British Embassy in Tel Aviv that had gone undetected for 17 years and the loss of satellite phones by the Foreign Office (Richard Bacon, interview; C&AG, 2005d, pp. 48–50, 2006d, pp. 57–60). Mark Etherton said to us that the Tel Aviv incident was an example of 'why you should look at the accounts of an embassy, quite seriously' (Mark Etherton, interview).

The most significant problems though occurred at the Home Office where Bourn reported in 2006 that for the year 2004–5, the 'pervasive and fundamental nature of the problems encountered in my audit of the Home Office's accounts for 2004-5 mean that I am unable to reach an opinion as to whether they [the accounts] show a true and fair view' (C&AG, 2006e, p. 28). Sir John Gieve,[38] Permanent Secretary for the year for which the accounts were prepared, attended the PAC and said he was 'mortified' that the department had got into this position (PAC, 2006a, Q128). Bourn worried that the NAO might not detect such cases: musing that the 'arrogance of inexperience' affected some senior civil servants and might lead them to undervalue corporate governance (Bourn, 2001a). The early years of resource accounting were therefore made up of an effort by the NAO to actually get departments into a position where their accounts would technically comply and to make them take corporate governance seriously. It is in this context that the NAO began issuing what was called the C&AG's general report, which summarised the progress of departments in delivering their accounts on time. This ceased publication in 2004, a decision regretted by the Public Affairs and Constitutional Committee some 13 years later (PACAC 2017, p. 40)

The technical challenge of resource accounting had consequences for the NAO's audit too. Sharman concluded in his review of audit and accountability that 'the technical quality of the C&AG's work is probably not something that parliamentary committees are best placed to comment on' and recommended more technical scrutiny of the NAO's audit(Sharman, 2001, p. 55). The NAO accepted Sharman's recommendation, and the Joint Monitoring Unit's (the unit was at that time responsible for monitoring the quality of audit work undertaken by member firms of the Institutes for Chartered Accountants in England and Wales, Scotland and Ireland) first visit to the NAO took place in 2002 (C&AG, 2002d, p. 25). That decision had huge consequences for his successors. Initially, though, this decision and the NAO's investment in its technical financial audit capability put it into a position of primacy on financial accounting amongst UK public sector auditors. By 2004, experienced insiders at the Audit Commission noted that 'the NAO had come much more to the fore on the technical accounting side' (Campbell-Smith, 2008, p. 565).

Resource accounting though was only a partial revolution. For Bourn, resource accounting had to, as discussed in the previous chapter, help reveal departmental underperformance. He warned financial auditors that 'accounting will be politicised as resource accounts come in e.g., the showing of contingent liabilities for medical insurance claims something previously obscured by income and expenditure accounts' (Bourn, 1998). He was concerned that 'creative accounting . . . is so much more possible under resource accounting' (Bourn, 2001a). This warning should not be seen as an argument against resource accounting: Bourn's advocacy for resource accounting was based upon an argument that accounting should be more political. Hence, he thought that resource accounting should be accompanied by validated reporting on the performance of departments. Bourn's position was influential in Parliament.

The PAC stated in 1998 that 'if we are to have good, clear accounts for the public sector, we also need to have a similar system of good, clear performance information to go with it' (PAC, 1998[39]). After the 1997 election, the PAC and the Treasury Select Committee endorsed his view that the NAO should validate this performance information in accounts (PAC, 1998; Treasury Select Committee, 1998; PAC, 2000a, p. 127).

The Treasury Committee stated that all of the witnesses they had heard from were in favour of performance metrics published alongside accounts being audited (Treasury Committee, 1998). Sharman agreed. In his report, Sharman suggested a phased implementation of performance reporting:

> The move to regular performance reporting for departments is a very important step in improving accountability, and there should be external validation of departmental information systems as a first step in a process towards validation of key published data.
>
> *(Sharman, 2001, p. 2)*

The government accepted this staged approach. For Sharman, Bourn and the select committees, the key point was that validating the data systems underpinning performance metrics in the accounts was always a first step to the NAO validating the data itself. Even after the government had accepted Sharman's first stage, MPs continued to insist that their eventual aim was that the published performance metrics should be subject to 'independent assessment by the National Audit Office of whether and how far targets have been met' (Public Administration Committee, 2003, p. 4).

The vehicle for this audit of performance were the Public Service Agreement targets. Gordon Brown as chancellor of the Exchequer introduced these agreements between departments and the Treasury in 1998, setting out indicators that departments would seek to achieve, though the number of indicators was reduced in 2000 and in 2002 (Gay, 2005). Initially, the government envisaged that these agreements would be subjected to audit by the executive (Treasury, 1998). The government's response to Sharman's recommendation about the audit of the data systems underpinning performance data grudgingly allowed that 'there should be some form of external validation of data systems which relate to these targets' and said they would ask the C&AG to perform the role (Treasury, 2002, p. 2). The government chose not to respond to Sharman and Bourn's suggestion that the data itself should be validated by the NAO eventually. The process of validating the data started in the NAO after the Treasury's response: in 2004, the NAO published its first compendium report assessing the quality of the data systems supporting Public Service Agreements (C&AG, 2005e). However, the reports on the data systems underpinning Public Service Agreements were never linked to the accounts: they were published separately, and the NAO never moved into auditing the actual data as Bourn, the PAC, the Treasury Committee, the Public Administration Committee and Sharman had initially intended. Consequently, the type of holistic audit and accounts covering both finance and performance envisaged by Bourn and Sharman never came to pass.

Parliament did not stop pressing for more. In 2009, just after Bourn had left office, the Public Administration Committee reported on good government in the UK. Tony Wright,[40] the chair of the committee, was an influential advocate for the power of Parliament, and his reforms became the basis for the select committee reforms of 2010. The committee took evidence about the NAO from a number of commentators including Sir Michael Bichard, Professor Colin Talbot[41] and Sir John Bourn. The committee endorsed Bourn's view that the NAO should provide a more 'rounded type of performance assessment' for government departments and suggested that it should become the 'National Accountability Office' (Public Administration Committee, 2009, pp. 39–40). Bourn by this point had left, but the Public Administration Committee's report marked the culmination of thinking that had been going on inside and outside the NAO about how to extend financial and value-for-money audit to present a more holistic view of government accountability.

By the time of Bourn's resignation, resource accounting was in place in central government as was validation of the data systems underpinning reporting against public service agreement targets. But validation of performance data had not happened, and the NAO reported on data systems separately to its report on accounts. Bourn's vision of audit reporting which would bring together an assessment of financial and non-financial performance for departments remained only a legacy left to his successors to implement if they chose to: as he said in 2009, 'you could, as it were, do an analysis of the strengths and weaknesses of a department in the round. It was one of the things we were thinking about before I left and I think my successors will want to consider it' (Public Administration Committee, 2009a, Q51).

5.5.3 The government's advisor

The Sharman report had another consequence for the NAO and its relationship with government. After 1997, the government was concerned about the NAO's critique of new policies. In 1999, the Cabinet Office argued that 'audit and inspection processes may hinder cross cutting work' within government (Cabinet Office, 1999, p. 23) In the following year, the Cabinet Office (2000, p. 53) stated that 'there is a widely held perception, for example, that auditors and scrutiny bodies will criticise departments for undertaking new and risky policies'. Lord Bichard, Permanent Secretary for the Department for Education and Employment between 1995 and 2001,[42] said that when he was a permanent secretary, he was often frustrated that the NAO 'weren't giving enough attention to the positives, the good practice, and ensuring that that was communicated across government' (Lord Bichard, interview). Bourn saw challenges to the NAO emerging out of the increasing number of regulators and auditors elsewhere: he told an NAO conference that as these bodies increased, 'Ministers increasingly want their own [auditor] and we shall have to show that we are best' (Bourn, 1998).

In meeting this challenge, Sharman became part of a discussion about how the role of the public sector auditor should evolve. The 1983 Act had been clear that the NAO's main purpose was to hold government to account to Parliament for what it had spent. In response to criticisms about auditors' attitudes to reform, the NAO joined with the other public sector auditors in the UK to form the Public Audit Forum. The forum issued a statement in 1999, which set out what it considered audit in the public sector should do. Auditors should be, according to the Public Audit Forum,

> consistent with their independent role, providing advice and encouragement to managers implementing Modernising Government initiatives by drawing on their audit work in this area, seeking to identify and promote good practice so that experience can be shared and risks minimised.
>
> *(Cabinet Office, 1999, p. 39)*

In Sharman's report, he defined two roles for the auditor: a traditional accountability role and a role which was far more related to advising government:

> External audit of public money is undertaken primarily from the perspective of the watchdog – designed to provide assurance that taxpayers' money has been well spent – but to make the most of the work, auditors should seek to combine this role with that of advisor in ways that do not compromise independence.
>
> *(Sharman, 2001, p. 1)*

Sharman's assertion of the advisor role sat more naturally with the Audit Commission, who performed the role of regulating, acting as an external expert and sharing best practice (Kelly, 2003). The Commission's work functioned as a 'good spur' to the NAO especially 'because what the Audit Commission were excellent at doing, was producing reports that were easily digestible' (James Robertson, interview). However, the NAO itself shifted in the way it defined itself and its purposes.

The NAO's annual reports reflected Sharman's language: in 2004, the NAO said that it had two objectives:

> The formal statutory duty to provide independent information, assurance and advice to parliament on the use of public resources and a wider role helping to promote better financial management and value for money and to improve public services.
>
> *(NAO, 2004, p. 2)*

This contrasts sharply with the attitude of figures like David Myland in the 1980s (referred to in a previous chapter) who largely disdained an advisory role for the NAO. Bourn recognised that the traditional image of the auditor meant that the NAO's attempts to get impact from advice 'starts from a "one down position"' (Bourn, 1999a). The NAO continued to present figures on its financial impact arising both from value-for-money audit and from financial audit; by the early 2000s, these were independently audited by the NAO's external auditor. The NAO tried to raise its impact, increasing to 9 to 1 and then 10 to 1. The New Labour period had subtly changed the rhetoric on the NAO's independence from government, shifting it more in the direction that Howe had envisaged in 1983 of the government's advisor rather than the backbenchers' advocate.

The change in rhetoric did not stop accountability work (see the audit scope section below), but it did have consequences. Lonsdale (2008) argued that increasingly value-for-money studies were chosen by the NAO to reflect the priorities and needs of those that they audited as well as fulfil their accountability role (which was a given), helping to ensure that the studies had more impact because they reflected real problems facing civil servants.

As an example, in 2004, the NAO published a review of asylum data and statistics (C&AG, 2004). The NAO acknowledged in public that they had done the study at the request of the Home Office, and privately Bourn wrote that the terms of reference had even been set by the government (C&AG, 2004, p. 2; Bourn, 2004). Lonsdale recalled carrying out another piece of work on estimates of pensions lifetime allowances again at the behest of government (C&AG, 2004a) (Jeremy Lonsdale, interview). Clearance continued to be a way that the civil service could seek to influence value-for-money studies. As part of the ongoing intellectualisation of the NAO's work, staff started to think about what clearance lent their reports. Scharaschkin (2011) distinguished NAO work from the work of academics in the social sciences because although it used many of the same types of techniques, reports were the product of 'argument games' between the department concerned and NAO, and these games formed the basis for assertions of the validity of the underlying report.

Lonsdale (2008) argued similarly that clearance 'dictates that auditors must have robust evidence capable of withstanding challenge' and noted that this meant NAO reports remained resolutely empirical. A greater role intellectually and practically for departmental involvement in reports did end up with some departments exploiting their ability to delay the work of the NAO. Lonsdale described some departments indulging in 'deliberately obstructive behaviour' during clearance which 'affected our ability to churn stuff out and to budget for staff time and meet planned publication dates for reports' (Jeremy Lonsdale, interview). At one point, David Clarke recalled that the MOD attempted to claim that the number of Tornadoes in the Royal Air Force was classified although it had been declared to the Russians (David Clarke, interview)! Despite such behaviour, the NAO's advisor role gave an extra reason for auditors to respond positively to clearance comments: auditors would only be listened to if they had avoided annoying the client in the meantime (Sharma, 2007).

The newer role of government advisor and concerns about how to audit risky policies came together in the audit of the Private Finance Initiative (PFI). PFI was a policy which originated under the Conservatives but was expanded by Labour after 1997 (Hellowell, 2010). A PFI project involved the public sector contracting with a project company for the design, build, finance and operation of a building (or another asset) over a period of 30 years. The project company attracted investment and borrowed money to build and maintain the asset, and the repayments included both the costs of their financing of the deal and the costs of the construction and maintenance of the asset. Commentators saw it as a mechanism by which

Labour could construct new assets for the public sector without increasing the debt owed by government, as much of the PFI debt remained 'off balance sheet' (Hellowell, 2010).

The NAO began reporting on PFI deals just after the election of the new Labour government in 1997, but these early reports focussed on deals signed by the Conservative government such as the Skye Bridge (C&AG, 1997).

The perspective that the NAO adopted in its reports on PFI was not to criticise the mechanism but to identify lessons for the future. Unusually, this first report on a PFI project opened with a preface by the C&AG, in which he said that 'from their previous work both the National Audit Office and the Committee of Public Accounts are familiar with the problems which have arisen from more traditional procurement methods. We and others have been greatly interested in how successful the initiative would be in addressing such problems' (C&AG, 1997, unpaginated). The C&AG explained that the intention of the NAO's report was to identify

> several general lessons which departments and others will wish to consider for future privately financed projects. My intention is that the National Audit Office will continue to keep the initiative under review, so that these ideas can be added to and if necessary elaborated over time.
>
> *(C&AG, 1997, unpaginated)*

This tone was not unusual for reports on PFI. In 1999, the C&AG summarised the first set of reports on PFI: in his preface, Bourn argued that whilst PFI 'offers the prospect of better value for money than traditional publicly financed methods', it brought with it 'new pitfalls and new risks to value for money' (C&AG, 1999, unpaginated). NAO reports offered themselves as sources of advice to the public sector about 'key issues which authorities need to keep in mind when developing and managing relationships with private sector PFI contractors' (C&AG, 2001, p. 1).

The NAO's approach did have an impact. In 1997, the NAO submitted evidence to the Labour government about the operation of PFI and the government accepted all of the auditor's points (Bowerman et al., 2003, p. 7). A further example comes from the refinancing of PFI deals. One of the big issues on PFI deals in the 1990s was that when a project was initially financed by the private sector, it was done so with a long loan at a high interest rate. After the building was built, the rate at which banks would lend to the project company fell, and when they refinanced the loan, the project company and its shareholders received a windfall (Shaoul et al., 2006, 2008). The NAO highlighted this issue across a number of reports during the 1990s and early 2000s (C&AG, 2000a, 2002b, 2005c,

2006b). The Treasury eventually negotiated a clawback mechanism by which some of the gains from refinancing the deals returned to the private sector. However, in the 2010s, this was later abandoned in order to maintain the off-balance sheet nature of PFI deals (PACAC, 2018, p. 18).

The relationship of advisor and government did not always work well because the NAO was always concerned about appearing to be too close to government. For example, in the report about asylum statistics cited above, Bourn was concerned to steer between 'the Scylla of too much criticism of the government and the Charybdis of appearing to play to the gallery' (Bourn, 2004).[43] This concern was seen as well in the development of resource accounting. As already noted, resource accounting was proposed in the mid-1990s, and implementation then took place across the late 1990s into the early 2000s. Bourn was supportive of resource accounting with caveats. The NAO therefore took a supportive role with regard to it. Nevertheless, it had to reconcile its two roles as advisor and watchdog within this context. Sir Andrew Likierman told us of the frustrations he had in dealing with the NAO as it played these two different roles.

> Quite often I would get a rather blank answer from the NAO: saying in effect 'We don't know. You sort it out.' The clear implication was that the onus was on the Treasury to take the initiative. Only after we had done so would they comment. And you could argue, that's absolutely fine – it's not their role to decide such issues. It's their role to audit what emerges as a policy. But at the time, when the Government was developing something completely new, the NAO's notion that 'We're going to stand back from that' was not very helpful. It would have been better if they had got more involved, but it could be that the NAO did not want to be captured by the Treasury and lose their independence.
>
> *(Sir Andrew Likierman, interview)*

Martin Sinclair, viewing the same exchanges, said that he felt that the NAO's involvement in these discussions was 'what would naturally have been expected of an external auditor in the process, in that we only ever provided an auditor's views and opinion on proposals put to us by HMT and Departments' (Martin Sinclair, interview). Likierman's discussion of the NAO's role in standing back and refusing to be captured by the Treasury represents the disappointment of someone who could, justifiably based on the NAO's rhetoric, have expected more help from the auditor. NAO auditors keeping strictly to their line on independence, in this case, reduced their impact as advisors to the government.

In the cases of PFI and resource accounting, there were risks that the NAO would be perceived as endorsing the government's initiatives. Academics subsequently have criticised the NAO's work on PFI (Aldred,

2008; Smyth and Whitfield, 2017, p. 54). This was not the only occasion on which the NAO risked getting too close to government and appeared to endorse the government's approach to an issue. The NAO, for example, wrote that the Financial Services Authority was a 'highly regarded' regulator whose 'risk-based approach is increasingly seen as a model to follow by other regulators' (C&AG, 2007a, p. 5). This report was immediately followed by one of the largest financial crises in British history. Being an advisor built influence and helped protect the NAO, but it also brought risks.

5.6 Tim Burr

Bourn was replaced by Tim Burr. Burr had been deputy C&AG and was appointed C&AG between 2008 and 2009, that is, from the point at which Bourn resigned to the appointment of Amyas Morse. Burr was a 'full' C&AG: as Richard Bacon, then a member of the PAC, said, 'There is no post of acting C&AG' (interview, Richard Bacon). However, when he took up the role, his remit was clearly to keep the NAO functioning after John Bourn's resignation. The appointment was publicly acknowledged to be temporary and cover the period until a new C&AG could be appointed. Ed Humpherson, who was on the senior management team at the time, told us that

> Tim Burr's goal was to try to hold everything together. He wanted to stop the organisation going down further and steady the ship. He was an incredibly clever man, and he was driven by not wanting to put a foot wrong on his watch, and consequently it felt to me that it was sometimes difficult to get things done.
>
> *(Ed Humpherson, interview)*

Burr's risk aversion was reasonable in the context of his appointment. The NAO had suffered publicly because of the press stories about Bourn's expenses and questions had been raised in Parliament. It had also lost credibility with departments. Burr's task therefore as C&AG was a simple one: to ensure that the NAO was in a reasonable position to be handed on to his successor, who after an appointment exercise was Amyas Morse. Burr made it 'quite clear that he didn't apply' (Neil Sayers, interview). It was for Morse and his senior team to move on from the achievements of Bourn perhaps in different directions.

5.7 Chapter summary

The chapter examined the latter half of Bourn's time as C&AG from 1997 to 2008 during the New Labour government, through considering both the political context and categories of regulatory space concerning organisational context, capacities and audit scope.

Through this chapter and the previous one, it has been shown that Bourn's centrality to the history of the NAO between 1988 and 2008 cannot be overstated. For outsiders, Bourn *was* the NAO: Richard Bacon argued that 'he built it – that the NAO was the way it was, was down to John Bourn'. Internally, as Dunleavy et al. (2009) suggests, Bourn was the dominant figure within the NAO.

Bourn's dominance in the NAO had both good and bad effects: he was able to obtain funding from Parliament for a massive extension in the NAO's budget over his reign and to extend the remit of both value-for-money and financial audit. His NAO reframed what it meant by value-for-money audit: expanding on the work performed in the 1990s with regard to effectiveness so that in studies like the NAO's work on stroke care, the NAO had a discernible impact on the way in which services were run for individuals on the ground. Value-for-money work was increasingly influential in government: while Bourn never lost his appetite for what Michael Whitehouse described as the 'red meat' of parliamentary accountability, he was also much more attuned in the late 1990s and 2000s to the requirement, after Sharman, to advise government as well as holding the government to account.

As an advisor, the NAO promoted resource accounting, successfully implemented across government during the 2000s but did so in the context of a commitment to extending performance reporting at the same time which did not happen.

However, Bourn's vision of the NAO was dependent on his own presence as C&AG to steer the NAO through troubled political waters. For example, he preserved the public sector nature of the NAO's audit whilst allowing the NAO to be monitored by the private sector's audit regulator by chairing the relevant regulatory board. Similarly, value-for-money audit's extent was never codified: Bourn never liked to constrain NAO's value-for-money work through defining the terms used in the 1983 Act: Bourn held the roles of advisor and agent of accountability in balance and sought to extend the NAO's work into effectiveness, but there was no guarantee that a successor would see the role in the same way that he had. There were gaps even when Bourn was in charge: the NAO was publicly embarrassed when the occasional inadequacies of its work were exposed at the PAC.

Nevertheless, the innate flexibility of the NAO's founding settlement in 1983 ensured that Bourn could shape the organisation to his will, but it also ensured that the foundations he left could be built upon and changed.

Notes

1 Tim Burr, 1950–, HMT 1986–94, Treasury Officer of Accounts 1993–4, Assistant Auditor General 1994–2000, DC&AG 2000–8, C&AG 2008–9,

Member, South Downs Park Authority 2017–19, Deputy Chair, South Downs Park Authority 2020–.

2 Interestingly, despite having a highly developed political sense, Bourn never voted in any election (private information).

3 Elizabeth Filkin, 1940–, Parliamentary Commissioner for Standards 1999–2002. She was invited to be reapply for her role as Parliamentary Commissioner in 2002 rather than being automatically reappointed.

4 David Ramsbotham, 1934–2022, HM Chief Inspector of Prisons for England and Wales 1995–2001, Knighted 1987, created Lord Ramsbotham 2005.

5 Sheldon had to stand down because he was a Labour MP. Conventionally, the Chair of the Committee always is a member of the opposition, so after Labour won the 1997 election, a Conservative MP had to be the chair.

6 David Davis, MP for Boothferry and Haltemprice and Howden, 1987–, Chair of the PAC 1997–2001, Chairman of the Conservative Party 2001–2, Shadow Secretary of State for the Office of the Deputy Prime Minister 2002–3, Shadow Home Secretary 2003–8, Secretary of State for Exiting the European Union 2016–18. Knighted 2024.

7 Edward Leigh, MP for Gainsborough and Gainsborough and Horncastle, 1983–, Chair Public Accounts Committee 2001–10, Chair Public Accounts Commission 2010–17. Knighted 2013.

8 Mark Etherton, Clerk to the Public Accounts Committee.

9 George Osborne, MP for Tatton 2001–17, Shadow Chancellor 2005–10, Chancellor of the Exchequer 2010–16, First Secretary of State 2015–16.

10 Frank Field, 1942–, MP for Birkenhead 1979–2019, Member Public Accounts Committee 2002–5, Chair Work and Pensions Select Committee 2015–19, Created Lord Field 2020.

11 Charles Clarke, 1950–, MP for Norwich South 1997–2010, Minister without Portfolio and Chair of the Labour Party 2001–2, Secretary of State for Education and Skills 2002–4, Home Secretary 2004–6.

12 John Reid, 1947–, MP for Motherwell North, Hamilton North and Bellshill and Airdrie and Shotts 1987–2010, Secretary of State for Scotland 1999–2001, Secretary of State for Northern Ireland 2001–2, Minister without Portfolio and Chair of the Labour Party 2002–3, Leader of the House of Commons and Lord President of the Council 2003, Secretary of State for Health 2003–5, Secretary of State for Defence 2005–6, Home Secretary 2006–7, created Lord Reid 2010.

13 Jon Trickett, 1950–, MP for Hemsworth 1996–, Public Accounts Committee member 2001–6, Shadow Secretary of State for Communities and Local Government 2015–16, Shadow Secretary of State for Business, Innovation and Skills 2016, Shadow Lord President of the Council 2016–20, Shadow Minister for the Cabinet Office 2017–20.

14 Greg Clark, 1967–, MP for Tunbridge Wells 2005–, Shadow Secretary of State for Energy and Climate Change 2008–10, Secretary of State for Communities and Local Government 2015–16, President of the Board of Trade 2016, Secretary of State for Business, Energy, Trade and Industrial Strategy 2016–19, Chair of the Science and Technology Select Committee 2020–22, Secretary of State for Levelling Up 2022, Chair of the Science and Technology Select Committee 2022–.

15 Alan Williams, 1930–2014, MP for Swansea West 1964–2010, Shadow Secretary of State for Wales 1987–9, Member Public Accounts Committee 1989–2010, Chair of the Public Accounts Commission 2001–10.

16 Nick Wright, 1960–, Clerk to the Public Accounts Committee.

17 Private information.

18 Donald Dewar, 1937–2000, MP for Aberdeen South, Glasgow Garscadden and Glasgow Anniesland 1966–70, 1978–2000, MSP for Glasgow Anniesland 1999–2000, Shadow Secretary of State for Scotland 1983–92, Shadow Secretary of State for Social Security 1992–5, Shadow Chief Whip 1995–7, Secretary of State for Scotland 1997–9, First Minister of Scotland and Leader of the Labour Party in Scotland 1999–2000.
19 Peter Hain, 1950–, MP for Neath 1991–2015, Secretary of State for Wales 2002–8, 2009–10, Leader of the House of Commons and Lord Privy Seal 2003–5, Secretary of State for Northern Ireland 2005–7, Secretary of State for Work and Pensions 2007–8, Shadow Secretary of State for Wales 2010–12, created Lord Hain 2015.
20 Sean Connery, 1930–2020, actor.
21 Kirsty Wark, 1958–, BBC journalist.
22 John Humphries 1943–, BBC journalist.
23 Robert Black, 1946–2021, Chief Executive Stirling Council 1985–90, Chief Executive Tayside Council 1990–5, Controller of Audit, Accounts Commission in Scotland 1995–2000, Auditor General for Scotland 2000–2012.
24 Jeremy Colman, 1948–, National Audit Office 1993–2005 including a period as Assistant Auditor General, Auditor General for Wales 2005–10.
25 Huw Vaughan Thomas, 1948–, Chief Executive Gwynedd County Council, 1991–6, Denbighshire County Council 1996–2001, Auditor General for Wales 2010–18.
26 Owing to the asymmetrical nature of devolution in the UK, the UK Parliament ran at different points in time, public services for England, for England and Wales and at times for the entire UK.
27 Jack Straw, 1946–, MP for Blackburn 1979–2015, Shadow Education Secretary 1987–92, Shadow Home Secretary 1994–7, Home Secretary 1997–2001, Foreign Secretary 2001–6, Leader of the House of Commons and Lord Privy Seal 2006–7, Lord Chancellor and Secretary of State for Justice 2007–10, Shadow Deputy Prime Minister and Shadow Secretary of State for Justice 2010.
28 David Bell, 1959–, Chief Inspector of Ofsted 2002–6, Permanent Secretary, Department for Education 2006–12. Knighted 2007.
29 William Cash, 1940–, MP for Stafford and Stone 1984–, Shadow Attorney General 2001–3, Shadow Secretary of State for Constitutional Affairs 2003, Chair of the European Scrutiny Committee 2010–. Knighted 2014.
30 Colin Sharman, 1943–, Chairman of KPMG 1997–9 and other business posts subsequently, created Lord Sharman 1999.
31 The correspondence was released by the NAO, but the individual's name is redacted.
32 Alistair Darling, 1953–2023, MP for Edinburgh South West and Edinburgh Central 1987–2015, Shadow Chief Secretary to the Treasury 1996–7, Chief Secretary to the Treasury 1997–8, Secretary of State for Work and Pensions 1998–2002, Secretary of State for Transport 2002–6, Secretary of State for Scotland 2003–6, Secretary of State for Trade and Industry and President of the Board of Trade 2006–7, Chancellor of the Exchequer 2007–10, Shadow Chancellor 2010, created Lord Darling 2015.
33 Alan Milburn, 1958–, MP for Darlington 1992–2010, Chief Secretary to the Treasury 1998–9, Secretary of State for Health 1999–2003, Chancellor of the Duchy of Lancaster and Minister for the Cabinet Office 2004–5.
34 Budgets prior to 2003 are not comparable because they include the costs of the Welsh Audit Office. These costs were disaggregated in 2004, but it is impossible to obtain restated figures for 2002, which do not include these costs.

Including 2002 in these figures would underestimate the growth in spending across the two main functions of the NAO.

35 Peter Abbott, 1942–2015, Royal Navy 1963–97 including Commander in Chief Eastern Atlantic Area and Commander Naval Forces North Western Europe 1995–7, Vice Chief of the Defence Staff 1997–2001. Knighted 1994.

36 Alex Scharaschkin, National Audit Office, Director of Regulation Competition and Consumers 2008–14, Executive Director of Assessment, Research and Innovation AQA 2014–.

37 Edward Humpherson, 1970–, National Audit Office 1993–2013, Assistant Auditor General 2007–13, Director General Office of Statistics Regulation 2014–.

38 John Gieve, 1950–, Department for Employment 1974–8, Treasury 1979–2001, Permanent Secretary Home Office 2001–5, Deputy Governor Bank of England 2006–9. Knighted 2005.

39 Only a webpage was available for this report, so the web link is included as the reference.

40 Tony Wright, 1948–, Academic at various universities 1976–92, MP for Cannock and Burntwood and Cannock Chase 1992–2010, Chair Public Administration Committee 1999–2010, Chair Reform of the House of Commons Committee 2009, Visiting Professor in Government and Public Policy University College London 2010–.

41 Colin Talbot, 1952–, 1990–5, Senior Lecturer, London SBU, Professor, Public Policy and Management, University of Glamorgan, Professor, Social Sciences, University of Manchester 2017–, Professor Emeritus, Manchester. Former advisor to both the Treasury and Public Administration Select Committees.

42 Michael Bichard, 1947–, Chief Executive Brent Council 1980–6, Chief Executive Gloucestershire Council 1986–90, Chief Executive Benefits Agency 1990–5, Permanent Secretary Department for Employment 1995, Permanent Secretary Department for Education and Employment 1996–2001, Director Institute for Government 2008–10, Chair of the NAO 2015–21.

43 Scylla and Charybdis are entities located in the Straits of Messina according to Homer. Scylla was a many headed monster and Charybdis a whirlpool: steering to avoid one would mean an unwary sailor ended up being swallowed by the other.

References

Aldred, R. (2008). Flexible regulation: The birth of a quantitative audit society. *International Journal of Management Concepts and Philosophy, 3*(1), 48–65.

Armstrong, H. and Rhodes, C. (2023). *The Ministerial Code and Independent advisor on ministerial interests.* London: House of Commons Library.

Bacon, Richard, interview

Bechberger, E., Lane, D. C., McBride, T., Morton, A., Quintas, D. and Wong, C. H. (2011). National Audit Office uses OR to assess value for money of public services. *Interfaces, 41*(4), 365–374.

Bichard, Michael, interview

Bourn, Jonathan, interview

Bourn, Sir J. (1997). 19 June 1997. In *Diary of Sir John Bourn,* Unpublished MSS. John Bourn Private Archive.

Bourn, Sir J. (1997a). 20 February 1997. In *Diary of Sir John Bourn,* Unpublished MSS. John Bourn Private Archive.

Bourn, Sir J. (1997b). 7 October 1997. In *Diary of Sir John Bourn,* Unpublished MSS. John Bourn Private Archive.

Bourn, Sir J. (1998). 27 July 1998. In *Diary of Sir John Bourn,* Unpublished MSS. John Bourn Private Archive.
Bourn, Sir J. (1998a). *International value for money seminar, 29/30 September 1998.* Unpublished MSS. John Bourn Private Archive.
Bourn, Sir J. (1998b). 23 November 1998. In *Diary of Sir John Bourn,* Unpublished MSS. John Bourn Private Archive.
Bourn, Sir J. (1998c). 26 March 1998. In *Diary of Sir John Bourn,* Unpublished MSS. John Bourn Private Archive.
Bourn, Sir J. (1999). Audit 21–24 November 1999. In *Diary of Sir John Bourn,* Unpublished MSS. John Bourn Private Archive.
Bourn, Sir J. (1999a). *VFM through people*, 4 November 1999. Unpublished MSS, John Bourn Private Archive.
Bourn, Sir J. (2000). 30 March 2000. In *Diary of Sir John Bourn,* Unpublished MSS. John Bourn Private Archive.
Bourn, Sir J. (2001). 12 December 2001. In *Diary of Sir John Bourn,* Unpublished MSS. John Bourn Private Archive.
Bourn, Sir J. (2001a). *Financial Audit Conference*, 14 December 2001. Unpublished MSS, John Bourn Private Archive.
Bourn, Sir J. (2001b). 24 to 25 July 2001. In *Diary of Sir John Bourn,* Unpublished MSS. John Bourn Private Archive.
Bourn, Sir J. (2001c). *Sir John Bourn to Professor Peter Hennessey*, 15 January 2001. Unpublished MSS, John Bourn Private Archive.
Bourn, Sir J. (2002). 29 March 2002. In *Diary of Sir John Bourn,* Unpublished MSS. John Bourn Private Archive.
Bourn, Sir J. (2003). 8 October 2003. In *Diary of Sir John Bourn,* Unpublished MSS. John Bourn Private Archive.
Bourn, Sir J. (2004). 25 May 2004. In *Diary of Sir John Bourn,* Unpublished MSS. John Bourn Private Archive.
Bourn, Sir J. (2006). 6 December 2006. In *Diary of Sir John Bourn,* Unpublished MSS. John Bourn Private Archive.
Bowerman, M., Humphrey, C. and Owen, D. (2003). Struggling for supremacy: The case of UK public audit institutions. *Critical Perspectives on Accounting, 14*(1–2), 1–22.
BBC (2006). *Clarke is fired in cabinet purge.* Available at http://news.bbc.co.uk/1/hi/uk_politics/4975938.stm accessed on 18 December 2023.
BBC (2007). *Data disaster: Your queries answered.* Available at http://news.bbc.co.uk/1/hi/business/7105592.stm accessed on 14 January 2024.
Cabinet Office (1999). *Modernising government.* London: HMSO.
Cabinet Office (2000). *Wiring up: Whitehall's management of cross-cutting policies and services.* London: HMSO.
Campbell-Smith, D. (2008). *Follow the money: The Audit Commission, public money and the management of public services, 1983–2008.* London: Allen Lane.
Clarke, David, interview
Cohen, Gabrielle, interview
C&AG (1993). *The Office of Telecommunications – Licence compliance and consumer protection*, Session 1992-3, HC529. London: National Audit Office.
C&AG (1996). *The regulation of gas tariffs – The gas cost index*, Session 1995-6, HC287. London: National Audit Office.
C&AG (1996a). *The work of the Directors General of telecommunications, gas supply, water services and electricity supply*, Session 1995-6, HC645. London: National Audit Office.

C&AG (1997). *The Skye Bridge*, Session 1997-8, HC5. London: National Audit Office.
C&AG (1999). *Examining the value for money of deals under the Private Finance Initiative*, Session 1998-9, HC739. London: National Audit Office.
C&AG (1999a). *Progress on National Audit Office reports on Scottish matters*, SE/1999/55. London: National Audit Office.
C&AG (1999b). *Modernising procurement*, Session 1998-9, HC808. London: National Audit Office.
C&AG (2000). *Kosovo: The financial management of military operations*, Session 1999-2000, HC530. London: National Audit Office.
C&AG (2000a). *The refinancing of Fazakerley PFI prison contract*, Session 1999-2000, HC584. London: National Audit Office.
C&AG (2000b). *Supporting innovation: Managing risk in government departments*, Session 1999-2000, HC864. London: National Audit Office.
C&AG (2000c). *Compensating victims of violent crime*, Session 1999-2000, HC398. London: National Audit Office.
C&AG (2000d). *The National Blood Service*, Session 2000-2001, HC6. London: National Audit Office.
C&AG (2001). *Managing the relationship to secure a successful partnership in PFI projects*, Session 2001-2, HC375. London: National Audit Office.
C&AG (2001a). *Joining up to improve public services*, Session 2001-2, HC383. London: National Audit Office.
C&AG (2001b). *1999-2000 General report of the Comptroller and Auditor General*, Session 2000-2001, HC25-XIX. London: National Audit Office.
C&AG (2001c). *Educating and training the future health professional workforce for England*, Session 2000-2001, HC277. London: National Audit Office.
C&AG (2002). *Innovation in the National Health Service: The acquisition of Heart hospital*, Session 2002-3, HC157. London: National Audit Office.
C&AG (2002a). *Opening the post: Postcomm and postal services - the risks and opportunities*, Session 2001-2, HC521. London: National Audit Office.
C&AG (2002b). *PFI refinancing update*, Session 2001-2, HC1288. London: National Audit Office.
C&AG (2002c). *Better public services through e-government*, Session 2001-2, HC704-I. London: National Audit Office.
C&AG (2002d). *2000-2001 General report of the Comptroller and Auditor General*, Session 2001-2002, HC335-XIX. London: National Audit Office.
C&AG (2003). *Operation Telic: The United Kingdom operations in Iraq*, Session 2002-3, HC60. London: National Audit Office.
C&AG (2004). *Managing risks to improve public services*, Session 2003-4, HC1078-I. London: National Audit Office.
C&AG (2004a). *The Government's estimates of the pensions lifetime allowance, 9 March 2004*. London: National Audit Office.
C&AG (2005). *Returning failed asylum applicants*, Session 2005-6, HC76. London: National Audit Office.
C&AG (2005a). *Reducing brain damage: Easier access to stroke care*, Session 2005-6, HC452. London: National Audit Office.
C&AG (2005b). *Dealing with the complexity of the benefits system*, Session 2005-6, HC592. London: National Audit Office.
C&AG (2005c). *The refinancing of the Norfolk and Norwich PFI Hospital: How the deal can be viewed in the light of the refinancing*, Session 2005-6, HC78. London: National Audit Office.
C&AG (2005d). Report of the Comptroller and Auditor General to the House of Commons: Fraud at the British Embassy, Tel Aviv. In *Foreign and*

Commonwealth Office Resource Accounts, 2004-05, Session 2005-6, HC776. London: HMSO. 48-50.
C&AG (2005e). *Public service agreements: Managing data quality- compendium report*, Session 2004-5, HC476. London: National Audit Office.
C&AG (2005f). *Working with the third sector*, Session 2005-6, HC75. London: National Audit Office.
C&AG (2006). *Sure start children's centres*, Session 2006-7, HC104. London: National Audit Office.
C&AG (2006a). *Re-opening the post: Postcomm and the quality of mail services*, Session 2005-6, HC944. London: National Audit Office.
C&AG (2006b). *Update on PFI debt refinancing and the PFI equity market*, Session 2005-6, HC1040. London: National Audit Office.
C&AG (2006c). *Delivering successful IT-enabled business change*, Session 2006-7, HC33-I. London: National Audit Office.
C&AG (2006d). Report of the Comptroller and Auditor General to the House of Commons: Theft and misuse of satellite phones in Iraq. In *Foreign and Commonwealth Office Resource Accounts 2005-06*, Session 2005-6, HC1495. London: HMSO. 57-60.
C&AG (2006e). Report of the Comptroller and Auditor General. *Home Office, Resource Accounts 2004-5* (pp. 22–29), Session 2005-6, HC826, London: HMSO.
C&AG (2007). *Caring for vulnerable babies: The reorganisation of neo-natal services in England*, Session 2007-8, HC101, London: National Audit Office.
C&AG (2007a). *The Financial Services Authority: A review under section 12 of the Financial Services and Markets Act 2000*. London: National Audit Office.
C&AG (2008). *End of life care*, Session 2007-8, HC1043. London: National Audit Office.
C&AG (2008a). *Protecting consumers? Removing retail price controls*, Session 2007-8, HC342. London: National Audit Office.
C&AG (2009). *Assessment of the Capability Review programme*, Session 2008-9, HC123. London: National Audit Office.
Darling, A. (2011). *Back from the brink: 1000 days at Number 11*. London: Atlantic Books.
Davis, David, interview
Dewar, D. (1999). *Donald Dewar's speech at the opening of the Scottish Parliament 1 July 1999*. Available online at https://www.parliament.scot/-/media/files/history/donalddewarsspeech1july1999.pdf accessed on 8 January 2024.
Dunleavy, Patrick, interview
Dunleavy, P., Gilson, C., Bastow, S. and Tinkler, J. (2009). *The National Audit Office, the Public Accounts Committee and the risk landscape in UK public policy*, LSE Research Online, Discussion Paper. Available online at https://eprints.lse.ac.uk/25785/1/The_National_Audit_Office,_the_Public_(LSERO_version).pdf accessed on 13 January 2024.
Economist (2001). *Sacked, but so politely*, 1 November 2001. Available at https://www.economist.com/britain/2001/11/01/sacked-but-so-politely accessed on 22 December 2023.
Etherton, Mark, interview
Evans, A. (2023). 'There will be no shortage of Cabinet ministers taking part in the Scottish referendum campaign. The same is not true in Wales': New labour, old struggles, and the advent of welsh devolution. *Parliamentary Affairs*, 42(2), 255–273.

Ferry, L., Honeysett, L. and Midgley, H. (2021). Holding the government to account for its finances: The "Unsung" heroes of the UK parliament scrutiny unit. *Journal of Public Budgeting, Accounting & Financial Management, 33*(2), 109–113.

Foster, H. and Knox, C. (2022). The 'eyes and ears of parliament': Devolved public accounts committees in the UK. *The Journal of Legislative Studies.* DOI: 10.1080/13572334.2022.2079860

Foster, H. and Knox, C. (2023). Variegated accountability: Devolved public accounts committees in the UK. *Parliamentary Affairs, 76*(3), 641–661.

Gay, O. (2005). Public Service Agreements. London: House of Commons Library.

Heald, D. (2005). The implementation of resource accounting in UK central government. *Financial Accountability & Management, 21*(2), 163–188.

Hellowell M. (2010). The UK's private finance initiative: History, evaluation, prospects. In G. Hodge, C. Greve, A. E. Boardman (eds.) *International handbook in public-private partnerships.* Cheltenham, UK: Edward Elgar, 307–332.

Hencke, D. (2007). Sir John Bourn, guardian of the public purse. In three years he's run up bills of £365k on travel and £27k on meals. Then there's opera, grand prix, polo ..., *The Guardian*, 11 October 2007.

House of Commons (1997). *Hansard*, vol 302, 9 December 1997.

House of Commons (2000). Hansard, Vol. 354, 24 July 2000.

House of Commons (2006). *Written ministerial statements 23 March 2006.* Available at https://publications.parliament.uk/pa/cm200506/cmhansrd/vo060323/wmstext/60323m03.htm#60323m03.html_sbhd1 accessed on 4 January 2024.

Heald, David, interview

Humpherson, Ed, interview

Kelly, J. (2003). The Audit Commission: Guiding, steering and regulating local government. *Public Administration, 81*(3), 459–476.

Kuo, D., Shackman, A. and anonymous others (2007). Memorandum submitted by David Kuo, Alan Shackman and others. In Public Accounts Committee, *Department for Health: the National Programme for IT in the NHS, Twentieth report of session 2006-7*, HC390. London: House of Commons, Ev. 109-Ev 144.

Leigh, Edward, interview

Liaison Committee (2007). *Annual report for 2005-6*, Session 2006-7, HC406. London: House of Commons.

Liaison Committee (2009). *The work of committee in 2007-8*, Session 2008-9, HC291. London: House of Commons.

Likierman, Andrew, interview

Lonsdale, Jeremy, interview

Lonsdale, J. (2008). Balancing independence and responsiveness: A practitioner perspective on the relationships shaping performance audit. *Evaluation, 14*(2), 227–248.

Mawhood, C. (1996). Devolution for Scotland and Wales- implications for current audit and accountability arrangements. In *Devolution: General implications of and arrangements for devolution for the National Audit Office (NAO); key papers relating to devolution not specific to either Scotland or Wales*, AO39/18, unpublished MSS, National Archives, London.

Mawhood, C. (1997). Devolution possible audit arrangements, 20 May 1997. In *Devolution: General implications of and arrangements for devolution for the National Audit Office (NAO); key papers relating to devolution not specific*

to either Scotland or Wales, AO39/18, unpublished MSS, National Archives, London.
Mawhood, C. (2007). *Caroline Mawhood to David Hartnett*, 22 November 2007. Available at https://www.nao.org.uk/wp-content/uploads/2013/04/child_benefit_data.pdf accessed on 14 January 2024.
Midgley, H. (2019). The National Audit Office and the select committee system 1979–2019. *Parliamentary Affairs, 72*(4), 779–798.
Mulholland, H. and Tempest, M. (2006). System 'not fit for purpose' says Reid, *The Guardian*, 23 May 2006.
National Audit Office (1997). Note of meeting at the Treasury on the audit arrangements following devolution, 9 June 1997. In *Devolution: General implications of and arrangements for devolution for the National Audit Office (NAO); key papers relating to devolution not specific to either Scotland or Wales*, AO39/18, unpublished MSS, National Archives, London. AO39/18.
National Audit Office (2003). *International educational comparisons: A compendium of published information on education provision and achievement in 10 countries*. London: National Audit Office.
National Audit Office (2003a). *Resource Accounts 2002–3*. London: National Audit Office.
National Audit Office (2004). *National Audit Office resource accounts 2003–4*. National Audit Office: London.
National Audit Office (2004a). *Resource accounts 2003–4*. London: National Audit Office.
National Audit Office (2006). *Review of the experiences of United Kingdom nationals affected by the Indian Ocean Tsunami*. London: National Audit Office.
National Audit Office (2006a). *International educational comparisons: A compendium of published information on education provision and achievement in 10 countries*. London: National Audit Office.
National Audit Office (2007). *Resource Accounts 2006–7*. London: National Audit Office.
National Audit Office (2008). *National Audit Office Resource Accounts 2007–8*. London: National Audit Office.
Omand, David, interview
Power, M. (1999). *The Audit Society: Rituals of verification*. Oxford: Oxford University Press.
Public Accounts Commission (2000). *Tenth report*, Session 1999-2000, HC754. London: House of Commons.
Public Accounts Committee (1998). *Resource accounting and resource based supply*. Session 1997-8, HC731. London: House of Commons.
Public Accounts Committee (1999). *Fourth report: The Government Resources and Accounts Bill*. Session 1999-2000, HC127. London: House of Commons.
Public Accounts Committee (2000). *Ninth report: Government resources and accounts bill*. Session 1999-2000, HC159. London: House of Commons.
Public Accounts Committee (2000a). *Twenty-ninth report. Progress on resource accounting and the adoption of resource-based supply together with the proceedings of the committee relating to the report, the minutes of evidence and appendices*, Session 1999-2000, HC561. London: House of Commons.
Public Accounts Committee (2001). *National Audit Office Resource Estimate 2001-2, minutes of evidence 31 January 2001*, Session 2000-2001, HC219-I. London: House of Commons.
Public Accounts Committee (2003) *Minutes of evidence taken before the committee of public accounts Wednesday 15 January 2003*. Available at

https://publications.parliament.uk/pa/cm200203/cmselect/cmpubacc/299/3011501.htm accessed on 16 March 2024.

Public Accounts Committee (2006). *NHS Local Improvement Finance Trusts*, Forty Seventh report of Session 2005-6, HC562. London: House of Commons.

Public Accounts Committee (2006a). *Home Office Resource Accounts 2005–6*, Sixtieth report, Session 2005-6, HC1079. London: House of Commons.

Public Accounts Committee (2007). *Department for Health: The National Programme for IT in the NHS, Twentieth report of session 2006-7*, HC390. London: House of Commons.

Public Administration and Constitutional Affairs Committee (2017). *Accounting for democracy: Making sure Parliament, the people and ministers know how and why public money is spent, Fourteenth report of Session 2016–17*, Session 2016-17, HC 95. London: House of Commons.

Public Administration and Constitutional Affairs Committee (2018). *After Carillion: Public sector outsourcing and contracting*, Session 2017-19, HC748. London: House of Commons.

Public Administration Committee (2003). *On target? Government by measurement*, Session 2002-3, HC62. London: House of Commons.

Public Administration Committee (2009). *Good government*, Session 2008-9, HC97-I. London: House of Commons.

Public Administration Committee (2009a). *Good government Vol. II oral and written evidence*, Session 2008-2009, HC97-II. London: House of Commons.

Robertson, James, interview

Sayers, Neil, interview

Scharaschkin, Alex, interview.

Scharaschkin, A. (2011). Evidence and argument. In J. Lonsdale, P. Wilkins and T. Ling (eds.) *Performance auditing: Contributing to accountability in government.* Cheltenham: Edward Elgar, 118–134.

Second Director, HMRC Audit (2007). *Letter to HMRC, our audit of child benefit, 9 November 2007.* Available at https://www.nao.org.uk/wp-content/uploads/2013/04/child_benefit_data.pdf accessed on 14 January 2024.

Shaoul, J., Stafford, A. and Stapleton, P. (2006). Highway robbery? A financial analysis of design, build, finance and operate (DBFO) in UK roads. *Transport Reviews, 26*(3), 257–274.

Shaoul, J., Stafford, A. and Stapleton, P. (2008). The cost of using private finance to build, finance and operate hospitals. *Public Money & Management, 28*(2), 101–108.

Sharma, N. (2007). Interactions and interrogations: Negotiating and performing value for money reports. *Financial Accountability & Management, 23*(3), 289–311.

Sharman, C. (Lord) (2001). *Holding to account: A review of accountability and audit in central government.* London: HMSO.

Sinclair, Martin, interview

Smyth, S. and Whitfield, D. (2017). Maintaining market principles: Government auditors, PPP equity sales and hegemony. *Accounting Forum, 41*, 44–56.

Speaker's Counsel (1997). Speaker's Counsel to J. Ashcroft, 27 June 1997. In *Devolution: General implications of and arrangements for devolution for the National Audit Office (NAO); key papers relating to devolution not specific to either Scotland or Wales*, AO39/18, unpublished MSS, National Archives, London. AO39/18.

Stolk, Christian van, interview

Summers, D. (2007). Auditor general to retire after expenses row. *The Guardian*, 25 October 2017.

Telegraph (2022). General Lord Ramsbotham, soldier who became a controversial chief inspector of prisons – obituary. *Daily Telegraph*, 16 December 2022.
The Scotland Act (1998). *The Scotland Act 1988*. Available at https://www.legislation.gov.uk/ukpga/1998/46/contents accessed on 1 August 2023.
Treasury (1998). *Modern Public Services for Britain: Investing in reform. Comprehensive Spending Review: New public spending plans 1999-2002*, Session 1997-8, Cm. 4011. London: HMSO.
Treasury (2002). *Audit and Accountability in Central Government: The Government's response to Lord Sharman's report "Holding to Account"*, Session 2001-2, Cm. 5456. London: HMSO.
Treasury Select Committee (1998). *Seventh report*, Session 1998-9, HC738. London: House of Commons.
Turnbull, Andrew, interview
Whitehouse, Michael, interview
Wright, Nick, interview

6

AMYAS MORSE 2009–19 - PLOTTING A COURSE THROUGH AUSTERITY AND BREXIT

6.1 Introduction

In 2008, after the resignation of John Bourn, the *Times* published a short announcement piece commenting on the adverts for both his successor and the new chair of the NAO. The journalist, Martin Waller, described the circumstances of Bourn's resignation and then commented that 'Both jobs require "political sensitivity," the ads say. Yes, I can see they might' (Waller, 2008).

In 2009, Amyas Morse was appointed as C&AG of the NAO. Waller was right: the new C&AG, then Mr, later Sir, Amyas Morse, and his two chairs, Sir Andrew Likierman and Lord Bichard, would indeed require political sensitivity, but the direction of the threat Waller identified was wrong. The threat came not from the circumstances which had led to Bourn's resignation, but from the wider political crisis of the late 2000s and 2010s.

Amyas Morse was the first qualified accountant to become C&AG, the first to be interviewed for the post and the first to have a term limit for his period in office (of 10 years). Mark Etherton said as regards Morse's appointment, 'My memory is that there was a very strong feeling that you couldn't just tap someone on the shoulder anymore and there had to be a proper process and it had to be advertised and there had to be a formal interview' (Mark Etherton, interview). Lord Macpherson said that being a qualified accountant was not a formal requirement when Morse was appointed. However, Sir Edward Leigh told us that it was important to his judgement of Morse as a candidate. The circumstances of Morse's

DOI: 10.4324/9781003520085-6

appointment largely underlay his entire time at the NAO. He brought to the role of C&AG his skills and worldview formed as an accountant with a highly successful career at a Big Four firm. He also brought with him the political skills which had enabled him to function at senior roles in business and at the Ministry of Defence (MoD).

The years from 2009 were shaped not by politics, but by the aftermath of the financial crisis 2007–8 and then subsequent crises such as austerity and Brexit. The NAO found itself auditing Alistair Darling's decisions (Labour Chancellor 2007–10) to safeguard and stabilise the financial system of the UK by massive infusions of capital and extensive government guarantees and from 2010 the efforts by the coalition and subsequent Conservative governments to reduce public expenditure often described in the UK as austerity. Later, these challenges were compounded with the UK's decision in 2016 to leave the EU and its aftermath (Brexit), which had not reached its end by the time Morse left the NAO in May 2019. As the political system which the NAO sat within struggled, the NAO's position also became strained. The pressures increasingly bearing down on the NAO came from all directions: parliamentary, regulatory and governmental.

The purpose of this chapter is to examine the 10 years of Morse's term as C&AG from 2009 to 2019. To do so the chapter sets out the political context and then considers the NAO within the categories of regulatory space: organisational context (including independence), capacities and audit scope. This enables us to show that Morse's response was to extend the NAO's remit and to anticipate and respond to potential criticisms of the organisation before they happened where he was able. The convulsions of the 2010s changed the way that the NAO operated constitutionally and practically and reshaped the NAO's relationship with both Parliament and government.

6.2 Political context

Morse's tenure as C&AG between 2009 and 2019 was unusually turbulent. The UK saw four general elections (2010, 2015, 2017, 2019). There was a referendum on Scotland's membership of the UK in 2014 and on the UK's membership of the EU in 2016. Politically, the decade divided neatly in two, with the first half focussed on the financial crisis and its aftermath and the second on the UK's decision to leave the EU.

The government led by Gordon Brown had taken unprecedented action to stabilise the financial system in 2008–9. The financial crisis of 2008–9 hit the UK hard, and its impact on politics was profound (Gamble, 2009). Whilst many of these decisions predated Morse, it was his regime that then had to audit them from 2009 onwards, and due to their scale and nature, they confronted the NAO with issues it had never faced before. The UK nationalised major banks including Lloyds and the Royal Bank of Scotland. Public spending rose from 38.9% of national income in 2007–8 to 44.9% in 2009–10, whilst tax revenues fell from 36.2% of national income to 35% (Cribb and Johnson, 2018). The UK economy was massively impacted by the crisis: it began contracting in 2008 and fell by 2.6% in one quarter of 2009. Cumulatively, the UK went through its deepest recession since the Second World War (Allen, 2010). The Labour government became very unpopular, and the credibility of the establishment was further damaged by the MPs' expenses scandal in 2009–10.

In the May 2010 election, Labour received its lowest proportion of the votes cast (29%) since 1983 and were replaced by a Conservative-led coalition government with the Liberal Democrats, with David Cameron[1] as Prime Minister. The Conservatives argued that the only response possible in the circumstances was to reduce public expenditure: as David Cameron put it in the Conservative manifesto, 'our belief in responsibility with public finances is the starting point of our plan for economic recovery and growth. We want your consent for a programme of public spending control' (Conservative Party, 2010, p. vii).

After the election, the coalition government (formed by a coalition of the Conservative and Liberal Democrat parties) adopted the rhetoric of the Conservatives on spending reductions: stating that 'the most urgent task facing this coalition is to tackle our record debts because without sound finances, none of our ambitions will be deliverable' (HM Government, 2010). The UK government's position was not endorsed by all economists (e.g., Krugman, 2015). Public spending fell as a percentage of GDP, declining to just under 40% of GDP by 2019 (Talbot and Talbot, 2019). This commitment to reducing government expenditure lay behind a suite of policies which involved reforms to public service delivery, the skills and capacities of Whitehall, local government accountability and cuts (in real and nominal terms) to some public sector programmes. Despite the massive effort involved, Conservative commentators noted that it was the pace of growth of public spending that was reduced rather than its actual level (Bacon and Hope, 2013, p. 1).

In 2015 Cameron won a majority of ten and governed as Prime Minister of a purely Conservative government for a year. He resigned in 2016 following the loss of the referendum on the UK's membership of the EU.

Cameron was replaced by Theresa May. In 2017, May began negotiations with the EU by activating article 50 of the Lisbon Treaty commencing the process of the UK's departure from the EU: she also called a general election to give her a larger majority to enable passing her Brexit deal through the House of Commons. However, after losing 13 seats, she had to make a confidence and supply arrangement with the Democratic

Unionists, a small Northern Irish party, to continue in government. She was unable to present a deal on Brexit, which commanded the support of the House of Commons and subsequently resigned. She was replaced by Boris Johnson, but one of May's last acts was to appoint Gareth Davies as C&AG of the NAO.

6.3 Organisational context

Within this turbulent political context, questions about the NAO's organisational context in terms of its independence focussed on three areas: its new governance system, the politics of the era with austerity and Brexit, and the election of the chair of the PAC. Firstly, in the aftermath of John Bourn's resignation, a new governance structure had to be created to ensure that the weaknesses in the governance of the NAO were addressed, especially surrounding the person of the C&AG exposed by the Bourn exit. There were concerns internally and externally that improved governance could restrict the C&AG's independence. Secondly, after 2008, the NAO had to react both to the politics of austerity and to Brexit. Thirdly, after 2010, in common with other select committees, the chair of the PAC was elected by the House of Commons for the first time. Both of the post-2010 chairs, Margaret Hodge[2] and Meg Hillier,[3] therefore had an automatic authority and independence that previous chairs had not had. Hodge in particular was the highest profile chair since David Davis and arguably since Harold Wilson. We will examine how the NAO's independence was shaped and reshaped by these three factors in this section.

6.3.1 Establishing the new governance system

Morse's tenure started amid a crisis about the independence of the NAO. Initially, as discussed in the previous chapter, the integrity of the C&AG himself was questioned. This led to questions about the NAO's integrity: NAO staff were ridiculed by some staff in departments who saw it as an opportunity to reflect on the audit office's processes. Michael Whitehouse told us that he thought 'that was a really, really dangerous point' in the NAO's history. Bourn's expenses opened up a further problem: ultimately, his resignation could only be obtained by a vote in Parliament, and there was no clear person charged with telling him that he must resign. The then Cabinet Secretary, LordO'Donnell, said that

> it was up to the PAC to appoint the C&AG and that it didn't make any sense to do it any other way but that the PAC all thought John Bourn's

time was up and it was time to change but none of them wanted to tell him so I got the short straw and had a conversation with John.

(O'Donnell, interview)

While O'Donnell's involvement was secret at the time, the fact that the crisis concerned Bourn's expenses and hospitality focussed attention on the question of whether the senior management at the NAO could ever be independent enough to provide a proper check on the C&AG's activities and hospitality. This confronted Parliament with uncongenial choices. In 2008, the dilemma had been resolved by the Cabinet Secretary deciding to tell the C&AG to go: but that was constitutionally, as O'Donnell recognised, problematic.

Parliament began to move towards improving oversight over the C&AG during the process of Bourn's resignation. The Public Accounts Commission discussed the C&AG's expenses in 2007 and stated,

> The Commission discussed the matter. It concluded that there was no evidence of impropriety in the use of public money, and that the expenditure had been in accordance with the existing rules on such expenditure. But it agreed that, in the light of the public concern, there was a need for a more transparent system for the Comptroller and Auditor General's travel expenses.
>
> *(Public Accounts Commission, 2007a)*

They then reported publicly on the C&AG's expenses later in 2007 setting out the basic dilemma: on the one hand, the C&AG had complete discretion in carrying out his functions under the Act, but on the other, the Commission was clear that the C&AG should 'follow the rules and practices of Permanent Secretaries of government departments' (Public Accounts Commission, 2007, p. 3), which of course had changed over time, particularly post the introduction of freedom of information. The Commission initially suggested that the NAO's own Director of internal assurance and the chair of its Audit Committee should oversee the C&AG's planned expenses and have access to the Commission if they required it (Public Accounts Commission, 2007, p. 3). This was unsatisfactory still: as Martin Sinclair told us, the senior members of the office always felt 'for most of my time [on the leadership team] most of us really felt we were only there at the whim of the C&AG' (interview, Martin Sinclair).

The Public Accounts Commission recognised that this was only a temporary expedient, and they commissioned John Tiner[4] to review the NAO's corporate governance. Tiner's remit was to examine how to ensure that the NAO could 'maintain systems of governance and internal controls consistent with good practice' whilst at the same time allowing the C&AG 'the authority to form completely independent judgements about the audits and value for money and other studies conducted by the NAO and the presentation of these to Parliament' (Public Accounts Commission, 2008, p. 3). The Commission itself asserted the 'fundamental importance of preserving the independence of the C&AG' (Public Accounts Commission, 2008a, p. 3). This was particularly important as some in the press speculated that Bourn had been hounded out of office (Halligan, 2008).

Tiner's main suggestion was that a new chair and Board should be appointed for the NAO, but should not have involvement in operational matters. The Commission agreed and summarised his argument: 'there is a need for an NAO board which includes members and a Chairman with sufficient authority and independence from the C&AG to challenge him or her when necessary' (Public Accounts Commission, 2008a, p. 4). The Commission saw the way to do this was by empowering the new board to challenge the C&AG on the strategy of the NAO but ensuring that the Board could neither force the C&AG to conduct an audit nor stop the C&AG doing an audit which they wished to do (Public Accounts Commission, 2008, p. 5). Internally, staff felt that the board was a concept proposed by the C&AG, Tim Burr, who served for a short period between Bourn and Morse (interview, Martin Sinclair). This new board could therefore, because of its increased independence, perform the role that Lord O'Donnell had performed with John Bourn with a future C&AG if similar circumstances arose.

The Commission originally envisaged legislation passing before the 2010 election; however, the clauses in the Constitutional Reform and Governance Act were dropped because of a lack of parliamentary time.

The coalition government of 2010 eventually created the new structures via the Budget Responsibility and National Audit Act in 2011, but despite the belated introduction of the legislation, the new structure had been functioning in shadow form for some time. Sir Andrew Likierman, the new chair of the NAO, was appointed prior to Morse's appointment in 2009. Likierman understood walking into the role, the challenges of what he was taking on. He told us that

> I think the incentive was here is a really interesting challenge, how do we get the organisation onto a more conventional footing with the Board and with the Chief Executive and accountabilities but with ambiguities?
>
> *(Sir Andrew Likierman, interview,)*

Likierman was not alone in his perception of the change: Lord O'Donnell told us that 'it was certainly something that surprised me' in the NAO before 2009 (O'Donnell, interview). This sense of a more conventional governance structure parallels the language that Tiner used in his review. For Tiner though the obligation on the chair was to be the NAO's fail-safe mechanism: the job in Likierman's words 'wasn't necessarily a positive brief. It was "Let's sort out the problems"' (Sir Andrew Likierman, interview). Likierman's description of the role of chair as creating 'some balance to the C&AG' brought into question how the C&AG would respond to being 'balanced'. Lord Bichard, who succeeded Likierman in 2015, thought that 'my task coming in was to try and mend the relationship, frankly, which I didn't think was healthy' (Lord Bichard, interview). Bichard inherited a board which understood its role but, in his view, needed to be closer to the C&AG. He saw the board as having two roles: first, to ensure, as Likierman had done, that there was an independent check upon the C&AG, but secondly, to be 'a sounding board you can trust' for the C&AG and the wider NAO. This evolution of the board's role brought it closer to the C&AG and the NAO, even though the office retained its independence.

The introduction of more conventional governance did not stop at creating an NAO Board. Lord Macpherson told us that the entire process of appointing the C&AG became more formalised and 'more open' (Macpherson, interview). Morse was appointed partly because he did not belong to a 'cosy Whitehall club' (Macpherson, interview) and was not, as many of his predecessors had been, a career civil servant. His status as a qualified chartered accountant mattered to Sir Edward Leigh, for example, who drew a parallel with the move to professionalise Whitehall's finance departments (Sir Edward Leigh, interview). Morse was brought in also because of his robustness and independence: Sir Geoffrey Clifton-Brown[5] described him as 'light hearted, but underneath it all he had a mind of steel' (Clifton-Brown, interview). He was seen as a new start for the organisation (Peter Riddell, interview) and a 'breath of fresh air' (Sir Edward Leigh, interview). The Act created a term limit of 10 years for C&AGs to ensure that no C&AG would have the depth and range of influence over the NAO that Sir John Bourn had had.

One of Morse's challenges was to repair the reputation of the NAO after the criticisms made of Bourn's expenses. Many of the changes he made to the NAO's spending (referred to later) were a necessary response to the situation into which he arrived.

6.3.2 The NAO and the politicians during austerity

Issues around Sir John Bourn's departure notwithstanding, the greater challenges to the NAO's independence under Morse arose out of the changing political climate in 2009–10.

As discussed above, the Conservative governments of the 2010s adopted a number of reform programmes collectively described as austerity, and ministers were critical of the NAO's response to some of these change programmes. In 2012, Michael Gove,[6] the Education Secretary under Cameron, in a speech to the think-tank Politeia blasted the NAO and the PAC as 'forces of conservatism'. Gove developed his point thus,

> Time after time the NAO and PAC report in a way which treats any mistake in the implementation of any innovation as a scandalous waste of public money which prudent decision-making should have avoided. And yet at the same time it treats the faults of current provision as unalterable facts of nature.
>
> *(Civil Service World, 2012)*

Gove's critique of the NAO was not repeated often in public. Political criticisms were tempered by the fact that value for money existed in a 'separate universe' (Macpherson, interview). However, behind the scenes, Morse perceived that some within government were hostile to the NAO; he told us of rumours that Francis Maude,[7] then Paymaster General and Minister for the Cabinet Office, was intent on revising or abolishing the NAO (Amyas Morse, interview). Gabrielle Cohen told us that the coalition government 'clip the wings of the more assertive PAC under Hodge's leadership' (Gabrielle Cohen, interview). Michael Whitehouse heard from his contacts that 'there was certainly a time around 2012, 2013, when people were saying the NAO is becoming a nuisance' (Michael Whitehouse, interview). Marcial Boo[8] told us that he felt there was a 'nagging doubt or latent threat that the government might want to privatise some of the financial audit services that the NAO was providing' (Marcial Boo, interview). Lord O'Donnell agreed with Macpherson but thought that political attitudes to the NAO were framed by the fact that for politicians, the NAO 'didn't feature on their radar 99% of the time and then when it did, they just got irritated because it was never good news' (O'Donnell, interview).

The NAO's fear of the threat from government was leant credibility by events at its sister organisation, the Audit Commission, which was abolished in 2015. In Lord Kerslake's[9] view, any threat to the NAO had to be seen in the light of the government's general resentment of independent sources of criticism like the Audit Commission. In August 2010, the Secretary of State for local government, Eric Pickles,[10] announced plans to close the Audit Commission, abolish its role in the audit of local government along with the whole performance management regime for local government and replace it with a new local audit regime. We will examine the impact of those decisions on the NAO later in this chapter. Advocates for the abolition of the Audit Commission suggested that 'many local authority staff estimate that millions more will be saved as staff can focus on their jobs as opposed to satisfying the Audit Commission' (Taxpayers Alliance, 2010). Other criticisms came from MPs like Bob Neill[11] that the Audit Commission had focussed too much on improvement and too little upon audit: 'it had become so much of an improvement agency that it had moved away from its core function' (quoted in Timmins and Gash, 2014). The government said at the time that their motivation was to reinvigorate accountability at a local level and replace national priorities with local. Professor Tony Travers[12] told us that

> the last thing the government wanted in a period of austerity was an official agency publishing reports to say this council can't deliver services. I think the Audit Commission would have been a profound embarrassment to the government so they got rid of it.
>
> *(Tony Travers, interview)*

The Audit Commission's abolition was not supported by senior civil servants: Lord O'Donnell, the Cabinet Secretary, told us that he had opposed it at the time (O'Donnell, interview). The NAO might have been more protected due to its influential backers in Parliament; in contrast, Timmins and Gash (2014) found few supporters for the Audit Commission in public, and those that did exist, such as Margaret Hodge, were opposition MPs. Marcial Boo, then Director of Policy at the Audit Commission, told us that the senior management of the Audit Commission were 'responsible for misjudging the political landscape' and were 'dismissive of Pickles and the Conservatives' (Marcial Boo, interview).

The NAO had to avoid the same fate. Morse did so through some of his changes to the NAO's capacity (discussed below), but he was also keen to ensure that the NAO and Audit Commission were not tied together in politician's minds. Marcial Boo told us that

> I got the strong sense that the senior leadership at the NAO wanted to put a barge pole between them and the Audit Commission. They wanted to play down my personal background and they didn't want to hire staff from the Audit Commission. A few people came across later but very few. The NAO wanted to create a distance so that they were not tarred with any similar behaviour. They were very different cultures though with respect to politics.
>
> *(Marcial Boo, interview)*

Boo told us that the cultures of the NAO and Audit Commission were radically different. He said that 'there was a much stronger understanding of political neutrality at the NAO than at the (Audit) Commission' (Marcial Boo, interview). After his arrival at the NAO, Boo asked Morse if he could go to the party conferences: something he did annually as a director at the Audit Commission to observe, and Morse said, 'no, you can't do it, you are a director at the NAO, it would be wrong if you were at a party conference' (Marcial Boo, interview). The NAO's cultural aversion to political involvement was only strengthened by the Audit Commission's demise.

Nevertheless, this did not mean that Morse's NAO did not comment on the implications of austerity. As we will come to in the section on audit scope, NAO did comment extensively. Events at the Audit Commission and the overall hostility described by Kerslake and others contributed to an NAO that was very focussed on its own remit. Within that remit, Morse was robust. To deal with the tactics of civil servants like Sir Richard Packer (described in the previous chapter), Morse shortened clearance timetables, writing to the Treasury to explain that the leisurely process was 'a waste of everybody's time' (Jeremy Lonsdale, interview). He found support from the Treasury permanent secretary, who agreed and wrote round to departmental heads in support of a faster turnaround of reports. Internally, Morse would often insist on a report's conclusions to a department and refuse to back down if the evidence said the NAO was right. He saw his role as ensuring that the NAO stayed consistent to its remit: ensuring its independence under a tightly defined sense of what public sector audit meant.

6.3.3 Brexit

Brexit represented a second and more profound challenge to the NAO's independence. The NAO did not, of course, take a public position on the UK's membership of the EU when the referendum was announced. However, as soon as the UK voted to exit the EU on 23 June 2016, it created a potential issue for the NAO in retaining its reputation for independence and non-partisan comment. Brexit created massive administrative challenges for government, varying depending on the type of Brexit decided on by government and approved by Parliament. Some forms of Brexit, for example, remaining in the single market and customs union, would have involved less disruption than others, where more of the existing arrangements at the border or in regulation would have survived. The NAO therefore had to comment on the value for money of the UK's arrangements for leaving the EU as a key part of its role holding the government to account for its expenditure. But it did so against two important confounding factors which made fulfilling its role very difficult. Firstly, Theresa May's failure to achieve a deal that could get parliamentary consent created a febrile political atmosphere. Taking a neutral and objective stance became fraught in an increasingly polarised atmosphere, in which numerous civil servants became portrayed as opponents of Brexit, notably Sir Ivan Rogers,[13] Sir Jeremy Heywood[14] and Oliver Robbins[15] (examples of attacks include Pierce, 2017; Maddox, 2018; Tombs, 2019). As Lord Bichard, chair of the NAO at the time, commented,

> The problem with Brexit is that it was very, very, difficult for anyone to get involved in any conversation, whether it was over the dinner table or, you know, in Parliament, which didn't – wasn't challenged on the basis of 'you're prejudiced'.
>
> *(Lord Bichard, interview,)*

Secondly, between 2017 and 2019, there was considerable doubt about what kind of Brexit the UK would eventually opt for. The demise of the May government meant that up until the autumn of 2019, the UK was still unclear about whether it wished to leave the EU without a deal, with a deal involving a distant relationship with the EU or a closer relationship with the EU (or a potential referendum on rejoining the EU (as advocated by Labour in the 2019 election (Labour Party, 2019, p. 90)). Given the NAO's unique remit, this posed challenges to Morse in devising a course of action which respected his mandate, to ensure Parliament was informed of the achievement (or not) of value for money in implementing Brexit whilst retaining the NAO's reputation for impartiality.

Morse saw his and the Office's role in this quite distinctly. Firstly, he saw the NAO as providing transparency to show what was going on within government and bring that knowledge to the outside world. Typical reports might examine issues which affected all departments like the number of civil servants and with what skills would be required to deliver Brexit (Comptroller and Auditor General, 2017), issues which affected a central administering body (Comptroller and Auditor General, 2017a, 2017c) or the way a single department dealt with Brexit (Comptroller and Auditor General, 2018, 2018e). The reports were cautiously worded: for example, in its review of the Department for Environment, Food and Rural Affairs (DEFRA) in 2018, the NAO concluded that 'Defra has achieved a great deal in difficult circumstances and to a very demanding timescale', despite the fact that the report also pointed out, 'Defra's plans for its individual work streams are improving, but many are of poor quality and lack maturity' and that it had missed 39% of its milestones for preparing for EU exit (C&AG, 2018, p. 3). This treatment of Brexit recognised, from Morse's point of view, the difficulties for the civil service of delivering against it. He told the EU Exit Committee that

> people have not sat down and said, 'I know what; we will have a Brexit project'. What has happened is the civil service has been landed with a very challenging task. You would not set out to do it this way from the management point of view. What you are dealing with here is something where you cannot put your ducks in the row in the time that you ought to be able to. You do not put your plans in place and have a clear objective. You cannot do all that. You just have to start running, but that is not an argument for not getting those things in place later.
>
> *(Exiting the European Union Committee, 2018, Q2709)*

From this point of view, Morse saw his role as making transparent what the civil service were doing, while understanding and conveying to the wider public the pressures they were under. Morse attempted to do this through intervening in the debate occasionally: infamously, he told the press that the government's plans for Brexit could fall apart 'like a chocolate orange'[16] and criticised the co-ordination of Brexit policy by the Cabinet Office, the Department for Exiting the EU and Treasury (Syal, 2017).

The focus on transparency and central co-ordination meant that the NAO's influence on the debate was limited, but subtle. Key actors in the discussions between 2017 and 2019 did not feel that the NAO had much of an impact at all upon what was happening: David Davis (EU Exit Secretary 2016–8 and PAC chair 1997–2001), when asked what he thought of the NAO's response to Brexit, answered by saying, 'truthfully, I mean I don't know', and suggesting that had he been able to, he would have liked to have commissioned work by the NAO to speed up Whitehall's preparations for a no-deal Brexit (interview, David Davis). The NAO's agenda harmonised with Meg Hillier (chair of the PAC) who wanted to keep her committee together in approaching the subject. She told us that 'I always point out that on Brexit, we had 12 reports. And we had every range of opinion from hard line Brexiteers to hardline remainers. You couldn't have had a broader range of opinion. And yet we agreed reports unanimously' (Meg Hillier, interview). The NAO and PAC therefore succeeded in charting a course through the Brexit debates that at one and the same time combined an administrative critique with making information transparent and also maintaining their reputation for impartiality. The NAO did this by sacrificing some of the usual immediate political impact of its work and letting itself fade into the role of a provider of information to others who then would interpret and make use of it. This subtle adaptation in role was Morse's response, supported by Bichard and Hillier, to the dilemmas caused by the political divisions and uncertainty over Brexit.

6.3.4 The Public Accounts Committee (PAC)

Morse also faced tension from a new PAC Chair, Margaret Hodge. Hodge said in her memoirs that she and Morse had a 'somewhat fractious relationship' early on (Hodge, 2016, p. 33). She had been elected to Parliament in 1994 and had been a minister, but she owed her appointment as PAC chair to her re-election battle in 2010, during which she took on and defeated the British National Party. Hodge derived incredible prestige from this in the Commons; her victory gave her 'a national profile at the time' (Margaret Hodge, interview). Meg Hillier, MP, told us that 'everybody coming into Parliament knew Margaret Hodge off the back of the Barking election. Her strong reputation and name recognition undoubtedly helped her win in the first ever election, hotly contested, of chair of the PAC'.

As chair, this gave Hodge extensive power to shape the role as she wished. She 'was determined not to be a mere mouthpiece for the National Audit Office', and early conflicts with Amyas revolved around her desire to bring in alternative sources of advice to the committee (Hodge, 2016, pp. 33–34). Hodge even proposed running an inquiry into the entire system of public audit in the UK off the back of the demise of the Audit Commission (Hodge, 2016, p. 36). In these conflicts, she was seen as being 'pretty antagonistic [and] combative' (Sir Andrew Likierman, interview). Philip Aylett, one of her clerks, told us that Hodge's main frustration was that 'the NAO was doing too much of the work in the sense that the committee would not put its own stamp on things' (Phillip Aylett, interview). She felt that the NAO was often 'too timid in its approach or in its criticism' (Adrian Jenner, interview). Sarah Petit, another clerk of PAC, thought that Hodge was more independent than the NAO's preferred model of chair: 'there was perhaps sometimes a slight tension where the committee wanted to do something, approach something in a different way to how the NAO would've done it, and I felt that the committee should be able to do that but the NAO didn't always' (Sarah Petit, interview). The NAO too was frustrated with Hodge: Gabrielle Cohen recalled that at times the PAC had requested the NAO should provide tax details relating individual taxpayers. She said,

> Hodge in particular, was frustrated by the constraints imposed by the legal and constitutional framework governing the NAO's work. For example, in the context of the Committee's work on tax avoidance and evasion, she was keen to see details of the tax affairs of large corporates. She was concerned that NAO's interpretation of tax law and its own governing legislation and conventions prohibited it from passing such information to the Committee. It was perhaps the time of greatest tension between the Committee and the NAO.
>
> *(Gabrielle Cohen, interview)*

Hodge had a powerful agenda of her own. It was based around her experience in Barking. She spoke passionately about the way in which it influenced her conduct at PAC:

> And I thought, it is our money. It is taxpayer's money. And we should understand where it goes. My constituents care about their money. So, I was very conscious of that sort of accountability back to the taxpayer, to the constituents and I didn't want civil servants to hide behind technical jargon.
>
> (*Margaret Hodge, interview*)

This link between the committee's work and the experience of ordinary people was one Hodge was keen to make. We will discuss how this affected the scope of the NAO's work later, but the political impulse that Hodge gave to the PAC's work definitely changed the environment within which the NAO operated.

Hodge's approach to accountability affected the attitudes of senior civil servants towards the PAC and the NAO. Lord O'Donnell said that 'from a permanent secretary's perspective, you should never underestimate the fact that they are driven by what happens when they appear before the PAC' and argued that 'some felt there wasn't enough pushback from the official NAO to try and put across a balanced message' (O'Donnell, interview). The most important example of Hodge's assertiveness in holding government departments and their officials to account came in November 2011. During a PAC session, she forced the general counsel at HMRC, Anthony Inglese, to take an oath that his evidence to the committee would be true and complete after the committee accused Mr Inglese of refusing to either disclose information to them or justify why he would not disclose information to them (Public Accounts Committee, 2011, Q294). Lord O'Donnell, the then cabinet secretary, described the hearing as 'a theatrical exercise in public humiliation'. He told Hodge that 'there is now a serious issue about the way that you are perceived by the wider civil service' (Hodge, 2016, p. 72). Within the NAO, Hodge's attempt to put Inglese on oath was seen by some as unprecedented.

O'Donnell's words illustrated the way in which Hodge's assertiveness created a potential problem on two fronts for the NAO: firstly, there was the obvious tension between the PAC chair, who wanted to make the committee more clearly independent of the NAO, and the NAO, with its own agenda which was used to working with a less assertive committee, and secondly, there was the question of how far her poor relationship with some permanent secretaries would affect the NAO's audit relationship with government departments. If O'Donnell was right and Hodge had discredited the process in the eyes of the civil service through her level of combativeness, then senior civil servants might lose trust in the NAO as well, seeing them as Hodge's adjunct.

Meg Hillier, who replaced Hodge after the 2015 general election, had a much less combative personality and reputation within Whitehall and the NAO. As Nick Smith, MP, told us, within the committee, 'Both Margaret and Meg have great strengths: Margaret was challenging for witnesses and others and broke new ground. She provided new substance to the Committee's work, as well as bringing bit of theatre to committee room 15. Meg is collegiate and that helps build an esprit de corps amongst committee members'. Smith thought that Hodge and Hillier had very different styles regarding the NAO as well but that the 'NAO bent into it and that's part of its role' (Nick Smith, interview).

One way for the NAO to ensure that it was not tied to any particular PAC chair was for the organisation to expand its work with other select committees in the Commons. Whilst the NAO had engaged with select committees under Sir John Bourn, this activity expanded greatly under Morse (Midgley, 2019). Clive Betts, chair of the Communities and Local Government Select Committee (and its successor committees) between 2010 and 2024, told us that he thought better engagement with the NAO had started after 2010: the NAO 'had become a lot brighter', and 'was offering to come and brief us about things that were very useful (Clive Betts, interview). A reason for this decision to engage more with select committees was to build the NAO a wider reputation within the House of Commons. It differed by committee, but certainly contact between some NAO directors and the select committee clerks 'increased considerably' during this period (Jeremy Lonsdale, interview). And the NAO perspective on a department's work was not always in tune with the interests of members, some finding briefings on aspects of the accounts, for example, 'rather dry and arcane' (Jeremy Lonsdale, interview).

However, there were risks. Whereas the PAC stays away from policy, other select committees are appointed to 'examine the expenditure, administration and policy' of government departments (House of Commons, 2023). Members often seemed ignorant of the NAO in sessions with Morse. For example, the experienced Conservative MP, Sir Peter Bone, asked him once whether he was a civil servant (Exiting the European Union Committee, 2018, Q2704).

Morse's greater number of appearances before other select committees could have caused a threat to the NAO's independence if he were to be commenting on policy; however, he and his officials were careful always to stay on the right side of the 1983 Act. For example, in 2018 he was invited by Stephen Timms, MP, to speculate on the state of negotiations between the UK and the EU in the Exiting the EU Committee. Morse responded by saying,

> I cannot comment on how effective it has been at improving the negotiations, because that is not a subject I look at. What I call the in-principle negotiations going on at Government level is not something I review, so I cannot say how effective it has been at that, which I suspect was the primary objective.
>
> *(Exiting the European Union Committee, 2018, Q2721)*

Morse's reluctance to comment on the effectiveness of the negotiations was similar to his reluctance to comment on the end to which the negotiations were being addressed: when asked by Sammy Wilson, MP, to speculate on the likelihood of a no-deal Brexit, Morse confined his comments to saying that he did 'not think it is a mistake to pay an insurance premium against a risk' (Exiting the European Union Committee, 2018, Q2724).

6.4 Capacity

The story of the NAO's independence is woven into the story of austerity after 2010, and the same is true concerning capacity.

Morse told the Public Accounts Commission in 2010 that he had opted to cut the NAO's spending by 15%: he said that he had chosen this figure as

> we looked at the overall rate of reduction in the public sector and we thought, 'Well, there's a degree of practising what you preach. We're talking to departments about efficiency; we need to think about that'.
>
> *(Public Accounts Commission, 2011)*

Morse clearly thought that the NAO should cut to imitate Whitehall. Not all of the NAO's staff agreed. Christian van Stolk said that senior staff told him that the NAO had decided without external pressure to adopt the cuts that Morse proposed (Christian van Stolk, interview). Others thought that many of these early cuts only eliminated excessive spending on consultancy and unnecessary additional work without damaging the core value-for-money reports (Michael Whitehouse, interview).

Whatever the reasons for Morse's cuts, they were real. In 2007–8, the NAO's gross spend was £98 million: this figure was actually falling before 2010 and had fallen to £95 million in 2009–10 (NAO, 2008, p. 32, 2010a, p. 95). After that, though, the reductions were much greater: spending fell to £83 million by 2014–15 (NAO, 2015, p. 88). Net spending fell too: from £74 million in Morse's first year of operations to £62 million in 2014–15 (NAO,2009, p. 82, 2015, p. 88). In nominal terms, the NAO, despite taking on new responsibilities, only reached its 2008 total of net expenditure in 2022 (£81 million in 2007–8 compared to £83 million in 2022–3 (NAO, 2008, p. 32, 2023, p. 85). These cuts meant fewer staff were working at the NAO in general during Morse's period as C&AG than before. Whereas under Bourn, staff levels had increased over the decades, under Morse that increase stopped. In 2009, the NAO employed 921 people: it would not be until 2022 under Morse's successor that the total would be exceeded (NAO, 2009, p. 94, 2022, p. 88). Staffing numbers fell quite dramatically: until in 2015 they reached 791 members of staff working at the organisation and they settled around 810 between 2016 and 2019, fewer than had worked in the NAO in 2004 (NAO, 2015, p. 90, 2019, p. 76).

Morse achieved these cuts to expenditure and staffing largely through cutting the amount dedicated to value-for-money audit within the budget. In Bourn's last full year as C&AG, the NAO had spent £25 million on value for money (NAO, 2008, p. 32). By 2010–11, that figure had fallen to £19 million under Morse, and by 2017–18, it had further reduced to £13 million (NAO, 2011, p. 70; 2018a, p. 104). This decline is exaggerated potentially by the fact that the NAO changed the way it categorised its spending several times in this period. Another way of seeing the same trend, therefore, is to examine spending that was not focussed on financial audit: in Bourn's last full year (2007–8), excluding the Comptroller function and the cost of moving buildings, the NAO spent £44 million net on non-financial audit activities (NAO, 2008, p. 32). In 2014–15, after Morse's cost cutting, that figure had reduced by 32% to £31 million (NAO, 2015, p. 88). In contrast, spending on financial audit sat at a net £27 million in 2007–8 and by 2010–11 had risen to £35 million, and whilst it reduced slightly to £30 million in the mid-2010s, by the end of Morse's term, it was climbing again to reach £38 million in his last year (NAO, 2008, p. 32, 2011, p. 70, 2014, p. 85, 2019, p. 99). The focus of the cuts was changing the nature of the organisation itself: in 2008, 41% of the NAO's gross expenditure had gone on financial audit; by the end of Morse's period in office, 68% of the NAO's gross expenditure was on financial audit (NAO, 2008, p. 32, 2019, p. 99).

There were clear consequences to this shift in resources, firstly, within value for money as a discipline. Richard Bacon raised this with Morse in 2010: 'what steps have you taken to ensure that, notwithstanding that they [value for money reports] are being done more quickly, that quality is maintained?' (Public Accounts Commission, 2011). Whilst Morse offered reassurance, Bacon's question was apt. Much of the service provided by value-for-money audit did not change. Margaret Hodge reflected, in terms reminiscent of David Davis 10 years before, that 'it was a joy to work with the NAO because there were a lot of bright people in the NAO' (interview, Margaret Hodge). However, Morse's focus in audit was different.

Christian van Stolk thought that value-for-money audit scope had been significantly affected by the change in budgets: he said that 'the NAO's methods became much more "plain vanilla" and the "studies had to be simpler and much more efficient"' (interview, Christian van Stolk). There was 'a disruption of traditional relationships with organisations like RAND' (interview, Christian van Stolk). Morse decided to dispense with most of the consultants the NAO were using and build up in-house capacity. Patrick Dunleavy, who had worked as an academic with the NAO under Bourn, noticed that Morse was 'more conservative' (interview, Patrick Dunleavy). Under Morse, the NAO kept to a much more traditional set of subjects using a much more traditional set of methods than they had at the end of Bourn's time as C&AG.

The change in resources going to value for money was driven thus by Morse's view of what value-for money-audit was as well as constraints on resources. The same was true on financial audit. The key driver in financial audit lay in the way that the NAO defined the capacity they required. They defined it, as we described above, as the capacity to conduct a private sector audit. This made the NAO even more concerned about salaries keeping pace with the private sector. The NAO were aware that staff on financial audit could easily move to the private sector if they chose: as Michael Whitehouse said, 'if someone has the financial audit qualification, they can easily get a job in the firms. If they have got experience in value for money and not financial audit, it was a bit more difficult for them to move as the private sector would ask "well, what have you actually done?"' (Michael Whitehouse, interview). Furthermore, the increasing technical complexity of the audits that the NAO were trying to provide and the desire to match private sector standards meant that financial audit expenditure had to be maintained.

The evolution in the type of organisation that the NAO represented was matched by a change in the staffing of the organisation. In 2014, Michael Whitehouse reported to the Public Accounts Commission that 'Forty people left the NAO last year at quite a senior level, and that had a significant impact; it had never happened before in the time of the NAO, to my knowledge' (Public Accounts Commission, 2014, Q21). This change in senior management was led by a desire to reduce the NAO's spend. Ed Humpherson believed that Morse thought that the 'organisation needed a huge shake up' and that there was a 'slight degree of sleepiness' within the NAO (Ed Humpherson, interview). Neil Sayers told us that Morse wanted to 'get this organisation by the scruff of the neck and shake it very hard and refocus it' (Neil Sayers, interview). Morse was given this remit by others as well. Lord Macpherson said that under Bourn, 'there was a risk that the NAO was becoming stale' and

Morse was 'a change of air' for the organisation (Macpherson, interview). Internally, this necessitated a change in culture. Martin Sinclair said,

> Amyas really pushed that cultural change forward. And also you had people who understood that if we were to be a really effective organisation, we did have to pay more concerted attention to organisational developments, how do you manage a professional staff, how do you make it an attractive place to work, how do you deal with equality and diversity issues.
>
> *(Martin Sinclair, interview)*

These changes in culture had other effects. The NAO became more interested under Morse in issues like diversity, publishing its first assessment of its gender pay gap in 2017. Sinclair also noted that they had begun to investigate why staff from ethnic minorities did not get promoted at the same rate as staff from white backgrounds:

> we did a big piece of work and it showed that staff from ethnic minorities were absolutely like for like with white staff on recruitment. However, when you looked at their probationary reports 6 months on and twelve months on, as a cohort they were falling behind. So, we asked why was that happening? We found that they weren't getting the opportunities, to shine and be identified for promotion. We devised a programme to change things.
>
> *(Martin Sinclair, interview)*

Sinclair's recollection demonstrates that the NAO was moving with the times under Morse and becoming a comparable organisation to other professional organisations.

6.5 Audit scope

Morse was faced with, from the NAO's viewpoint, a set of unprecedented situations during his time as C&AG. The UK reacted to the financial crisis of 2007–8 by cutting the public sector in the 2010s, and then in 2016, the British public voted that the UK leave the EU.

As we have discussed above, this had consequences both for the NAO's independence and for the capacity to audit the public sector; here, we move on to discuss the consequences of these events, and the way that Morse interpreted them, for the scope of the NAO's audit.

There are four sections to our consideration of audit scope including accountability, value for money, financial audit and extension of scope.

Firstly, we examine the ways in which Morse's (and Tim Burr's) view of the new situation changed the NAO's view of accountability: accelerating a trend to see accountability in managerial rather than parliamentary terms. Secondly, the changes to capacity in value for money and Morse's vision of managerial accountability altered the type and content of the value-for-money reports that the NAO produced. Thirdly, we set out how the NAO's professionalisation of financial audit and its view of accountability as a managerial rather than a parliamentary construct reinforced the trend towards seeing accounting best practice as the proper aim of financial audit in the public sector. Finally, the extension to the scope of activities during this period will be considered.

6.5.1 Accountability

The evolution of the NAO's view of accountability during this period was partly down to Morse, though elements of it could be seen in the short time Tim Burr held the post of C&AG. In this section, we will document different ways in which this perspective on accountability evolved. Firstly, we will demonstrate that the NAO's reaction to the financial crisis, which began under Tim Burr and continued under Amyas Morse, demonstrated the ways in which the Gladstonian tradition of parliamentary accountability was less important to the NAO than it had been before. Rather, Morse saw accountability in terms of good public management and democratic transparency (C&AG, 2016). We will trace these principles of accountability – good public management and democratic government – through the NAO's responses to the financial crisis, austerity and the Brexit negotiations between 2017 and 2019.

6.5.1.1 Parliamentary accountability

The NAO reported on the UK's response to the global financial crisis in 2007–8 (C&AG, 2009), which serves to illustrate how its view of accountability had shifted since the days of the E&AD as significantly it no longer saw itself as purely an enforcer of parliamentary authority (which the E&AD under Gladstone (see Chapter 2) had seen itself as doing).

In response to the financial crisis, the UK's decision to nationalise and support the banks was unprecedented. The Treasury can spend money (as with any other government department) only on matters included in its estimate's ambit. In previous times, the auditors would have examined the ambit and concluded that the Treasury needed additional authorisation from Parliament before it could spend money on something that it did not envisage doing when Parliament voted the money. However, the NAO in 2009 did not adopt this approach, as the estimate ambit was so wide that it could be interpreted to include any possible action aimed at the stability of the financial system. Steve Corbishley told us,

> So, we continued with this approach in our examination of the banking interventions ensuring that government had the appropriate authorities, such as through the ambit of the Appropriation Act.
>
> *(Steve Corbishley, interview)*

The vagueness of the wording of the estimate therefore meant that the NAO did not really need to consider the question of regularity. The NAO concluded that the Treasury could in effect spend money on anything that it wished, providing that the Treasury thought that by doing so it was securing financial stability, which contrasts with the Gladstonian view that the ambit should tightly constrain what a department could or could not do without Parliamentary authorisation.

HM Treasury could in effect override parliamentary procedure without apparently much criticism from the NAO. For example, in its 2009 survey of the Treasury's guarantees to the banks, the NAO stated that

> The indemnity for the Bank of England's emergency support to RBS and HBOS was not reported to Parliament, as would normally be expected under long-standing procedures put in place by the Treasury to control the use of public money. This indemnity would normally have been notified to Parliament as a contingent liability before it was granted. Because of the considerable sensitivity of the support operation at the time, the Treasury judged that it was not in the public interest to follow procedures that allow for confidential notification to the chairs of the Committee of Public Accounts and the relevant departmental select committee.
>
> *(C&AG, 2009a, p. 6)*

Parliamentary procedure had clearly ceased to be the focus of the NAO's work as it would have been a hundred years before. These questions were not as relevant to the audit of austerity or even of Brexit. There are reasons for this: in general, governments knew that austerity was happening as it happened so were able to seek approval from Parliament. Secondly, in the case of Brexit, no constitutional issues arose in which the NAO had to make a call as to whether Parliament's instructions to the government had been faulted. This situation could have arisen: in July 2019, Dominic Grieve[17] and Margaret Beckett[18] tried to pass a motion that would have deprived the government of funding for four departments had they gone ahead with Brexit, but the motion was not passed (Faulconbridge, 2019).

Neither in the case of the bank bailouts, where the government was carrying out a novel financial bailout, nor in the case of austerity or Brexit, where the issue of parliamentary approval arose, did the NAO see its role as mainly upholding the rights of the House of Commons over government finance.

6.5.1.2 Accountability as good public management and democratic government

So the question, therefore, is how did the NAO see its role with respect to accountability as being, if it was not to uphold a constitutional system of safeguards and systems of accountability?

The answer to this came in the NAO's own report about public sector accountability: they said that 'accountability to Parliament for taxpayers' money is an inextricable part of good public management and democratic government' (C&AG, 2016, p. 4). In this statement, the NAO did not connect accountability to the practices of Parliament but to two abstract ideas: public management and democratic government. These two ideas informed the NAO's response to the financial crisis: austerity and Brexit. We cover how the NAO implemented this approach, through each of the crises that Morse experienced as C&AG.

Although the NAO had not yet published its report on accountability when the financial crisis hit the UK, it followed the approach to accountability set out in 2016. For example, in its 2010 report on the banking schemes, all three of the NAO's recommendations focussed on the Treasury's capacity. The NAO suggested that the Treasury needed to ensure that it identified how many staff it needed, ensured they were sufficiently expert and preserved an institutional memory of the crisis (C&AG, 2010c). This was not uncommon: the C&AG's report on the sale of Northern Rock focussed on technical issues such as whether the Treasury had challenged with 'sufficient rigour' Northern Rock's forecasts for future trading conditions, whether it had restricted the company's lending activities, had 'struggled to maintain continuity in staffing' and queried its agreement with Goldman Sachs on advisory work (C&AG, 2009, pp. 7–10). Similarly, in assessing the sale of Lloyds nine years later, the NAO report stated that

> This review does not form a judgement on the value for money of the share sales. However, our view of the process as a whole is positive: UK Financial Investments Limited (UKFI) and its advisers prepared for, and executed, the transactions professionally; and in cash terms the sale returned the taxpayers' original investment. We found some areas

> where improvements could be made for future sales, and this report summarises those more technical observations and recommendations arising from our work.
>
> *(C&AG, 2018a, p. 4)*

Policy questions were avoided: the NAO's report on Northern Rock accepted the government rationale for extraordinary intervention: 'Treasury had no choice but to put in place guarantee arrangements for the retail depositors, once a run on deposits was underway' (C&AG, 2009, p. 6). In terms of democratic government, Steven Corbishley told us that the Treasury's financial accounts, as audited by the NAO and supplemented by the C&AG's reports, 'set out the nature of the schemes put in place to rescue the banks and their evolution over time' (Steve Corbishley, interview). The NAO concluded that it was important for there to be an independent commentary which would show 'how large the guarantees were and what the impact of their failure could be as the guarantees that were in place were valued in the hundreds and hundreds of billions of pounds' (Steve Corbishley, interview). The C&AG kept up a steady stream of annual reports to Parliament on HM Treasury's financial statements, supplementing value-for-money work, which showed the government's financial exposure to the banking system was changing (C&AG, 2011, 2012, 2013, 2014, 2015). Interestingly, on its own website, the banking reports are set out in order and conclude with a 2016 report on managing the government's balance sheet (NAO, 2023). The NAO's work on the financial crisis therefore reflects an attitude to public accountability that broke down the concept into democratic government – identified largely with transparency – and good public management.

The same approach is obvious when the NAO's work on austerity is examined. Following the 2010 general election, the NAO published a pamphlet focussed on structured cost reduction: it was clearly aimed at departments and its lessons were very managerial,

> Cutting spending effectively requires departments to take a strategic overview to avoid an erosion of service quality in priority delivery areas. Departments should clearly prioritise what matters most, based on an accurate, realistic assessment of the costs, benefits and risks of the options.
>
> *(NAO, 2010, p. 3)*

The NAO followed up this point with later reports on cost reduction, all of which were couched in the same managerial language. In 2012, for example, the NAO recommended that departments should implement austerity 'as part of a well-managed change programme' which would 'minimise impacts on services' (C&AG, 2012b, p. 5). Whilst the NAO called on departments to understand better the impact of their cuts, they phrased this aspiration in the language of cost drivers:

> Departments' financial data on basic spending patterns is sufficient to manage budgets in-year, but information about the consequences of changes in spending is less good. There are few examples of systems that link costs to performance. Without improvements in impact measurement, departments will not be able to track or manage the impact of cost reduction on service provision. Not understanding the factors driving cost and the consequences of spending cuts makes it difficult for departments to forecast future spending.
>
> *(C&AG, 2012b, p. 7)*

All these reports analysed aspects of the government's processes to see whether they could reduce the cost of services. This approach to austerity – seeing it as a challenge for the civil service to manage and to develop a 'target operating model' for public services – had two impacts (C&AG, 2012b, p. 31).The first was it meant that the NAO largely avoided the political controversy about austerity, but secondly, the NAO did not provide an analysis of the impact of austerity on the lives of ordinary Britons. Given that austerity is widely seen by some as contributing to the instability of the UK state after 2015, it could be argued that this was a gap in the UK's accountability system during this period (Murphy et al., 2019; Fetzer, 2019).

The NAO saw public services as systems managed from Whitehall. This was the implication of an early group of studies by the NAO conducted just after the 2010 election called landscape reviews. These reviews were described well in 2010 in the context of the criminal justice system:

> This management report takes a strategic view of the whole of the criminal justice system. It has been prepared to inform the debate on future developments and, in particular, on how the Government can achieve better services for less expenditure. As such, it differs from the value for money reports to Parliament that the Comptroller and Auditor General carries out under the National Audit Act, 1983. Instead of focusing on the economy, efficiency and effectiveness of individual departments or programmes of expenditure, we have taken an end-to-end view of the offender 'journey' and aimed to highlight long-standing and challenging issues that need to be considered.
>
> *(C&AG, 2010b, p. 4)*

As the quotation sets out, the review was intended to see the system – in this case criminal justice – as a whole entity, managed from the Home Office and Ministry of Justice, rather than as a set of single programmes or projects. (In doing this, Morse's NAO was unknowingly continuing something that Bourn's NAO had begun, though in the earlier case, the impetus had come from Sir David Omand and the civil service.) Seeing public sector delivery in this way had implications for the ways in which the NAO saw austerity.

The focus on whole systems of public sector delivery began with the NAO's analysis of outsourced services. The NAO's approach to auditing outsourcing and using markets in the public sector was more holistic than a pure reading of the contract might imply. Principles papers on delivering through markets, the failure of service providers and payment by results identified the need for government to understand the impact of its delivery models upon the users of the services involved (NAO, 2012; C&AG, 2015a, 2015b). Frequently in the 2010s, the NAO found that the government had achieved cost reductions by passing them on to providers, and it highlighted the risk that services would collapse if contractors withdrew (NAO, 2012a). In some cases, the risk materialised, and the government was found to have contracted either with inexperienced contractors or at rates which did not enable the contractor to perform the required work (C&AG, 2012a; NAO, 2012a; C&AG, 2013e). At PAC, Robert Devereux (Permanent Secretary at the Department for Work and Pensions (2011–18) and Morse clashed over this very argument. Devereux argued that the NAO recommended that the department spend more money on services to the unemployed than they had, and Morse explained that he was concerned about the risk that contractors would walk out (PAC, 2012, Q101). The implications of this point could easily be transferred from the situation in which a contractor contracted with the private sector to deliver something to the situation where central government devolved the management of a service to another part of government.

The NAO developed this argument over a long period of time, in combination with the PAC. And of course, the NAO were able to examine outsourced markets due to the precedent set in the 1990s that the auditors' access rights were built into contracts. In 2012, the NAO said that it was concerned that

> Departments do not always understand the cost drivers and cost value ratios of devolved bodies sufficiently to make good decisions about changes in funding. Nine departments spend more than 50 per cent of their budget through arm's-length or devolved bodies. Departments that deliver through others need to have a coherent strategy to deliver their objectives at lower cost, which takes into account the value delivered by

> different funding streams. The departments we have looked at do not have full capability to do this. Generally their strategy combines cuts to lower priority funding with an expectation that delivery bodies will manage their own costs down.
>
> *(C&AG, 2012b, p. 7)*

The NAO identified specific examples in its reports during the period. For example, in its 2013 report on capital funding for new schools, the NAO assessed that the Department for Education risked not funding local authorities enough to supply places required for new primary school children (C&AG, 2013c). The NAO saw its role as alerting departments and the PAC to concerning trends in the finances of bodies who delivered locally: for example, in 2013, it reported that 'more NHS trusts and foundation trusts reported deficits in 2013-14 than in 2012-13' and that 'the average earnings before interest, tax, depreciation and amortisation for NHS trusts and foundation trusts has fallen in the past 4 years' (C&AG, 2014d, p. 7). Further reports on the NHS's financial position identified that additional funding intended for the reform of services was spent on coping with financial pressures instead (C&AG, 2018b) and documented issues with the funding settlement for the NHS (C&AG, 2019).

The NAO also expected departments to analyse the effect of their policies on the parties they interacted with. In its report on the New Homes Bonus, the NAO criticised the Department for Communities and Local Government for the fact that 'the Department's impact assessment did not cover the potential financial risk for local authorities that lose funding as a result of the bonus [scheme]' (C&AG, 2013d, p. 25). Departments were told that they had to monitor and understand their own delivery chains and could not rely on local accountability arrangements if they were insufficient:

> The new arrangements [to local government accountability] provide departments with less direct information on how local authorities spend government grants and whether they achieve their outcomes. Departments rely more on systems of local accountability to ensure relevant local authority spending meets with Parliament's intentions and is value for money.
>
> *(C&AG, 2014a, p. 5)*

As Rob Whiteman told us, this opened up a new avenue of thinking about accountability:

> Quite a lot about this, I think, is saying, 'Here is a set of policy goals, oh, Minister. Here is a set of costing data that tells us how much those

> policy goals cost. . . . And here is the budget that you've set. This does not match'.
>
> *(Whiteman, interview)*

Whiteman's point is important. The auditor was almost becoming an auditor of the spending that had not happened as well as the spending that had. For some this was an outrage: an attempted extension of central government accountability down to a constitutionally inappropriate level (Jones and Stewart, 2012). However, for Morse and the NAO more generally, these constitutional questions were less relevant than the clarity that responsibility and accountability for decisions should rest at the same point: if central government reduced funding and did not change the ambitions it had for the system, it was responsible for the mismatch between the resources and ambitions.

It is key to realise what this approach was not: it was not a systematic criticism of austerity from a policy perspective, but rather what Morse had arrived at was a critique of austerity framed around departments facing austerity as a management challenge. If austerity was an external event, then departments should manage and adjust to it. The NAO recommended they should cope by redesigning their management structures to ensure planning long term and that cross-departmental challenges were met (C&AG, 2018g). This message was aligned with what politicians wanted as well. The PAC produced its own report on accountability in 2012, noting that

> Greater confidence is needed in the capacity and skills of oversight bodies. Where decision making is devolved to the local level, to the bodies directly providing services, there needs to be a clear and appropriate structure for the regulation and review of the performance of those local delivery bodies.
>
> *(PAC, 2011a)*

The approach taken was particularly true in local government. The NAO had taken on new responsibilities in this area (described later) and used them to analyse local authority financial sustainability. The auditors saw local 'authorities' ability to deliver their statutory services as the defining test of their financial sustainability' (C&AG, 2018h, p. 5).

However, the analysis of financial sustainability in local government crossed over to become an analysis which also supported democratic government. The NAO's role in detecting this gap – between statutory services, on the one hand, and the funds committed to resource them, on the other – was crucial to the parliamentary scrutiny of local government finance. Clive Betts (chair of the Local Government Committee, 2010–) told us that he thought the NAO's role here was crucial:

> it was important we could verify what we knew what was happening instinctually but wanted the information and figures to show what was happening that couldn't really be challenged.
>
> *(Clive Betts, interview)*

Betts' argument in this quotation demonstrates the strength of Morse's focus on responsibility and accountability in a managerial rather than a constitutional sense: it enabled the NAO and Parliament more widely to hold ministers and senior officials to account for the decisions they made, rather than misallocating that accountability to local bodies who were dealing with the consequences of decisions made elsewhere. The development of the Accounting Officer Systems Statement pinned responsibility firmly to central departments.

More widely, the NAO responded to austerity with further transparency. The experiment in producing guides to the accounts which had begun under John Bourn was strengthened and institutionalised (Midgley, 2019). Departmental Overviews, as they were now described by the NAO, were published for all departments and some other areas including local government. The overviews contained no new information but purely summarised and placed in context information from other sources with a particular focus on the NAO's value-for-money reports and the financial accounts published by the departments. They were also part of Morse's desire for the NAO to be more strategic in the way it thought about departments and for individual pieces of work to be seen in context and to be understood contextually.

The NAO during the financial crisis and austerity had maintained the two pillars of accountability it described in its 2016 report.

The third great event of Morse's period in charge was Brexit. As we have already discussed, the NAO published a stream of studies during the aftermath of the referendum campaign and the negotiations by Theresa May and then Boris Johnson about the UK's exit and future relationship with the EU. The NAO's approach to accountability was suited to the topic. Pre-exit, most of what could be discussed was how departments were setting up systems to cope with the UK's departure: for example, the NAO's report on customs preparations explained delays to the timetable for preparing the customs system for a border with the EU. The report focussed on 'how HMRC is managing' the programme, 'technical challenges' to implementing new systems and 'HMRC's actions to ensure that traders and others involved in customs' were ready by January 2019 (C&AG, 2018d, p. 8).

The focus on Brexit as a management challenge leant a particular tone to the NAO's efforts to make Brexit transparent. The NAO assessed departments' progress against the requirements of EU exit, and they used an internal government concept of 'work streams' to do so. For example, the NAO's report on the Foreign Office's approach to Brexit explained that the Foreign Office was responsible for 11 of these workstreams and then identified progress (C&AG, 2018e). Seeing its role as making the management challenge of Brexit as transparent as possible ushered the NAO into new territory. In 2017, the NAO explained that Brexit meant the UK would require a large amount of new legislation to be passed. Indeed, the NAO noted that this would be challenging as the UK needed to pass about 1,000 statutory instruments before Brexit, which would effectively double the number the Commons needed to pass in that year (C&AG, 2017, p. 10). Seeing the process of Brexit through the lens of good public management and democratic accountability allowed Morse to set a precedent by commenting for the first time on the legislative timetable adopted by the Commons.

6.5.2 Value for money

The new attitude to accountability changed the way that the NAO performed value-for-money reports. As opposed to the more academic approach that John Bourn, in his later years, valued, Morse's focus was on 'are the senior civil servants doing a good job of delivering the programmes they said they would' (interview, Ed Humpherson). Morse's approach was far more traditional in that sense. Humpherson had the impression that Morse's original sense was that the organisation was 'far too academic' (Humpherson, interview). Morse put it himself even more clearly than Humpherson, when he told us,

> At the NAO, you are not running with research programmes. That's not what it says on the tin. What we're actually there for is to protect taxpayers' interest in terms of value for money. So, I wanted the ammunition, I didn't want all this other stuff.
>
> *(Amyas Morse, interview)*

Morse wanted reports that would fulfil the twin mandates set out above. Christian van Stolk detected what he described as of 'more of the hand of God' and 'much more control being exercised' in all the NAO's products at this time (interview, Christian van Stolk). Morse cut the size of reports: 10,000 words and no more (though as in any organisation exceptions were made occasionally). Jeremy Lonsdale, who was responsible for overseeing value-for-money audit methodology and practice at the time, recalled him saying that he 'wanted to cut reports right back and sharpen up the summaries' when he arrived as C&AG, which forced teams to think more carefully about what was important. In the 2000s, the cost and complexity of NAO studies had both become considerable, with multiple methods, elements contracted out, long fieldwork stages and large surveys, for example, which generated long reports which took time to write and to clear. Michael Whitehouse said Morse complained that the NAO's earlier reports had been 'too woolly' (Michael Whitehouse, interview). Alex Scharaschkin recalled this move too: 'towards the end of my time there, we had shorter reports and shorter timescales and so on' (Alex Scharaschkin, interview). Morse's desire for concise reports with granular financial information was matched by his desire that the reports should have clear conclusions. He placed great emphasis on making sure that the report's message was clear and saw his job as C&AG as ensuring that the value-for-money conclusion was absolutely clear. Morse was also willing to challenge ministers publicly when they mischaracterised the work of the NAO. For example, in 2018, when Esther McVey,[19] then Secretary of State for Work and Pensions, made statements in the House of Commons about an NAO report on Universal Credit, stating that 'the NAO's report did not take into account recent changes to the programme', Morse wrote to her saying that his report 'was based on the most accurate and up to date information from your department' and other statements she had made were 'also not correct'. His letter was published (Morse, 2018).

Humpherson and Morse both suggested that Morse wanted to move the NAO away from academic or research reports and towards doing more focussed reports (as discussed above under capacity). This had a clear consequence of the types of methods that the NAO used and led to a sharp reduction in the involvement of external resources in NAO value-for-money audit work. Instead of contracting out large elements of fieldwork as had been the norm under John Bourn, under Amyas Morse there was a more systematic effort to recruit technical specialists: economists, sector specialists and different types of analysts in order to enhance in-house capacity, including at senior levels.

The NAO's reporting on effectiveness returned often to the template used by Sir Gordon Downey, when the NAO really audited the arrangements that the department had put in place to secure effectiveness rather than the achievement of effective spending by a programme. Reports would concentrate on the performance data collected by departments themselves (C&AG, 2014e, 2016b, 2018f), or at most, the NAO might conduct surveys of the ultimate providers of public services, for example, prison governors (C&AG, 2017d, p. 48), local authorities (C&AG, 2013e, p. 41, 2016c, p. 40) or contract managers within a department (C&AG, 2014e, p. 48) rather than service users. Interviews with representative organisations or academics would substitute for trying to get evidence about how people using the programmes actually felt about them (C&AG, 2014f, p. 42). Frequently, therefore, the NAO would not conclude on the effectiveness of services but that departments should collect better data to understand whether services were effective (C&AG, 2013e, p. 11) or equitable (C&AG, 2013e, p. 11, 2015d, p. 9).

The NAO turned from effectiveness to focussing on management. David Clarke told us that Morse 'was interested in how the mechanics of the machine worked, the governance, management information and efficiency all worked and gave me the impression that he wasn't as interested in policy outcomes' (David Clarke, interview). Clarke was not alone. Jill Rutter,[20] for example, told us that she had been particularly shocked by the NAO's failure to report promptly about evaluation (the report was published but was not a value-for-money report and was published three working days before Christmas, when most of Whitehall had gone home (NAO, 2013a)). Rutter diagnosed this case in the same terms as Clarke,

> I think the NAO, under Amyas Morse, had a too limited conception of its role and a narrow view of what value for money means. I remember being absolutely surprised when I discovered at Institute for Government that a report on policy evaluation by government departments sat on Amyas's desk from April to December because he didn't think evaluation had anything to do with value for money. That is what government spends most of its money on – programmes to achieve outcomes not big kit procurement – the NAO seemed to have defined itself into a hole looking at big kit procurement or looking at systems without thinking about what the government's trying to achieve with this money and whether it is succeeding.
>
> *(Jill Rutter, interview)*

Clarke's and Rutter's comments are supported by the structure of NAO reports in the 2010s. They often reflected a managerial agenda focussed on, as Rutter said, big procurement or looking at systems. For example, a report on assurance for major projects took a framework of good practice principles, applied it to a clearly demarcated system run by the government and identified flaws in the process. Departmental systems of assurance were excluded from the scope of the study, so only HM Treasury and the Major Projects Authority were included, and there was no discussion of any of the individual projects that were assured through this system. (C&AG, 2012e)

The report on assurance for major projects reflected the NAO's interest in pursuing back office topics. This was a continuation from Downey and Bourn, but insiders like Clarke saw a greater emphasis on these topics and thought it marked a retreat from evaluating the effectiveness of government programmes themselves. There were studies of how central government managed early departure schemes (C&AG, 2012c), rationalised their corporate functions through shared services centres (C&AG, 2012d, 2016a), reformed their IT systems (C&AG, 2013a) and improved centralised procurement and contract management (C&AG, 2013b, 2014b, 2014c). These reports often saw government as a form of business: for example, the NAO pursued the idea that the Cabinet Office and Treasury should be constituted as a strategic centre of government with 'unarguable responsibilities' to coordinate departments, achieve cost savings and manage common functions (C&AG, 2014g, p. 7). This approach could yield significant insights: for example, the NAO published in 2013 an assessment of the work of four of the government's major contractors – Atos, Capita, G4S and Serco – which revealed the size of the businesses of these four contractors in both central government (and in each central department) and local government for the first time (C&AG, 2013g).

Morse's focus with these reports was on making an impact inside Whitehall. The NAO declared that some reports existed to suggest issues for Parliament to scrutinise (NAO, 2012b, p. 4; C&AG, 2013f) or 'inform the debate' about their subject (C&AG, 2011a, p. 5). In one case, the NAO went so far as to contribute to the consultation on the government's development of a contracting mechanism for probation (NAO, 2013). Morse thought that the NAO could leverage its 'unique insight into the whole of government that no one else has' (Morse, 2016). Christian van Stolk told us that the

> reports became a lot more focussed, more of a project with a product that is delivered to a government department which was in part a choice that Amyas made, which he may have been comfortable with due to his consulting background.
>
> *(Christian van Stolk, interview)*

This perspective supported doing reports early on in projects: the NAO published reports on how government was preparing for the Olympic Games in London in 2012 long before the games took place (C&AG, 2010). For Ed Humpherson, Morse wanted the NAO to be 'much more central to how government was run' (Ed Humpherson, interview). Civil servants often responded to this approach positively. Those who did identified the NAO's technocratic reports as the system learning lessons. Lord Macpherson saw the NAO's reports on the financial crisis as 'important that we learnt the lessons' from the crisis and thought that the Treasury had improved its dealings with the banks through, in part, the NAO's reports (Macpherson, interview). Others though pointed to the NAO's lack of technical expertise in the areas that they were examining. On the financial crisis, contrasting to Lord Macpherson, Lord O'Donnell pointed out that the banking rescues were very technical and were being examined by a large number of different people and told us he 'wasn't sure that the NAO added a lot of value to be honest' (O'Donnell, interview). There is evidence of this influence in key areas during austerity: the NAO's work on contracting took advantage of the development of functional leadership within the civil service, but it also had an impact on guidance produced by the Cabinet Office for use in government (Cabinet Office, 2023). At times, though, the NAO could almost act like a lobbyist for Whitehall. For example, in 2016, Morse warned politicians that they were demanding too much of the civil service (Morse, 2016).

The approach had costs though too. Patrick Dunleavy argued that NAO reports increasingly read as addressed to an elitist audience: 'Morse didn't want to make the reports more accessible. He didn't really care what they looked like. He didn't really worry about who was reading them. He basically wanted to, I thought, restrict the audience to a narrower circle of elite readers' (Patrick Dunleavy, interview). David Clarke told us that 'we weren't doing reports that the Press Office could work with, they wanted to get coverage on papers and tv but we weren't doing those sort of reports' (David Clarke, interview).

To understand their comments, it is worth contrasting how two reports – one written under Bourn and the other under Morse – examined the same issue. In 2001, the NAO published a report on impact assessments, and in 2010 it provided the PAC with an update. This enables us to compare the pre- and post-Morse style of report. The first paragraph of the 2001 report read:

> Each year the Government brings forward many regulatory proposals which may affect the daily lives of citizens and the costs borne by business, charities and voluntary organisations. Some of these effects are specifically intended and outcomes of Government policy – others result from the implementation of the policy. For some years the Government have been concerned that the policy making process does not routinely include an informed consideration of these effects. For instance, in 1999 the Government stated that: 'regulation for its own sake is too often seen as an easy answer, without proper consideration being given to better ways of achieving the outcome'.
>
> *(C&AG, 2001, p. 1)*

Contrast to the first paragraph of the 2010 report:

> Impact Assessments assess the need for, and likely impact of, proposed government policies. They help policy makers think through and understand the consequences of proposed policy interventions; and enable government to weigh and present publicly the relevant evidence on the likely impacts of such interventions. Impact Assessments are required

> for all government interventions which affect the private sector and for interventions with costs of over £5 million affecting the public sector, including UK implementation of European Union directives and rulings.
> *(C&AG, 2010a, p. 4)*

Both statements convey roughly the same information, but do so very differently. The 2001 report begins with an introduction for a citizen to the subject of impact assessments. The 2010 report is addressed to those who want to understand the rules and bureaucratic process of the assessment, and it moves beyond definitions for the general public very quickly. The point of the first report was accountability to the citizen: anyone interested in the managerial detail had to wade through waffle such as justifications for the purpose of these statements. The point of the second report was improving management first: a citizen might easily be stranded in the technocratic language about EU directives and different sectors, but for a civil service manager, the message was direct, free from extraneous explanation and clear.

To some extent, this new managerial focus on the NAO's part was compensated for by the PAC. The committee did this in two ways. They diversified their evidence base by beginning to ask pre-panels to attend. Traditionally, a PAC session would focus on a department and the government representatives would be questioned on the basis of the NAO's report. Hodge brought in additional witnesses before the government witnesses appeared, who provided a different and often service user–based perspective to the committee. But MPs also translated the NAO's technical language into something much more accessible. Take, for example, the NAO's 2016 report on the sale of Northern Rock shares, which concluded that

> Customers who have loans and mortgages that were sold in the transaction have been protected in the short run. Treatment of customers was one of the criteria in selecting bidders and was a pass or fail test. UKAR (UK Asset Resolution)[21] also included protections in the sale agreement, such as a 12-month restriction on changes to the standard variable rate and maintaining UKAR's debt management principles.
> *(C&AG, 2016d, p. 9)*

In the PAC, Meg Hillier, the chair, translated this question into a much more democratically acute question:

> We are just a bunch of MPs who are not financial experts. Our constituents who have got mortgages are concerned about their rates.
> *(PAC, 2016, Q2)*

Hillier had translated technical language about concern for the customers of the sold-off bank into a statement that could be understood by ordinary voters.

A new use of value-for-money powers related to investigations. By 2015, the NAO's annual report stated that amongst its missions was 'providing integrated assurance with products tailored more appropriately for Parliament's needs' (NAO, 2015, p. 11). The point of this concept was to see assurance as the product the NAO provided rather than any particular type of audit. Consequently, the NAO expanded what it did for Parliament. We have described some of the consequences for this already: departmental overviews were one major new form of report, as were investigations as the NAO called them, which Morse had developed as a second strain of work after 2012.

Investigations are short pieces which the NAO could publish under its value-for-money powers, which sought only to present the facts of what had happened in a particular incident to Parliament. The purpose of investigations was set out in a published NAO document in 2018: investigations sought to 'establish the facts' rather than offer a conclusion about them and were justified because

> Parliament and the public want facts they can trust and believe in, and which they can use to develop their own views and arguments.
>
> *(NAO, 2018)*

These shorter pieces of work could be published urgently, with an example being the NAO's work on Kids Company[22] that was published on 29th October 2015, a mere 86 days after the charity closed. The report did not set out any findings about why the charity had failed or whether the government had been wrong to award the charity grants; instead, it merely 'sets out the facts relating to the government's funding of Kids Company. It covers the funding that Kids Company received from the government; the government's reasons for funding Kids Company; and how the government monitored the grants made to Kids Company' (C&AG, 2015, p. 4).

The report into Kids Company by the NAO was the basis for evidence sessions before two parliamentary committees (PAC, 2015; PACAC, 2016). Investigations were swift. The NAO would often provide an investigation in response to concerns within the House of Commons and calls for an inquiry. For example, in 2016, allegations that the charity Broken Rainbow might collapse were brought to the attention of Bernard Jenkin,[23] then chair of the Public Administration and Constitutional

Affairs Committee. He wrote to the C&AG requesting an investigation which Morse then performed (Jenkin, 2016; C&AG, 2017b).

Investigations importantly allowed the NAO to fulfil its democratic mandate, identifying cases where there had been mistakes, but they also allowed the NAO to produce its quota of reports whilst maintaining the cuts in capability to the value-for-money budgets sustained over previous years.

6.5.3 Financial audit

The technical professionalisation of the NAO's financial audit function continued and deepened under Amyas Morse. Staff understood that 'Amyas came in with a private sector view point and wanted us to be like a private sector big four accountancy firm' (Neil Sayers, interview). The impetus for this development came from two directions: from Whitehall and the profession. Firstly, Whitehall continued to professionalise its finance function. In 2009–10, Whitehall adopted International Financial Reporting Standards (IFRS) (Scrutiny Unit, 2009). Secondly, there was a more generalised concern though from Morse that the audit profession as a whole was under pressure:

> we had this developing criticism of the profession as a whole that has been mounting and mounting and mounting outside and we were, I was worried about that. Plus, because of the pressure, the financial pressures on the government, people might start to try and monkey around with their accounts. Consequently, I began to realise that [financial] audit was a real risk, really serious risk, getting to be more and more so.
>
> *(Amyas Morse, interview)*

The NAO perceived parliamentary pressure to keep the standard of financial audit high as well. Martin Sinclair told us that 'Hodge just wanted the accounts to be done well' (Martin Sinclair, interview). Martin Sinclair told us that parliamentary pressure would be used internally as a spur to greater professionalism: he recalled that Andrew Tyrie, then chair of the Treasury Select Committee, was 'demanding' of the NAO. Morse, Sinclair and the rest of the NAO's senior management team therefore had a clear sense that they were required to maintain a professional standard of financial audit for Parliament and had to assure Parliament that this was what they were doing. The NAO internally recognised that the increasing interest in its audit quality was driven by the increased complexity of the tasks that it had taken on. For example, organisations like the BBC which the NAO had recently taken on (see the next section) meant that it inherited an audit from the private sector directly, which brought the pressure of comparison with the previous private sector auditor.

The biggest extension of financial audit comprised the Whole of Government Accounts (WGA) (a single set of accounts, presenting consolidated figures for the entire UK government). Morse inherited WGA from Bourn as a project. The task of auditing WGA was hugely complex: the NAO needed to both organise its own audit teams to a single timetable but also to liaise with audit teams for local government, healthcare and other public sector organisations. The NAO was conscious of a need to explain what the numbers actually meant as well. During austerity, as we discussed above, the C&AG's reports on the relevant financial statements from the Treasury explained movements in them due to the financial crisis. In WGA, the NAO continued this practice. Steve Corbishley explained to us that

> The NAO made a conscious decision to publish an annual C&AG's report with these financial statements given the importance of the WGA in setting out what the government spends, receives, owns and owes. We wanted to inform PAC of the importance of WGA so they could hold government to account. The NAO's report shows the government's significant undertakings and points PAC to their significance, such as the liabilities in the public sector pension schemes. It was there to shine a light.
>
> *(Steve Corbishley, interview)*

The initial reports from the C&AG featured international comparisons (Treasury, 2013, p. 47), charts explaining the difference between the accounting debt and deficit and the national debt and deficit (Treasury, 2013, pp. 52–53), breakdowns of government expenditure by type and taxation by type (Treasury, 2013, pp. 54–55) and other data. It became the basis for several PAC sessions which focussed on new issues such as the provision for the potential costs of clinical negligence which WGA showed were much more substantial than anyone had thought. For the NAO, WGA became a key justification of their entire approach to auditing across government over many years. Martin Sinclair spoke, for example, of the benefits of financial reporting in government being done on an accruals basis and identified the WGA as a key source of benefits from the practice:

> What helps Parliament is the improved reporting because you can see the balance sheets and highlighted issues such as the atrocious management of the working capital in some areas and the scale of investment in some of the departments. This did support, particularly at the Whole of Government Accounts some very good hearings on asset

> management, nuclear decommissioning, coal industry liabilities, and the clinical liabilities within the NHS.
>
> *(Martin Sinclair, interview)*

Sinclair's identification of the strength of WGA on an accruals basis was supported by the way that the document was scrutinised. The PAC repeatedly turned to WGA.

The mechanism to assure Parliament that the NAO's financial audit was competent involved inviting private sector regulators in to examine the NAO's audits. Central technical teams acted as a key constituency for using technical quality of accounts and financial audits as an index of their actual quality. Neil Sayers explained what this meant:

> The technical team were extreme about technical issues and the whole of that team were made up of people that were just technical experts and would dance on the head of a pin for months about an accounting judgement with no sense of context or that time matters.
>
> *(Neil Sayers, interview)*

Sayers' point was supported by how the NAO faced crises like the financial crisis early on in Morse's tenure. We have covered already the NAO's audit of the Treasury financial statements in these years, but crucially the NAO saw this as a moment that required expertise. Steve Corbishley, the responsible director, told us that the NAO brought in some of the private firms to help them with these audits because, 'the government financial reporting framework largely follows FRS (Financial Reporting Standards) and then IFRS and if you set that as the rule to follow, you need to make sure either as an account preparer or an auditor that you know what you've got to do to bring these things to account in a true and fair way' (Steve Corbishley, interview). The NAO corporately defined the expertise required to audit the public sector's financial statements as expertise in applying standards derived from the private sector.

There were critics of this approach to financial audit in the wider world and in the NAO itself. The Public Administration and Constitutional Affairs Committee (PACAC) held an inquiry into government accounts in 2016–17. The government responded, and the Committee issued a follow-up report in 2018, which led to a government review of departmental accounting and a further session of the committee in 2019. Morse appeared as a witness before the inquiry in 2016. What is noticeable about the PACAC's approach to accounts was how far the committee were from the official line of the NAO: in their initial call for evidence, they stated that 'it is not clear that they [government accounts] are of any use to Select Committees, or to the public, in holding the government to account'

(PACAC, 2016a). The committee's focus was on the utility of the accounts rather than on their technical quality (Ferry and Midgley, 2024). (This did parallel work commissioned at senior levels within the NAO, involving a working group of directors and research conducted in the NAO by some junior staff, particularly Richard Ratcliffe[24] and Sen Rudran,[25] on the users of the accounts. This work never went anywhere inside the NAO but privately PACAC staff were aware of it and it helped inform PACAC's approach to its work (Neil Sayers, interview, private information).) This mismatch between MPs' expectations of the accounts and the NAO's own account of the accounts became clear when Morse and Kate Mathers[26] gave evidence. For Morse, the use of private sector accounting standards gave the accounts more authority with taxpayers:

> If they are prepared to put themselves through the same disciplines as the private sector, the advantage is it gives it more credibility. It does not mean that it should be clearer and more concise, but it just gives it more credibility, perhaps to taxpayers who might want to see that.
> *(PACAC, 2016b, Q140)*

Sir Bernard Jenkin, the committee chair, reacted with incredulity: asking 'What evidence do you have that this improves the credibility of the Government's accounts?' (PACAC, 2016b, Q151). PACAC's final report argued that the quality of accounts should be measured against whether they succeeded in achieving three objectives: to act as a starting point for debate about value for money, to outline whether the government had met the commitments it had made to Parliament and to be credible (PACAC, 2017, p. 5). Credibility, for the committee, was a supporting purpose: consequently they asked the NAO to go further with its audit, to look at the performance information which was published by departments to support the value-for-money purpose of accounts (PACAC, 2017, p. 45). Morse's NAO, abandoning the position established by Bourn and proposed by Lord Sharman, described this as a 'significant new requirement . . . which would involve significant audit costs' and 'may sit better within the existing assurance arrangements' (PACAC, 2018, p. 84). The NAO's sense of its role was not tied to the purposes PACAC had described for government accounts. The NAO did not disagree with PACAC about those purposes: in 2016, they noted that accounts 'enables Parliament to track how effectively taxpayers' money has been used' (C&AG, 2016, p. 40). However, they saw their audit purely in technical terms.

PACAC was not alone. The Institute for Government endorsed the PACAC report when it was published (Freeguard, 2017). Others privately agreed with the thrust of both PACAC and the Institute for Government's views. Margaret Hodge, for example, agreed that accounts required reform and thought that the financial audit of them was 'pretty low grade' and that the relationship between the auditors and departments was 'very cosy' (Margaret Hodge, interview). Lord O'Donnell told us that 'I think what you need is a reform programme for the financial audit and lets all sit down and think about what we really want from these [audits] and how do we deliver it' (Lord O'Donnell, interview). Macpherson argued that the accounts were 'really problematic' to use and 'pretty incomprehensible' because of the complexities around accrual accounting and its relationship with categories like DEL (Departmental Expenditure Limit) and AME (Annually Managed Expenditure)[27] (Macpherson, interview). Lord O'Donnell said,

> as a working official, you don't really use the financial accounts. You create your own numbers and if you are doing public spending you wouldn't start with the accounts. Nobody starts with the accounts and in fact you might never ever go near them.
>
> *(Lord O'Donnell, interview)*

These comments from senior civil servants were reflected in the recollections of people from the NAO. For them, the NAO's focus on audit was wrong: Neil Sayers said that 'the accounts existed for their own purposes, irrelevant to anything wider and therefore what matters is how gleamingly clean and pristine that set of accounts are, not what that set of accounts can tell us about the organisation or how they can inform a discussion about how government has utilised its resources' (Neil Sayers, interview). Ed Humpherson (head of the Office of Statistical Regulation and previously Assistant Auditor General) noted that the NAO never really discussed who used the accounts: he said that the NAO had a 'notion of this user of the accounts as an abstracted taxpayer who is a just a notion' and said that 'now I know what it's like to be in a community in statistics where users are so central, but I regret not thinking through what and who resource accounts are for' (interview, Ed Humpherson). The scope of the NAO's audit did not address these criticisms – little changed after PACAC had reported; indeed one of the authors was told in 2019 by a junior member of the NAO technical team that PACAC's concerns were 'not relevant' to the financial audit community and references in the NAO's own assessment of the Treasury's progress in improving its spending framework were minimal and grudging (C&AG, 2018g).

The NAO's general approach to financial audit became increasingly parallel to that of the firms during this period. As David Clarke, who left the NAO in 2013, argued, financial audit had a very clear identity internally: the 'financial audit part of the NAO had got a very strong sense of what it was supposed to be doing, it was trying to be like a firm and doing a quasi firm type work' (David Clarke, interview). This comparison to the private sector gave the NAO a nickname amongst Supreme Audit Institutions in Europe of the fifth of the Big Five (Khalid Hamid, interview).[28] This identity meant that the interests of the senior management including Morse and the interests of the financial auditors who saw their work as the priority for the office were aligned.[29]

6.5.4 Extensions to scope

So far, we have mainly dealt with the evolution in the NAO's audit, but the NAO also increased the range of organisations that it audited during Morse's period as C&AG. These changes were largely the expansion of audit into new areas, including the BBC and Bank of England, which had remained as anomalies since the 1983 Act was passed. In local government, the NAO acquired new powers consequent to the abolition of the Audit Commission and work in this area increased. The NAO also lost some functions, either those that Morse viewed as peripheral or those that were acquired by other bodies in the public sector. Despite these losses, the NAO after 2015 was the only public sector auditor in England and more and more of the public sector's audits were being conducted by the NAO.

The NAO under Bourn had a huge impact internationally as we have described, but Morse gave us his view on that:

> I thought it was a distraction. I thought it was a really easy way of avoiding doing really hard challenging work on what really mattered and what we actually just do, and little on what governments do.
>
> *(Amyas Morse, interview)*

Morse continued, 'I always believed that the NAO's focus on central government and how it functions is a huge responsibility that matters to the country, and to our national constitutional balance. Any commitment that could undermine that focus, be it international involvement, or local government audit, has to be very critically examined' (interview, Amyas Morse). This statement helps us understand Morse's view of what the NAO should be doing. For him, its key role was as a national auditor of both financial accounts and value for money. For Morse, other activities could spin off from that key role, for example, commentary to help government improve or publications which advanced transparency, but Morse thought the NAO should focus on those key objectives. Consequently, he did not, as Bourn had done, acquire other roles (such as being an advisor on ministerial interests), which could have conflicted with what he thought of as the key role of the NAO, nor did he see international work as a means of improving governance standards more broadly. The UK's withdrawal from the international auditing community was noticed: Khalid Hamid told us that Morse 'didn't listen to anyone' and that he heard from contacts inside the NAO that 'he thought it was a nonsense and had no respect for the international audit community' (Khalid Hamid, interview).

The growth of the NAO for Morse, therefore, had to be consistent with the NAO's role as the national public sector auditor of preference. There are two main expansions that happened under Morse's aegis. Firstly, the NAO acquired the rights to conduct value-for-money investigations into the Bank of England. These investigations were limited in that they could not deal with the merits of policy decisions taken by the Financial Policy Committee, the Monetary Policy Committee or Prudential Regulatory Committee or any other body regarding certain specific areas such as the supervision of payment systems (Bank of England and Financial Services Act, 2016, Section 7D). Crucially, an initial provision that the NAO had to receive approval from the bank before conducting value-for-money studies, something that Lord McFall[30] suggested 'challenge[d] the independence of the office . . . to the great disadvantage of Parliament and the taxpayer', was taken out (House of Lords, 2015, col. 1862). The NAO's first studies on the Bank of England were cautious, for example, looking at the bank's central services (C&AG, 2018c).

Similarly, in 2017, the NAO also acquired the financial audit of the BBC (BBC, 2017, p. 74). In both of these two cases and others, the NAO saw itself as having to demonstrate the credibility to do the audit: as Lord Bichard put it to the Public Accounts Commission, 'it is very important that we start off on the right foot and that they see us as credible auditors' (Public Accounts Commission, 2016, Q44). The audit of the BBC in particular encouraged the NAO to invest in and investigate raising its capability through technology, for example (Ferry and Midgley, 2023).

One unique set of new responsibilities arose out of the abolition of the Audit Commission in 2014. Morse believed that the NAO could not (and should not) take on all of the audit, performance management and inspection work of the Audit Commission: as he told us, in language strikingly reminiscent of what he said about the NAO's previous international work:

> we were not stylistically aligned. We could have still done it, if it really made sense but I didn't think it did. I think it distracted us a lot from our work.
>
> *(Morse, interview)*

Morse continued, 'you have to remember that the Commission was a very large organisation, relative to the size of NAO. A large part of its activity was running local government audit. If we had taken over its responsibilities, this job of running the local audit system would have demanded a substantial refocus of the NAO's balance of effort' (Amyas Morse, interview).

Jones and Stewart (2012) (who had both sat on the Layfield Commission in the 1970s) argued that the NAO's direct involvement in local council audits would have been a 'constitutional outrage'. The NAO did not therefore become involved in the audit of local councils individually, but took a national role instead. For example, it did take on two new roles as a result of the 2014 abolition of the Audit Commission. Firstly, the NAO produced the Code of Audit Practice which set out 'the way local auditors are to carry out their functions' (C&AG, 2015c, p. 4). Secondly, the Local Audit and Accountability Act 2014 amended the NAO's responsibilities for value-for-money studies. The C&AG was given the right to conduct studies of any bodies that were audited by the Audit Commission; however, this right was limited. The C&AG was allowed to conduct value-for-money studies 'end to end' of programmes which involved local authorities. Secondly, the NAO could publish reports of 'general interest' so long as they applied to 'all relevant authorities' or to 'particular descriptions of authorities' (Parliament, 2014). In practice, this meant that the C&AG and the NAO could now conduct studies examining the value for money of local authority spending, but only through examining the bodies as a class rather than examining the value for money of spending in a particular council. Again, the development of the NAO's audit into local government encouraged the construction of capacity to support it, especially around the interpretation of local authority data.

6.6 Chapter summary

Morse skilfully guided the NAO through a turbulent period: despite the serious events affecting the UK polity during his time in office, austerity and Brexit, the NAO emerged with its non-partisan reputation enhanced.

Morse's political skill was matched by a very clear vision of what the NAO existed to do: he saw public sector audit as a professional activity committed to professionalising the public sector and driving it into the 21st century. He did not see the value that John Bourn had seen in wider activities like international support, and he was clearly affiliated to the accounting industry's vision of what accounts were for. The NAO saw itself between 2009 and 2019 as the provider of an assurance service to central government rather than as a parliamentary constitutional authority.

The change in approach had consequences for the types of audit that the NAO did in this period. Morse's office focussed more and more on financial audit: a move driven by the regulator's opinions but also by the NAO's commitment to enhancing the technical quality of their audits. On the other hand, Morse opted for a far more focussed and managerially orientated value-for-money report: for Morse, MPs and departmental managers were the natural audience for NAO reports, which were shortened and sharpened to make an impact, whereas the public were not the intended audience. Morse's reports looked far more like those published by Downey's NAO than by Bourn's. This retrenchment of the meaning of audit back to a core focussed on public sector process, and financial accounting enabled the NAO to examine issues like Brexit from a pure project management perspective and enabled the NAO to make large cuts to their own spending during the decade.

The assertiveness towards the new approach to audit by the NAO though should be framed within an overall political approach that recognised austerity as the government's goal. For example, in 2010, the NAO's initial response to austerity was to publish a guide for departments on how to save money (NAO, 2010). Civil servants were resistant and 'increasingly prickly because it [achieving austerity] was sensitive to them' (Peter Riddell, interview). This was not a universal experience: Sir Bob Kerslake, head of the Home Civil Service and Permanent Secretary at the Department for Communities and Local Government, said that he found his relationship with the NAO to be 'challenging but not adversarial' and attributed his comfort with the auditors to his prior experience in local government (Kerslake, interview).

Notes

1 David Cameron, 1966–, MP for Witney 2001–16, Shadow Secretary of State for Education 2005, Leader of the Conservative Party 2005–16, Leader of the Opposition 2005–10, Prime Minister 2010–16, Foreign Secretary 2023–, created Lord Cameron 2023.
2 Margaret Hodge, 1944–, Leader Islington Council 1982–92, MP for Barking 1994–, PAC Chair 2010–15.
3 Meg Hillier, 1969–, MP for Hackney and Shoreditch, PAC Chair 2015–.
4 John Tiner, 1957–, Arthur Anderson 1976–2001, Financial Services Authority 2001–7 including Chief Executive 2003–7, Private Sector roles 2007–.
5 Geoffrey Clifton-Brown, MP for Cirencester and Tewkesbury, subsequently the Cotswolds 1992–. Knighted 2018.
6 Michael Gove, 1967–, MP for Surrey Heath 2005–, Shadow Secretary of State for Children Schools and Families 2007–10, Secretary of State for Education 2010–14, Chief Whip 2014–15, Secretary of State for Justice and Lord Chancellor 2015–16, Secretary of State for Environment, Food and Rural Affairs 2017–19, Chancellor of the Duchy of Lancaster 2019–21, Minister for

the Cabinet Office 2020–21, Secretary of State for Levelling Up, Housing and Communities and Minister for Intergovernmental relations 2021–2, 2022–.

7 Francis Maude, 1953–, MP for North Warwickshire and Horsham, 1983–92, 1997–2015, Shadow Secretary of State for Culture Media and Sport 1997–8, Shadow Chancellor of the Exchequer 1998–2000, Shadow Foreign Secretary 2000–2001, Chairman of the Conservative Party 2005–7, Shadow Minister for the Cabinet Office 2007–10, Minister for the Cabinet Office and Paymaster General 2010–15, Minister for Trade 2015–16, created Lord Maude 2015.

8 Marcial Boo, Director Street Crime Initiative Home Office 2002–5, Director of Policy, Knowledge and Studies, Audit Commission, 2005–10, Director of Strategy, Knowledge and Communications National Audit Office 2010–13, Chief Executive Independent Parliamentary Standards Authority 2014–20, Chief Executive Equality and Human Rights Commission 2021–.

9 Robert Kerslake, 1955–2023, Chief Executive London Borough of Hounslow 1990–7, Sheffield Council 1997–2008, Chief Executive Homes and Communities Agency 2008–10, Permanent Secretary Department for Communities and Local Government 2010–15, Head of the Home Civil Service 2012–14. Knighted 2005, created Lord Kerslake 2015.

10 Eric Pickles, 1952–, Leader of Bradford Council 1988–90, MP for Brentwood and Ongar 1992–2017, Shadow Secretary of State for Local Government and the Regions 2002–7, Shadow Secretary of State for Communities and Local Government 2007–9, Chairman of the Conservative Party 2009–10, Secretary of State for Local Government and Communities 2010–15, created Lord Pickles 2018.

11 Robert Neill, 1952–, MP for Bromley and Chislehurst 2006–, Chair of the Justice Select Committee 2015–.

12 Tony Travers, 1953–, academic posts and advisory posts to select committees 1992–7, Member of the Audit Commission 2010–15 Advisor to the Public Accounts Committee, Director, LSE London and visiting professor, LSE, 1998–.

13 Ivan Rogers, 1960–, Prime Minister's Advisor for European and Global Issues 2012–13, UK representative to the European Union 2013–17. Knighted 2016.

14 Jeremy Heywood, 1961–2018, Downing Street Chief of Staff 2008–10, Downing Street Permanent Secretary 2010–11, Cabinet Secretary 2011–2018, Head of the Civil Service 2014–18. Knighted 2011, created Lord Heywood 2018.

15 Oliver Robbins, 1975–, Permanent Secretary Department for Exiting the European Union 2016–17, Prime Minister's Europe Advisor and Chief Negotiator with the European Union 2017–19. Knighted 2019.

16 There was much discussion in the NAO at the time, which one of the authors was a party to, as to the fact that chocolate oranges do not just fall apart; indeed, they are amongst the most difficult chocolate structures to get into. One press officer was heard commenting at the time that they doubted that Amyas Morse had ever seen a chocolate orange! The NAO press office was decorated with chocolate oranges for about a week afterwards, placed there by mischievous members of staff. Morse himself was faced with a desk filled with chocolate oranges when he returned to the office, and there was a shortage in the Victoria area for a couple of days after his comment.

17 Dominic Grieve, KC PC, 1956–, MP for Beaconsfield 1997–2019, Shadow Home Secretary 2008–9, Attorney General for England and Wales 2010–14, Chair, Intelligence and Security Committee 2015–19.

18 Margaret Beckett, 1943–, MP for Lincoln 1974–9, MP Derby South, 1983–, Deputy Leader of the Labour Party 1992–4, Leader of the Opposition 1994,

Secretary of State for Trade & Industry 1997–8, Leader of the House 1998–2001, Secretary of State for MAFF then DEFRA 2001–6, Foreign Secretary 2007–8.

19 Esther McVey, 1967–, MP Wirral West and Tatton 2010–15 and 2017–, Secretary of Sate for Work and Pensions 2018, Minister of State for Housing and Planning 2019–20, Minister without Portfolio 2023–.

20 Jill Rutter, HM Treasury 1978–97, British Petroleum 1998–2003, Director of Strategy, Department for the Environment Food and Rural Affairs 2004–9, Senior Fellow Institute for Government and subsequent posts 2009–, Director UK in a Changing Europe 2019–.

21 UK Asset Resolution Limited (UKAR) owned NR's legacy assets. The government established UKAR in 2010 to facilitate the orderly management of NR's assets and those of another bailed-out bank, Bradford & Bingley. HM Treasury owned UKAR, and UK Financial Investments Limited (UKFI) supervised it. UKFI managed the government's shareholdings in the financial sector. It was part of UK Government Investments (UKGI), which HM Treasury also owned.

22 Kids Company was a charity that operated in the UK between 1996 and 2015. The charity closed in 2015. It had been in receipt of several government grants. When the charity closed, there was a political controversy about whether the charity should have been funded by the government continuously and whether the charity's governance arrangements were appropriate.

23 Bernard Jenkin, 1959–, MP for Colchester North, North Essex and Harwich and North Essex 1992–, Shadow Defence Secretary 2001–3, Shadow Secretary of State for the Regions 2003–5, Chair of the Public Administration and Constitutional Affairs Committee 2010–19, Chair of the Liaison Committee 2019–.

24 Richard Ratcliffe, NAO 2009–15.

25 Senthuran Rudran, NAO 2009–15.

26 Kate Mathers, NAO including Director 2010–17, Executive Leader 2017–.

27 HM Treasury manages public spending within two 'control totals' of about equal size:

- departmental expenditure limits (DELs) – mostly covering spending on public services, grants and administration ('resource' spending) and investment ('capital' spending), planned over periods.
- annually managed expenditure (AME) – categories of spending less amenable to multi-year planning, such as social security spending and debt interest.

28 The largest accounting firms globally (PWC, Ernst and Young, KPMG and Deloitte) are often referred to as the Big Four.

29 This was a phrase used to one of the authors during this period when considering allocating staff between value-for-money and financial audit.

30 John McFall, 1944–, MP for Dumbarton and West Dumbartonshire 1987–2010, Chair of the Treasury Select Committee 2001–10, Lords Speaker 2021–, created Lord McFall 2010.

References

Allen, G. (2010). *Recession and recovery.* London: House of Commons Library.

Aylett, Philip, interview

Bacon, R. and Hope, C. (2013). *Conundrum: Why every government gets things wrong- and what we can do about it.* London: Biteback Publishing.

Bank of England and Financial Services Act (2016). *Bank of England and Financial Services Act 2016.* Available at https://www.legislation.gov.uk/ukpga/2016/14/enacted accessed on 5 August 2023.

Betts, Clive, interview
Bichard, Michael, interview
Boo, Marcial, interview
British Broadcasting Corporation (2017). *BBC Annual report and accounts 2016–17.* London: BBC.
Cabinet Office (2023). *The sourcing playbook: Government guidance on service delivery, including outsourcing, insourcing, mixed economy sourcing and contracting.* London: HMSO.
Civil Service World (2012). Gove brands PAC and NAO the 'fiercest forces of conservatism'. *Civil Service World.* Available at https://www.civilserviceworld.com/professions/article/gove-brands-pac-and-nao-the-fiercest-forces-of-conservatism accessed on 5 August 2023.
Clifton-Brown, Geoffrey, interview
Cohen, Gabrielle, interview
Comptroller and Auditor General (2001). *Better regulation: Making good use of regulatory impact assessments*, Session 2001-2, HC329. London: National Audit Office.
Comptroller and Auditor General (2009). *Maintaining financial stability across the United Kingdom's banking system*, Session 2009-10, HC91. London: National Audit Office.
Comptroller and Auditor General (2009a). *The nationalisation of Northern Rock*, Session 2008-9, HC298. London: National Audit Office.
Comptroller and Auditor General (2010). *Preparations for the London 2012 Olympic and Paralympic Games: Progress report*, Session 2009-10, HC298. London: National Audit Office.
Comptroller and Auditor General (2010a). *Assessing the impact of proposed new policies*, Session 2010-12, HC185. London: National Audit Office.
Comptroller and Auditor General (2010b). *Criminal Justice System: Landscape Review.* London: National Audit Office.
Comptroller and Auditor General (2010c). *Maintaining the financial stability of UK banks: Update on the support schemes*, Session 2010-12, HC676. London: National Audit Office.
Comptroller and Auditor General (2011). *The financial stability interventions.* London: National Audit Office.
Comptroller and Auditor General (2011a). *Information and communications technology in government: Landscape review*, Session 2010-12, HC757. London: National Audit Office.
Comptroller and Auditor General (2012). HM Treasury Resource Accounts 2011-12: The Comptroller and Auditor General's Report to the House of Commons. London: National Audit Office.
Comptroller and Auditor General (2012a). Department for Work and Pensions: The introduction of the Work Programme, Session 2010-12, HC1701. London: National Audit Office.
Comptroller and Auditor General (2012b). *Cost reduction in central government: Summary of progress*, Session 2010-12, HC1788. London: National Audit Office.
Comptroller and Auditor General (2012c). *Managing early departures in central government*, Session 2010-12, HC1795. London: National Audit Office.
Comptroller and Auditor General (2012d). *Efficiency and reform in government corporate functions through shared services centres*, Session 2010-12, HC1790. London: National Audit Office.
Comptroller and Auditor General (2012e). *Assurance for major projects*, Session 2010-12, HC1698. London: National Audit Office.

Comptroller and Auditor General (2013). *HM Treasury Resource Accounts 2012-13 the Comptroller and Auditor General's Report to the House of Commons*. London: National Audit Office.
Comptroller and Auditor General (2013a). *The impact of government's ICT savings initiatives*, Session 2012-13, HC887. London: National Audit Office.
Comptroller and Auditor General (2013b). *Improving government procurement*, Session 2012-13, HC996. London: National Audit Office.
Comptroller and Auditor General (2013c). *Capital funding for new school places*, Session 2012-13, HC1042. London: National Audit Office.
Comptroller and Auditor General (2013d). *The New Homes Bonus*, Session 2012-13, HC1047. London: National Audit Office.
Comptroller and Auditor General (2013e). *Programmes to help families facing multiple challenges*, Session 2013-14, HC878. London: National Audit Office.
Comptroller and Auditor General (2013f). *Early action: A landscape review*, Session 2012-13, HC683. London: National Audit Office.
Comptroller and Auditor General (2013g). *The role of major contractors in the delivery of public services*, Session 2013-14, HC810. London: National Audit Office.
Comptroller and Auditor General (2014). *HM Treasury Annual Report and Accounts 2013-14: The Report of the Comptroller and Auditor General to the House of Commons*. London: National Audit Office.
Comptroller and Auditor General (2014a). *Department for Communities and Local Government: Local government funding: Assurance to Parliament*, Session 2014-15, HC174. London: National Audit Office.
Comptroller and Auditor General (2014b). *Home Office and Ministry of Justice: Transforming contract management*, Session 2014-15, HC268. London: National Audit Office.
Comptroller and Auditor General (2014c). *Cabinet Office: Transforming government's contract management*, Session 2014-15, HC269. London: National Audit Office.
Comptroller and Auditor General (2014d). *The financial sustainability of NHS bodies*, Session 2014-15, HC722. London: National Audit Office.
Comptroller and Auditor General (2014e). *The Work Programme*, Session 2014-15, HC266. London: National Audit Office.
Comptroller and Auditor General (2014f). *Personal Independence Payment: Early progress*, Session 2013-14, HC1070. London: National Audit Office.
Comptroller and Auditor General (2014g). *The centre of government*, Session 2014-15, HC171. London: National Audit Office.
Comptroller and Auditor General (2015). *Report on Accounts: HM Treasury 2014-15: The Report of the Comptroller and Auditor General to the House of Commons*. London: National Audit Office.
Comptroller and Auditor General (2015a). *Principles paper: Managing provider failure*, Session 2015-16, HC89. London: National Audit Office.
Comptroller and Auditor General (2015b). *Outcome-based payment schemes: government's use of payment by results*, Session 2015-16, HC86. London: National Audit Office.
Comptroller and Auditor General (2015c). *Code of Audit Practice*. London: National Audit Office.
Comptroller and Auditor General (2015d). *Progress in improving cancer services and outcomes in England*, Session 2014-5, HC949. London: National Audit Office.

Comptroller and Auditor General (2016). *Accountability to Parliament for taxpayers' money*, Session 2015-16, HC849. London: National Audit Office.

Comptroller and Auditor General (2016a). *Shared service centres*, Session 2016-17, HC16. London: National Audit Office.

Comptroller and Auditor General (2016b). *Training new teachers*, Session 2015-16, HC798. London: National Audit Office.

Comptroller and Auditor General (2016c). *Local welfare provision*. London: National Audit Office.

Comptroller and Auditor General (2016d). *The £13 billion sale of former Northern Rock assets*, Session 2016-17, HC513. London: National Audit Office.

Comptroller and Auditor General (2017). *People and skills: The role of the centre of government*, Session 2017-19, HC626. London: National Audit Office.

Comptroller and Auditor General (2017a). *Implementing the UK's exit from the European Union: Infrastructure and Projects Authority*, Session 2017-19, HC606. London: National Audit Office.

Comptroller and Auditor General (2017b). *Report on the funding and governance of Broken Rainbow*, Session 2016-17, HC1060. London: National Audit Office.

Comptroller and Auditor General (2017c). *Implementing the UK's exit from the European Union: The Department for Exiting the European Union and the centre of government*, Session 2017-19, HC593. London: National Audit Office.

Comptroller and Auditor General (2017d). *Mental health in prisons*, Session 2017-19, HC42. London: National Audit Office.

Comptroller and Auditor General (2018). *Department for Environment, Food and Rural Affairs: Progress in implementing EU exit*, Session 2017-19, HC1498. London: National Audit Office.

Comptroller and Auditor General (2018a). *HM Treasury and UK Government Investments limited: The return of Lloyds Banking Group to private ownership*, Session 2017-19, HC1127. London: National Audit Office.

Comptroller and Auditor General (2018b). *Sustainability and transformation in the NHS*, Session 2017-19, HC719. London: National Audit Office.

Comptroller and Auditor General (2018c). *Managing the Bank of England's central services*, Session 2017-19, HC1784. London: National Audit Office.

Comptroller and Auditor General (2018d). *The Customs Declaration Service: a progress update*, Session 2017-19, HC1124. London: National Audit Office.

Comptroller and Auditor General (2018e). *Implementing the UK's exit from the European Union: The Foreign and Commonwealth Office*, Session 2017-19, HC899. London: National Audit Office.

Comptroller and Auditor General (2018f). *Improving children and young people's mental health services*, Session 2017-19, HC1618. London: National Audit Office.

Comptroller and Auditor General (2018g). *Improving government's planning and spending framework*, Session 2017-19, HC1679. London: National Audit Office.

Comptroller and Auditor General (2018h). *Financial sustainability of local authorities 2018*, Session 2017-19, HC834. London: National Audit Office.

Comptroller and Auditor General (2019). *NHS financial sustainability*, Session 2017-19, HC1867. London: National Audit Office.

Conservative Party (2010). *Invitation to join the government of Britain: Conservative Party Manifesto, 2010*. London: Conservative Party.

Corbishley, Steve, interview

Clarke, David, interview

Cribb, J. and Johnson, P. (2018). *10 years on – have we recovered from the financial crisis?* Available at https://ifs.org.uk/articles/10-years-have-we-recovered-financial-crisis accessed on 29 October 2023.
Davis, Davis, interview
Dunleavy, Patrick, interview
Etherton, Mark, interview
Exiting the EU Committee (2018). *Oral evidence: The progress of the UK's negotiations on EU withdrawal 10 October 2018*, Session 2017-19, HC 372. Available at https://committees.parliament.uk/oralevidence/8417/pdf/, accessed on 28 July 2023.
Faulconbridge, G. (2019). Some British lawmakers to seek to block no-deal Brexit: The Sun. *Reuters*. Available at https://www.reuters.com/article/britain-eu-parliament-idUKL9N22X01P/ accessed on 22 November 2023.
Ferry, L. and Midgley, H. (2023). Institutional entrepreneurship in a Supreme Audit Institution: The National Audit Office and the use of data in financial audit. In T. Rana and L. Parker (eds.) *The Routledge Handbook of Public Sector Accounting*. New York: Routledge.
Ferry, L. and Midgley, H. (2024). Are public sector accounts trusted? Exploring the verdict of the Public Administration and Constitutional Affairs Committee in the United Kingdom. *Public Administration*. https://doi.org/10.1111/padm.12983.
Fetzer, T. (2019). Did austerity cause Brexit? *American Economic Review, 109*(11), pp. 3849–3886.
Freeguard, G. (2017). *Why reforming government accounts matters*. Available at https://www.instituteforgovernment.org.uk/article/comment/why-reforming-government-accounts-matters accessed on 30 October 2023.
Gamble, A. (2009). British politics and the financial crisis. *British Politics, 4*, 450–462.
Halligan, L. (2008) Economic Agenda: Bourn away on a tide of ministerial spin. *Sunday Telegraph*, 20 January 2008.
Hamid, Khalid, interview
HM Government (2010). *The Coalition: Our programme for government*. London: HMSO.
Hillier, Meg, interview
Hodge, Margaret, interview
Hodge, M. (2016). *Called to account: How corporate bad behaviour and government waste combine to cost us millions*. London: Abacus.
House of Commons (2023). *Standing Orders of the House of Commons*. Available at https://publications.parliament.uk/pa/cm5803/cmstords/blue-add-so_03-07-2023/so-orders.html#_idTextAnchor597 accessed on 1 August 2023.
House of Lords (2015). *Hansard*, Vol. 765, 9 November 2015.
Humpherson, Ed, interview
Jenkin, B. (2016). *Letter to Amyas Morse*. Available at https://www.parliament.uk/globalassets/documents/commons-committees/PACAC/Correspondence/Sir-Amyas-Morse-Broken-Rainbow-12-07-16.pdf accessed on 26 November 2023.
Jones, G. and Stewart, J. (2012). *The National Audit Office should not be responsible for the audit of local authorities*. Available at https://blogs.lse.ac.uk/politicsandpolicy/public-audit-jones-stewart/, accessed on 5 August 2023.
Kerslake, Bob, interview
Krugman, P. (2015). The case for cuts was a lie. Why does Britain still believe it? *The Guardian*, 29 April 2015.

Labour Party (2019). *It's time for real change: The Labour Party Manifesto, 2019.* London: Labour Party.

Leigh, Edward, interview

Likierman, Andrew, interview

Lonsdale, Jeremy, interview

Macpherson, Nicholas, interview

Maddox, D. (2018). 'It fails the sniff test!' Anger as Remainer civil servant granted TOTAL CONTROL of Brexit. *Daily Express*, 25 July 2018.

Midgley, H. (2019). The National Audit Office and the select committee system 1979–2019. *Parliamentary Affairs, 72*(4), 779–798.

Morse, Amyas, interview

Morse, A. (2016). *C&AG speech at the Institute for Government*, 22 July 2016. Available at https://www.instituteforgovernment.org.uk/sites/default/files/CAG%20speech%20at%20the%20Institute%20for%20Government%20070716.pdf, accessed on 28 November 2023.

Morse, A. (2018). *Letter to Esther McVey*, 4 July 2018. Available online https://www.parliament.uk/globalassets/documents/commons-committees/work-and-pensions/Correspondence/180704-Amyas-Morse--E-McVey-Universal-Credit.pdf, accessed on 29 March 2024.

Murphy, P., Ferry, L., Glennon, R. and Greenhalgh, K. (2019). *Public service accountability, rekindling a debate.* London: Springer International Publishing.

National Audit Office (2008). *National Audit Office Resource Accounts 2007–8.* London: National Audit Office.

National Audit Office (2009). *Annual Report 2009.* London: National Audit Office.

National Audit Office (2010). *A short guide to structured cost reduction.* London: National Audit Office.

National Audit Office (2010a). *Annual Report 2010.* London: National Audit Office.

National Audit Office (2011). *Annual Report 2011.* London: National Audit Office.

National Audit Office (2012). *Delivering public services through markets: Principles for achieving value for money.* London: National Audit Office.

National Audit Office (2012a). *The Ministry of Justice's language services contract.* London: National Audit Office.

National Audit Office (2012b). *Regulating charities: A landscape review.* London: National Audit Office.

National Audit Office (2013). *Response to the Ministry of Justice consultation on its proposals outlined in Transforming Rehabilitation- a revolution in the way that we manage offenders.* Available at https://www.nao.org.uk/wp-content/uploads/2013/03/Response_MoJ_consultation_Transforming_Rehabilitation.pdf accessed on 5 August 2023.

National Audit Office (2013a). *Evaluation in government.* London: National Audit Office.

National Audit Office (2014). *Annual Report and Accounts 2013–14.* London: National Audit Office.

National Audit Office (2015). *Annual Report and Accounts, 2014–15.* London: National Audit Office.

National Audit Office (2018). *Investigations: Information on our approach to undertaking investigations.* Available at https://www.nao.org.uk/wp-content/uploads/sites/12/2018/06/NAO-approach-to-investigations.pdf accessed on 26 November 2023.

National Audit Office (2018a). *Annual report and accounts 2017–18.* London: National Audit Office.

National Audit Office (2019). *Annual report and accounts 2018–19*. London: National Audit Office.
National Audit Office (2023). *Taxpayer support for UK banks: FAQs*. Available at https://www.nao.org.uk/taxpayer-support-for-uk-banks-faqs/#other-related-nao-reports accessed on 29 July 2023.
O'Donnell, Gus, interview
Parliament (2014). *Local Audit and Accountability Act (2014)*. Available at https://www.legislation.gov.uk/ukpga/2014/2/enacted, accessed on 30 November 2023.
Petit, Sarah, interview
Pierce, A. (2017). Sir Jeremy Heywood is the die-hard Remainer who really runs Britain (aided and abetted by his influential Europhile wife). *Daily Mail*, 14 October 2017.
Public Accounts Commission (2007). *Thirteenth report*, Session 2006-7, HC915. London: House of Commons.
Public Accounts Commission (2007a) Minutes of meeting on Wednesday 13 June 2007. Available at https://www.parliament.uk/globalassets/documents/commons-committees/publicaccountscommission/Mins13June07.pdf accessed on 18 January 2024.
Public Accounts Commission (2008). *Review of the National Audit Office's corporate governance: Fourteenth report*, Session 2007-8, HC328. London: House of Commons.
Public Accounts Commission (2008a). *Corporate governance of the National Audit Office: Response to John Tiner's review, fifteenth report*, Session 2007-8, HC402. London: House of Commons.
Public Accounts Commission (2011). *Transcript of hearing held on 9 November 2010*. Available online at https://www.parliament.uk/globalassets/documents/commons-committees/publicaccountscommission/Transcript9November2010.pdf accessed on 30 October 2023.
Public Accounts Commission (2014). *Uncorrected transcript of oral evidence, 2 December 2014*. Available online at Microsoft Word - PACm 02 12 14.doc (parliament.uk) accessed on 10 March 2024.
Public Accounts Commission (2016). *Oral evidence: NAO's Supplementary Estimate for 2016-17 and NAO's strategy for 2017-18 to 2019-20*. Available at https://www.parliament.uk/globalassets/documents/public-accounts-commission/TPAC-minutes-13.12.16.pdf accessed on 17 March 2024.
Public Accounts Committee (2011). *Oral evidence*, HC1531. Available at https://publications.parliament.uk/pa/cm201012/cmselect/cmpubacc/1531/11110701.htm accessed on 28 July 2023.
Public Accounts Committee (2011a). *Accountability for public money, 28th report of session 2010-12*, Session 2010-12, HC740. London: House of Commons.
Public Accounts Committee (2012). *Oral evidence*, HC1814. Available at https://publications.parliament.uk/pa/cm201012/cmselect/cmpubacc/1814/120208.htm accessed on 23 November 2023.
Public Accounts Committee (2015). *The Government's funding of Kids Company, 8th report of Session 2015-16*, Session 2015-16, HC504. London: House of Commons.
Public Accounts Committee (2016). *Oral evidence: Granite and Northern Rock*. Available at https://committees.parliament.uk/oralevidence/5977/pdf/ accessed on 17 March 2024.
Public Administration and Constitutional Affairs Committee (2016). *The collapse of Kids Company: Lessons for charitable trustees, professional firms,*

the Charity Commission and Whitehall, Fourth report of session 2015-16, Session 2015-16, HC433. London: House of Commons.

Public Administration and Constitutional Affairs Committee (2016a). *Inquiry into government accounts launched*. Available at https://committees.parliament.uk/work/5979/inquiry-into-government-accounts/news/101718/inquiry-into-government-accounts-launched/ accessed on 29 October 2023.

Public Administration and Constitutional Affairs Committee (2016b). *Oral evidence: Government accounts*, HC 95 Tuesday 24 May 2016, available at https://committees.parliament.uk/oralevidence/5706/pdf/ accessed on 29 October 2023.

Public Administration and Constitutional Affairs Committee (2017). *Accounting for democracy: Making sure Parliament, the people and ministers know how and why public money is spent, Fourteenth report of session 2016-17*, Session 2016-17, HC95. London: House of Commons.

Public Administration and Constitutional Affairs Committee (2018). *Accounting for democracy revisited: The Government response and proposed review, sixth report of session 2017-19*, Session 2017-19, HC1197. London: House of Commons.

Riddell, Peter, interview

Rutter, Jill, interview

Sayers, Neil, interview

Scharaschkin, Alex, interview

Scrutiny Unit (2009). *Adoption of IFRS by central government: Briefing note by the House of Commons Scrutiny Unit*. Available at https://www.parliament.uk/globalassets/documents/upload/ifrsbriefing.pdf accessed on 7 August 2023.

Sinclair, Martin, interview

Smith, Nick, interview

Stolk, Christian van, interview

Syal, R. (2017). Brexit plans could fall apart 'like a chocolate orange', says auditor general. *The Guardian*, 13 July 2017.

Talbot, C. and Talbot, C. (2019). *UK public spending the long view*. Available at https://www.bennettinstitute.cam.ac.uk/blog/uk-public-spending-long-view/ accessed on 19 November 2023.

Taxpayers Alliance (2010). *Justifying their existence*. Available at https://www.taxpayersalliance.com/justifying_their_existence_z0qp85obnpryub84ltbgher6xtk accessed on 30 July 2023.

Timmins, N. and Gash, T. (2014). *Dying to improve: The demise of the Audit Commission and other improvement agencies*. London: Institute for Government.

Tombs, R. (2019). *What Sir Ivan Rogers gets wrong about Brexit*. Available at https://www.spectator.co.uk/article/what-sir-ivan-rogers-gets-wrong-about-brexit/, accessed on 28 July 2023.

Travers, Tony, interview

Treasury (2013). *Whole of Government Accounts: Year ended 31 March 2010*. London: HM Treasury.

Waller, M. (2008). Two jobs at the National Audit Office, City Diary. *The Times*, 30 September 2008.

Whitehouse, Michael, interview

Whiteman, Rob, interview

7

GARETH DAVIES 2019 – AUDIT DURING AND AFTER THE PANDEMIC

7.1 Introduction

In 2019, Gareth Davies was appointed Comptroller and Auditor General. He was approved by the PAC on 22 January 2019 (PAC, 2019) but was not appointed until March 2019 (House of Commons, 2019). Davies's appointment took longer than it should have done, not due to any fault in the candidate, but because the C&AG's appointment requires the approval of the Prime Minister. At the start of 2019, Theresa May as Prime Minister had other things to focus on rather than approving the appointment of a C&AG, including the state of her government.

Within months of his appointment, the established British political parties were in chaos, following the 2019 European elections, and May herself, the prime minister who appointed him, had resigned. These events positioned his arrival at the NAO in the context of escalating political and parliamentary chaos.

On the surface, this chaos was halted by the election of Boris Johnson as leader of the Conservative Party and his success in the 2019 general elections, but Johnson's election did not resolve the crisis of government which had begun in 2009 with the financial crisis and the UK's response to it: his administration was charged with taking the UK out of the EU and then was struck by the COVID-19 pandemic.

Davies, unlike Downey, Bourn or even Morse, was thus faced with escalating crises immediately in his tenure, crises which had a huge effect on the NAO, closing the physical office for the first time in its history.

DOI: 10.4324/9781003520085-7

The purpose of this chapter is to examine the first half of Davies' tenure as C&AG from 2019 to 2024 (5 years of his 10-year tenure). To do so, the chapter sets out the political context of the period and then considers the NAO using the categories of regulatory space: organisational context (including independence), capacities and audit scope. This allows us to show that Davies met these crises by focussing the NAO on providing advice to departments, concentrating on its core interests in improving the management of public services and financial audit by sharing insights from audit and developing best practice guidance and trying to maintain parliamentary accountability during crises.

7.2 Political context

As referred to above, Davies became C&AG at a volatile time in British political history. Theresa May was unable to get a majority for a Brexit deal with the EU during 2018–19, and in 2019 she was finally forced out. She was replaced by Boris Johnson. Johnson immediately began further negotiations with the EU, reaching a deal in the autumn of 2019. After failing to see that deal be approved by the House of Commons, Johnson called a general election in 2019, which he won with a majority of 80 then passing the withdrawal agreement with the EU soon after. He negotiated a trade and future relationship treaty with the EU during 2020.

In March 2020, Johnson locked down the UK following the arrival of the COVID-19 pandemic from China. This decision became increasingly controversial in the UK with critics arguing that either Johnson did not lock down early enough or locked down too late or that the pandemic revealed vulnerabilities in the UK state which had arisen in the past 10 years of Conservative government. The UK then went through a series of lockdowns and social distancing measures during 2020 and 2021 (Institute for Government, 2022).

In 2022, Russia invaded Ukraine. The UK was one of the leading countries in opposing the Russian invasion and supplied Ukraine with defence equipment. The invasion, however, raised energy costs through 2022 due to market turbulence caused by the gap in supply of Russian gas. Johnson, however, did not survive in office long enough to meet this new domestic policy challenge. In 2022, Johnson was forced to resign after scandals about breaches of lockdown in Downing Street during the COVID-19 pandemic and due to the behaviour of some Conservative MPs.

Johnson was replaced by Elizabeth Truss, but she was Prime Minister only between September and October 2022. In September 2022, Truss and her Chancellor Kwasi Kwarteng[1] announced a series of measures including an energy price guarantee and a series of tax changes. After panic on the bond markets, first Kwarteng and then Truss were forced to resign.

High inflation exacerbated a cost of living crisis for most citizens in the UK, deepening the government's political difficulties. In October 2022, Truss was replaced by Rishi Sunak as Prime Minister. Bringing inflation under control and re-balancing the economy were seen as priorities.

In effect, during only five years, the UK had had four prime ministers. These prime ministers were faced with a series of crises. Scholars have described the early 2020s as a period of polycrisis: in which governments faced crises on different fronts simultaneously – healthcare related, economic, geopolitical – and struggled against them (Tooze, 2021).

7.3 Organisational context

Despite ongoing political crises, Davies was the first C&AG to be appointed since the 1983 Act into position when the NAO's independence was neither under threat nor novel. Downey was appointed before the Act was passed, and John Bourn came in when the NAO was only four years old. Amyas Morse was appointed to a role which was being reshaped in the light of the appointment of a new NAO board and the resignation of his predecessor. Davies was appointed into a position that was stable, and there was no suggestion, unlike in 2011, of a new Act to set out the governance of the NAO. Threats when they came arose from the technical regulation of the NAO's audit or tensions between the NAO and the government of the day.

The one exception to this came in the form of a recommendation from the Kingman review into financial audit, which reported in 2018. This review, led by Sir John Kingman,[2] a former Treasury official, was established in the aftermath of scandals, such as the collapse of the construction company Carillion, to examine the role and activities of the Financial Reporting Council (FRC), the regulator of private sector financial audit in the UK. It largely focussed within that remit, proposing the creation of a new regulator, the Audit Reporting and Governance Authority (ARGA), which would replace the FRC. The review also included a section on the C&AG's financial audits which noted that some were regulated by the FRC, namely audits of publicly owned companies. The NAO also invited the financial audit regulator in to review other audits, but this was at the discretion of the C&AG.

The review concluded that there was 'no credible justification' for excluding the NAO's financial audits from the remit of the new regulator and that 'the regulator should quality assess all the NAO's financial audit work' (Kingman, 2018, p. 16).

The issue with this from a constitutional perspective was simple; as Davies told us, the Kingman review 'would put the NAO in the unacceptable position of being accountable to a government body' (interview,

Gareth Davies). (This was distinct from previous arrangements under which the C&AG voluntarily accepted monitoring from an audit regulator – an arrangement from which theoretically the C&AG could withdraw.) Under Morse, the NAO began to lobby against this change and propose its own preferred solution; however, Morse's term ended six months after the Kingman review was published. Davies addressed these issues in March 2020 before the Public Accounts Commission: he told them that

> We disagreed with the specific recommendations included in the Report that were aimed at the NAO, because they would have brought us to be directly accountable to a body that is part of Government, a ministerial body – the new regulator.
>
> *(Public Accounts Commission, 2020, Q18)*

He said that the NAO was involved in 'constructive dialogue' with the government and the Commission about next steps forward (Public Accounts Commission, 2020, Q18).

The solution proposed by the NAO and accepted by the government was that the NAO would not be subject to the new regulator; rather the Commission, assisted by expert advisors, would hold the NAO to account for the quality of its financial audits. Davies described this proposal as a 'neat solution', which preserved 'our proper accountability, which is to you in Parliament' (Public Accounts Commission, 2020, Q19). He enlarged on this point in 2021: linking the solution back to the 1983 Act:

> As an officer of Parliament, I am already accountable to the Commission for the oversight of the NAO, its budget, and the delivery of its functions, so it seems appropriate for this Commission to hold me to account for the quality of the NAO's audit work.
>
> *(Public Accounts Commission, 2021, Q1)*

These hearings commenced in 2021 and continued in subsequent years (Public Accounts Commission, 2021, 2022). We will discuss the effects of this scrutiny later, but the key point was that the NAO had continued to reinforce the 1983 Act. The measures agreed by the government and the NAO, and the Commission, went further than the Act, in that they gave Parliament a direct, if limited, ability to hold the C&AG to account for what the NAO audited as well as the way it spent its money. This was a move which Sir Geoffrey Howe and the Treasury had resisted in 1983.

Davies came with a second important personal history when it came to analysing the independence of the NAO, as he had been a senior member of staff at the Audit Commission, the NAO's 'so-called' sister organisation. The NAO already had, as we have noted previously, taken on several staff with backgrounds in the Audit Commission during the 2010s, especially to staff its local government work. Davies, as C&AG, was shaped by the Audit Commission's approach to public audit, as will be discussed below but also by the experience of the Audit Commission's demise between 2010 and 2015. Davies himself reflected on this when he discussed with us his reasons for taking the job:

> it's not as if this is my first exposure to public audit – this has been my career and it's a top job in public audit in the UK.
>
> *(Gareth Davies, interview)*

Davies was probably the first C&AG to conceptualise his own career as a career in public sector audit. Morse, Downey and Bourn, to differing extents, came to the role versed in the mechanisms of parliamentary accountability as they had all (albeit in Morse's case briefly) served as civil servants. For Davies, this was different: he viewed the NAO as part of a system of public sector audit which had included the Audit Commission until 2015 and therefore brought ideas about independence from this whole system to his approach. Davies's language like Morse's was as much about the role of auditor as it was about a parliamentary auditor. For example, in speaking to the Public Accounts Commission about the Kingman review, he told them

> That [the Kingman proposal] is just in principle not right for an organisation like mine, which has to be independent of the organisations that it audits.
>
> *(Public Accounts Commission, 2020, Q18)*

Notice the reference to the principle that the auditor has to be 'independent of the organisation that it audits' – an appeal to a generic principle – rather than to the Act or the constitution. Davies did mention the link to Parliament at other points, but anchoring the NAO's sense of itself in the broad tradition of audit and public audit was an important rhetorical shift.

Davies' rhetorical shift becomes clearer when analysing the NAO's own view of independence. In the 2019 strategy, the word 'independence' is used three times to describe the NAO. Firstly, the NAO, the strategy says, is the UK's 'independent public spending watchdog' (NAO, 2020a, pp. 3, 8). Secondly, the strategy sets out accurately that the NAO 'scrutinise[s] public spending for Parliament and are independent of government and the civil service' (NAO, 2020a. p. 9). The third reference though is the only one in which the new strategy advanced an objective for the NAO and linked it to the organisation's objectives: the NAO would now focus on 'providing more accessible independent insight' (NAO, 2020a, p. 10). Davies himself thought of independence in this way: as an attribute which helped the auditor be more effective. In an interview with *Civil Service World*, he described the importance of audit independence:

> when the auditor becomes part of the management process, it becomes very difficult to audit that process later. So, staying on the right side of the line while also producing constructive work is part of the challenge.
>
> *(Johnstone, 2019)*

This focus on the need to be independent, not as a constitutional guarantor (though his NAO definitely acknowledged that role), but as an important part of performing 'constructive work', represented a deepening of Morse's interest in impact. Not all observers believed this was possible: Sir Bernard Jenkin believed that during the 2019 Parliament, civil servants remained 'very defensive' in front of PAC (Sir Bernard Jenkin, interview). Running through Davies's approach to the NAO and its independence is the idea that independent audit represents 'a rich source of learning' for the executive; in this sense, his concept of independence reaches back to Thatcher and Wilson and makes the auditor the teacher of the civil service (Davies, 2022).

Davies also described a different impact of the Audit Commission upon his own mindset as C&AG in his pre-appointment hearing in 2019. In response to a question from Anne Marie Morris, MP,[3] Davies explained that he was concerned that the NAO did not become subject to 'the risk of mission creep which is a serious risk for an organisation' (PAC, 2019, Q35). Mike Newbury[4] said to us that he felt the Audit Commission had become the 'Swiss army knife of local government audit and regulation', and that for both the Conservatives and Liberal Democrats, specific aspects of the Commission's activity had become irritating or seen as wasteful (Mike Newbury, interview). Whether the Audit Commission's demise was caused by overreach or not, the link between the Audit Commission's end and a threat to the NAO was already visible to Morse and his leadership team. For Morse, the threat had been a direct one from the government and met through political leadership. By 2019, the tale of the Audit Commission's demise had become more cautionary: prompting the auditors to consider how they might avoid its fate. It is in that context, that in 2019, the new NAO strategy reflected on the purpose of the organisation. Davies set up a bespoke team within the NAO which interviewed MPs, civil servants and members of staff. The NAO strategy (which we will discuss more when we discuss the way that the audit scope changed) focussed the organisation on what it described as the NAO's purpose: 'we support Parliament in holding government to account and we help improve public services through our high-quality audits' (NAO, 2020a). Concentrating the NAO on its purpose could help it avoid the fate of its sister organisation, the Audit Commission.

7.4 Capacity

Regarding capacity, Davies continued the commitment to increasing the NAO's professionalisation in both financial audit and value for money, and to boost its financial audit practice whilst reducing the resource deployed to value for money, as Morse did in the 2010s. This in many ways was to be expected as the NAO sought to build a modern professional image both externally and internally.

As we will show, these long-term developments strengthened the NAO, but also created weaknesses in the organisation's sense of itself. These weaknesses were exacerbated by the NAO's response to the COVID-19 pandemic, which whilst inevitable weakened the cohesion of the organisation, which was notable since 1983.

The effects of financial audit regulation were felt beyond the scope of the NAO's financial audit, as increased attention to the bureaucratic process of audit required more auditors and therefore took up a larger share of funding. From Davies's first year in 2018–19 to 2022–3, the NAO significantly increased the amount it spent on financial audit: in 2018–19 the NAO spent £57.9 million on its financial audit function, whilst in 2022–3 it spent £78.3 million (NAO, 2019, 2023).[5] This increase has to be put into the context of an organisation whose total expenditure in the period went from £87 million to £110 million (NAO, 2019, 2023). It is noticeable that not only did funding rise, but the NAO increasingly moved resources into financial audit: in 2019, under Morse, the NAO spent 66% of its resources on financial audit; by 2023, that proportion had risen to 71%. Under Morse, the trajectory (as we described in the previous chapter) had been rising anyway, but Davies kept concentrating resources on financial audit.

Some of this increase in funding for financial audit was driven by the COVID-19 pandemic: the NAO requested and obtained an additional £2.1 million to audit the accounts of bodies including the Department of Health and Social Care, whose activities had become more complicated and extensive due to the pandemic (NAO, 2022a, p. 7), but inevitably, however, the NAO also invested money due to pressures it saw within the marketplace for financial auditors. As Davies and Dame Fiona Reynolds[6] wrote in 2022:

> Our estimate [budget submitted to Parliament for approval] also reflects the costs associated with meeting new standards and making more complex audit judgements, including the next stage of modernising our audit methodology and software; and the need to increase pay to mitigate the risk of higher staff turnover following last year's public sector pay freeze.
>
> *(NAO, 2022a, p. 5)*

The NAO's additional finance for financial audit was partly devoted to auditors. Prior to Davies, the NAO funnelled its financial audit and value-for-money staff through the same career structure: they would advance to manager and then director. Davies introduced in 2023 a new financial audit manager grade, boosting both the prestige and the pay of many financial auditors, and signalling clearly the priority and importance the NAO put on its financial audit practice (NAO, 2023a, p. 69). Investment also went into the NAO's development of new technologies as part of the NAO's Audit Transformation Programme, intended to refresh the organisation's audit methodology in light of the regulator's criticisms (NAO, 2022a, p. 27).

Funding to other areas of the organisation remained much flatter as a proportion of the NAO's overall spend, such as spending on value for money. It merely increased from £14.6 million in 2019 to £18.3 million in 2023 (NAO, 2019, 2023a). Furthermore, this increase only reversed some of the previous decline in expenditure on value-for-money audit under Morse. For example, in 2023 expenditure on value-for-money audit was still £8.5 million less in nominal terms than it had been in 2009 (£26.8 million compared to £18.3 million) (NAO, 2009, 2023a). Some of this reduction could have arisen from a change in the way that the NAO reports its spending.

However, another way of looking at the spending on value for money is to examine what the NAO spent on non-financial audit activity which includes all its value for money audit and central functions. In 2009, the NAO spent £46.6 million on non-financial audit activity; by 2019 following Morse's tenure, that had reduced to £29.2 million (NAO, 2009, 2019). Under Davies it recovered slightly to £31.7 million in 2022–3 (NAO, 2023a). Again, the picture is that under Davies this figure recovered but from a low base.

Tim Phillips,[7] Director of Health Value for Money, told us that whilst budgets for the average value-for-money study when he joined in 2004 had been around £280,000, which included the costs of buying in extra research, in 2023 he was asked to work typically with budgets of

£250,000, all of which would ordinarily be staff costs (both figures are nominal and exclude inflation).[8] As a proportion of the NAO's spend, the recovery under Davies becomes marginal: from 2019 onwards, the NAO consistently spent 17% of its resources on value for money (as defined in NAO's accounts). The decline in resources devoted to non-financial audit work as a proportion of the NAO's overall work continued under Davies: from 34% of the NAO's budget to 29% between 2018–19 and 2022–3 (NAO, 2019, 2023). Compared to 2009, when non-financial audit work had consumed half the NAO's budget, the decline is particularly steep (NAO, 2009). This has had important effects: the NAO has been deprioritising its work on value for money over time and moving towards being focussed on financial audit rather than value for money. Low spending led to often young and inexpert teams running value-for-money projects. Interestingly, this lack of specialism was reflected on by Kate Bingham,[9] who ran the government's vaccine taskforce during the pandemic and was the subject of an NAO report, who scoffed in her memoirs at any suggestion that the 'youthful generalists [of the NAO] would be able to sharpen our thinking' and said the NAO's attempt to advise her was, based on their skills, a 'foolish and expensive joke' (Bingham and Hames, 2022, p. 121).

The transition in capacity away from value for money and towards financial audit meant that after 2019 the intellectual freedoms visible under Bourn's leadership of the NAO did not return. The main innovation after 2019 in terms of the NAO's value-for-money capacity came in the form of hubs. Morse had established centres of excellence for the various skills he saw as important within government during the 2010s. Hubs were different for two reasons: firstly, they sat outside the general structure of the NAO (Morse's centres had sat within clusters of departmental teams), and secondly, they focussed as much on topics such as commercial and contracting and digital as much as they did on the skills departments needed. Davies described his hubs in evidence to the Public Accounts Commission:

> Our new strategy came up with the concept . . . [of] our knowledge hubs. Those operate regardless of professional discipline. They bring together all of our knowledge in areas like digital transformation, major project delivery and so on. They draw on the expertise of both financial auditors and V[alue] F[or] M[oney] specialists.
>
> *(Public Accounts Commission, 2021a, Q17)*

They were designed explicitly because Davies and other senior managers saw that government failed in similar ways: as Dame Fiona Reynolds[10] put it, 'this is where the hubs come in. They give us the ability to look across different functions of government at cross-cutting issues like project management and IT transformation programmes' (Fiona Reynolds, interview). These hubs were designed to look outwards as well as inwards. Reflecting Davies's interest in influencing government, they produced summaries of previous NAO work that sought to build the NAO's influence with departments.

Turning from the NAO's position on value for money and financial audit, the NAO had faced challenges like all organisations in becoming more diverse in terms of ethnicity, class and disability. This was something that Davies emphasised on his appointment. For Lord Bichard, there was a clear continuity between Morse and Davies in their recognition of the importance of making the NAO more diverse. Davies did take more action though: in October 2019, for example, the NAO launched a diversity mentoring scheme for senior managers (NAO, 2020a, p. 56). The NAO put in place a race equality action plan (2020), a disability equality action plan (2021) and a social mobility equality action plan (2022) to help it address diversity issues (NAO, 2023a, p. 131).[11] The NAO began to publish ethnicity and disabled pay gap data from 2020 (NAO, 2023a, p. 69). The gender pay gap fell from 9.9% in 2019 to 6.4% in 2023 and the NAO targets eliminating the gap by 2027 (NAO, 2020a, p. 46, 2023a, p. 70). Despite these signs of progress, the NAO admitted in 2021 that 'we have not made as much, nor as quick, progress as we would have liked over the course of our previous D&I Strategy and have fallen below some of the expectations our people rightly have of us' (NAO, 2021, p. 2).

Across this picture of capacity though, the COVID-19 pandemic created unprecedented challenges for the NAO as it did for all organisations. The immediate challenge was sizeable. By 24th March 2020, 10% of the NAO's workforce was directly affected by COVID-19 either because they were infected or because they were self-isolating (Public Accounts Commission, 2020, Q1). As government issued the order to stay at home, the NAO complied, and the office was effectively shut in March 2020 and remained shut until the lockdown was released. However, even after the immediate lockdown in 2020 ended, the NAO maintained staff working from home (in common with other organisations) for the next 18 months (Lonsdale and Barrados, 2023). Most staff therefore spent very few days in the office between March 2020 and the effective end of the acute phase of the pandemic in the autumn of 2021. Additionally, several departments, due to the COVID-19 pandemic, faced issues with their accounts (Lonsdale and Barrados, 2023). The immediate question for Davies and his senior management was whether the NAO could continue to present audits to Parliament. The investment under Morse and Davies in IT was successful in enabling the organisation to continue: working in the cloud became possible on most financial audits, for example. As Steve Corbishley told us, even the Comptroller function, which in previous years the NAO had thought was impossible to function with staff at home, continued to function through the pandemic and authorised expenditure in the normal way (Corbishley, interview). The conduct of much value-for-money audit, according to Lonsdale and Barrados (2023), also carried on despite the pandemic, with reports still published and PAC hearings still supported via online briefings. When restrictions eased, some work that had to be carried on an in-person basis, such as site visits to conduct stocktakes, could resume but this happened slowly. The main risk was that the informal relationships which auditors developed when visiting departments and which helped to elicit valuable insights would be lost, to the detriment of the NAO's understanding of its audit clients. There was no sense that the NAO took any shortcuts and audits largely continued.

The longer-term issue that the NAO's pandemic period brought to light though was around the culture of the office. In previous years, NAO trainees, researchers and analysts had joined an office with an incredibly strong culture, nurtured through staff being together in the same building and being sent off together either on audit trips or, as trainees, to college. The NAO of 2019 focussed socially on areas like the staff canteen and gym, where networks and links were built between staff and a strong identification with the organisation was nurtured. The pandemic interrupted that. Nevertheless, for existing staff, their identity continued: the two years of the pandemic failed to expunge earlier experience. Furthermore, staff gradually returned, and whilst this return was not complete, it was complete enough for relationships to be rebuilt. There are some questions in the organisation, however, about whether the same thing has happened for those who joined shortly before or during the pandemic. This dynamic added to a sense described by Neil Sayers that the NAO has not prioritised preserving its culture under either Morse or Davies:

> Institutional memory has certainly declined. There's not a lot of historical knowledge at the top of the office, there are a few older directors but not many and most are retiring. This started to be a problem twenty years ago and we promoted too many people too young, who didn't have full knowledge and understanding, and we still like to promote people too early because we are afraid that otherwise they will run away.
>
> *(Neil Sayers, interview)*

In this sense, there is a risk that the NAO's knowledge of its own history and its culture may well have been disrupted by the patterns of promotion since 2000 and more recently by COVID-19.

7.5 Audit scope

Within months of Davies's appointment, the NAO like the rest of the UK was blown off course by the COVID-19 pandemic. Davies's NAO approached audit similarly to Morse's NAO but with distinctions. Firstly, Davies' NAO approached the situation that the UK found itself in with a deeper sense of the crises (both short and long term) facing the country. This was related of course to the pandemic but with a broader context in the development of climate change policy. Analysing the state through the medium of crisis revealed both the strengths of the NAO's audit and the weaknesses of its approach. Secondly, Davies' NAO concentrated on improving government: more reports and more resources were devoted to thinking about lessons that could be learnt from previous work rather than bringing out new value-for-money studies. This reflected Davies's emphasis on improvement rather than accountability alone as the purpose of audit. Thirdly, Davies's NAO redoubled the efforts of the previous 20 years to embed professionalisation into the financial audit practice. Taken together, the Davies' NAO therefore sits within the traditions of both Bourn and Morse but represents development in an era when British government and governance are less confident and state capacity is struggling.

7.5.1 Deeper sense of crises

Crisis was the motif of Davies' NAO from the moment he was appointed. He singled it out in speeches especially after the COVID-19 pandemic. For example, in 2022, Davies reflected on the need for government to be a better risk planner: having described so-called 'black swan events', he argued that 'I don't think we can accept that any longer I don't think [that] these are going to be so rare [that they have] to be put in a separate category' (Davies, 2022a). Seeing government as uniquely afflicted in the 2020s by crisis both short and long required an audit response. Davies, in his interview with us, spoke of the need to analyse the state's approach to systemic risk rather than just auditing the money the state spent:

> I think a big strategic question that we're starting to think about coming out of the pandemic experience, also informed by Brexit and the prospective challenge around net zero, is whether as well as auditing money that government has decided to spend, we should also be reviewing how well government has set itself up to mitigate systemic risks.
>
> *(Gareth Davies, interview.)*

This 'big strategic question' predated COVID-19 in Davies's thinking, as he argues, linking both Brexit and the pursuit of efforts to control climate change. It conditioned his approach to the kinds of topics that he wanted the NAO to pursue.

This focus on crisis was particularly visible in climate change. For Davies, a central fact about British politics and life is that 'we are living through the early phases of a climate crisis which is now well accepted and is government policy to tackle': a crisis that he described as 'equally systematic, if not more so [compared to the COVID-19 pandemic] and shaping economies across the entire planet and every aspect of government policy too' (Davies, 2022a). The NAO recognised the scale of the effort required to achieve net zero: as a blog in 2020 suggested,

> Almost every individual will also have some role to play, whether that is changing the type of car they drive, updating their household heating system or even reducing the amount of meat and dairy products they consume.
>
> *(Bittlestone, 2020)*

Although the NAO conceived of this as a radical whole society project, they also saw it as a project which could be audited in the traditional way, as one of the 'numerous cross-government projects and programmes in the past, ranging from the 2012 Olympics to preparations for EU Exit' which the NAO had previously audited (Bittlestone, 2020). For example, the NAO examined preparations for the risk management of the climate crisis and based their analysis on a survey of audit committee chairs:

> To gauge the level of climate change risk maturity in government we surveyed Chairs of Audit and Risk Assurance Committees (ARACs). While four out of five ARAC Chairs considered climate risks to be relevant to their organisation, over half noted that their organisation did not have a climate or sustainability risk policy or a dedicated employee accountable for either. Additionally, seven in ten Chairs said that climate change risks had either never been discussed at an ARAC meeting or had been discussed less than annually.
>
> *(Akpan et al., 2022)*

In examining the crisis, the NAO therefore domesticated it: it was something that Audit and Risk Committees could look at in the same way that they might look at any other risk to the organisation. These commitments also led the NAO to seek to influence others to see these crises in the same way: for example, in 2022, they reported in their annual report that

> Our Financial and Risk Management hub produced a guide for audit and risk assurance committees on climate change risk. We identified this as an emerging risk area across government which was not attracting the level of attention we expected. Our guide was aimed at audit and risk assurance committees, to help them support and challenge management on how climate change risk was being managed.
>
> *(NAO, 2022b, p. 61)*

The NAO was seeking to shape the lenses through which government would look at climate change: seeking to impose a business or project-based lens in which the crisis is conceptualised as needing risk management. This conceptualisation places the auditor and the manager at its centre with technical experts, the outside population and experts in governing populations providing inputs to that managerial process.

The NAO had covered climate change and the environment since the 1990s. For example, the NAO had begun offering the Environmental Audit Committee sustainability reviews of departments before Davies was appointed (e.g. the NAO's 2017 report into the sustainability of the Ministry of Justice) (NAO, 2017). Davies's efforts were supported by a cadre of staff who had already developed an interest in environmental issues under Morse. Davies's emphasis on climate change as a driver of government activity made it much more central to the NAO's overall activities. Internally, the NAO, as in previous times with other initiatives such as austerity, sought to signal its interest in net zero by committing to a target of net zero by the end of Davies's term as C&AG in 2029 (NAO, 2019, p. 15). Externally, the NAO's reporting on climate change became more high profile and more expansive. In 2020, the NAO published an assessment of the way that the government was organised, cross-departmentally, to perform its environmental objectives and published a report into the government's management of progress towards the goal of making the UK a net-zero country by 2050 (C&AG, 2020, 2020a). The NAO followed this up with further reports, for example, examining how the government regulated to support environmental outcomes (C&AG, 2023). These topics did not represent an advance in terms of the powers of the NAO, but they did represent a change in tone led by Davies's insistence that the government should be seen as a manager of future flows to and from the exchequer as well as current ones. Arguably, Davies's approach to the environment was a natural development of the NAO's long embrace of accrual accounting: in both cases, government was to be held accountable for its future as well as current spending.

If climate change was the crisis which Davies arrived at the NAO already considering, then COVID-19 came to the NAO as it did to everyone else, as a surprise. We have already highlighted earlier the NAO's response to COVID-19 as a managerial challenge, which required staff to work from home for extended periods. As with Brexit, the pandemic raised questions of parliamentary scrutiny (Ferry et al., 2024). There were particular concerns in the UK involving questions of fraud of public funds (Sian and Smyth, 2022). The NAO responded to COVID-19 in four different ways. Much of its approach derived from work conducted under Morse and even Bourn, which was repurposed for the new context of the pandemic. We outline these four different approaches to the NAO's view of the pandemic, before drawing together the NAO's thinking about crisis as a whole.

Firstly, Davies saw COVID-19 as a crisis to which the NAO had to respond. He thought it was key that the NAO continued to perform its function despite the challenges it faced due to the pandemic and the general political sentiment that the country should rally around the government. He set this out in a blog from April 2020:

> My colleagues and I are committed to providing Parliament and the public with the evidence they need to understand how public money has been used in tackling this crisis. We will also help ensure that the appropriate lessons are learned for the future.
>
> *(Davies, 2020)*

As Tim Phillips said,

> It is to Gareth's credit that the NAO's institutional response to the pandemic was as swift and thorough as it was. For the first six weeks we got out of the way of government but then we began a large programme of publications on pandemic-related issues. My recollection is that other bodies radically reduced or suspended their inspection regimes for much longer, even years in some instances. Gareth took the decision in late April that we should audit from the start.
>
> *(Tim Phillips, interview)*

This brought difficulties: the NAO had to 'ask social care and NHS for evidence at the height of the pandemic', but 'in terms of the institution, we provided a full service throughout the pandemic' (Tim Phillips, interview). Phillips was not alone in seeing this scrutiny as vital: Sarah Olney[12] told us that 'as opposition we simply didn't have the tools to provide any effective scrutiny of what was done' and the NAO and PAC were crucial to filling some of that gap and providing transparent information (Sarah Olney, interview). The NAO published its first report on COVID-19 in May 2020 (C&AG, 2020b), and by July, Davies could report that 'we have published reports on the scale and nature of the public spending commitments and on readying the NHS and social care for the pandemic' (Davies, 2020a).

This was welcomed by the PAC where Meg Hillier recalled that she and the committee wanted 'to get into COVID straightaway' (Meg Hillier, interview). Davies was keen to emphasise the timing of his interventions. He commented in 2021 to the PAC on how the NAO's work differed at each stage of the pandemic: he contrasted 'our work on the acute phase of the pandemic, those initial schemes that had to be launched very quickly with little preparation' with subsequent work examining 'longer-term' issues such as 'the backlogs in many public services, the recovery of fraudulent payments and so on' (PAC, 2021, Q5). The crisis element of COVID-19 meant that Davies and the NAO recognised that some projects could not be run in the same way as before. Davies told us, 'What was important in auditing that situation, was demonstrating that you understood the context and why the standard way of operating was not possible. It isn't helpful to say why doesn't this fit my checklist if the answer why not is staring you in the face' (Gareth Davies, interview). Davies's point was absorbed by PAC: Sarah Olney said she felt PAC 'were really getting under the bonnet of people making decisions in a crisis with poor or very little information available' (Sarah Olney, interview). There are NAO reports which make precisely this point: the NAO's first investigation of procurement acknowledges the need for emergency procurement regulations. But Davies was equally insistent that the crisis 'makes it more not less important that you are completely transparent about what you're doing, and you do that promptly and accurately' (Davies, interview). An emergency for Davies and the NAO was a reason for providing assurance that government was being run appropriately.

Secondly, focusing on COVID-19 as a crisis also required the NAO to examine the pandemic as a cross-government event which touched all departments rather than just proceeding to audit it department by department. Under Davies and previous C&AGs, the NAO was used to this cross-government method of reporting its work: reports on climate change had already adopted this perspective, addressing themselves to the entirety of government rather than any department (C&AG, 2020, 2020a). Fiona Reynolds identified the fact that the NAO 'regularly highlights that the governments are not good at working laterally across departments' as one of the themes of Davies' tenure more widely. During Brexit, Peter Gray,[13] the Director responsible for the Department for Exiting the European Union, had also coordinated work within the NAO on the UK's exit. The NAO fused these two models when approaching the pandemic as a crisis: firstly, Lee Summerfield[14] (Director for Investigations), Tim Phillips (Health Value for Money Director) and Sian Jones[15] (Cross-Government Value for Money Director) convened a group of directors internally to coordinate work on the pandemic which met weekly. The NAO joined an international group of Supreme Audit Institutions to share lessons on how different governments were responding to the crisis (Lambauer, 2020). Secondly, the NAO, beginning with its first overview of the government's response to the pandemic in May 2020, continued to report in a cross-government fashion when required, for example, examining cross-government procurement or identifying lessons from the pandemic experience overall (C&AG, 2020b, 2020c). The logic of this position – that the crisis was a cross-government event – led the NAO into seeing the emergence of the COVID-19 crisis as a cross-government risk. In 2021, the NAO reported that

> This pandemic has exposed a vulnerability to whole-system emergencies – that is, emergencies that are so broad that they engage the entire system. Although the government had plans for an influenza pandemic, it did not have detailed plans for many non-health consequences and some health consequences of a pandemic like COVID-19.
>
> *(C&AG, 2021b, p. 10)*

The NAO's view that the government needed a more systematic view of emergencies tied to this much more systematic view of accountability.

Thirdly, the NAO viewed the pandemic as a challenge to public sector management. Early on, the NAO published its own guide for Audit and Risk Committees, in which it defined two ambitions for it as an organisation during the pandemic:

> to report in a risk-based way on programmes and activities being undertaken by government departments and other organisations and also to support organisations' own internal scrutiny and challenge.
>
> *(NAO, 2020)*

This approach at the departmental level resembled the NAO's work under Morse pre-pandemic. The NAO drew liberally on its previous intellectual capital in responding to the crisis. For example, in 2021, the NAO published a report on local government finance during the pandemic. In the report, the NAO applied its thinking about financial sustainability during the 2010s in local government to the situation in the sector after the pandemic's arrival. The report clearly identified that the department was responsible for what it described as a 'funding gap' for local government between the pressures created by COVID-19 and a shortfall in revenue due to the pandemic (C&AG, 2021, p. 9). The NAO did recognise the difficulty of the department's position due to the unexpected nature of the pandemic:

> In unprecedented circumstances, the Department did not have a ready-made strategic framework to apply at the outset of the pandemic and early initiatives, such as the initial tranche of funding provided in March, were based on the limited information available.
>
> *(C&AG, 2021, p. 8)*

Ultimately, though, the message of the report harked back to reports under Morse: as Dame Fiona Reynolds told us, the pandemic touched on a 'vulnerability' that the auditors had already known about (Fiona Reynolds, interview). This phenomenon, in which the NAO applied its previous toolkit of methods and findings to the novel crisis of the pandemic, was not unique. Individual departments continued to fail to deliver in similar ways to previous failures: for example, the NAO's report on programmes to help vulnerable adults with food and medicines during lockdown identified flaws in data, coordination and a lack of departmental assurance that food and medicine were actually getting through to the right people (C&AG, 2021c). Yvonne Gallagher,[16] Director of IT Value for Money audit, published a comment piece on the NAO's website that made this claim clear: after commenting on the flaws in the government's data during the pandemic, she wearily observed that 'these challenges are examples of broader issues that we have previously highlighted' (Gallagher, 2021). Similarly, the NAO's report on procurement in November 2020 identified familiar flaws such as poor documentation, but these were exacerbated by a situation in which departments were moving quickly and often discarding previously existing processes (C&AG, 2020c). Although the NAO's approach to the crisis was novel in that Davies and senior management clearly saw COVID-19 as an exceptional event which affected the whole of government, Tim Phillips argued much of the NAO's response was a traditional one (Tim Phillips, interview).

However, the NAO could have taken a different approach, and its traditionalism was criticised during the pandemic. A different C&AG and a different NAO could have argued that the government's interventions into the people's lives through lockdowns resembled regulation: a small amount of spending was supposed to have a large impact on society. It was possible therefore for the NAO to have audited decisions about lockdown, and it could have examined the advice offered by civil servants to ministers concerning that decision, following precedents set in Gordon Downey's time. It decided not to do that, a decision which may well have been wise, and thereby directed a key parliamentary instrument away from what some consider the key decisions of the pandemic. Critics of the NAO's approach did not identify this caution as a problem: rather they focussed on the NAO's over-eagerness to apply its traditional auditing approach to the novel problems of the pandemic. Kate Bingham, the head of the government's vaccine taskforce (VTF), was critical of the timing of the NAO's work on her taskforce, which started two months after she had launched it (Bingham and Hames, 2022, p. 121). For Bingham, the NAO had 'multiple shortcomings, including a profound lack of understanding of what the VTF was doing, the timing and scope of the audit, and a failure to understand or adequately reflect the extraordinary environment in which the VTF has been operating' (Bingham and Hames, 2022, p. 123).

Fourthly, the NAO saw itself during the pandemic as providing transparent data for others to use. The NAO had done this in the past and much of this activity continued. Traditional investigations were still run: for example, in 2022, the NAO published an account of delays in driving licence applications during the pandemic, identifying the scale and nature of delays in processes within the Driver and Vehicle Licensing Authority (DVLA) and measures the authority had taken to address those issues (C&AG, 2022). This gave the public and Parliament the information to push and scrutinise the activities of the DVLA further. Similarly, the NAO provided accounts of the ways in which government departments managed the aftermath of the pandemic, from the collection of taxation to the government's efforts to get long-term unemployed people back to work (C&AG, 2021a, 2022a). However, the NAO also embraced novel methods to provide Parliament with data about the pandemic in particular. From September 2020, the NAO published a regular COVID-19 Cost Tracker which set out the costs of the pandemic to the UK government (the final version is available at NAO, 2022). The NAO published a total cost for the promises made by ministers during the pandemic, which it drew together from a number of sources. Both press and academics used the information to scrutinise government (Partington, 2020; Appleby, 2022). The COVID-19 Cost Tracker represented an extension of the NAO's pre-existing role, both as a public spending focussed accountability body and increasingly from the late 2000s onwards as a compiler or producer of information intended to make government more transparent. The COVID-19 Cost Tracker's existence led to pressure on the government to publish its own figures about the costs of COVID-19 (PAC, 2022, p. 6). Subsequently, they began to publish some of this data (Treasury, 2023). The cost tracker represented a change in the nature of the NAO's activity: it became for the first time the publisher of information about government to the public. The NAO identified a gap in accountability for Parliament and filled it.

However, this development raised questions firstly about the auditor's role: should it adopt this role in future crises? It also raised questions about how the pandemic was accounted for. In 2017, the Public Administration and Constitutional Affairs Committee suggested that if the accounts were the chief accountability document for public expenditure, they should incorporate information about programmes and clearly identify it for transparency purposes (Public Administration and Constitutional Affairs Committee, 2017). Sir Bernard Jenkin identified the major projects report as a positive example of this: 'the equipment plan is a really good report because that's continuously monitoring some very large projects on an ongoing basis' (Sir Bernard Jenkin, interview). In 2022, the PAC recommended that the government should 'integrate the positive attributes of the cost tracker to further increase transparency and accountability around other large areas of spending' (PAC, 2022, p. 8). Their suggestion implied the accounts were not the final word on public spending accountability, but it did not state it.

None of these addresses the Gladstonian question about the control of government expenditure during the pandemic. Interestingly, as in the case of the financial crisis, Steve Corbishley, who had returned to the Comptroller function, told us that COVID-19 'didn't cause us any Comptroller issues' (Steve Corbishley, interview). There were amendments to the parliamentary funding process which were passed in March 2020, authorising the Contingencies Fund to be expanded from 2% of government expenditure to 12% and making available a huge amount of extra money to government departments in advance of their estimates being approved in July 2020. However, these changes did not impact upon the NAO (HM Treasury, 2020). Within the NAO, there was some expectation that accounts would need to be qualified due to the pandemic, but again by the time of the accounts publication for the first year of COVID-19, there were fewer excess votes than expected (Steve Corbishley, interview).

If anything, the sense of urgency in public accountability came not through the financial audit side, but from value for money. Meg Hillier told us that the pandemic focussed the committee on the propriety with which money was spent:

> we were very, very, focused on the money because it was something that's more than double the normal NHS budget. Staggering amounts of money were being spent. The civil service let itself down at times on Brexit and COVID because it didn't say no limits, wait a day or two, we can give you some better anti-fraud measures. And they didn't keep proper records of some of the contracts which then became a rod to beat government with whether or not it actually broke the rules. It gives people the impression that something bad is going on. And the civil service should have just been better at that. And we were quite shocked at how they weren't.
>
> *(Meg Hillier, interview,)*

Interestingly, for Hillier and for the NAO too, issues around ethics and propriety were now issues that value for money focussed on. The C&AG reported on 'the extraordinary financial impact' in the 2020–21 Department for Health and Social Care Accounts and outlined issues with inventory, procurement, fraud and internal controls (Department for Health, 2022, pp. 198–205). These accounts though were published after the NAO had already published several value-for-money reports on the same issues. With respect to procurement, for example, the NAO argued in 2020 that there was 'inadequate documentation' in many instances about how the risks of procuring suppliers without competition had been mitigated and that this undermines 'public trust in the fairness of the process' (C&AG, 2020c, p. 10).

Joshua Reddaway,[17] an NAO director, commented on this before a House of Lords Committee in 2021 and explained that the reason that the report's conclusions about documentation and process were so important was 'You need the system to prove to the public that it is clean, that it is safe, and that these decisions are being made properly. Unfortunately, they were not in a position to show to us that they had met that standard' (Select Committee on Public Services, 2021, Q1). It is unclear what the subsequent reports on the Department of Health's accounts added to Reddaway's words or indeed the NAO's value-for-money reports. Parliamentary and public assurance for the traditional subject matter (the propriety and regularity of spending) of financial audit during the pandemic thus flowed through the NAO's value-for-money reports as much as through financial audit.

7.5.2 Focus on improving government

Beyond the crises of COVID-19, climate change and Brexit, Davies came to the NAO with the intention of continuing its existing trajectory towards being a professional advisor to government as well as the body which held it to account. This had impact on value for money and financial audit work.

In value-for-money audit, Davies focussed even more on the impact of the NAO's work. On arrival in 2019, he announced a new strategy for the organisation (NAO, 2020a). Davies argued that the NAO had strengths in 2019, but he wanted the NAO to achieve more impact. He told the Public Accounts Commission that the NAO's focus should be on 'retaining our strengths but also delivering maximum value for the knowledge in the organisation' (Public Accounts Commission, 2020, Q8). For Davies this meant,

> making better use of the cumulative knowledge in the NAO. People have said, 'Why is it that I have to read six of your Reports on a particular theme across different Departments to really extract the learning? Can't you do more of that for us?' As you will see, that is an important strand in what we are now setting out to do.
>
> *(Public Accounts Commission, 2020, Q8)*

Davies' language here mirrors Bourn's and Morse's earlier desire to understand the systematic reasons for failure. Davies's focus on improving public services included deepening the NAO's own accountability for the impact of its work. He commissioned a new webpage on the NAO website which set out all the reports published since April 2019 with detail about whether recommendations had been accepted and further narrative data for reports published after October 2022 (NAO, 2023). By commissioning the tracker, Davies clearly indicated a deepening of the NAO's commitment to improving public services and seeing that as a key outcome for the organisation.

7.5.3 Embedding professionalisation in audit

In terms of financial audit, the NAO continued to strengthen its professional approach to financial audit. Private sector audit had been criticised in the late 2010s after a series of corporate failures including that of Carillion. The NAO saw a crisis in public sector audit with potential to parallel the crisis in private sector audit. This perspective had its roots under Morse (as described in a previous chapter), but Davies's NAO continued this approach. In its strategy, the NAO refers to the Kingman and Brydon reviews of private sector audit, but does not refer to PACAC's review of the parliamentary status of accounts (referred to in the previous chapter):

> Our financial audit work will continue to respond to developments in auditing standards and regulation following the Kingman and Brydon reviews, while also addressing some of the unique challenges in financial reporting arising from the impact of COVID-19.
>
> *(NAO, 2020a, p. 2)*

There is no question in this quotation as to whether the auditing standards or regulatory standards for private sector audit are suitable for public sector audit.

The NAO in 2019 could have perceived a public sector audit crisis which focussed on the auditor's role in ensuring the accounts play their proper part in parliamentary scrutiny. It could have thought following

Sir Douglas Henley in the 1970s and Sir Gordon Downey in the 1980s that its role was to support Parliament in achieving the vision set out in the PACAC reports of 2017 and 2018. It could have seen the underuse of financial information in Parliament as a crisis that reflected on public sector audit. Some within the NAO did understand this issue: Neil Sayers told us that

> no one is looking at the set of accounts of an organisation in the round and saying what does this mean, in a way this should be the job of select committees but select committees need help in doing this, and how far the administration of select committees can do this I don't know. My feeling is that they need support and that should be the job of the NAO.
>
> *(Neil Sayers, interview)*

Discussions about the way that public sector audit should be regulated were covered above from the perspective of independence. Davies and Morse and the NAO more widely were keen that the auditor should be regulated by Parliament rather than by a government body. However, Davies also believed that the appropriate assistance to that parliamentary select committee should come from the regulators of the private sector auditing industry. As he put it in discussions with TPAC,

> We already compare ourselves with the top firms in the audit market in the country, and in fact in the world. That seems to be the only relevant standard, because we audit hugely complex and large organisations and it is right that, when we ask somebody to inspect the quality of our work, they are people who are equipped to assess those kinds of audits. That is why the voluntary arrangement that we have had with the FRC in the last few years has been in place, because the FRC, as you know, inspect the biggest firms.
>
> *(Public Accounts Commission, 2021, Q3)*

Davies very clearly says that the private sector regulator should be inspecting the NAO's work. Kate Mathers, one of the NAO's executive leaders (board members) responsible for financial audit, described her view of what audit quality was and how she could see it improving and tied it to the view of the private sector regulator (referred to as AQR – the audit quality review team) in her answer:

> The ultimate indicator for us will be the scores from the AQR review,[18] so we want to see those improving. We want to see the level of comments

> in this area diminishing. That is the ultimate key performance indicator for us.
>
> *(Public Accounts Commission, 2021, Q9)*

Davies later explained that he agreed with Mathers and that the NAO 'now publish[es] our AQR scores on our website in a way that was not happening before two years ago' (Public Accounts Commission, 2021, Q32). Both Mathers and Davies conceptualised quality, not in terms of the scrutiny that the accounts made possible, but the ratings for the audit from the regulator.

For the NAO's financial audit, the sense was that their peer organisations were private sector audit firms and that the regulator measured quality had measurable impacts upon the way that financial audit was done and its scope. This is true as it had been under Morse for the NAO's increasing use of digital technology to perform its audit. As Ferry and Midgley (2023) argue, the use of data analytics in financial audit was partly driven by the demand from the private sector regulator for the technology to be used more. Its influence, however, went wider. The regulator made detailed recommendations about how the NAO's financial audit should develop. And in terms of proximity, the regulator was the most frequent external commentator on the NAO's audits. In 2021, for example, the reviewers spent six months (from January to July) inside the NAO inspecting the organisation's financial audits (Audit Quality Review Team, 2021). In contrast, few parliamentary or media commentators focussed on the NAO's financial audits, so there was little discussion or criticism from any other perspectives.

This had an impact on the NAO's audit scope. We can see some of the effects and reasons for the regulator's views by examining what they did in local government. Davies told a select committee that the regulator's technical approach was driven by private sector scandals:

> my observation is that the ratcheting up of the requirements from the regulator on what must be audited to get sufficient assurance in some of these areas – quite rightly those expectations have gone up as a result of the scandals in the private sector.
>
> *(Levelling Up, Housing and Communities Select Committee, 2023, Q109)*

Rob Whiteman agreed, describing the regulator as the 'Taliban' and saying that he felt they were 'auditing purists' (Levelling Up, Housing and Communities Select Committee, 2023, Q133). The same technical approach to audit can be seen in their reviews of the NAO's audits and those reviews also indicate that they influenced the conduct of the NAO's audit. For example, in 2019–20, the NAO agreed to strengthen its monitoring of 'risky' audits, adjusted its guidance on credit losses, developed a new approach to the audit of estimates, raised the level of audit required on low risk areas of the accounts, developed their guidance on the going concern of the entities they audited and on the acceptance of engagement, training and HR rules (Audit Quality Review Team, 2020). These reviews were purely technical: the audience for the audited accounts – the select committee – or the purpose of the audited accounts are not mentioned at all. For example, the 2021 report has four mentions of Parliament: two of which refer to the governance of the NAO itself (Audit Quality Review Team, 2021, pp. 7–8) and two of which are generic definitions of the C&AG's role and the concept of regularity (Audit Quality Review Team, 2021, p. 3). The NAO itself described how its financial audit developed in this period:

> In our financial audit work, we are continuing to respond to developments in auditing standards and regulation. We are also addressing several new and changing audit risks, for example challenges in valuing assets and inventories following the COVID-19 pandemic; increased vulnerability of public spending to fraud and error and the increased use of financial instruments by public bodies.
>
> *(NAO, 2023a, p. 16)*

Note how again, progress is described as technical improvement and in terms of the improvement of the process rather than with any reference to the outcome of the audit (such as improved accountability).

This did not mean that any agenda about parliamentary interest in audit fell away. Audit had by the period Davies was C&AG lost its underlying Gladstonian purpose. Although the NAO strategy reaffirmed the importance of auditing that 'income and expenditure are in accordance with Parliament's intentions' (NAO, 2022a, p. 14) and although there were qualifications due to regularity, normally as Parliament would never have intended fraud, the audit of regularity had lost any of its specificity.

One particular instance illustrates this development. In 2022, Boris Johnson, the prime minister, was accused of lying about parties in Downing Street during the period when the UK population was under coronavirus restrictions. Johnson eventually resigned and the Procedure Committee held an inquiry. Johnson's legal advice for his appearance before the committee was paid for by the Cabinet Office, and at the time questions were raised about whether a ministerial direction should have been sought (Nevett and Seddon, 2023). The C&AG examined the expenditure as part of his examination of the Cabinet Office's accounts, and in his certificate, he criticised the Cabinet Office for failing to seek Treasury advice about the issue. However, he did not refer to the fact that the PAC after the Lamont affair (described in Chapter 4) had said that expenditure on such arrangements should be rare.

This decision reflected a wider cultural trend on which some aspects of the fiscal constitution were no longer given the importance it had had previously. And so, counter-intuitively perhaps, ministerial directions have become much more common in recent years and, as Lord Butler told us, are perhaps not working as they should as a curb on decisions by ministers which risk propriety, regularity or value for money:

> Whereas directions were the very occasional nuclear weapon in my day, now they are very much more frequent, ministers have got used to giving such a direction and the reason why this currency has been debased and this has been inherent to the issue, is that the Public Accounts Committee don't do anything about it. What should happen is that the PAC should call the minister before them to say the accounting officer can't justify this, so how do you justify this. So, the use of the direction as a way of supporting efficiency, effectiveness and propriety has been greatly debased.
>
> *(Lord Butler, interview)*

Under Davies, therefore, the movement begun under Morse and Bourn to professionalise audit became even more intense partly through the regulator's influence. Audit under Morse and Davies had separated itself from its roots as a parliamentary activity and became a process of assessing controls and risks similar to that going on in any other major business.

7.6 Chapter summary

The chapter examined the first half of Davies's 10-year term as C&AG from 2019 to 2023, through considering both the political context and categories of regulatory space concerning organisational context, capacities and audit scope. Gareth Davies has not yet brought about a revolution in the way that the NAO operates, nor has he yet sought to.

Much of Davies' NAO continued what Morse's had done: in terms of capacity, financial audit continued and extended its domination of the organisation's work and budget. That financial audit's scope became more and more allied to the type of financial audit seen in the private sector: focussed on the process of ensuring that valuations in the accounts and other complex accounting judgements were correct. It evolved away from its parliamentary origins either as a check on regularity or as a process of transparency and the NAO were willing to allow the Treasury to dominate the conversation about what accounts should do or be (and were unwilling to take up suggestions by Parliament for reform). Davies, like Morse, approached the public sector as a set of managerial challenges: a perspective the NAO was intrinsically positioned to take both because of its statutory inability to comment on policy and because of the skills of those working in the office. In terms of organisational context, Davies has sought to extend the NAO he had been left, to make it more influential and a more powerful commentator. Critiques of the NAO's competence as a commentator on management were therefore a powerful threat to the organisation's credibility even if they were rare (Bingham and Hames, 2022).

However, the other side of Davies's inheritance and the context for the organisation was a British state struggling to cope with a multitude of crises. When he arrived at the NAO, the country was struggling to deal with Brexit, and months after his appointment, the Prime Minister who appointed him fell. The political legacies of Brexit then underpinned the swift rise and fall of a further two prime ministers during the first half of his term as C&AG. In March 2020, the UK was again struck by crisis as the pandemic arrived and government lockdowns hit the country economically and socially, including workplaces.

Climate change presented a new form of crisis which also threatened to transform the politics of the UK. The NAO's approach to these crises – through the lens of project management – brings it into more potentially contentious arenas. One of Morse's key skills was his ability to move around the crisis of Brexit, which transformed government during his period. The NAO was largely unscathed by COVID-19 due to the approach taken by Davies and his senior managers, which avoided the controversial topic of lockdown and focussed on the NAO's traditional terrain of contracting and financial sustainability. However, it will be interesting to see whether the NAO and Davies will be able to navigate the increasingly contentious politics of climate change in the same way. The urgency of crisis, the apolitical nature of a managerial narrative and the ideological division over basic facts are all potentially combustible for the NAO.

Notes

1 Kwasi Kwarteng, 1975–, MP for Spelthorne 2010–, Secretary of State for Business, Energy and Industrial Strategy 2021–2, Chancellor of the Exchequer 2022.

2 John Kingman, 1969–, HM Treasury 1991–4, 1999–2008 including Second Permanent Secretary 2007–8, 2012–16, Chief Executive UK Financial Investments Ltd 2008–9, Chair UK Research and Innovation 2016–21. Knighted 2016.

3 Anne Marie Morris, 1957–, MP for Newton Abbott 2010–.
4 Michael Newbury, Audit Commission 2003–11, National Audit Office Director 2012–.
5 These figures are both gross of income. In 2018–19, the NAO took £19.9 million of income from financial audit, and in 2022–3, it took £25.9 million worth of income from financial audit.
6 Fiona Reynolds, 1958–, Director Women's Unit Cabinet Office 1998–2000, Director General National Trust 2001–12, Master Emmanuel College, Cambridge University 2013–21, Chair National Audit Office 2021–, made a Dame 2008.
7 Tim Phillips, NAO 2004–, NAO Director including Education Value for Money and Health Value for Money Director 2016–.
8 Internal budgets in the NAO relate to projects and include any cash costs but are mostly devoted to staff costs with staff billing their hours to a project and the recorded hours being charged to the project in question.
9 Kate Bingham, 1965–, Chair UK Vaccine Taskforce 2020.
10 Fiona Reynolds, Director Women's Unit, Cabinet Office 1998–2000, Director General, National Trust 2001–12, Master Emmanuel College, Cambridge University 2013–21, Chair, National Audit Office 2021–, created Dame Fiona Reynolds 2008.
11 These plans were announced in the referenced document but are internal documents only, so not available to outside readers.
12 Sarah Olney, 1977–, MP for Richmond Park 2016–17, 2019–.
13 Peter Gray, NAO, Director Exiting the EU 2016–20.
14 Lee Summerfield, NAO 2000–, Director Defence and Investigations 2012–.
15 Sian Jones, NAO 2004–, Value for Money Director 2016–.
16 Yvonne Gallagher, NAO Director of Digital 2013–.
17 Joshua Reddaway, NAO 2002–, Director of Commercial and Contracting 2014–17, Head of Practice Commercial and Contracting 2017–21, Director, Work and Pensions Value for Money 2016–23, Director of Fraud and Propriety 2023–.
18 This stands for Audit Quality Review Team: a team of reviewers that the regulator brings into organisations to review their financial audits.

References

Akpan, M., Coyne, C. and Ip Tat Kuen, C. (2022). *Climate change risk: Are we doing enough, fast enough?* Available at https://www.nao.org.uk/insights/climate-change-risk-are-we-doing-enough-fast-enough/ accessed on 23 August 2023.

Appleby, J. (2022). The public finance cost of covid-19. *British Medical Journal.* https://doi.org/10.1136/bmj.o490

Audit Quality Review Team (2020). *National Audit Office: 2019/20 Audit Quality Inspection.* Available at audit_quality_inspection_report_2019-20.pdf (nao.org.uk) accessed on 11 September 2023.

Audit Quality Review Team (2021). *National Audit Office: 2020/21 Audit Quality Inspection.* Available at Audit-Quality-Inspection-2020-21.pdf (nao.org.uk) accessed on 11 September 2019.

Bingham, K. and Hames, T. (2022). *The long shot, the inside story of the race to vaccinate Britain.* London: Oneworld Publications.

Bittlestone, S. (2020). *Government has increased its climate change ambition, now it must step up to the challenge.* Available at https://www.nao.org.uk/

insights/government-has-increased-its-climate-change-ambition-now-it-must-step-up-to-the-challenge/ accessed on 23 August 2023.
Butler, Robin, interview
Comptroller and Auditor General (2020). *Achieving government's long-term environmental goals*, Session 2019–2021, HC 958. London: National Audit Office.
Comptroller and Auditor General (2020a). *Achieving net zero*, Session 2019-21, HC1035. London: National Audit Office.
Comptroller and Auditor General (2020b). *Overview of the UK government's response to the COVID-19 pandemic*, Session 2019-21, HC366. London: National Audit Office.
Comptroller and Auditor General (2020c). *Investigation into government procurement during the COVID-19 pandemic*, Session 2019-21, HC959. London: National Audit Office.
Comptroller and Auditor General (2021). *Local government finance in the pandemic*, Session 2019-21, HC1240. London: National Audit Office.
Comptroller and Auditor General (2021a). *Managing tax debt through the pandemic*, Session 2021-2, HC799. London: National Audit Office.
Comptroller and Auditor General (2021b). *The government's preparedness for the COVID-19 pandemic: Lessons for government on risk management*, Session 2021-2, HC735. London: National Audit Office.
Comptroller and Auditor General (2021c). *Protecting and supporting the clinically extremely vulnerable during lockdown*, Session 2019-21, HC1131. London: National Audit Office.
Comptroller and Auditor General (2022). *Investigation into the management of backlogs in driving licence applications*, Session 2022-3, HC851. London: National Audit Office.
Comptroller and Auditor General (2022a). *The Restart scheme for long-term unemployed people*, Session 2022-3, HC936. London: National Audit Office.
Comptroller and Auditor General (2023). *Regulating to achieve environmental outcomes*, Session 2022-3, HC1283. London: National Audit Office.
Corbishley, Steve, interview
Davies, Gareth, interview
Davies, G. (2020). *COVID-19: What it means for the NAO*. Available at https://www.nao.org.uk/insights/covid-19-what-it-means-for-the-nao/ accessed on 31 August 2023.
Davies, G. (2020a). *Auditing the government's response to COVID-19*. Available at https://www.nao.org.uk/insights/auditing-the-governments-response-to-covid-19/ accessed on 31 August 2023.
Davies, G. (2022). *Efficiency savings require learning past lessons*. Available at https://www.nao.org.uk/insights/efficiency-savings-require-learning-past-lessons/#conclusion, accessed on 23 August 2023.
Davies, G. (2022a). *From COVID-19 to net zero: How can regulation respond to change?* Available at https://www.nao.org.uk/wp-content/uploads/2022/08/covid-net-zero-transcript-4.txt, accessed on 23 August 2023.
Department for Health and Social Care (2022). *Annual report and accounts 2020–21 (For the period ended 31 March 2021)*, Session 2021-2, HC1053. London: House of Commons.
Ferry and Midgley, H. (2023). Institutional entrepreneurship in a Supreme Audit Institution. In T. Rana and L. Parker (eds.) *The Routledge Handbook of Public Sector Accounting*. Abingdon: Routledge.
Ferry, L., Midgley, H. and Green, S. (2024). Accountability, emergency and liberty during COVID-19 in the UK 2020–22. *Accounting, Auditing and Accountability Journal, 37*(1), 2024

Gallagher, Y. (2021). *Better data means better services – so how can government get there?* Available at https://www.nao.org.uk/insights/better-data-means-better-services-so-how-can-government-get-there/, accessed on 31 August 2023.
Hillier, Meg, interview
House of Commons (2019). *Hansard*, Vol. 655, 6 March 2019.
Institute for Government (2022). *Timeline of the UK government coronavirus lockdowns and measures March 2020 to December 2021, Institute for Government.* Available at https://www.instituteforgovernment.org.uk/sites/default/files/2022-12/timeline-coronavirus-lockdown-december-2021.pdf, accessed on 21 November 2023.
Jenkin, Bernard, interview
Johnstone, R. (2019). 'Timing your intervention is part of the art' – NAO head Gareth Davies on the role of auditors in ensuring value for money in government. *Civil Service World.* Available at https://www.civilserviceworld.com/professions/article/timing-your-intervention-is-part-of-the-art-nao-head-gareth-davies-on-the-role-of-auditors-in-ensuring-value-for-money-in-government accessed on 16 April 2024.
Kingman, Sir J. (2018). *Independent review of the Financial Reporting Council.* London: HMSO.
Lambauer, D. (2020) *Auditing COVID-19: An international perspective.* Available at https://www.nao.org.uk/insights/auditing-covid-19-an-international-perspective/ accessed on 31 August 2023.
Levelling Up, Housing and Communities Select Committee (2023). *Oral evidence: Financial reporting and audit in local authorities*, 5 June 2023, Session 2022-3, HC1196. London: House of Commons.
Lonsdale, J. and Barrados, M. (2023). Knowledge production in a pandemic supporting accountability at pace in the United Kingdom and Canada. In P. Elliadis, I. A. Naidoo and R. C. Rist (eds.) *Policy evaluation in the era of COVID-19.* New York: Routledge, 83–100.
National Audit Office (2009). *Annual report.* London: National Audit Office.
National Audit Office (2017). *Ministry of Justice: Environmental sustainability overview.* London: National Audit Office.
National Audit Office (2019). *Annual report and accounts 2018–19.* London: National Audit Office.
National Audit Office (2020). *Guide for audit and risk committees on financial reporting and management during COVID-19.* London: National Audit Office.
National Audit Office (2020a). *The National Audit Office's five-year strategy 2020 to 2025.* Available online at https://www.nao.org.uk/wp-content/uploads/2020/05/nao-strategy-2020-25.pdf accessed on 5 September 2023.
National Audit Office (2021). *Diversity & Inclusion Strategy 2021–2025.* Available online at https://www.nao.org.uk/wp-content/uploads/2021/06/NAO-DiversityInclusion_Strategy_2021-25.pdf, accessed on 23 September 2023.
National Audit Office (2022). *Covid cost tracker.* Available online at https://www.nao.org.uk/overviews/covid-19-cost-tracker/ accessed on 24 August 2023.
National Audit Office (2022a). *NAO strategy: Progress update and estimate memorandum for 2022–23.* London: National Audit Office.
National Audit Office (2022b). *Annual report and accounts 2021–2.* London: National Audit Office.
National Audit Office (2023). *Recommendations tracker.* Available at https://www.nao.org.uk/recommendations-tracker/ accessed on 5 September 2023.
National Audit Office (2023a). *Annual report and accounts 2022–23.* London: National Audit Office.

Nevett, J. and Seddon, P. (2023). *Boris Johnson's taxpayer-funded legal bill rises to £245,000*. Available at https://www.bbc.co.uk/news/uk-politics-65401587, accessed on 23 September 2019.
Newbury, Michael, interview
Olney, Sarah, interview
Partington, R. (2020). Coronavirus bill has cost UK government £210bn, spending watchdog says. *The Guardian*, 8 September 2020.
Phillips, Tim, interview
Public Accounts Commission (2020). *Oral evidence: Public Accounts Commission*, Tuesday 24 March 2020. Available at https://committees.parliament.uk/oralevidence/251/pdf/ accessed on 23 August 2023.
Public Accounts Commission (2021). *Oral evidence: National Audit Office audit quality*, Tuesday 23 November 2021. Available at committees.parliament.uk/oralevidence/3096/pdf/ accessed on 23 August 2023.
Public Accounts Commission (2021a). *Oral evidence: NAO Estimate and strategy*, Thursday 11 February 2021. Available at https://committees.parliament.uk/oralevidence/1707/default/ accessed on 5 September 2023.
Public Accounts Commission (2022). *Oral evidence: National Audit Office Audit quality 2021–22*. Available at committees.parliament.uk/oralevidence/12415/pdf/ accessed on 23 August 2023.
Public Accounts Committee (2019). *Oral evidence: Pre-appointment hearing, preferred candidate for Comptroller and Auditor General*, Wednesday 16 January 2019. Available at https://committees.parliament.uk/oralevidence/8880/pdf/ accessed on 23 August 2023.
Public Accounts Committee (2021*). Oral evidence: Covid-19: Cost tracker update*. Available at https://committees.parliament.uk/oralevidence/3365/default/ accessed on 16 March 2024.
Public Accounts Committee (2022). *COVID-19 cost tracker update, Thirty Eighth report of session 2021–2*, Session 2021-2, HC640. London: House of Commons.
Public Administration and Constitutional Affairs Committee (2017) *Accounting for democracy: Making sure Parliament, the people and ministers know how and why public money is spent, Fourteenth report of session 2016–17*, Session 2016-17, HC95. London: House of Commons.
Reynolds, Fiona, interview
Sayers, Neil, interview
Select Committee on Public Services (2021). *Uncorrected oral evidence: Procurement and public services, Wednesday 20 January 2021*. Available at committees.parliament.uk/oralevidence/1493/pdf/ accessed on 22 September 2023.
Sian, S. and Smyth, S. (2022). Supreme emergencies and public accountability: the case of procurement in the UK during the Covid-19 pandemic. *Accounting, Auditing and Accountability Journal, 35*(1), 146–157.
Tooze, A. (2021). *Shutdown: How covid shook the world's economy*. London: Allen Lane.
Treasury (2020). *Explanatory notes*. Available online at https://publications.parliament.uk/pa/bills/cbill/58-01/0123/en/20123en01.htm accessed on 31 August 2023.
Treasury (2023). *2023 COVID-19 cost tracker update*. Available at https://www.gov.uk/government/statistics/hm-treasury-2023-covid-19-cost-tracker-update accessed on 24 August 2023.

8

CONCLUSION

The evolution of democratic audit

8.1 Chapter overview

In terms of the evolution of democratic audit in the UK and National Audit Office (NAO) specifically, an obvious question is: how did we get here? To some extent, this question of causation stands at the heart of all history, but with it comes a warning. As Maitland (1897) argued, we must go back into the past by taking small steps, with caution, so that we do not end up committing the sin of anachronism.

The study of institutions and the ideas that those institutions embody are particularly subject to anachronism: it is easy to assume that because such a thing as public sector audit existed in 1983 before the NAO was established, it means the same thing as it does today. It is easy to see a continuity between the words of Gladstone and those of Gareth Davies spoken over a century and a half later.

In this book, what we have tried to show is that the NAO has evolved over time and that the substance of public sector audit, public sector accountability and hence democracy has evolved too. Just because words remain the same does not mean their definition has also remained the same. Nor does it mean that there has been progress: different regimes require a different form of auditor. The kind of auditor described by Gladstone (which we describe in Chapter 1) would have been completely inappropriate for creating the kind of godly republic that the New Model Army had in mind when it proposed an audit of the state in 1652 (Midgley, 2016). Given that accountability does different things, it is pointless to discuss whether a changed audit system is more or less successful than its predecessors: rather changes in the way that audit supports accountability

DOI: 10.4324/9781003520085-8

reflect wider changes in accountability and hence in democracy in the UK since 1984.

By studying the process of change over the past 40 years, we can also isolate why the NAO has changed, what the motivations for change were and how far the NAO met the expectations of its founders and those who formed it.

To understand this change, we have used a theoretical framework from accounting scholarship called regulatory space. Regulatory space is used by accounting scholars to understand how institutions have changed and to categorise that change.

We have followed Ferry et al. (2023), who described this regulatory space for Supreme Audit Institutions (SAIs). They described a theoretical framework in which the regulatory space of SAIs could be defined in three themes: organisational context, capacity and scope.

Regulatory space and its three themes of organisational context, capacity and scope have run through each of the chapters of this book, and in this conclusion, we summarise the book through these themes. Then, we look more broadly at the history of the NAO in the context of world events.

8.2 Regulatory space

8.2.1 Organisational context

Since its creation in 1984, the NAO's organisational context has been defined by the relationship between the executive and legislature in the UK's democracy. It was created to redress that balance by a backbench rebellion in the early 1980s, and much of its subsequent history, as described in the previous chapters of this book, has been surrounded by these issues. There were several stages in the evolution of the NAO's context which we summarise below.

When the NAO first opened its doors in 1984, two things affected its organisational context. Firstly, Downey, senior managers within the NAO and many other staff were aware that the 1983 Act was the product of a backbench rebellion to restore the powers and rights of the House of Commons against the executive. The 1983 Act was the last in a sequence of reforms, beginning with the creation of the Parliamentary and Health Service Ombudsman in 1967 and the 'Crossman' select committees of the late 1960s through the creation of the modern select committee system in 1979 and then to the creation of the NAO in 1983. The political climate and the specifics of the debates in 1983 affected how the NAO conducted its work and managed its relationships with Parliament and government.

The relationship with Parliament has always been essential to the NAO. The NAO's role in relation to Parliament expanded over time. The fact that the 1983 Act said that the NAO had to report to Parliament and not just to the Public Accounts Committee (PAC) enabled the NAO to expand its work to support other committees. This move began slowly under Bourn, gained pace in the 2000s and, finally under Morse, the NAO regularly supported other committees and Morse was frequently a witness in parliamentary inquiries by other select committees (Midgley, 2019).

Parliamentarians pushed at the boundaries of this relationship. After Sheldon retired in 1997, David Davis was a much more assertive and media savvy PAC chair. Davis raised the NAO and PAC's profile considerably. MPs like Jon Trickett and Richard Bacon also pushed back on NAO work where they did not feel that the NAO had been critical enough of departments in the mid-2000s. The most assertive figure in this history is Margaret Hodge. Hodge had been a minister and a council leader before being elected PAC chair, and she took those habits into the PAC role, endeavouring to make the committee more independent of the NAO. During her period as chair, she forced the NAO to focus on tax and tax collection. And at that time, when the NAO was moving more towards examining government as a business, Hodge was sufficiently independent that she focussed PAC on the users of the public services.

The parliamentary figures who pushed the NAO forward did not work independently but often inspired each other to use the NAO to extend Parliament's scrutiny. Assertive chairs inspired young MPs to join the PAC and respect the NAO: Richard Bacon and George Osborne joined the committee, for example, because of David Davis. These alliances went across party political divides. Sheldon provided advice to Davis, and Davis pursued the causes that Sheldon had begun. Davis advised Hodge that she should examine tax. There were significant alliances on the committee. Davis and Leigh benefitted from the presence of Alan Williams on the committee (also chair of the Public Accounts Commission) and fought for the NAO from that position. Similarly, Margaret Hodge and Meg Hillier depended upon Conservative MPs who backed them, most notably Richard Bacon and Sir Geoffrey Clifton-Brown. The cross-party and collegiate nature of the PAC strengthened the NAO at several points through the 1980s, when Sheldon shepherded the new organisation through its first year, to the 1990s and 2000s, when persistent campaigning by Sheldon and Davis influenced the direction of the Sharman report, through to the 2010s, when Hodge, Bacon, Clifton-Brown and Hillier helped shape its response to austerity, Brexit and COVID-19.

The NAO, however, always maintained its independence from Parliament. Downey's NAO was concerned that it did not become the prisoner of PAC's agenda in the 1980s. Perhaps more interestingly, under Morse and Davies, the NAO felt itself in a position to ignore a parliamentary committee's recommendations. For example, the Public Administration and Constitutional Affairs Committee's reports on financial accounting and auditing in government departments were ignored by the NAO, which did not see them as relevant to accounting and auditing as it believed they should be. Parliament might be a key influence on the NAO, but it was not in charge.

If the relationship with Parliament was one of the key pillars of the NAO's organisational context, then the second key pillar was its relationship with government. When backbench MPs proposed the creation of the NAO, the government initially objected. Permanent secretaries resisted efforts by Downey and his staff to extend accountability, and there was some dissatisfaction within the civil service with the partnership between the NAO and PAC (and complete resistance early on to any idea that the NAO would cooperate with other select committees). In 1986, the civil service won a considerable victory, when PAC emphasised that all reports used as part of its evidence sessions should normally be agreed. If the C&AG and the Accounting Officer could not reach agreement, the nature and extent of the disagreement would be noted in the report. During the 1990s, permanent secretaries like Sir Richard Packer were able to exploit clearance to ensure that reports were only published after a long process of negotiation and accommodation of civil service critiques. Clearance became an arena of extensive battles between civil servants and the NAO.

A significant turning point came with the arrival of Amyas Morse in 2009: Morse refused to let civil servants delay his reports and was much more willing to publish disagreed reports. This was crucial in shifting the balance of power between auditor and auditee and making audit teams feel supported at the highest level in making unpopular judgements. Taking his stand on professional competence, Morse was often willing to disagree with permanent secretaries, and therefore, the NAO's reports came out more quickly and the organisation became generally more assertive about its findings.

However, the government were still able to influence reports and ensure that they were at least factually accurate and 'balanced', although accuracy is the key point of clearance. Underlying these tensions between different C&AGs and the government of the day was the fundamental difficulty of separating policy from administration: as Sir Bernard Jenkin said to us, 'if a policy can't be implemented, you haven't got viable policy. If a policy is difficult to implement, what can be learned from those difficulties so that the policy objective can be achieved in a different way' (Sir Bernard Jenkin, interview).

The government's approach to the NAO was not purely defensive. In the 1960s, Harold Wilson had argued that a public sector auditor had to recognise that in the UK there was no real separation of powers: it had instead to report to Parliament on whether the parliamentary majority's wishes were being effectively executed. Wilson's executive formulation of the auditor's responsibilities found echoes in later arguments of ministers. In 1979, the Thatcher government came to power with a hostile agenda towards the civil service. One of her advisors, Leslie Chapman, wrote about how the Exchequer and Audit Department (E&AD) was an ineffective scrutineer of the civil service. Chapman envisaged an auditor who would force the civil service to deliver government policy far more effectively. When in government, Sir Geoffrey Howe and Clive Priestley, both close to Thatcher, came to similar conclusions. For them, the auditor was the government's mechanism to control the civil service, rather than Parliament's to control the government. This fundamentally different sense of what the auditor's role should be echoes through the story of the NAO.

Governments from Thatcher forward feared that the NAO would become a brake on reform. In fact, the NAO was cautiously neutral about the 'Rayner' and Next Steps reforms of the 1980s: the development of New Public Management (NPM) in the 1990s and 2000s and the civil service reform agenda developed by the coalition and Conservative governments after 2010. Nevertheless, critics from Tony Blair to Michael Gove suggested that the NAO was in some sense a brake on innovation in the public sector. The NAO's response to this, over time, was to suggest that it would not block reform but act as an advisor to the government on how best to implement reform. This rhetoric originated in the Sharman report of 2001 but was taken up by Sir John Bourn in the 2000s: a period marked by Bourn's decision to produce cross-cutting reports which examined systemic issues and how government had addressed them and which at times came close to endorsing aspects of the 'Modernising Government' agenda. Sir Amyas Morse responded in the 2010s in exactly the same way: the NAO's expertise could support Whitehall's efforts to change. The rhetoric of Gareth Davies in the 2020s continues this strain of thinking. The NAO in this sense could be transformed from a constitutional guardian into Whitehall's consultant of choice: exploiting its range of expertise and access to provide insights that others could not manage.

The relationship with Parliament and the government were the two key relationships shaping the NAO's behaviour across the 40 years of its existence. However, the NAO was not the only public sector auditor in the UK. In 1983, the Audit Commission was created as the key body for auditing local government. The Commission's relationship with the NAO between 1983 and 2015 was complex. The organisations often, as we have described, collaborated, especially in areas like health where their remits overlapped. However, they were also in competition, and NAO staff acknowledged that at times the Audit Commission appeared to be ahead of the NAO. The Audit Commission often had a higher profile and more vocal supporters and, because of its remit, was able to do more sophisticated comparative work than the NAO. However, the Audit Commission was abolished by the coalition government: a decision which meant the NAO became involved in local government for the first time in its history, but which also reminded the NAO of its own vulnerability.

From 1997, the NAO serving the Westminster Parliament was not the only auditor in the UK due to the creation of the Scottish, Welsh and Northern Irish legislatures. The NAO had to develop relationships with the devolved auditors and to understand that it could not serve as the sole auditor of all government organisations at the same time. The NAO began its existence with the concept of a separate auditor for local government but was slow to realise that these other auditors had to be constitutionally independent: in 1997–8, the NAO suggested that it should audit the devolved governments, and until 2005, Bourn remained auditor general of Wales. From 2005, the NAO and the devolved auditors had to work out arrangements between them to ensure that devolution settlements were incorporated into public sector audit. This is one area where potentially the role of auditor will change, as the nature of devolved audit in the UK changes.

The relationship between government and Parliament and the inevitable strains shaped the way the NAO has developed over the past 40 years. The two opposing aspects of the role of the NAO, that it serves as Parliament's chief instrument of accountability and is the executive's preferred consultant, remain as core principles of the NAO's strategy even today. Relationships between the executive and Parliament form the indispensable context for the NAO's role: for example, in the 2010s, the NAO had to preserve its relationship with government despite the open hostility between the senior civil service and the Chair, Margaret Hodge. Likewise, splits in Parliament limit the NAO's ability to speak freely: the NAO was very cautious over Brexit, recognising that both PAC and Parliament were divided both between parties and across party lines. In 1988, John Bourn commented that the NAO's role was naturally political. This is true in both the terms Bourn meant, that the C&AG and the NAO had to understand the political forces swirling around them (the failure to do so doomed the Audit Commission) and make their way through and that understanding the NAO's role turns on understanding the role of the legislature within the UK constitution.

8.2.2 Capacity

The second of our key themes is capacity. One reason for the E&AD's demise was its lack of capacity. The Crown Agents scandal of the 1970s and wider critiques of the E&AD's ability to conduct value-for-money examinations and criticism from select committees undermined its credibility. There was a sense that the organisation was a backwater. This was compounded by the fact that the Treasury controlled the funding of the department: from 1966 onwards, there were allegations that the Treasury had restricted the E&AD's funding to limit its effectiveness. In 1979, the E&AD conducted a management review which was endorsed by the PAC: this called for further professionalisation of its financial audit function and raising the priority of financial audit within the organisation. Sir Douglas Henley, C&AG between 1976 and 1981, sponsored the management review and argued strongly that E&AD needed complete reform so that it could become an auditor fit for purpose for the 1980s.

After 1984, Parliament acquired the responsibility for funding the NAO through the Public Accounts Commission. The first chair of the Commission, Sir Edward Du Cann, was insistent on ensuring that the new NAO was properly financed. In the context of the early 1980s, with the creation of two new public sector auditing bodies (NAO and the Audit Commission), the NAO found itself facing increasing competition for staff. Downey's main focus was on ensuring that the NAO got the funding necessary for the tasks it had taken on. John Bourn carried on Downey's campaign for increased finance into the 1990s, and both found support on the Public Accounts Commission. Between 1984 and 1993, the NAO's gross expenditure rose from £25 million to £42 million. After a pause in the mid-1990s, spending rose even faster in the 2000s: the NAO's budget went from £43 million in 1997 to £98 million in 2008.

The increased funding supported expansion in both financial and value-for-money audit. In financial audit, more money was funnelled into obtaining commercial qualifications for the NAO's staff. From 1991, new NAO staff trained with the Institute of Chartered Accountants in England and Wales qualification rather than the Chartered Institute of Public Finance and Accountancy qualification that they had had previously taken. The NAO took on new financial audits too: including government companies and non-departmental public bodies especially as a consequence of the Sharman report. By 2010, the NAO had emerged as the public sector's most technically competent financial auditor: causing concerns in the Audit Commission that they were being outgunned technically by central government's auditor.

The effect on value-for-money audit was, if anything, more dramatic. Up until the 1990s, NAO staff did both financial and value-for-money audit. From the early 1990s, the NAO separated the two streams: staff could opt to specialise in either form of audit. Value-for-money became thus something which staff could specialise in. The NAO in the 1990s and 2000s expanded the methodologies it used and the skills of its staff. Value for money in this period had a high status internally. Bourn recruited staff from Whitehall and beyond to support its development. The NAO's success in developing the status of its audit was reflected in decisions within government to rely more on the C&AG's auditors: for example, in 1997, when Gordon Brown decided to have an independent examination of the assumptions underlying the budget, he turned to the NAO, who had recruited Whitehall economists to deliver it. Similarly, the NAO by the 2000s was increasingly influential on areas of policy like Private Finance Initiative (PFI) and health policy because of its recruitment of staff with a complex mix of skills. Bourn's boasts that the NAO's methodologies were not purely economic, or management focussed, but extended to political science and botany were not idle ones; in making the comment, he was emphasising how much insight the NAO had to offer.

The financial crash had a dramatic effect on the NAO's capacity. Amyas Morse had a different, more restrictive vision than Bourn of what public sector audit, especially value-for-money audit should be. His view was more traditional. The NAO's expenditure did not recover its 2008 level until 2021, and the cost reductions were mostly on value-for-money audit, which was cut back: in 2003, the NAO spent £16.8 million on value-for-money audit; in 2021, £16.7 million. Financial audit, on the other hand, continued to expand as both Morse and his successor, Gareth Davies, saw it as essential that the organisation complied with commercial best practice in financial audit. Their focus was therefore on meeting regulatory requirements on financial audit, which meant that financial audit spending increasingly dominated the organisation. Whereas in 2008, Bourn left with an office roughly evenly divided between value-for-money and financial audit, Davies in 2024 presided over an organisation that was dominated by a commercialised financial audit practice.

These shifts had inevitable consequences for the internal character of the organisation. The NAO of the 1980s was largely based on the E&AD: most of the same staff were in position and cultural divisions within the organisation focussed on the distinction between staff recruited into the sleepier backwater of the E&AD and those recruited into and motivated by the NAO's greater reputation and importance. These divisions continued into the 1990s. During the 1990s and 2000s, increased funding led to increased confidence: the NAO was braver and more willing to take on new methods and recruited staff from Whitehall. The advent of staff with ICAEW qualifications introduced a subtle change, with more and more staff having a much more commercial attitude to audit. After 2010, Morse and Davies presided over an organisation which was increasingly focussed on commercial-style audit judgements and a value-for-money practice which tended to produce shorter, more factual reports with fewer innovative methodologies and in many cases concentrating on economy and efficiency rather than effectiveness, focussed only on outputs rather than full value-for-money evaluations. The change in value for money became a weakness for the NAO more generally as the NAO was criticised in private and in public by senior figures in government and politics.

The last important development in the story of the NAO was that its culture modernised across the entire period. All staff from all periods of the office's development discussed how each C&AG individually sought to modernise and professionalise management within the NAO from its 'Edwardian' state under the E&AD. This trend goes back to Sir Douglas Henley but continued under Downey, Bourn, Morse and Davies. The NAO wanted to be the best managed organisation in Whitehall, and under Morse in particular, the NAO sought to set an example (through its adherence to austerity) to the rest of the public sector. Modernisation for the NAO meant professionalisation, but it also meant that the NAO sought in this period, imperfectly, to become more diverse. Under Morse and Davies, in particular, the NAO made efforts to recruit more female staff at senior levels and to improve its recruitment, retention and promotion of non-white staff. These ambitions were intended to make the NAO reflect the society it served better and also improve the talent pool that the organisation drew from.

Changes in the NAO were driven from various directions. The individual C&AGs clearly had a massive effect on the NAO: their personality was obvious in all the reports published during their periods of office. Decisions taken by C&AGs had a huge effect on the way that the NAO functioned. Downey's interest in pursuing access rights established precedents for the NAO to rely on into the following century. Bourn's intellectual interests steered the NAO's value-for-money work to become more academic, and his courage enabled studies on issues such as the Iraq War. Morse's tactical skill steered the NAO through austerity and Brexit, and Davies insisted on the role that the NAO had to play during COVID-19 and encouraged the organisation to look to existential risks such as climate change. However, this was only possible because of the work conducted by staff: two examples demonstrate this. The NAO was only created in the 1980s because of a campaign beginning in the 1960s by Normanton, a former member of E&AD staff to bolster the independence of the UK's SAI (Normanton, 1966). Likewise, young, enthused staff enabled the NAO to digitalise key aspects of its financial audit in the 2010s (Ferry and Midgley, 2023).

Nevertheless, the story of capacity in the NAO is not a simple one of continuous advance. The NAO of the 1980s inherited from the E&AD a hierarchical organisation which was largely a backwater within Whitehall. By 2005, the NAO had completely changed: its financial audit function and its value-for-money function were funded to an extent they had never been before. This had consequences: the technical quality of the NAO's financial audit had risen and value for money became a diverse and varied practice, employing hugely different techniques. Looking two decades on, the picture had changed again: the NAO was now largely an organisation focussed on technical financial audit quality with value for money moving backwards to something more similar to the value-for-money audit as practiced by Gordon Downey. These changes reflected changes in the conception of the relationship between the NAO, Parliament and government, but they also reflected changes in the conception of what the audit and audit report were about that can be seen across the decades.

8.2.3 Audit scope

The scope of the NAO's audit changed hugely between 1984 and 2024. The basic structure of what the NAO was doing did not change, but the contents of audits did. The National Audit Act 1983 brought forward one crucial innovation, which had a huge effect on the NAO into the 1980s and beyond. The Act stated that the C&AG could report to Parliament in his own right and in his own name. Prior to 1983, reports were published with the accounts of the organisation that they focussed on; from 1983 onwards, the NAO published its value-for-money reports separately. This decision had huge consequences because it meant that the NAO's reports now were published individually and could gain attention from Parliament, commentators and the media. The NAO enjoyed the immunity of parliamentary privilege, and the C&AG's remit was circumscribed but undefined: allowing each C&AG to deploy the power of reporting using parliamentary privilege as they themselves chose.

The NAO initially continued to do the work that the E&AD did. Downey's NAO made it clear that they were following the precedents set by the E&AD in both their financial auditing and value for money. E&AD's audits in this regard were often seen as relatively ineffective, but Downey pushed forward cautiously so as not to lose the support of the government for his office. Senior civil servants did notice more assertiveness from the NAO and complained about it. The NAO pursued the audit of significant government policies such as the Rayner efficiency drives or privatisation of nationalised industries but did so without challenging the principles behind them; rather, they focussed on the technical quality of the transactions and reporting from departmental records of events. On appropriation audit too, the NAO continued where the E&AD had left off: they continued to audit accounts in the same way that they had been audited in the 1970s.

However, as the 1980s continued and into the 1990s, the level of challenge from the NAO rose especially in value-for-money audit. Value for money was never defined externally, so successive generations of auditors developed it within the terms of the 1983 Act. This process was already underway by the early 1990s. To quote Sir Richard Wilson, there was a sense abroad in the civil service that the NAO and PAC had changed. This change was cemented by the mid-1990s by what Bourn was doing. Studies were increasingly focussing on the users of public services, and the NAO was using techniques like focus groups and surveys to discern their views and report them. This innovation was a product of bigger budgets for studies and continued into the 2000s. Bourn's NAO was increasingly deploying these methods to provide recommendations to the government, which were not solely generic on improving management but particular advice on how to improve specific services. For example, in the 1990s, they gave advice to the Metropolitan Police about how phone operators should approach answering calls from members of the public. Similarly in the 2000s, the NAO advised the NHS on how it could campaign to ensure that victims of stroke got to hospital more quickly than before. These kinds of recommendations went far beyond traditional audit advice on how to improve costing or project management which Downey's NAO had offered. They also meant that the NAO was increasingly focussed on effectiveness as well as economy and efficiency (and through that, though never explicitly on what academics refer to as equity, 'the distribution of outcomes across different individuals' (Johnsen, 2005)).

Bourn's NAO began in its work on regulation to push the boundaries of those definitions even further: reports redefined the meaning of economy to include the cost to the user of the service as well as the cost to the Treasury. These tentative steps reflected a more holistic view of what value for money might or should be and consequently offered a much greater challenge to the government.

Bourn's decision to change the nature of value-for-money audit and bring service users into the audit remit was largely abandoned after the financial crisis. The restriction in resources meant that the NAO moved to a much more managerial approach when examining programmes. Reports were impactful because Morse was less likely to accept clearance comments, but they were far less focussed on effectiveness than they were on efficiency and traditionally defined economy. Where Morse did make a difference was in extending the NAO's examination of local services: Morse's NAO began to look into what they described as financial sustainability. The NAO defined financial sustainability as the relationship between the budgets allocated by central government to local services (including to local government) and the statutory minimum service that central government also mandated that local services should provide. A whole series of reports spanning local government, health, the police and universities examined this in different contexts and suggested a gap between the budget and expectations of service levels. Through this work, the NAO became one of the most important commentators on the effects of the fiscal consolidation that the UK pursued after 2010.

The 2000s saw a further development of value for money. Following on from Sharman's points about advice, the NAO began to produce reports which included more generic lessons on topics like risk management and contracting. Whereas the expansion of value for money into user perspectives was discarded in 2010, this managerial grouping of lessons learnt was harnessed by Morse and Davies and extended. Morse did it through reports in systemic areas including contracting out and commercialisation and the implementation of digital technology in government. Davies specifically embraced this approach to audit, creating expert hubs within the NAO which were supposed to lead on this kind of work and ensure that the NAO was in the best place possible to advise government. In this sense, for Bourn, Davies and Morse, the mission of governmental advisor helped reframe what value-for-money audit meant post-2010. This chimed with the views of Lord O'Donnell and other senior civil servants:

> There are big things like HS2 or Hinkley Point which it would be nice, not too many you know, but three or four really big projects where it would be nice to say, 'couldn't the NAO just do some kind of looking at the business case early on' so that we saved billions.
>
> *(O'Donnell, interview)*

Whether this broadening of the NAO's work has been successful is a different matter: even under Gareth Davies. Sir Bernard Jenkin said that when he served on the PAC, he thought that the NAO's analysis was 'very perceptive but it does not feel entitled to look at for example attitude or behavioural problems in departments' and the incentives that drive bad outcomes (Sir Bernard Jenkin, interview).

For Morse and Davies, value-for-money work was carried out within the context of a developing set of crises within the British state. We have already seen that Morse was faced with the problematic issue of how to audit austerity. Both faced crises which taxed the resources of the British state: the financial crisis in 2007–8, Brexit in 2017–20 and finally the COVID-19 crisis. Interestingly, in all three cases, the NAO responded in the same way. Firstly, there was an attempt to avoid direct criticism of the policy choices made by politicians. The NAO stuck to its remit as set out in the 1983 Act that it could not and did not criticise policy. Secondly, the NAO made it clear that it had a role in providing information to Parliament as each of the crisis continued. During the Brexit negotiations, Morse continued to provide Parliament with information throughout the process. During the pandemic, the NAO was very swift to publish reports.

Davies made it clear that the NAO's service to Parliament would continue regardless of the crisis and from the summer of 2020 the NAO began to evaluate the government's response to the COVID-19 pandemic.

Financial audit too was being reshaped in the 1990s. This began with the establishment of the Executive Agencies in the early 1990s which accounted on an income and expenditure basis rather than the old appropriation account cash basis. In 1993, Ken Clarke moved the UK to resource accounting. This process took several years to complete, but by the early 2000s government departments were publishing financial information on an accruals basis, using accounting standards that were more comparable with those used in the private sector. The NAO supported this change, and it had a massive impact on the organisation. By 2005, the NAO led in the UK on the technical audit of financial statements, but at the same time, it had drawn back from some of its earlier ambitions. Downey in 1986 proposed a financial audit which would be much more holistic and be driven by Parliament's needs, not the requirements of technical accounting. Bourn accepted resource accounting because he argued it would deepen accountability and thought it should be combined with audited performance measurement by departments.

By the 2000s, the effect of the move to ICAEW and to resource accounting created a constituency within the NAO, which saw financial audit as simply a matter of technical compliance. Under Sir Amyas Morse and Gareth Davies, the NAO saw audit as predominately a matter of technical rectitude and judged the success of their financial audit by the verdict of the regulator, the Financial Reporting Council. The NAO was privately dismissive of the Public Administration and Constitutional Affairs Committee's reports on government accounts, even though the committee proposed measures that were entirely consistent with Downey's insistence that accounts should reflect the needs of Parliament and Bourn's suggestion that audit should examine non-financial as well as financial performance. An NAO that viewed its performance by reference to the regulator found this impossible to cooperate with. Consequently, during the pandemic, when PAC recommended that the government publish more data about programmes and their achievements, neither they nor the NAO seemed to realise that parliamentary committees and auditors had been suggesting publishing performance information about programmes since the 1980s!

In 1983, a key question about the new National Audit Office was about what it should cover. MPs wanted the auditor to examine the BBC, the Bank of England, local government and nationalised industries. In different ways, by 2024, this ambition had been realised. The NAO became the auditor of the BBC and the Bank of England during the 20002 and 2010s by Acts of Parliament. After the abolition of the Audit Commission, the NAO acquired responsibility for some aspects of the audit of English local government. The durability of these arrangements is under question due to the crisis in local public audit in England. With nationalised industries, the NAO never became their auditor, but after privatisation, it did audit the regulators. The consistent efforts of PAC chairs, C&AGs and others within and without the NAO thus led to the expansion of parliamentary scrutiny within the public sector.

8.3 The NAO and the history of the UK

John Bourn was very conscious, drawing on the work of Braudel,[1] Wittgenstein[2], Foucault[3] and Derrida that the structure of audit reports depended on 'deep movements in society: the longue durée'[4] he was also conscious that audit was embedded within political language that determined how power was thought of at particular times and was subject to the same limitations of its ability to cope with reality that faced all human beings (Bourn, undated). For Braudel, the history of events was much less important than the history of the deep geological, biological and social structures within which those events were embedded (Braudel, 1972, 1973). It is to these contexts that we now turn to explore what the history of the NAO means.

8.3.1 The NAO and reform

From the 1980s onwards, successive UK governments aimed to reform the British state. Most of these reform agendas were attempts to professionalise the state, to raise its commercial skills, its understanding of the environment it operated within and the technical proficiency of its civil servants. In both central and local governments, officials increasingly became commissioners who were responsible for buying in services from either the private or the charitable sector. The UK led the world in privatising the utilities and investing huge amounts of intellectual capital in devising approaches to regulating them. Figures such as John Hoskyns, Francis Maude and Dominic Cummings arrived in government with a dismissive attitude to civil servants who were often seen as brakes on both ministerial ambition and good performance of public services. Accounting scholars linked this development to the development of an audit society in which all public servants including professionals like doctors and teachers were subjected to a regime of performance management and measurement (Power, 1999). The UK was conceptualised as a shop, a PLC or even a household by politicians keen to drive the state to be more efficient and effective.

These changes commonly described as New Public Management, which incorporated some private sector disciplines into the way that the public sector was managed, came to prominence with the election of Margaret Thatcher in 1979. However, they did not originate with Thatcher or her time in power. The idea that the traditional civil service needed reconstruction was a far earlier pre-occupation shared by Harold Wilson amongst others. Recent evaluations have stressed the degree to which Britain in the 1970s experienced a geo-strategic re-orientation, away from a nationalist, socialist concept of the economy and towards a European liberal model of state and society (Edgerton, 2018). In this discussion, scholars are beginning to perceive how the 'hidden politics of Whitehall' played a role in deprioritising some aspects of the state, seen as key by the postwar generation such as investment in technology and prioritising the creation of a liberal economy (Kelsey, 2023). Specific institutions of government have been tied to this turn to economic liberalism including the Treasury and the Central Policy Review Staff amongst others (Davis, 2022; Turnbull, 2022). From the 1980s, these institutional sources of expertise were supplemented by consultants and other experts in public sector reform (Cooper et al., 2023). In economic policy, the same dynamic can be observed with key changes towards liberalism being made within the Treasury and by ministers prior to the arrival of Thatcher, even if she pushed those changes further (Hickson, 2002, pp. 175–6). Rogers (2012, p. 148), for example, suggests that the International Monetary Fund (IMF) reforms to public expenditure in the late 1970s were part of a deliberate strategy by the British elite to reposition the UK's economic policy.

The NAO fitted neatly into this description of the UK state. In the 1980s, 1990s, 2000s and 2010s, it cast itself as a friendly critic of the government's reform agenda. It fitted into what Steve Richards, the political journalist, told us was a constant across the Thatcher, Major and Blair eras, that 'the state, its structure and spending, needed to be constantly kept under scrutiny' (Steve Richards, interview). It surveyed whether the government's reforms were working in their own terms and suggested technocratic adjustments. For example, its reports on the Rayner scrutinies (covered in Chapter 3) outlined how they could be better implemented within departments, and its work on contract management in the 2010s (covered in Chapter 6) examined the way that the government could improve contract management practices without questioning their rationality in public services. The NAO interpreted the statutory restriction on policy created by the 1983 Act and Lord Sharman's advice to act as an advisor as endorsing this approach to public sector reform. Furthermore, from John Bourn's time as C&AG, the NAO embraced the analogy between government departments and companies, especially in its financial audit. Eventually, especially under Bourn's successors, its model of successful accountability through financial accounts was that of a company making known its financial performance and position to a market. In this sense, as Clive Priestley and Geoffrey Howe had envisaged (Chapter 2), the NAO became a constraint not on reform, but on deviation from reform.

This is not to say that the NAO did not criticise different governmental reform initiatives over the years. It did. Examples include John Bourn's criticisms of the failures of regulation to recognise consumer interests in the 2000s and Amyas Morse's criticisms of the failure of government to maintain financially stable services in the 2010s. A valedictory interview article with Morse in 2019 captured this well by describing him simultaneously as a 'Cassandra' and a 'force for change' (Bowie, 2019). These were criticisms from within the established ideological settlement set by the British state. Radcliffe (1998) argued that auditors adopted rationalities in Canada of good government from the contemporary political and intellectual climate in order to legitimate their work: we would agree and add that often NAO staff and C&AGs also agreed with the rationality they espoused. At its most abstract, we might consider the NAO as part of a system of rules or critiques which bound the UK state to see problems in a particular way rather than to make fundamental criticisms of the prevailing intellectual model for British capitalism and more narrowly government (Roberts, 2011). The NAO has functioned as, what scholars of Eastern Europe describe, the 'treadmill' of ideological development: forcing governments not to rethink reform, but to do it better, with more information, more coordination, better design and better plans (Innes, 2023, p. 49). Its attention was focussed on what government can do and how it can improve that rather than the problems that the government has missed. As Jill Rutter said,

> there is a real bias towards looking at when government tries to do things and messes it up rather than ducks looking at an issue and the real problems in the UK are not when we've slightly overspent on something but when we've just not bothered to deal with something at all or let things fester and I don't think the NAO sees itself as having a role in untackled problems.
>
> *(Jill Rutter, interview).*

In doing this, the NAO is closely allied with those at the centre of government, especially its natural allies in the Treasury: an alliance which goes back to the 1860s and attests the difficulty described by Rutter (2021) that the centre of the UK government has in trying to get departments, let alone other agencies within the state, to go along with its programme of reforms. The disciplining effect of the NAO's adherence to the government reform mindset is not purely ideological; it also provides reinforcement to the often weak centre of the UK government.

8.3.2 The NAO and democracy

Some of these models of rules-based governance see the invention of new modes of governance as an explicit constraint on democracy (Streeck, 2017; Slobodian, 2018). In order to assess the NAO's relationship with the development of the UK's constitution in this period, we have to go further into assessing exactly how things were changing between 1984 and 2024.

There are many reasons to suggest that the UK state is more accountable and democratic than it was in 1984. The creation of political assemblies and Parliaments in Scotland, Wales and Northern Ireland did accomplish some real devolution of powers to the nations of the UK. The Human Rights Act codified the UK's legislation on rights and was heralded at the time for being constitutionally revolutionary. Between the late 1960s and 2010, Parliament acquired new powers to see into government and correct abuses: the creation of an ombudsman (in 1967), of standing select committees monitoring departments (who took their final form in 1979 and acquired independent chairs in 2010) and the development of the NAO all suggest greater accountability. These reforms have been heralded by scholars who see them as part of a democratic transition within the UK (Foster and Knox, 2022, 2023; Norton, 2019). Although others have commented that the change has not gone in one direction alone, there is significant evidence that trust in Parliament is weaker than it was and that Britons generally are more uncertain about how their democracy should be governed (White, 2022).

The NAO is definitely seen as part of this infrastructure of democratic accountability. Richard Bacon, MP, told us that

> It is perfectly proper to see the (National) Audit Office as one of the constitutional pillars of a well-constructed polity. I have always been extremely aware of that. There is a painting when you come into St. Stephen's Hall, you go up the steps into central lobby, look at the painting on the right, it's Thomas More talking to Cardinal Wolsey and the quote underneath says, 'Sir Thomas More, as Speaker of the Commons, in spite of Cardinal Wolsey's imperious demand, refuses to grant King Henry VIII a subsidy without due debate'. The painting makes the point that the people shall not be taxed without a say and that is the centre of what we are doing on the Public Accounts Committee and of what the NAO does. I carry these things around in my head every time I walk into the Public Accounts Committee or The Public Accounts Commission.
>
> *(Richard Bacon, interview)*

Steve Richards said that 'a consequence of the 1983 Act is that there was a mechanism, the new NAO, for the select committees who, without the resources themselves to scrutinise and analyse to the same extent, had this ammunition for their reports' (Steve Richards, interview). Academic studies agree (Ferry and Midgley, 2022). Interviewee after interviewee stressed to us, as the previous pages have revealed, how far the NAO built upon that Act to strengthen Parliament's power against the executive and properly scrutinise it. The NAO played this role in the pandemic, where its continued scrutiny ensured that Parliament remained informed about the progress of COVID-19, despite the challenges in auditing the pandemic response. However, this is not the only story that can be told about the NAO and its development over the past 40 years, nor is it the only way that auditors themselves think about their links to democracy.

C&AGs including Morse and Bourn retreated to a technical concept of what audit meant: a set of neutral guidelines which aided governments of all complexions in achieving their aims, whenever challenged. In the late 1980s, the early 2000s, the early and late 2010s, C&AGs saw this role of technocratic advisor as a way of surviving political controversy. This reflexive return to the role of technocratic advisor, justified by improvement of process, was only strengthened by the demise of the Audit Commission. Bourn had been, by most accounts, an incredibly courageous C&AG and was pushing the organisation to develop more of a role in stimulating accountability across the piece, finishing the work begun by Gordon Downey in his 1986 report into financial accountability.

This agenda did not interest Morse. Morse and Davies, who came from contrasting accounting backgrounds in the private and public sector, nevertheless saw the NAO through the lens of the accounting profession rather than through the lens of Parliament and what they evolved was a politically defensible organisation devoted to the improvement of public sector processes. Elston and Zhang (2023) provide evidence of this in Morse's early years: documenting that the most common type of recommendation from PAC in 2010–12 was the improvement of management in the public sector. If the NAO wanted to measure itself, by the late 2010s, it did so by using the benchmarks of a private sector regulator looking at the audit profession. The constitutional aspect of financial audit, so important to Gladstonian visions of public sector audit, was muted in favour of this technocratic perspective.

This development happened at the same time as the weakening of value-for-money audit. One of the striking developments of the post-2010 public sector audit landscape is the way in which the histories of the audit of local and central government have converged. Public sector audit in the UK has increasingly become a financial, compliance-based audit and moved away from assessing value for money. In local government, this happened after the abolition of the Audit Commission in 2015. In national government, the change was not as dramatic but still important. The NAO's studies became less ambitious in their focus and were less well funded than before, although the number of reports produced stayed steady and NAO's remit expanded to cover the BBC and Bank of England and gained new powers to examine local government. This evolution was not purely tactical. The NAO has often seen democracy as playing a secondary role when compared to the importance of commercialising the way that government operates. Apart from under Downey, the NAO has stuck closely to a format of financial accounts, which according to Parliament itself makes scrutiny harder. Despite the attentions of the Public Administration and Constitutional Affairs Committee in the late 2010s and the NAO's own report in 1987, the NAO sees accounts largely as a technocratic effort and seems to pay more attention to a non-parliamentary regulator than to Parliament. Calls from civil servants, parliamentarians and others interested in scrutiny go unheard as opposed to those from the professional accounting bodies. For staff in the NAO, the reflex has often seemed to subordinate democratic accountability to the requirements of efficiency: for example, it is notable that under John Bourn, the NAO wanted to become the auditor of the Scottish and Welsh governments because it felt that this would be more efficient without regard to the constitutional principles at stake. This political and constitutional naivety is reflected in an increasing forgetfulness about the reasons that the NAO was established.

Bacon's quote is fascinating but can feel anachronistic: an appeal to a parliamentary authority that is obsolete and more an instrument to achieve the NAO's true goal, promoting the commercialising and efficiency of the public sector, rather than a fundamental postulate of the NAO's politics. In this sense, the NAO talks about accountability rather than democracy, illustrating what Peter Mair described as a hollowing out of democratic politics in the West, as politics and the administrative classes of the civil service move ever further away from anything except the most limited engagement with the public (Mair, 2013). Hence, the NAO can embrace an increasingly technocratic value-for-money audit and an almost inaccessible set of financial accounts because these are documents by experts, for experts, ignoring a growing level of distrust in the institutions of Parliament, whilst claiming it upholds democracy (White, 2022, p. 7). And there are those that doubt the efficacy of the NAO/PAC process in improving government and public services. Sir Richard Packer said, 'we've got this system which has an effect on Permanent Secretaries and Departments, but does it cut right through to decision-making and policy? I'm not sure it does' (Sir Richard Packer, interview).

The wider changes to the UK's constitutional landscape are often seen within the NAO as peripheral. Human rights law has limited application to the administrative questions the NAO seeks to answer. Scottish and Welsh devolution have led to changes in remit (as discussed in Chapter

5) but not to fundamental changes in the way that the NAO operates. However, this may not remain true forever. For example, it is not clear that Scottish independence has been finally defeated given the generational profile of Scottish voters (Patterson, 2023).

8.3.3 The NAO and the UK's place in the world

The UK's position in the world changed hugely in the 20th century. In 1900, the UK was the metropole of a vast empire which spanned every continent and extended further after the First World War. After 1945, the UK retained much of the military capacity that it had during the Second World War. Into the 1950s, the UK continued to invest in industries purely because they were required for the purposes of war; for example, the UK maintained a publicly subsidised clock-making industry largely so to maintain the mechanical capacity for war. This military state was itself being pruned down. From 1948 onwards, the UK decided to abandon progressively its imperial possessions. Whilst there were colonial wars, for example in Malaya during the 1950s, largely the UK focussed its military efforts on Europe. This continental strategy was made even more of an emphasis after the embarrassment of Anthony Eden during the Suez crisis of 1956 and culminated in Harold Wilson's government's decision in the late 1960s to withdraw UK forces from 'east of Suez'. Furthermore, from 1960 onwards, the UK's military became increasingly technological: with a defence doctrine based on the possession of nuclear weapons and advanced machinery rather than a large conscript army. The kind of accountability that Gladstone had envisaged, which was designed to prevent the creation of a standing army which could overawe Parliament, was inappropriate in a world where the state's military capacity was a defence against a perpetual threat to Europe from Russia. Harold Wilson recognised this as PAC chair and spoke about it to the Commons in 1960. He saw the redefinition of the way that Britain fought wars and might fight a war with the Soviet Union as requiring a transformed audit office.

The UK continued to be a significant military power in Europe during the 1980s and 1990s. British forces were engaged in major combat operations in Yugoslavia, especially Kosovo, Sierra Leone, Iraq and Afghanistan. They often played a junior role alongside armed forces from the USA and NATO, with the minor exception of the Falklands War (a conflict fought between the UK and Argentina). Many of these later wars, especially after 1989, embraced a sense of the world that most countries were en route to some form of democratic capitalism. Tony Blair, for example, justified the wars in Kosovo, Iraq and Afghanistan by arguing that the UK was supporting and promoting human rights and democracy (Hoggett, 2005). This attempt to continue to project power included the

UK's membership of the European Union. For example, in 2016, remainers like David Cameron and Gordon Brown argued that Britain could only be a diplomatic leader in the world within the European Union; thus, departure was seen as a diminishing move (Saunders, 2020). The UK's membership of the European Union thus was not just a source of work for the NAO (as we have discussed, the NAO worked on British entry into the single market in 1992) but also presented a frame for Britain to use its soft power worldwide.

The period from the Iraq War in 2003 onwards saw a recalibration of the UK's role in the world, especially after the UK voted to leave the European Union in 2016. This decision to depart had in part been coming for a while. The UK's repeated decisions not to participate in European Monetary Union, especially after its departure from the European Exchange Rate Mechanism in the autumn of 1992, made the UK's membership problematic, especially during the Eurozone crisis of 2010–12 (Thompson, 2016, 2017). What appears true is that whereas advocates for the UK's membership in the European Union stressed a vision of the world that was continental in scope and focus, advocates for Brexit embraced a much more maritime vision where the UK linked either to the United States or to the old and new Commonwealth. These competing visions of the UK's diplomatic and geopolitical future were taking place against the background of the UK's relative economic decline versus countries like China, Brazil and India and the UK's own decisions to opt for financial retrenchment after the financial crisis. The UK on both counts had less money to spend on defence than it had in the 1980s. Although British ministers made much of their opposition to the Russian invasion of Ukraine in 2022, it was clear that the UK operated as a junior partner to the USA with very little room for independent manoeuvre.

The NAO participated in these shifts. The E&AD had been the traditional auditor of the warfare state. Created by Gladstone as part of Parliament's constitutional machinery to control military expenditure, it accomplished the move in the 20th century to become the scrutineer of waste in the military machine. During the 1980s, just under 20% of value-for-money work still concerned the warfare state. This continued to be true of the NAO: a fact reinforced by the appointment of two figures from the warfare state – John Bourn and Amyas Morse – as C&AGs after 1983. But there were changes. The percentage of studies devoted to defence drifted downwards across the 40 years we analyse, although the 20 or so reports which have been published in recent years have done much to draw attention to the difficulties that the residual warfare state has had in delivering serviceable equipment, recruiting, retaining and motivating its personnel, and maintaining the infrastructure needed to support its capabilities.

John Bourn followed the Blair government in attempting to spread democratic audit through organisations like the International Organisation of Supreme Audit Institutions (INTOSAI). He believed that the NAO should be part of efforts to spread and build democracy especially in Eastern Europe. Morse never had the same geopolitical vision and saw the international work conducted by the NAO as an unnecessary extravagance, and whereas Davies returned to the international sphere, he did so in a different geopolitical context. The NAO aimed under Davies to be a participant rather than a leader. The NAO's own work increasingly shifted to scrutinising domestic rather than defence politics: the shape of the state decreed that the sights of both the UK's auditor and its Parliament shifted from grand strategy to the strategy of national renewal and the management of the disintegration of public services through austerity. In this context, it may be significant that Bourn's eventual successor, Gareth Davies, made his reputation in local government audit. Safeguarding, scrutinising and improving the public realm, within the context of an ageing society, an economy that refused, stubbornly, to grow and a politics that increasingly seemed unable to create consent were tasks enough for the British establishment without thinking about what happened beyond the seas.

8.4 Chapter summary

We began this chapter with Maitland's (1897) warning about anachronism. The problem with the NAO and E&AD is that it is tempting to imagine that just because both organisations carried out an activity which retained the same name – audit – they have been doing the same thing for the same purposes. Actually, nothing could be further from the truth. The NAO's audit has been reshaped several times by the ideological preferences of its leaders and its staff: the wider politics that surrounds it and its interaction with the political community at any one time. Given that audit is always in flux, this means that it is open for the political community more widely and the NAO itself, in reaction to that, to redefine its meaning. This has happened before: for example, financial audit was redefined by the introduction of resource accounting in the 1990s and 2000s; value-for-money audit was redefined by John Bourn and then Amyas Morse, and whilst never achieved, Bernard Jenkin's PACAC and Tony Wright's Public Administration Committee indicated how public sector accountability could be reconfigured in the 2000s and 2010s (Ferry and Midgley, 2024).

In understanding this evolution, we have used the categories of regulatory space as defined by Ferry et al. (2023). They suggest three themes through which the regulatory space which Supreme Audit Institutions inhabit could be understood: organisational context, capacities and audit scope. We have charted the evolution of the E&AD and the NAO by using these themes to group our analysis. The NAO's organisational context, shaped by the beliefs and intentions of politicians, has influenced how it developed. Early on, Parliament was willing to allow the NAO to spend more money than its predecessor. The Thatcher, Blair and Cameron reform efforts affected the intellectual climate in which the NAO operated. Equally, its capacity shaped the type of work that the NAO did: from the early days, where C&AGs were worried about whether the NAO could perform any wider function say for select committees and hence restricted their role, to the later period where austerity imposed on government forced the NAO to decide to reduce its budget. But lastly, the NAO's vision of its audit scope shaped how others responded to it and how it responded to the constraints on its capacity. Morse could have decided to reduce budgets for financial audit but chose not to because of his sense of the organisational context (regulation) he faced and his sense of what financial audit should be.

The questions facing the political system in the UK are the same as in 1983. How can the administration of government be made accountable to Parliament, and how does Parliament receive information about government? How can those who provide that information and advice to MPs be made immune from political controversy? Have the efforts to do this narrowed the vision of what accountability means in the UK, and how do we avoid that in the future? How can we ensure that accountability is not captured by a commercial professional view which is uninterested in democratic development? How does accountability, restricted by the need to be politically impartial, not result in channelling attention to making the administrative machine turn a treadmill of repeated failed approaches as opposed to opening up new vistas? How will accountability change as the challenges faced by the state, whether from renewed geopolitical pressures, environmental change or even unexpected crises in the future, alter? These great questions should frame how we approach both what organisational context the NAO should be placed within, what capacities it requires and what the scope of its work should be. The question facing the NAO and us as citizens out of the last 40 years of its history is therefore not 'what kind of NAO do we need', but 'what kind of constitutional democracy do we want, how much do we wish to pay for it, and what should a public sector auditor do within it?'

Notes

1 Fernand Paul Achille Braudel 1902–85, French historian and leader of the Annales School. His scholarship focused on three main projects: the Mediterranean, Civilization and Capitalism, and the unfinished Identity of France.

2 Ludwig Josef Johann Wittgenstein 1889–1951, Austrian philosopher who worked primarily in logic, the philosophy of mathematics, the philosophy of mind and the philosophy of language. From 1929 to 1947, Wittgenstein taught at the University of Cambridge.
3 Paul-Michel Foucault, 1926–84, French philosopher, historian of ideas, writer, political activist and literary critic. Foucault's theories primarily address the relationships between power and knowledge, and how they are used as a form of social control through societal institutions.
4 Jacques Derrida, 1930–4, Algerian-born French philosopher. He developed the philosophy of deconstruction, which he utilised in his texts, developed through close readings of the linguistics of Ferdinand de Saussure and Husserlian and Heideggerian phenomenology.

References

Bacon, Richard, interview
Bourn, J. (undated). *Notes*. Unpublished MSS, John Bourn Private Archive.
Bowie, J. (2019). Sir Amyas Morse valedictory interview with civil service world. *Civil Service World*. Available at https://www.civilservant.org.uk/library/2019-Sir_Amyas_Morse-CSW_Valedictory_Interview.pdf accessed on 17 March 2024.
Braudel, F. (1972, 1973). *The Mediterranean and the Mediterranean world in the age of Phillip II, Vol. 1 and Vol. 2* (S. Reynolds, trans.). New York: Harper and Row.
Cooper, C., Tweedie, J., Andrew, J. and Baker, M. (2023). The new "corporate state": The meshing of corporate and political power and the erosion of democratic accountability in the UK. *Financial Accountability & Management, 39*(2), 268–285.
Davis, A. (2022). *Bankruptcy, bubbles and bailouts: The inside history of the Treasury since 1976*. Manchester: Manchester University Press.
Edgerton, D. (2018). *The rise and fall of the British nation*. London: Allen Lane.
Elston, T. and Zhang, Y. (2023). Implementing Public Accounts Committee recommendations: Evidence from the UK Government's 'progress reports' since 2012. *Parliamentary Affairs, 76*(3), 662–693.
Ferry, L., Hamid, K. and Dutra, P. H. (2023). An international comparative study of the audit and accountability arrangements of supreme audit institutions. *Journal of Public Budgeting, Accounting and Financial Management, 35*(4), 431–450.
Ferry, L. and Midgley H. (2022). Democracy, accountability and audit: The creation of the UK NAO as a defence of liberty. *Auditing, Accounting and Accountability Journal, 35*(2), 413–438.
Ferry, L. and Midgley, H. (2023). Institutional entrepreneurship in a Supreme Audit Institution: Ihe National Audit Office and the use of data in financial audit. In T. Rana and L. Parker (eds.) *The Routledge Handbook of Public Sector Accounting*, 49–62. Abingdon: Routledge.
Ferry, L. and Midgley, H. (2024). Are public sector accounts trusted? Exploring the verdict of the Public Administration and Constitutional Affairs Committee in the United Kingdom. *Public Administration*. https://doi.org/10.1111/padm.12983.
Foster, H. and Knox, C., (2022). The 'eyes and ears of parliament': Devolved public accounts committees in the UK. *The Journal of Legislative Studies*. https://doi.org/10.1080/13572334.2022.2079860

Foster, H. and Knox, C. (2023). Variegated accountability: Devolved public accounts committees in the UK. *Parliamentary Affairs, 76*(3), 641–661.
Hickson, K. (2002). *The IMF crisis and British politics*, unpublished PHD thesis, University of Southampton.
Hoggett, P. (2005). Iraq: Blair's mission impossible. *The British Journal of Politics and International Relations, 7*(3), 418-428.
Innes, A. (2023). *Late Soviet Britain: Why materialist utopias fail?* Cambridge: Cambridge University Press.
Jenkin, Bernard, interview.
Johnsen, A. (2005). What does 25 years of experience tell us about the state of performance measurement in public policy and management? *Public Money & Management, 25*(1), 9–17.
Kelsey, T. (2023). The retreat from high technology in twentieth century Britain. *English Historical Review*. https://doi.org/10.1093/ehr/cead183
Mair, P. (2013). *Ruling the void: The hollowing of Western democracy*. New York: Verso.
Maitland, F.W. (1897). *Doomsday Book and beyond: Three essays in the early history of England*. Cambridge: Cambridge University Press.
Midgley, H. (2016). Political thinking and the creation of the Assembly of 1653. *Seventeenth Century, 39*(1), 37–56.
Midgley, H. (2019). The National Audit Office and the select committee system 1979–2019. *Parliamentary Affairs*, 72(4), 779–798.
Normanton, E. (1966). *The audit and accountability of Government*. Manchester: Manchester University Press.
Norton, P. (2019). Departmental select committees: The reform of the century? *Parliamentary Affairs, 72*(4), 727–741.
O'Donnell, Gus, interview
Packer, Richard, interview
Paterson, L. (2023). Independence is not going away: The importance of education and birth cohorts. *Political Quarterly, 94*(4), 526–534.
Power, M. (1999). The Audit Society. Oxford: Oxford University Press.
Radcliffe, V. (1998). Efficiency audit: An assembly or rationalities and programmes. *Accounting, Organizations and Society, 23*(4), 377–410.
Richards, Steve, interview
Roberts, A. (2011). *The logic of discipline: Global capitalism and the architecture of government*. Oxford: Oxford University Press.
Rogers, C. (2012). *The IMF and European economic policy: Crisis and conditionality*. London: Palgrave Macmillan.
Rutter, Jill, interview
Rutter, J. (2021). The hole in the centre: A comment on Lowe and Pemberton, the official history of the British civil service, Volume II: 1982–1997. *Political Quarterly, 92*(1), 90–94.
Saunders, R. (2020). Brexit and empire: 'Global Britain' and the myth of imperial nostalgia. *The Journal of Imperial and Commonwealth History, 48*(6), 1140–1176.
Slobodian, Q. (2018). *Globalism: The end of Empire and the beginning of neo-liberalism*. Cambridge, MA: Harvard University Press.
Streeck, W. (2017). *Buying time: The delayed crisis of democratic capitalism*. New York: Verso.
Thompson, H. (2016). Inevitability and contingency: The political economy of Brexit. *The British Journal of Politics and International Relations, 19*(3), 434–449.
Thompson, H. (2017). How the City of London lost at Brexit: A historical perspective. *Economy and Society, 46*(2), 211–228.

Turnbull, T. (2022). 'No solution to the immediate crisis': The uncertain political economy of energy conservation in 1970s Britain. *Contemporary European History, 31*(4), 570–592.
White, H. (2022). *Held in contempt: What's wrong with the House of Commons.* Manchester: Manchester University Press.

INDEX

Note: Page numbers in *italics* indicate figures, **bold** indicate tables in the text, and references following "n" refer notes

www.ingramcontent.com/pod-product-compliance
Ingram Content Group UK Ltd.
Pitfield, Milton Keynes, MK11 3LW, UK
UKHW022349190926
475702UK00015B/2192
9781032858371